MW01064006

PHILO
SUPPLEMENT II

PHILO

IN TEN VOLUMES
(AND TWO SUPPLEMENTARY VOLUMES)

SUPPLEMENT

II

QUESTIONS AND ANSWERS ON EXODUS

TRANSLATED FROM THE ANCIENT ARMENIAN
VERSION OF THE ORIGINAL GREEK BY

RALPH MARCUS, Ph.D.

PROFESSOR OF HELLENISTIC CULTURE, UNIVERSITY OF CHICAGO

CAMBRIDGE, MASSACHUSETTS
HARVARD UNIVERSITY PRESS
LONDON
WILLIAM HEINEMANN LTD
MCMLXXXVII

American
ISBN 0-674-99442-6

British
ISBN 0 434 99401 4

First published 1953
Reprinted 1961, 1970, 1987

CONTENTS OF SUPPLEMENT II

CONTENTS OF SUPPLEMENT II

v

LIST OF PHILO'S WORKS

SHOWING THEIR DIVISION INTO VOLUMES IN THIS EDITION

LIST OF PHILO'S WORKS

EXODUS

BOOK I

*1. (Ex. xii. 2) [a] " This month (shall be) for you the be-
ginning of months ; it is the first in the months of the
year." [b]

(Scripture) thinks it proper to reckon the cycle of months
from the vernal equinox. [c] Moreover, (this month) is said
to be the " first " and the " beginning " by synonymy, [d]
since these (terms) are explained by each other, for it is
said to be the first both in order and in power ; [e] similarly
that time which proceeds from the vernal equinox also
appears (as) the beginning both in order and in power, in
the same way as the head (is the beginning) of a living
creature. And thus those who are learned in astronomy
have given this name ; [f] to the before-mentioned time.
For they call the Ram the head of the zodiac [g] since in it
the sun appears to produce the vernal equinox. [h] And in
addition to this, it was fitting for it to be (the beginning) [i]

[a] Philo comments on this verse, without quoting it literally,
in De Vita Mosis ii. 222-223 and De Spec. Leg. ii. 151-152.
[b] lxx ὁ μὴν οὗτος ὑμῖν ἀρχὴ μηνῶν, πρῶτός ἐστιν ὑμῖν ἐν τοῖς
μησὶν τοῦ ἐνιαυτοῦ.
[c] ἀπὸ τῆς ἐαρινῆς ἰσημερίας.   [d] κατὰ συνωνυμίαν.
[e] καὶ τάξει καὶ δυνάμει.   [f] i.e. of " head."
[g] κεφαλὴν τοῦ ζωφόρου . . . τὸν κριόν.
[h] Cf. De Opif. Mundi 116 ἧλιος ὅπτος καθ᾽ ἕκαστον ἐνιαυτὸν ἀποτελῶν ἰσημερίας . . . τὴν μὲν ἐαρινὴν ἐν κριῷ.
[i] I follow Aucher in supplying the words " the beginning "
(Aucher " exordium "), to which nothing corresponds in the
Arm. text.

2

EXODUS

BOOK I

*1. (Ex. xii. 2) [a] " This month (shall be) for you the beginning of months; it is the first in the months of the year." [b]

(Scripture) thinks it proper to reckon the cycle of months from the vernal equinox. [c] Moreover, (this month) is said to be the " first " and the " beginning " by synonymy, [d] since these (terms) are explained by each other, for it is said to be the first both in order and in power [e]; similarly that time which proceeds from the vernal equinox also appears (as) the beginning both in order and in power, in the same way as the head (is the beginning) of a living creature. And thus those who are learned in astronomy have given this name [f] to the before-mentioned time. For they call the Ram the head of the zodiac [g] since in it the sun appears to produce the vernal equinox. [h] And in addition to this, it was fitting for it to be (the beginning) [i]

[a] Philo comments on this verse, without quoting it literally, in *De Vita Mosis* ii. 222-223 and *De Spec. Leg.* ii. 151-152.

[b] lxx ὁ μὴν οὗτος ὑμῖν ἀρχὴ μηνῶν, πρῶτός ἐστιν ὑμῖν ἐν τοῖς μησὶν τοῦ ἐνιαυτοῦ.

[c] ἀπὸ τῆς ἐαρινῆς ἰσημερίας.   [d] κατὰ συνωνυμίαν.

[e] καὶ τάξει καὶ δυνάμει.   [f] *i.e.* of " head."

[g] κεφαλὴν τοῦ ζωοφόρου . . . τὸν κριόν.

[h] Cf. *De Opif. Mundi* 116 ἥλιος διττὰς καθ᾽ ἕκαστον ἐνιαυτὸν ἀποτελῶν ἰσημερίας . . . τὴν μὲν ἐαρινὴν ἐν κριῷ.

[i] I follow Aucher in supplying the words " the beginning " (Aucher " exordium "), to which nothing corresponds in the Arm. text.

2

of the times that come into being during the year. Accordingly, when the fruits of things that are sown become
full grown on the trees; then they receive the beginning
of hearing, in order that the gracious acts of God may be
prolonged perpetually as they replace one another, and as
they join the ends to the beginnings and the beginnings
to the ends. But in the first creation of all things,
which He also made that of His constituted [all] things
at the same time to be filled with their fruits and great
thoughts. For it was proper that this be so, since the
Father left no appearance of superfluity or deficiency.
And this was especially for the sake of man, to whom He
was about to entrust the beginning of customs, that he
might immediately find all things perfect and perfectly
produced.

For it ministers to the earth by giving it rest and
And that (Scripture) presupposes the vernal equinox
to be the beginning of the cycle of months is clear from the
notions of time in the ordinances and traditions of
various nations. And one may make certain of this from
the sheaves of first-fruits, which (Scripture) commands
to (the rest of) the universe, so among the seasons the

a Only slightly different is the wording of the Greek fragment (which contains only this sentence of the section),
οἱ τῶν σπαρτῶν καρποὶ τελειωθῶσιν, οἱ τῶν δένδρων γενέσεως
ἀρχὴν λαμβάνωσιν ἵνα δουλεχεύωσιν ὡς τοῦ θεοῦ χάριτες τὸν αἰῶνα
παρ᾽ ἀλλήλας διαδεχόμεναι καὶ συμπλέκουσι τέλη μὲν ἀρχαῖς,
ἀρχὰς δὲ τέλεσιν, ἀτελεύτητοι. The last two words appear
to be an addition to the original text of Philo.

b Prob. δημιουργία: Aucher "productione."
c τὸν κόσμον.
d Of Unleavened Bread or Passover.
e Aucher "suspicionem."
f ἔθων. g τελειογονηθέντα.
h ὑποτίθησι.
Aucher renders more
literally, "de retentione
certans id revivificet."
Leg. ii. 162, 175.

(us) to bring on the second day of the festival [a] for the needs of the service, [b] and spring is the season of harvest.

But one may be in doubt why it is that since there are two equinoxes, the vernal and the autumnal, which nature established as the just canons [c] of the equinoxes, it was not from the autumnal one but from that which falls in spring that (Scripture) begins to reckon time. [d] For it is in the spring that every fertile place both in mountain and plain grows and blossoms and bears fruit, but in the autumn, so soon as there is gathered whatever fruit the earth has borne, the plants lose their leaves and dry up. But it is necessary to attribute the beginning to the better and more desirable (season). To me, moreover, it seems that the autumnal equinox is to the vernal as a servant is to a queen. For it ministers to the earth by giving it rest and by making lighter the trees which have been suffering hardship in their nature, and by fighting like a brave athlete, it enables them to gather together their strength and to make a new start from the beginning. [e] Now if this is so, no one will err in saying that in the same way as heaven (is superior) to (the rest of) the universe, [f] so among the seasons the spring is prior to and more sovereign than the autumn.

But not all (peoples) treat the months and years alike, but some in one way and some in another. Some reckon by the sun, others by the moon. And because of this the initiators of the divine festivals have expressed divergent views about the beginnings of the year, setting divergent

[a] Of Unleavened Bread or Passover.

[b] Aucher "is used in ministration." According to Lev. xxiii. 20 the sheaves are to be given to the priests.

[c] *i.e.* of barley.

[d] ἡ φύσις.   [e] κανόνας.

[f] See *QG* ii. 17 notes.

Aucher renders somewhat differently, *hoc enim colit terram, quiete ei data, et arbores levitate donat; quum defatigata fuisset earum natura, luctatoris instar generose certans, qui velut pugil cum adversario optime congressus foret, sinit ut lassus renovetur rursum ex principio.*

[g] τῷ ὅλῳ: Aucher "mundo."

4

beginnings to the revolutions of the seasons suitable to the beginnings of the cycles. Wherefore (Scripture) has added, " This month (shall be) to you the beginning," making clear a determined and distinct number of seasons, lest they follow the Egyptians, with whom they are mixed, and be seduced by the customs of the land in which they dwell.[a] For He wishes this season to be (the beginning) of creation for the world, and the beginning of months and years for the race.[b] Now the season in which the world was created, as anyone will ascertain in truth who uses a proper method of inquiry (and) deliberation, was the season of spring, since it is at this time that all things in common blossom and grow, and the earth produces its perfected fruits. And, as I have said, nothing was imperfect in the first creation of the universe.[c] For special care was taken that the race should be civilized [d] and receive a special portion of excellence in honour of (its) piety,[e] (namely) this megalopolis, the world,[f] and civilization,[g] by which it manages its economy.[h] Wherefore He thought it proper that the same season (should be) a memorial both of the creation of the world and of that which is kin to it,[i]

[a] Aucher renders slightly more freely, " ne in Aegyptiorum abirent mores, mixtim in regione eorum habitantes consuetudine seducti."

[b] τῷ γένει. Apparently the human race, not merely the Israelite nation, is meant.

[c] οὐδὲν ἀτελὲς ἦν ἐν τῇ πρώτῃ τοῦ ὅλου γενέσει.

[d] The original probably had πολιτεύεσθαι, in the sense given above rather than its more usual senses " to behave politically " or " to be governed ": Aucher " optime conversaretur in mundo."

[e] τῆς εὐσεβείας.

[f] Cf. De Spec. Leg. i. 34 τὸν οὖν ἀφικόμενον εἰς τὴν ὡς ἀληθῶς μεγαλόπολιν, τόνδε τὸν κόσμον . . . ἔννοιαν λήψεσθαι δεῖ τοῦ ποιητοῦ καὶ πατρὸς καὶ προσέτι ἡγεμόνος.

[g] πολιτείαν: Aucher " urbanitatem."

[h] οἰκονομίᾳ χρῆται: Aucher " qua dispensatione bene conversatur."

[i] Apparently time is meant as that which is kin to the world.

5

again in order that the spring might be the beginning of every time, for time came into being together with the creation of the world. And the race,[a] following nature and the whole dispensation of heaven,[b] reckoned [c] the seasons similarly and in harmony with the months and years, giving the same priority to the spring as it has in the creation of the world. For at the command of the Lord,[d] wherever it was arranged [e] that they should change their dwelling from Egypt, being persuaded by clear words, He prescribed [f] the first month as the time of migration.[g] But this is the same as the seventh (month) in the solar period, for the seventh (month) from the autumnal equinox is described as the time of migration, and it is the first (month) according to the solar reckoning.[h]

2. (Ex. xii. 3, 6) Why does (Moses) command that from the tenth (day of the first month) a sheep be kept for the fourteenth (day), which was to be sacrificed ?[i]

[a] See note b on p. 5.

[b] ἀκόλουθον τῇ φύσει καὶ ὅλῃ τῇ τοῦ οὐρανοῦ οἰκονομίᾳ.

[c] Aucher " aptavit."

[d] The Arm. reads aɣ aɣn ʒain, lit. " at the voice of the man," but I have ventured to emend aɣn " man " to tearn " Lord."

[e] Lit. " it was made " : Aucher " oportebat."

[f] Lit. " wrote."   [g] ἀποικίας.

[h] Nisan (March-April) is the first month of the vernal or festival calendar, and the seventh month of the autumnal or civil calendar, which begins with Tishri (Sept.-Oct.). The above passage has a close parallel in De Spec. Leg. ii. 150 ἕβδομος ὢν ὁ μὴν οὗτος (Nisan) ἀριθμῷ τε καὶ τάξει κατὰ τὸν ἡλιακὸν κύκλον δυνάμει πρῶτός ἐστι, διὸ καὶ πρῶτος ἐν ταῖς ἱεραῖς βίβλοις ἀναγέγραπται.

[i] LXX τῇ δεκάτῃ τοῦ μηνὸς τούτου λαβέτωσαν ἕκαστος πρόβατον κατ' οἴκους πατριῶν, ἕκαστος πρόβατον κατ' οἰκίαν . . . (vs. 6) καὶ ἔσται ὑμῖν διατετηρημένον ἕως τῆς τεσσαρεσκαιδεκάτης τοῦ μηνὸς τούτου, καὶ σφάξουσιν αὐτὸ πᾶν τὸ πλῆθος συναγωγῆς υἱῶν Ἰσραὴλ πρὸς ἑσπέραν. Philo quotes part of vs. 3 and comments on it differently in De Congressu 106-108 ; he also alludes to vs. 6 in De Vita Mosis ii. 224-225.

6

In the first place, (this was commanded) in order that
he who offered sacrifice might perform the sacrifice not
offhandedly [a] and on the spur of the moment and without
preparation but with care and thought as if rendering
thanks to God, the saviour and benefactor of all (men).[b]
In the second place, by this allusion [c] to the sacrifice which
was to be prepared beforehand he wishes to teach this
first, (namely) that he who was about to offer the sacrifice
should first prepare his soul and body [d]—the latter by
abstaining from uncleanness in holiness and purity, and
the former by quietly giving himself up to God [e] in order
that it might be released, even though not altogether, from
the passions that disturbed it, for, according to the saying,
one should not enter with unwashed feet on the pavement
of the temple of God.[f] In the third place, he wishes to
test the nation for several [g] days as to just how it stands
in respect of faith,[h] since he clearly knew (them to be) of
two minds,[i] not having been prepared beforehand for
sacrifice and through negligence not having taken thought
as was suitable and fitting. In the fourth place, he clearly
introduces the defeat of the Egyptians, for though they
were not altogether crushed and dismayed by the things
which had happened to them, he was referring to the evils
which were about to overtake them in five days and which
they would have to endure one after another [j] when the
enemy would prepare to offer the sacrifices of victory.
That is the literal meaning.[k] But as for the deeper meaning,[l] it was fitting that this should be, (namely) that the
numbers and the nature of all things should be brought

---

[a] The Arm. uses two expressions to render παρέργως.
[b] τῷ σωτῆρι καὶ εὐεργέτῃ πάντων θεῷ.
[c] αἰνιττόμενος.　　　[d] τὴν ψυχὴν καὶ τὸ σῶμα.
[e] τῷ ἐνθουσιᾶν or ἐπιθειάζειν.
[f] Cf. De Vita Mosis ii. 138 on Ex. xxx. 19.
[g] Aucher " multis."　　　[h] πρὸς πίστιν.
[i] Aucher " dubio actos."
[j] Aucher renders slightly differently, " illud quoque
futurum eis malum quod post certos quoque dies debuissent
perpeti."　　[k] τὸ ῥητόν.　　　[l] τὸ πρὸς διάνοιαν.

together.[a] For when souls [b] appear bright and visible, their visions [c] begin to hold festival,[d] hoping for a life without sorrow or fear as their lot and seeing the cosmos [e] with the weight of the understanding [f] as full and perfect, in harmony with the decad.[g] That is to say, what else would its experience [h] be but festive ? [i]

3. (Ex. xii. 3b) Why is it that (Moses) commands a sheep to be taken " in accordance with the houses of the clans " [j]?

In the first place, because clans are a kind of great kin-group and a large number of men,[k] but small are those (clans) which in accordance with the houses and by blood are reduced to a small number of men. And so, bringing those (groups) which are small into kinship with the large

[a] Apparently Philo is thinking of the numbers ten and fourteen in relation to the lunar calendar.

[b] ψυχαί (see note d).

[c] Or " forms " : Aucher " visus."

[d] One is tempted to restore the apparently corrupted original as, " For when bright and visible visions appear to souls, they (i.e. " the souls ") begin to hold festival." It seems that the original had ψυχαῖς, not ψυχαί.

[e] Arm. zard, which Aucher renders literally by " ornamentum," obviously reflects κόσμον in the sense of " cosmos."

[f] Slightly emending the Arm. which seems to reflect τοῦ λόγου ὁλκῇ, cf. De Plantatione 21 τὴν πρὸς τὸ ὂν διανοίας ὁλκήν.

[g] This is the best sense which I can get from the obscure clause, which Aucher renders, " vitam tristitia et timore carentem sperantes sortiri certo in decimo plenum, et perfectum cernentes ornamentum rationis perpensionisque."

[h] πάθος.

[i] ἑορτῶδες.

[j] LXX λαβέτωσαν ἕκαστος πρόβατον κατ' οἴκους πατριῶν (Heb. " of the fathers "), ἕκαστος πρόβατον κατ' οἰκίαν. In De Congressu 106 Philo quotes part of the verse, δεκάτη τοῦ μηνὸς τούτου λαβέτωσαν ἕκαστος πρόβατον κατ' οἰκίαν, and comments in part as here, see below. See also De Vita Mosis ii. 224.

[k] μεγάλαι τινὲς συγγένειαι καὶ πολυανθρωπία. Philo here anticipates his comments on vs. 4 in § 5 below.

8

ones, he makes them worthy to be table-companions [a] and to come together in one place for the sharing of salt and offerings and sacrifices, which makes for harmonious affection [b] and binds it more firmly. For law is always a maker of peace and unity, [c] especially as they were about to go on a journey. But on a journey tent-mates [d] are useful, and he thought it right for them to make this after beginning with sacrifice. In the second place, he commands that everyone's sacrifice shall be made " in accordance with the house," (and also the sacrifices) of defenders and allies, [e] since in every house of their adversaries the death of the first-born was to take place, so that anyone seeing one (death) after another may at the same time praise and fear the beneficence and just acts (of God). For unexpected things [f] happened within a short time : among some there would be the offering of sacrifices, among others the destruction of the first-born ; for some there would be festivals and rejoicing, for others mourning and sorrow ; for some there would be blessings and hymns, for others wailings and groans and incessant lamentations. That is the literal meaning. [g] But as for the deeper meaning, [h] it is this. The sheep is " progressive," as the name itself shows, being so called in accordance with the progress [i] of the soul, and it indicates improvement. [j] And he wishes that not in one part but in all their parts, by which I mean their nature, [k] they may progress and grow in virtue [l] in respect of their senses and words and sovereign mind, [m]

[a] ὁμοτραπέζους.   [b] Prob. φιλίαν : Aucher " amorem."
[c] εἰρήνης καὶ ἑνώσεως ἀεὶ δημιουργός ἐστιν ὁ νόμος.
[d] σύσκηνοι, rendered by two Arm. nouns.
[e] Apparently this is a reference to the Israelites' " neighbours " mentioned in vs. 4, see § 5.
[f] παράδοξα.   [g] τὸ ῥητόν.   [h] τὸ πρὸς διάνοιαν.
[i] προκοπήν, expressed by two Arm. nouns.
[j] The same connexion between *pascha*, the Paschal lamb, and spiritual progress is made in *De Congressu* 106 τὸ ψυχικὸν Πάσχα, ἡ . . . διάβασις πρὸς τὸ δέκατον . . . ἱερουργεῖν ἤδη δύνηται τὰς ἀσινεῖς καὶ ἀμώμους προκοπάς.
[k] φύσιν.   [l] ἀρετῇ.
[m] κατὰ τὰς αἰσθήσεις καὶ τοὺς λόγους καὶ τὸν ἡγεμόνα νοῦν.

9

in order that their natural kinship,[a] admitting a stronger likeness,[b] may more firmly bring about a harmony consisting of counsel and justice.[c]

4. (Ex. xii. 11) [d] But what is the Pascha,[e] which is interpreted as " Passover " [f] ?

They make the Passover sacrifice while changing their dwelling-place in accordance with the commands of the Logos,[g] in return for three beneficent acts (of God), which are the beginning and the middle of the freedom to which they now attain.[h] And the beginning was that they were able to conquer the harsh and insupportable masters of whom they had had experience and who [i] had brought all kinds of evil upon them, and this (came about) in two ways, by having their force [j] and their numbers increase. And the middle was that they saw the divinely sent punishments and disasters which overtook their enemies, (for) it was not the nations which fought against them but the regions of the world and the four elements [k] which came against them with the harmfulness and violence of beasts. That is the literal meaning.[l] But the deeper meaning [m] is this. Not only do men make the Passover sacrifice when they change their places but so also and more properly [n] do

---

[a] ἡ φυσικὴ συγγένεια.　　　　　[b] οἰκειότητα.

[c] Aucher " copiam prudentiae et justitiae."

[d] Since the name Pascha does not occur before vs. 11 in Ex. chap. xii, the present section should follow § 18.

[e] Arm. P'esek (Heb. Pesah).

[f] διάβασις or διαβατήρια as elsewhere in Philo, e.g. Leg. All. iii. 154, De Sacr. Abelis 63, De Migratione 25, De Vita Mosis ii. 224. See also De Spec. Leg. ii. 146-148 for an allegorical explanation of the name.

[g] τοῦ λόγου : Aucher " verbi (divini)."

[h] Aucher " quae sunt principium et medium et proxima consecutio libertatis."

[i] Reading Arm. ork' for the meaningless oyk'.

[j] δύναμιν : Aucher " virtutem."

[k] τὰ τοῦ κόσμου μέρη καὶ τὰ τέτταρα στοιχεῖα.

[l] τὸ ῥητόν.　　[m] τὸ πρὸς διάνοιαν.　　[n] οἰκειότερον.

10

souls when they begin to give up the pursuits of youth and
their terrible disorder [a] and they change to a better and
older state. And so our mind [b] should change from ignorance and stupidity to education and wisdom,[c] and from
intemperance and dissoluteness to patience and moderation,[d] and from fear and cowardice to courage and confidence,[e] and from avarice and injustice to justice and
equality.[f] And there is still another Passover of the soul [g]
beside this, which is its making the sacrifice of passing
over from the body ; and there is one of the mind, (namely,
its passing over) from the senses [h] ; and as for thoughts,[i]
(their passing over consists) in one's not being taken with
oneself [j] but in willingly thinking further of desiring and
emulating prophetic souls.[k]

5. (Ex. xii. 4a) Why is it that (Moses) commands that
" if there are few in the house," they shall take their
neighbours " in accordance with the number of souls " [l] ?

[a] στάσιν : Aucher " insipientia."   [b] ὁ νοῦς.
[c] ἐξ ἀπαιδευσίας καὶ ἀνοίας εἰς παιδείαν καὶ σοφίαν.
[d] ἐξ ἀκρασίας καὶ ἀκολασίας εἰς ὑπομονὴν καὶ σωφροσύνην.
[e] ἐκ φόβου καὶ δειλίας εἰς ἀνδρείαν καὶ θάρσος : Aucher
renders incompletely, " ex timore in fortitudinem."
[f] ἐκ πλεονεξίας καὶ ἀδικίας εἰς δικαιοσύνην καὶ ἰσότητα.
[g] τῆς ψυχῆς.   [h] τῶν αἰσθήσεων.
[i] τῶν λογισμῶν.
[j] i.e. with one's own importance : Aucher " ut non a se
capiatur."
[k] προφητικῶν ψυχῶν or πνευμάτων : Aucher " spirituum
propheticorum."
[l] LXX ἐὰν δὲ ὀλιγοστοὶ ὦσιν οἱ ἐν τῇ οἰκίᾳ ὥστε μὴ εἶναι ἱκανοὺς
εἰς πρόβατον, συλλήμψεται μεθ' ἑαυτοῦ τὸν γείτονα τὸν πλησίον
αὐτοῦ· κατὰ ἀριθμὸν ψυχῶν κτλ. : the Heb. reads somewhat
differently " And if the house (i.e. household) be too small
for a sheep, then it and its near neighbour shall take (it) for
its house by the number of souls." In Quis Rer. Div. Heres
193 Philo quotes the verse in the following form, ἐὰν ὀλίγοι
ὦσιν οἱ ἐν τῇ οἰκίᾳ ὥστε μὴ ἱκανοὺς εἶναι εἰς τὸ πρόβατον, τὸν
πλησίον γείτονα προσλαβεῖν, κατ' ἀριθμὸν ψυχῶν κτλ.

QUESTIONS AND ANSWERS

From the literal text [a] you see how much love of mankind and common feeling [b] he shows, since the divine Word gives the command [c] not only to keep (the festival) [d] but also to take thought about giving a share in it [e] to their neighbours and those near by, both in equality and in likeness. For it is about a most honourable thing—and what is more honourable than sacrifice ?—and about that which is held in honour and is a matter of sharing in the smallest things that he seems to be legislating [f] in the present passage.[g] That is the literal meaning. But as for the deeper meaning,[h] there are some souls which have a full and complete kinship,[i] being adapted to the nobility of concord,[j] their thoughts being in accord with their words, and their words with their deeds.[k] And there are others which lack the elements [l] of eternity, being deficient in nobility. Now these elements pour out love,[m] always [n] receiving neighbours and those who come near. For as a kind of neighbour and as near to us in respect of desire for virtue [o] (we may consider) the theories of the so-called school studies.[p] And one who is nourished by these and keeps in practice,[q] makes up for his deficiencies by receiving the common discipline of the mind.[r] And the instruction of the school studies should be not childish and puerile but rational [s] and

---

[a] ἐν τῷ ῥητῷ.
[b] φιλανθρωπίαν καὶ κοινωνίαν.
[c] προστάττοντος τοῦ θείου (or ἱεροῦ) λόγου.
[d] Aucher renders, " servare," without supplying an object.
[e] κοινωνίαν. [f] νομοθετεῖν.
[g] The meaning is not wholly clear.
[h] τὸ πρὸς διάνοιαν. [i] συγγένειαν.
[j] καλοκἀγαθίᾳ ὁμονοίας vel sim.
[k] τῶν βουλῶν τοῖς λόγοις καὶ τῶν λόγων τοῖς ἔργοις ὁμονοούντων.
[l] Lit. " parts."
[m] ἔρωτα ἐκχέει : Aucher " amore effluunt."
[n] Aucher renders the adverb freely, " humaniter."
[o] ἀρετῆς.
[p] τὰ τῶν ἐγκυκλίων λεγομένων θεωρήματα.
[q] Aucher " instructus . . . solido exercitio."
[r] τὴν κοινὴν τοῦ νοῦ παιδείαν. [s] λογική.

12

*6 (Ex. xiii. 4b) Why does (Moses) command that every-
one shall "number sufficient for himself" for the sacrifice?

In the first place, excess and defect of equality produce
inequality. And inequality, if I may use rather mytho-
logical terms, is the mother of injustice, just as, on the
other hand, equality is (the mother of) justice. But
sufficiency is midway between excess and defect. In this
passage Holy Scripture lays down (the rule), "Nothing
too much." But in the second place, one's own labour
in tilling the soil is a measure of moderation in the things
necessary and useful for bodily life. And it is natural
for it to have as sisters frugality and contentment, and

___

[a] Lit. "taken into account." Aucher " aestimatione
dignum."

[b] Aucher " quoniam secundum numerum animarum id
conciliat mentem," which does not make much sense.

[c] LXX ἕκαστος τὸ ἀρκοῦν αὐτῷ συναριθμήσεται· τὰ πρόβατον ·
Hebrew "everyone according to his eating you shall number
for the sheep." In Quis Rer. Div. Heres 192-193 Philo quotes
this verse as an illustration of "proportioned equality," the
wording of the latter part being ἵν' ἕκαστος τὸ ἀρκοῦν αὐτῷ
συναριθμῆται.   [d] ἰσότητος, rendered by two Arm. nouns.

[e] The Greek frag. reads more briefly ὑπερβολαὶ καὶ
ἐλλείψεις ἀνισότητα ἐγένησαν.

[f] Aucher mistakenly takes this noun as the second object
of " produce " in the preceding sentence.

[g] Here again ἰσότης is rendered by two Arm. nouns.

[h] Slightly emending the Arm. on the basis of the Greek
frag. ἀνισότης δέ, ἵνα αὐτὸς μυθικωτέροις χρήσωμαι τοῖς ὀνόμασιν,
μήτηρ ἀδικίας ἐστίν, ὡς ἔμπαλιν ἰσότης δικαιοσύνης. Cf.
see Aristotle.

[i] So the Greek frag. ὑπερβολῆς δὲ καὶ ἐλλείψεώς ἐστι τὸ
αὐταρκές.

[j] Similarly the Greek frag. (which ends here), ἐν ᾧ τὸ
ἱερὸν γράμμα περιέχεται τὸ " μηδὲν ἄγαν."

___

[k] σωφροσύνης or παραδόξως : Aucher " modestiae."   εἰκός

[l] Prob. εὐφροσύνη : Aucher " facilitas."   τέλειος, i.e. full-.

13

an excessive virtue; and everything which accepts the task
of attacking and overthrowing arrogance.

*7. (Ex. xii. 5a) Why does (Moses) command (them)
to take a "perfect male sheep of one year"?

(It is to be) perfect in two physical features,[c] (namely)
in the sensitive parts of the body and in the other
organs.[d] For an imperfect (sacrifice) is not worthy to be
brought to the altar of God. And (it is to be) male, first,
because the male is more perfect than the female. Wherefore it is said by the naturalists that the female is nothing
else than an imperfect male.[e] In the second place, since
it was commanded by the king of the land that the males
should die, he thought it right, in face of this and also for
the sake of thanksgiving, to make a sacrifice of male
animals. And third, because of the king's cruelty and
wickedness,[f] in ordering the proclamation against the
Hebrew children, (he thought it right) to nourish the female
and to kill the male (sheep). For since the (king's) command had been annulled by the friendliness and humaneness and power of God, it was proper to give thanks for
the males unexpectedly kept alive by making their
sacrifice. And (the sheep is to be) a year old, since the
males become perfect (in) a year. For having added the

[a] ἀναφερομένην.
[b] Γέγραπται—τελειοῦται· σαρφαγεῖν (τε) + τὰ
ὑμῖν.
[c] κατὰ φύσιν.
[d] τὰ ἄλλα τοῦ σώματος
ὄργανα.

[e] So the Greek frag. (which contains only this sentence
and the last sentence of this section) λέγεται τὸ θῆλυ οὐδὲν
ἕτερον εἶναι ἢ ἀτελὲς ἄρσεν. For the thought
see Aristotle, De Gener. An. 775 a. Cf. Plato, Timaeus 90 e. ff.
Aucher inadvertently omits the second clause in his
rendering.
[f] Aucher
"per humanissimum beneficium divinae potentiae."
[g] ἀπροσδόκητος or παραδόξως: Aucher "subito."
[h] τέλειοι, i.e. full-grown: Aucher "facti."

"perfect" as in those of prime consideration, he further adds those details in which it is perfect, namely that it is more perfect than the female; while the (year) old shows the time sufficient for the perfecting of such animals. That is the literal meaning. But as for the deeper meaning, progress toward piety (and worthy holiness) ought to be both made and of a year's (duration). But what this means must be shown. Some (men) who have progressed in virtue turn back and flee before they have reached the end; for the newly grown power of virtue in the soul is destroyed by ancient error, which after being quiet for a short while again returns to the attack with great power, forth new buddings[a] of prudence and moderation,[o] and sometimes bears and brings forth perfect fruits of wisdom.[m]

But as for the continuation (of the passage), perhaps these

8. (Ex. xii. 5b) Why is a sheep chosen?

Symbolically,[k] as I have said, it indicates perfect progress,[m] and at the same time the male. For progress is indeed nothing else than the giving up of the female gender by changing into the male, since the female gender

---

[a] Aucher " tamquam principale."
[b] τὸ ῥητόν...καὶ αἰσθητικόν καὶ...
[c] ...θεωρητικόν καὶ ἀσώματον...
[d] The Arm. uses two nouns to render τὰς προκοπάς...οἰκείου, see the preceding note...
[e] ...εὐλάβεια καὶ ἀξίαν ἁγιστείαν.
[f] So the Greek frag., ἔνιοι προκόψαντες ἐπ' ἀρετήν ὑπανάστασιν...ἐφικέσθαι. Cf. De Spec. Leg. iv. 235 τὸν ἑαυτοῦ...
[g] Slightly different is the reading of the Greek frag., ἄρτι φυόμενα...ἀριστοκράτειαν...τούτοις ὅμοια καὶ αἱ τοῦ...
[h] Here again the Greek frag. differs somewhat, καθολοῦντος τῆς παλαιᾶς ἀρεταιελείας (v.l. ὀχλοκρατίας)...
[i] So the Greek frag., ἣ πρὸς ὀλίγον ἠρεμήσασα...πάλιν ἀλλὰ ὑπ-αρχική μετὰ πλείονος...
[j] A ...(αὖθις τε)...
[k] LXX (πρόβατον) . . . ἀπὸ τῶν ἀρνῶν καὶ τῶν ἐρίφων (Heb. "from the sheep and from the goats").
[k] συμβολικῶς.
In the preceding section.
βλάστημα.
[o] εὐβουλίας (vel sim.) καὶ σωφροσύνης.
[m] προκοπὴν τελείαν. Perhaps the original was προκοπήν τελειότητος, as in De Ebrietate 82. On the word πρόβατον as a symbol of προκοπή see Leg. All. iii. 165 and De Sacr. Abelis 112.
i.e. ...ὑπεράνω τῆς...in De ...

is material, passive,[a] corporeal and sense-perceptible,[b] while the male is active, rational, incorporeal and more akin to mind and thought.[c] But not ineptly[d] has it added[e] of a year, "since the year is (so) called from the fact that it holds everything contained within itself.[f] But since in two of the four seasons,[g] (namely) in autumn and winter, plants lose their leaves and dry up; and, on the other hand, in two (seasons, namely) spring and summer, they flower and bear fruit, so do the souls of progressive men experience similar things.[h] For when they cast off the causes of life[i] they become almost entirely dry,[j] being changed by desires[k] and all the other sorts of passion. And the mind[l] brings forth new buddings[m] of prudence and moderation,[o] and sometimes bears and brings forth perfect fruits of wisdom. But as for the command to prepare lambs and kids,[p] perhaps it was given because the Egyptian considered these animals especially divine, in order that the protector and champion[q] might show the overthrow of their adversaries and by what power they were destroyed who were unable

---

[a] Aucher "vitiosum," see next note.

[b] ὑλικὸν καὶ πάσχον καὶ σωματικὸν καὶ αἰσθητικόν.

[c] δραστήριον καὶ λογικὸν καὶ ἀσώματον καὶ νῷ καὶ λογισμῷ οἰκειότερον. The Arm. uses two words to render τὰς προκοπάς.

[e] ἐνιαύσιον, see the preceding section on the first half of Ex. xii. 5.

[f] Cf. De Spec. Leg. iv. 235 τὸν ἐνιαυτόν, ὃς καθάπερ αὐτὸ μηνύει τοὔνομα, αὐτὸς ἐν ἑαυτῷ πάντα περιέχων ἀναφαίνεται.

[g] τούτοις ὅμοια καὶ αἱ τῶν προκοπτόντων ψυχαὶ πάσχουσιν.

[l] Aucher amplifies in rendering "post eam vero mutationem."

[m] βλαστήματα.

[o] εὐβουλίας (vel sim.) καὶ σωφροσύνης.

[p] i.e. God who is called ὑπερασπιστής in De Ebrietate 111.

26

...even their ancestral gods. And finally, the male (lambs) were chosen and appointed for the daily sacrifices, and the goats for the forgiveness of sins. These, however, are symbols of the virtuous soul which desires perfection. First it was necessary to pluck out sins and then to wash them out, and, being resplendent, to complete the daily (tasks) in the practice of virtue.

9. (Ex. xii. 6a) Why does He command (them) to keep the sacrifice until the fourteenth (day of the month)?

(Consisting of) two Sabbaths, it has in its nature a (special) honour because in this time the moon is adorned. For when it has become full on the fourteenth (day), it becomes full of light in the perception of the people. And again through (another) fourteen (days) it recedes from its fullness of light to its conjunction, and it wanes as much in comparison with the preceding Sabbath as the second (waxes) in comparison with the first. For this reason the fourteenth (day) is pre-festive, as though it were a road leading to festive rejoicings, during which it is incumbent upon us to meditate...

and of piety in the other. In the third place, because a temple had not yet been built. He showed that the dwelling together of several good persons in the house...

the Pascal lamb... following Heb... The Greek... see next note.

---

f Cf. De Spec. Leg. ii. 149.

g ἀπὸ πλησιφαοῦς εἰς σύνοδον, cf. De Spec. Leg. i. 178.

h Aucher renders obscurely, "diminuitur eo magis ... anterius sabbatum crescit, et quantum se habebat ... dum ad primum (vel, unitatem)."

i προέορτος, as in De Spec. Leg. ii. 176, which supports Aucher's emendation of Arm. ... progressive") to ...

10. (Ex. xii. 6b) And He says, "all the multitude shall sacrifice."

Now at other times the daily priests (chosen) from the people, being appointed for the slaughtering and taking care of them, performed the sacrifices. But at the Passover here spoken of, the whole people together is honoured with the priesthood, for all of them act for themselves in the performance of the sacrifice. For what reason? Because, in the first place, it was the beginning of this kind of sacrifice, the Levites not yet having been elected to the priesthood nor a temple set up. And in the second place, because the Saviour and Liberator, Who alone leads out all men to freedom, deemed them all equally worthy of sharing in the priesthood and in freedom as well, since all who were of the same nation had given evidence of equal piety. And because, I think, He judged all the Egyptians to be equally impious, unworthy and unclean, He intended to punish them. For they would not have suffered this if they had not been guilty of the same things before the Father (and) Judge and His justice, so that this (period of) time brought out the equality of both nations, the Egyptian and the Hebrew—an equality of impiety in one, and of piety in the other. In the third place, because a temple had not yet been built, He showed that the dwelling together of several good persons in the home was a temple and altar, in order that in the first sacrifices of the nation no one might be found to have more than any other. In the fourth place, He thought it just and fitting that before

note.

(Heb.) "Israel," for "congregation" or "community" as usually; cf. Philo comments more briefly and so unclearly on this half-verse in De Spec. Leg. ii. 145-146.

e ἀπὸ τηρολόφους εἰς σύνοδον, cf. De Spec. περα τι φηδιο.

f Aucher "obscurely," cf. De Spec. . . .

g Aucher . . . anterius sabbatum crescit, et diminutum . . . dum ad primum (sc. unitatem).

i χειροτονηθέντων."

h προσέωσεν, De Spec. ρόμφιμαν ἐκλιθερευσαι στος . . .

j Aucher's emendation . . . λικτεον τεστα . . .

k Aucher "coram Patre et in tribunali justitiae suae . . ."

choosing the particular priests? He should grant priesthood to the whole nation in order that the part might be adorned through the whole, and not the whole through a part—above all the popular element. And He permitted the nation, as the very first thing to be done, to prepare with their own hands and to slaughter the sacrifice of the so-called Passover (as) the beginning of good things. And He decided that there is nothing more beautiful than that the divine cult should be performed by all in harmony. And also that the nation might be an archetypal example to the temple wardens and priests and those who exercise the high-priesthood in carrying out the sacred rites. In the fifth place, because He wished every household and similarly (every) head of a household to act worthily and not to incur any profanation, (being) like a priest purified to do whatever he says or does or thinks. And in now speaking of the multitude as a " congregation " He uses opposite names for a more exact appearance of sobriety in the matters entrusted to them now at the present time. For when the whole multitude came together with harmonious oneness to give thanks for their migration, He no longer called them a multitude or a nation or a people but a " congregation."

---

a Aucher "Honorificaretur." *b* Aucher "populares,"
see below, QE i. 20 on ...

c Philo here refers to the LXX expression συναγωγῆς.

d Apparently the kindnesses of God are meant.

e (see above).

f τὴν θείαν λατρείαν (or διακονίαν) ...

g ὁ προφήτης, i.e. Moses, is treated as speaking for God.

h See note ... Aucher literally, "tempus mediocre ad vesperam," ...

k παράδειγμα ἀρχέτυπον.

m τῇ ἀρχιερωσύνῃ.

n οἰκοδεσπότην.

i Aucher "vigilantiae." *l* Aucher "nomenclaturam."

r Aucher "in rebus suppositis." " opinion "

And so it happened that they congregated and came together not only in body but also in mind—as being about to sacrifice with one character and one soul.

11. (Ex. xii. 6c) Why is the Passover sacrificed at evening?

Perhaps because good things were about to befall at night (and because) it was not the custom to offer a sacrifice in darkness, and for those who were about to experience good things at night it was not (proper) to prepare it before the ninth hour.[f] Therefore it was not at random but knowingly that the prophet[g] set a time between the evenings.[h] That is the literal meaning.[i] But as for the deeper meaning,[j] this should be said. The true sacrifice[k] of God-loving souls consists in abandoning an empty and visible splendour[l] and attempting to change to the unseen or (the object) of thinking. And I am now speaking of the multitude as a "congregation."[m] He (Moses) virtually says more exact appearance of sobriety, for every (soul as?) a whole multitude came together.

LXX πρὸς ἑσπέραν. Heb. "between the evenings" (dual) in Lev. xxiii. 5 LXX renders more literally, ἀνὰ μέσον τῶν ἑσπερινῶν, but in Num. ix. 3 it has πρὸς ἑσπέραν as here. In De Spec. Leg. ii. 145 Philo sets the time for sacrificing the Paschal lamb "from noon until evening."

[e] εὐπραγίαι, i.e. the judgment executed on the Egyptians, see below, QE i. 20 on Ex. xii. 12.

[f] i.e. 3 P.M. In Palestine the Paschal lamb was usually slaughtered at about 3 P.M., although theoretically the slaughtering might be done "between noon and twilight" (see above, note d).

[g] ὁ προφήτης, i.e. Moses, here represented as speaking for God.

[h] See note d. Aucher renders more literally, "tempus mediocre ad vesperam vergens."

[i] τὸ ῥητόν.

[j] τὸ πρὸς διάνοιαν.

[k] Philo here refers to the LXX expression θυσία.

[l] ἡ αὐλὴ καὶ ὁρατὴ . . . Aucher has "infallibile sacrificium."

[m] The Arm. park' may here reflect δόξα in the sense of "opinion." Aucher "in rebus suppositis."

apparent and invisible.[a] Now the time of evening does not have a refulgent brightness, such as occurs at midday, nor is it darkened, although while day is near and close to night, it is dimmed to a certain extent. Such happens to be [b] the state of progressive men.[c] For they do not completely change to virtue [d] nor do they remain unhindered [e] in the affairs of mortal life.

12. (Ex. xii. 7) Why does He command (them) to place some of the blood upon the doorposts and upon the lintel of every house ? [f]

That is (because), as I said a little earlier,[g] at that time every house became an altar and a temple of God for the contemplative,[h] wherefore He rightly deemed them worthy of making divine offerings of blood upon the front parts of each (house) [i] that they might at the same time, showing

[a] Aucher " in invisibilem studere transferri."

[b] πέφυκε : Aucher " habetur ex natura."

[c] τῶν προκοπτόντων.   [d] ἀρετήν.

[e] Aucher " sine obstaculo (vel, discrimine)." One would expect " nor do they remain completely immersed " or the like. The Arm. anargel renders ἀκώλυτος, ἀκόλαστος and ἀκρατής. Perhaps, therefore, we should here render, " incontinent."

[f] LXX καὶ λήμψονται ἀπὸ τοῦ αἵματος καὶ θήσουσιν ἐπὶ τῶν δύο σταθμῶν καὶ ἐπὶ τὴν φλιὰν ἐν τοῖς οἴκοις ἐν οἷς ἐὰν φάγωσιν αὐτὰ ἐν αὐτοῖς. The meanings of the two architectural terms in the Arm. and LXX texts are not precise, since both terms in both languages may render " doorpost " or " lintel " or " threshold." But the Philonic context and the Heb. original favour the rendering given above. Aucher, however, renders, " super limina et super postes."

[g] In QE i. 10.

[h] τοῖς θεωρητικοῖς (or ὁρατικοῖς)= Israel as elsewhere in Philo, e.g. Quis Rer. Div. Heres 78, De Somniis ii. 173 ; so, too, Aucher, " contemplativis (Israelitis)."

[i] As Aucher notes, the meaning is somewhat uncertain because of the ambiguity of two of the Arm. words ; he renders, " unde jure divini sacrificii ex sanguine offerendo super postes singulorum dignos eos afficit."

21

contempt of their enemies, sacrifice without fear and, as it were, bear testimony to and show confidence in the greatness and abundance of God's gracious acts.[a] That is the literal meaning.[b] But as for the deeper meaning,[c] it is this. Since our soul is threefold,[d] the heart is likened to the lintel, desire to the house, and reason to the two doorposts. And since each of these parts is destined [e] to move on [f] to righteousness and piety and worthy holiness [g] and to change to other virtues,[h] it is necessary for it to participate in virtue, to which it is kin by blood.[i]

13. (Ex. xii. 8a) Why does He command (them) to eat the flesh of the Paschal lamb [j] at night ? [k]

As for the literal meaning,[l] since good things [m] were ordered to take place at night, it was right [n] that the

---

[a] τῶν τοῦ θεοῦ χαρίτων. Aucher renders the last clause somewhat differently, " sed quasi ostentantes confidenter per magnitudinem copiamque Dei gratiae."

[b] τὸ ῥητόν.

[c] τὸ πρὸς διάνοιαν.

[d] Cf. Quis Rer. Div. Heres 225 ψυχὴ γὰρ τρισμερὴς μέν ἐστι. Philo here follows Plato in assuming that the soul has three faculties or parts, emotion (θυμός), appetite or desire (ἐπιθυμία) and reason (λόγος).

[e] μέλλοντος.

[f] Lit. " to migrate."

[g] εἰς δικαιοσύνην καὶ εὐσέβειαν καὶ ἀξίαν ὁσιότητα.

[h] ἀρετάς.

[i] The meaning of the last clause is uncertain. Aucher renders, " necesse habet ut participet sanguinem cognatum virtute," adding in a footnote, " vel, ut consanguineus participet virtutem." Apparently Philo means that blood is in general a symbol of kinship, cf. De Virtutibus 79.

[j] Arm. p'esxeki= τοῦ πάσχα.

[k] LXX καὶ φάγονται τὰ κρέα τῇ νυκτὶ ταύτῃ.

[l] τὸ ῥητόν.

[m] εὐπραγιῶν, i.e. the judgment executed upon the Egyptians, cf. QE i. 11 and 20.

[n] Aucher, in disregard of the Arm. word-order, renders, " rectum fuit secundum ordinem."

victims sacrificed in thanksgiving should be consumed by
the eaters at the same time. But as for the deeper meaning,[a] it was proper for those who wished truly to repent [b]
to effect the purification of their souls [c] invisibly and without making signs and not saying anything more but only
believing (themselves) to stand in night and darkness, in
order that no visible (and) visionary form of imaginary
idols might appear to be seen.[d] And none the less does
glory follow the humility of the worshippers,[e] for darkness
does not make the stars invisible ; rather do they appear
more clearly at night.

14. (Ex. xii. 8b) (Why) does He command that the flesh
of the Passover [f] sacrifice be offered roasted ? [g]

First, for the sake of speed, for He was hastening the
exodus. Second, for the sake of simplicity,[h] for that which
is roasted is prepared more simply [i] and without dressing.
In the third place, He does not permit (us) to lead a life

---

[a] τὸ πρὸς διάνοιαν.

[b] μετανοεῖν.

[c] *Cf. De Spec. Leg.* ii. 147 " But to those accustomed to
turn literal facts into allegory the Passover (τὰ διαβατήρια)
suggests the purification of the soul (ψυχῆς κάθαρσιν)."

[d] The text is somewhat obscure. Aucher renders a little
more freely, " eoquod nulla videatur imaginaria visio simu-
lacri idolorum instar." In *De Spec. Leg.* i. 319-323 Philo
inveighs agaiṇst the pagan mysteries celebrated in the darkness of night, while in *De Spec. Leg.* ii. 155 he points out that
the Passover sacrifice takes place in the clear light of the full
moon.

[e] Aucher less aptly, I think, renders, " quum non parva
sequitur religiosos humilitas ac gloria."

[f] τῶν διαβατηρίων, see *QE* i. 11, note c.

[g] LXX καὶ φάγονται τὰ κρέα . . . ὀπτὰ πυρί.

[h] The Arm. lit.=δι' ἀκρασίαν, which usu. means " intemperance " in Philo, but here means more literally " not
being mixed (with spices, etc.)." Possibly, however, the
original was ἀκηρασίαν " purity."

[i] ἁπλούστερον.

23

filled with luxury,[a] for boiling[b] is an indication of variety and seasoning.[c]

15. (Ex. xii. 8c) (Why) does He say that they shall offer[d] unleavened bread on bitter herbs together with the above-mentioned sacrifice ?[e]

Unleavened bread is (a sign) of great haste and speed, while the bitter herbs (are a sign) of the life of bitterness and struggle which they endure as slaves. That is the literal meaning.[f] But as for the deeper meaning,[g] this is worth noting, (namely) that that which is leavened and fermented[h] rises, while that which is unleavened is low.[i] Each of these is a symbol of types of soul,[j] one being haughty and swollen with arrogance, the other being unchangeable and prudent, choosing the middle way rather than extremes because of desire and zeal for equality.[k] But the bitter herbs are a manifestation of a psychic migration,[l] through which one removes from passion to impassivity and from wickedness to virtue.[m] For those who naturally and genuinely repent[n] become bitter toward their former way of life and are vexed with their wretched life, weeping, sighing and groaning because they have given over the most necessary part of time to that seductive

---

[a] τρυφῆς vel sim. : Aucher " voluptate."
[b] ἕψησις, as opposed to ὄπτησις.
[c] ποικιλίας καὶ ἀρτύματος.
[d] Scripture " eat," see next note.
[e] LXX καὶ ἄζυμα ἐπὶ πικρίδων ἔδονται. In commenting briefly on this phrase in *De Congressu* 162 Philo cites it as ἐπὶ πικρίδων τὰ ἄζυμα ἐσθίειν.
[f] τὸ ῥητόν.   [g] τὸ πρὸς διάνοιαν.
[h] τὸ ἐζυμωμένον ⟨καὶ⟩ ζέον vel sim. : Aucher " fermentatum pustulis."
[i] ταπεινόν : Aucher " desidet."
[j] ὧν ἑκάτερον σύμβολόν ἐστι τῶν ψυχῶν τρόπων.
[k] ἰσότητος.
[l] ψυχικῆς ἀποικίας : Aucher " spiritualis emigrationis."
[m] ἐκ παθῶν εἰς ἀπάθειαν καὶ ἐκ πονηρίας εἰς ἀρετήν.
[n] φύσει καὶ γνησίως μετανοοῦσι.

and deceitful mistress, Desire,[a] and have spent [b] the prime
of their youth in being deceived by her when they ought to
have renewed themselves and advanced [c] in the contemplation of wisdom [d] toward the goal of a happy, fortunate
and immortal life.[e] And so, we who desire repentance eat
the unleavened bread with bitter herbs, that is, we first
eat bitterness over our old [f] and unendurable life, and then
(we eat) the opposite of overboastful arrogance through
meditation on humility,[g] which is called reverence.[h] For
the memory of former sins causes fear, and by restraining
t through recollection brings no little profit to the mind.[i]

16. (Ex. xii. 9a) What is the meaning of the words,
You shall not eat (it) raw " [j] ?

And who of mankind will eat raw meat ? Carnivores
among beasts and eaters of raw flesh (alone do so). But
man is a tame animal by nature,[k] especially those who are
adorned with a character [l] in accordance with the divine
law.[m] Accordingly, He appears to allegorize [n] all this, for
He says that those who change from wickedness to virtue [o]
shall not eat of repentance [p] when it is raw and crude but
(shall do so) by heating it, that is, with hot and ignited
principles. For many men change unexpectedly to the
opposite by an irrational impulse,[q] from generosity to

[a] ἐπιθυμία.
[b] Aucher amplifies in rendering, " male traduxerunt."
[c] Aucher combines the two infinitives in rendering,
jucunde proficere."   [d] τῇ σοφίας θεωρίᾳ.
[e] Aucher renders less literally, " ad felicem immortalis
vitae statum."
[f] Lit. " oldness " (παλαιότητος) : Aucher " transactum
empus."   [g] ταπεινώσεως.
[h] Prob. αἰδώς : Aucher " pudor."
[i] Aucher renders less literally and less intelligibly, " et
n se recolligens mentem, non paucam utilitatem fert."
[j] LXX οὐκ ἔδεσθε ἀπ' αὐτῶν ὠμόν.
[k] ἥμερον ζῷον φύσει.   [l] Aucher " cunctis moribus."
[m] κατὰ τὸν θεῖον νόμον.   [n] ἀλληγορεῖν.   [o] ἀρετήν.
[p] μετανοίας, see the preceding section.   [q] ἀλόγῳ ὁρμῇ.

25

parsimony, and from a barbarous,[a] artificial and delicate
way of life to a harsh way of life,[b] and from love of glory
they fly to ingloriousness. These men no one will praise.
For, as one might say allegorically, their change is raw
and crude and unstable,[c] wherefore they are not aware
of changing, not to virtue but to the opposite vices. But
those who change by the principle of knowledge [d] and are
hardened [e] as though by the force of fire have acquired
a stable and unmoving usefulness.

17. (Ex. xii. 9b) Why was the head to be offered with
the feet and the entrails at the Paschal sacrifice ? [f]

The literal meaning [g] is, I believe, somewhat as follows.
Since He believes that the whole sacrifice should be consumed, He mentions all the parts, indicating [h] that it is
not proper to leave anything at all. But as for the deeper
meaning,[i] the head is the first, highest and principal (part).
But the internal (parts) He opposes to the external. For
He says that it is fitting for him who is purified to purify
his entire soul [j] with his inner desires,[k] and the words that
go outward and the deeds through serviceable instruments [l]
and through the head (as) chief, as it were.

18. (Ex. xii. 10) (Why) does He command that the
remainder of the Paschal sacrifice be burnt at dawn ? [m]

---

[a] Aucher " agresti."   [b] σκληραγωγίαν.

[c] Aucher renders inaccurately, " quoniam cruda et in-
constans est, ut aliquis diceret, summa commutatio eorum."

[d] λόγῳ ἐπιστήμης vel sim.

[e] Lit. " are fitted together " : Aucher " componuntur."

[f] LXX κεφαλὴν σὺν τοῖς ποσὶν (Heb. " legs ") καὶ τοῖς ἐνδοσ-
θίοις.   [g] τὸ ῥητόν.

[h] αἰνιττόμενος : Aucher " declarans."

[i] τὸ πρὸς διάνοιαν.

[j] The Arm. noun (= ψυχή) is strangely in the plural.

[k] ἐπιθυμίαις.

[l] διὰ τῶν ὑπηρετούντων ὀργάνων.

[m] τὰ δὲ καταλιπόμενα ἀπ' αὐτοῦ ἕως πρωὶ ἐν πυρὶ κατακαύσετε.

EXODUS, BOOK I

He did not think it right that the sun should first shine upon the Passover *a* because of His completing a good thing *b* at night, as I have said.*c* And why this was at night has already been said, where the manifestations of deeds took place and the praises of the deeds. And it was commanded that the sacrifice be prepared at this time in order that all the limbs of the sacrifice might be consumed. For many of the necessary things are wont to be overlooked in an unexpected and hurried exodus, especially by those who are hurrying to make the exodus with great speed. (And) it was not proper for the unworthy and unclean hands of the Egyptians to touch the remains. Wherefore, taking care that they should not be defiled in any way, He handed them over to an undefiled king, the fire.*d*

*19. (Ex. xii. 11) (Why) does He command (everyone) to eat, having a girdle and shoes and a staff ? *e*

All the things mentioned are an indication of the manner of journeying of those who are in haste. For it is the custom of those who are about to travel a long way to wear shoes and to be girt with a girdle and to take a staff for their needs, because shoes protect the feet, while girding oneself makes movement easier for the legs, and a staff is useful to lean on and to drive away poisonous reptiles and other beasts. This, then, suffices for the explanation of the literal meaning.*f* But as for the deeper meaning,*g* this must be said. The girdles represent drawing together *h*

---

a τῶν διαβατηρίων, cf. QE i. 4.

b εὐπραγίαν, *i.e.* the judgment executed on the Egyptians.

c In QE i. 11, 13. See also QE i. 20 on Ex. xii. 12.

d Apparently fire is here called " an undefiled king " in implied contrast to the unclean king of Egypt.

e LXX οὕτως δὲ φάγεσθε αὐτό· αἱ ὀσφύες ὑμῶν περιεζωσμέναι καὶ τὰ ὑποδήματα ἐν τοῖς ποσὶν ὑμῶν καὶ αἱ βακτηρίαι ἐν ταῖς χερσὶν ὑμῶν· καὶ ἔδεσθε αὐτὸ μετὰ σπουδῆς· πάσχα ἐστὶν κυρίῳ. Philo briefly allegorizes this verse in Leg. All. iii. 154 and De Sacr. Abelis 63. *f* τοῦ ῥητοῦ. *g* τὸ πρὸς διάνοιαν.

h The Greek frag. (which begins here) has στάσιν, while the Arm. more closely renders συστολήν or the like.

27

and the coming together of the sensual pleasures and other passions,[a] which, being, as it were, released and let go, overtake all souls.[b] Wherefore not ineptly does He add that one must have a girdle about the middle, for this place is considered as the manger of the many-headed beast of desire within us.[c]

And the staves seem to represent a royal, disciplinary [d] and stable form, for the rod is a symbol of kingship and an instrument of discipline for those who are unable to act prudently [e] without being scolded.[f] And it is a figure [g] of unmoving and stable souls which abandon whatever inclines to either side and in two (directions). And the shoes indicate the covering and protection of one who is engaged in hurrying not on a trackless way but on a well-travelled and worn path which leads to virtue.[h] Wherefore that which is (here) said is contrary to what (actually) takes place. For, He says, they must have shoes " in their feet " [i] which is impossible and cannot be done, for the feet of the wearers are different from the shoes. But it seems from this and many other (passages) that He is recalling the mind to the contemplation of natural ideas.[j] For shoes are inanimate while feet are animate, just as is each of the various other parts of the body. And so, He says, let not the inanimate be a covering for that which

[a] So the Greek frag., συναγωγὴν ἡδονῶν καὶ τῶν ἄλλων παθῶν.

[b] The Greek frag. reads more briefly ἃ τέως ἀνεῖτο καὶ κεχάλαστο.

[c] Similarly the Greek frag. (which ends here), οὐκ ἀπὸ δὲ σκοποῦ προσέθηκε τὸ δεῖν ζώννυσθαι κατὰ τὴν ὀσφύν· ὁ γὰρ τόπος ἐκεῖνος εἰς φάτνην ἀποκέκριται πολυκεφάλῳ θρέμματι τῶν ἐν ἡμῖν ἐπιθυμιῶν.

[d] Or " admonitory " : Aucher " monitivam."

[e] σωφρονίζεσθαι.

[f] Cf. De Mut. Nom. 175 ἡ ῥάβδος . . . ἡ νουθεσία, ὁ σωφρονισμός, ἡ παιδεία.

[g] τρόπος vel sim. : Aucher " exemplar."

[h] ἀρετήν.

[i] For homiletical purposes Philo dwells on the literal meaning of the LXX phrase τὰ ὑποδήματα ἐν τοῖς ποσίν.

[j] φυσικῶν ἰδεῶν, i.e. religious-philosophical concepts.

28

has a soul but, on the contrary, let the animate (be a cover) for the inanimate in order that the better may not be held and contained by the bad but the bad by the better. For the Creator has made the soul queen and mistress of the body, and the body the obedient servant and slave of the soul.

20. (Ex. xii. 12) (Why) does He say, " And on all the gods of the Egyptians I will take vengeance ; I (am) the Lord " *a* ?

(This is said) concerning all unstable and unworthy things, for (only) up to a certain point does the pretence of divinized idols *b* succeed by accidentally attaining knowledge in giving oracular responses *c* through persuasive words and parables and still other (devices) which have their source in chance. And these are all of short duration, for they never see the light of sacred truth, *d* by which alone the Creator of all, Who keeps created beings in security and is truly *e* their Lord, can naturally be comprehended. *f* And the comprehension *g* of Him immediately dissolves unstable and unworthy human beliefs and the power *h* by which men are overwhelmed because of the impotence within them. And so, just as are the words of idols, so in all things is the way of life of the foolish man. For he who has a false and erroneous opinion *i* concerning the best, (namely) God, also has an erroneous and false way of life. And as for those who have true knowledge without

---

a Philo here comments on only the last part of the verse which reads in full in the lxx text καὶ ἐλεύσομαι ἐν γῇ Αἰγύπτῳ ἐν τῇ νυκτὶ ταύτῃ καὶ πατάξω πᾶν πρωτότοκον ἐν γῇ Αἰγύπτῳ ἀπὸ ἀνθρώπου ἕως κτήνους, καὶ ἐν πᾶσι τοῖς θεοῖς τῶν Αἰγυπτίων ποιήσω τὴν ἐκδίκησιν (Heb. " judgments ")· ἐγὼ κύριος.

b τῦφος (vel sim.) τῶν θεοπλαστηθέντων εἰδώλων.

c Lit. " in places of questioning."

d Aucher, disregarding the Arm. word-order, renders, " sanctum lumen veritatis."

e ὄντως : Aucher " solus."

f καταλαμβάνεσθαι πέφυκε.

g ἡ κατάληψις.   *h* τὴν δύναμιν.   *i* δόξα.

29

error concerning the Existent One,[a] their truthfulness is honoured in every other matter.

*21. (Ex. xii. 17) What is the meaning of the words, " I will bring out your force from Egypt "[b] ? Why does He not say " you "[c] ?

" Force " is the godly piety of the seeing nation.[d] Now, so long as those who have this force dwell in cities and villages, the cities and villages act well and properly, for they are adorned at least with the virtue[e] of others if not with their own.[f] But when (these inhabitants) depart, the portion of common good fortune is changed. For good men are the pillars of whole communities, and they support cities and city-governments as if they were great houses.[g] That is the literal meaning.[h] But as for the deeper meaning,[i] it is this. Just as, when health leaves the body, illness immediately seizes it, so also, if godly piety, the force of the soul, departs, one must necessarily expect its waiting house-mate,[j] impotence and impiety, for not even a seed of decency[k] remains, but even if there is a small remaining spark, this too is driven out, and there supervenes a great and most severe affliction.

22. (Ex. xii. 22c) What is the meaning of the words,

---

[a] περὶ τοῦ Ὄντος : Aucher " de Deo."

[b] Philo here comments on only part of vs. 17, of which the LXX text reads καὶ φυλάξετε τὴν ἐντολὴν (Heb. " unleavened bread ") ταύτην· ἐν γὰρ τῇ ἡμέρᾳ ταύτῃ ἐξάγω (Heb. " I brought out ") τὴν δύναμιν ὑμῶν (Heb. " your hosts ") ἐκ γῆς Αἰγύπτου, καὶ ποιήσετε τὴν ἡμέραν ταύτην εἰς γενεὰς ὑμῶν νόμιμον αἰώνιον.

[c] i.e. instead of " your force."

[d] δύναμίς ἐστι ἡ τοῦ ὁρατικοῦ γένους (i.e. Israel) θεοσέβεια.

[e] ἀρετῇ. [f] ταῖς οἰκείαις.

[g] So, with one addition, the Greek fragment (which contains only this sentence), ἄνδρες ἀγαθοί, τροπικώτερον εἰπεῖν, κίονές εἰσι δήμων ὅλων, ὑπερείδοντες, καθάπερ οἰκίας μεγάλας, τὰς πόλεις καὶ τὰς πολιτείας.

[h] τὸ ῥητόν. [i] τὸ πρὸς διάνοιαν.

[j] Aucher " satellitem domesticum." [k] καλοκἀγαθίας.

30

" And no one shall go out through the doors of his house until morning " [a] ?

As for the literal meaning,[b] this must be said, (namely) that God wishes to accomplish His benefactions solely by His own hand without any human operator [c] both in punishing those who deserve every curse and in helping those to whom unjust and violent things happen.[d] But as for the deeper meaning,[e] " morning " is a figure of sense-perceptible light,[f] for the mind [g] until that time dwells in itself [h] alone, leaving the tumult of the senses. And sometimes, permitting itself to use the senses, it is wont to go about everywhere. Now this going about produces for it error and tracklessness,[i] for the doors, by which I understand the senses,[j] are opened to the streams of sense-perceptible things,[k] into which the mind throws itself down, as if from some high precipice, from the perfect, intelligible and incorporeal ideas.[l] But he who does not go out through the doors of the soul and experiences a good fear, sees only those things worthy to be seen, which shine forth [m] from thoughts stripped of the senses. Wherefore (Scripture) adds, " The Lord will pass over the door," [n] by which I understand both the senses and all sense-perceptible things. For so long as the senses are released

---

[a] LXX ὑμεῖς δὲ οὐκ ἐξελεύσεσθε ἕκαστος τὴν θύραν τοῦ οἴκου αὑτοῦ ἕως πρωΐ.　　　　[b] τὸ ῥητόν.

[c] Aucher " cooperatore."

[d] Aucher amplifies in rendering, " illos vero qui omnem maledictionem merent punire volens aut quibus iniqua quaedam per vim inferenda sint, id mediantibus aliis prosequi."　　　　[e] τὸ πρὸς διάνοιαν.

[f] σημεῖον τροπικόν (vel sim.) ἐστι φωτὸς αἰσθητοῦ.

[g] ὁ νοῦς.

[h] The Arm. demonstr. pron. here seems to be used as a reflexive. Aucher boldly renders, " in corpore."

[i] πλάνην καὶ ἀνοδίαν.　　　　[j] τὰς αἰσθήσεις.

[k] Slightly emending the Arm. which lit.= τῶν αἰσθήσεων instead of τῶν αἰσθητῶν.

[l] ἀπὸ τῶν τελειῶν καὶ νοητῶν καὶ ἀσωμάτων ἰδεῶν.

[m] Aucher " oriuntur."

[n] See LXX of Ex. xii. 23b καὶ παρελεύσεται κύριος τὴν θύραν.

QUESTIONS AND ANSWERS

and apart by themselves,^a they belong to the mind.^b But when they descend into the body, they give admittance to a baser idea, imitating, in a way, the nature of irrational creatures.^c

23. (Ex. xii. 23c) (Why) does (Scripture) say that He will not let " the destroyer enter your houses to strike "^d?

It weaves into the whole legislation ^e the faithful and worthy sentiment ^f that we are not to make the Deity the cause of any evil.^g For when it says that He will not suffer the destroyer, it makes plain that corruption and destruction are brought about through certain others as ministers but not through the sovereign King.^h There you have the literal meaning.ⁱ But as for the deeper meaning,^j this must be said. Into every soul at its very birth ^k there enter two powers,^l the salutary and the destructive.^m If the salutary one is victorious and prevails, the opposite

---

^a ὅσον ἅφεταί εἰσι καὶ ἴδιαι καθ᾽ ἑαυτὰς αἱ ἰδέαι : Aucher "quantum liberi sunt et in se collecti sensus."

^b Lit. "they are of the mind " : Aucher " mentis sunt."

^c ἀλόγων ζῴων φύσιν.

^d LXX καὶ οὐκ ἀφήσει τὸν ὀλεθρεύοντα εἰσελθεῖν εἰς τὰς οἰκίας ὑμῶν πατάξαι. Philo quotes this passage and comments on it very briefly in Leg. All. ii. 34.

^e νομοθεσίᾳ.

^f γνώμην : Aucher " voluntatem."

^g That God is not responsible for any evil is stated by Philo in several places, e.g. De Confus. Ling. 161, 182. Sometimes, however, he admits that God sometimes Himself inflicts evil as a punishment, see Wolfson, Philo, i. 282, 382.

^h διὰ τοῦ πρώτου βασιλέως.

ⁱ τὸ ῥητόν.   ^j τὸ πρὸς διάνοιαν.

^k ἅμα τῇ γενέσει.   ^l δυνάμεις.

^m ἡ μὲν σωτηρία, ἡ δὲ φθοροποιός. These powers are not to be identified with the two chief powers or attributes of God, the βασιλική or κολαστήριος δύναμις and the εὐεργέτις or ποιητικὴ δύναμις, on which see QG ii. 51, iv. 2, QE ii. 68 et al. They correspond more closely to the good and evil cosmic powers, identified with good and bad angels (or demons) respectively.

32

one is too weak to see.ᵃ And if the latter prevails, no
profit at all or little is obtained from the salutary one.
Through these powers the world ᵇ too was created. People
call them by other names : the salutary (power) they call
powerful and beneficent, and the opposite one (they call)
unbounded ᶜ and destructive. Thus, the sun and moon
and the appropriate positions of the other stars and their
ordered functions and the whole heaven together come
into being and exist through the two (powers). And they
are created ᵈ in accordance with the better part of these,ᵉ
namely when the salutary and beneficent (power) brings
to an end ᶠ the unbounded and destructive nature. Wherefore also to those who have attained such a state and a
nature similar to this is immortality given. But the
nation ᵍ is a mixture of both (these powers), from which
the heavens and the entire world as a whole have received
this mixture. Now, sometimes the evil becomes greater in
this mixture, and hence (all creatures) live in torment,
harm, ignominy, contention, battle and bodily illness
together with all the other things in human life, as in the
whole world, so in man. And this mixture is in both the
wicked man and the wise man ʰ but not in the same way.
For the souls of foolish men have the unbounded and

ᵃ The Arm. inf. may be either active or passive, hence we
may here render " to be seen." Moreover, the verb *tesanem*
renders φροντίζειν as well as ὁρᾶν, hence Aucher here renders,
" ad aliquid sibi providendum." I suspect, however, that
the original reading was not ὁρᾶν " to see " but ὁρμᾶν " to
attack."   ᵇ ὁ κόσμος.
  ᶜ Prob. ἄπειρον, perhaps here used in the sense of the
indeterminate, inferior principle of the Pythagoreans.
  ᵈ Arm. *stanam* here renders κτίζειν rather than κτᾶσθαι, as
Aucher supposes, see the next note.
  ᵉ Aucher renders less accurately, " acquiritur autem
melior eorum pars."
  ᶠ Form and meaning of the verb *katarem*, which usually
renders τελειοῦν, are here not certain : Aucher " subigit."
  ᵍ It is not clear whether this refers to the nation (γένος) of
Israel, as the Arm. glossator supposes, or to the human race.
  ʰ ἐν τῷ σοφῷ.

destructive rather than the powerful and salutary (power), and it [a] is full of misery when it dwells with earthly creatures. But the prudent and noble (soul) rather receives the powerful and salutary (power) and, on the contrary, possesses in itself good fortune and happiness,[b] being carried around with the heaven because of kinship [c] with it. Most excellently, therefore, does (Scripture) say that He will not let " the destroyer enter your houses to strike," and this is what (actually) happens, for the force which is the cause of destruction strives,[d] as it were, to enter the soul, but is prevented by the divine beneficences [e] from striking (it), for these are salutary. But those from whom the favours and gifts of God [f] are separated and cut off suffer the experience of desertion and widowhood.[g] The meaning is somewhat as follows. Into this soul there extend and enter visible appearances [h] which are mixed in accordance with various kinds of involuntary traits of character,[i] sometimes naked and unarmed, and sometimes armed and in a certain manner [j] threatening death, and they inflict mighty blows upon the thoughts.[k] Now, these blows are the admission [l] of appearances. But perfect good is not obtained from any of these.

[a] Lit. " which," referring to the destructive power rather than to the salutary one.
[b] Or " good fame."
[c] συγγένειαν.
[d] φιλοτιμεῖται vel sim. : Aucher " inhibetur."
[e] ὑπὸ τῶν θείων εὐεργεσιῶν.
[f] αἱ τοῦ θεοῦ χάριτες καὶ δωρεαί.
[g] ἐρημίας καὶ χηρείας.
[h] φαντασίαι : Aucher " imaginationes."
[i] ἀκουσίων τρόπων vel sim. : Aucher " mores involuntarios."
[j] τρόπον τινά.
[k] τοὺς λογισμούς.
[l] συγχώρησις vel sim. : Aucher " admissio."

BOOK II [a]

*1. (Ex. xx. 25b) What is the meaning of the words, " If thou strike thy hand-tool against it, then it is defiled " [b] ?

Those who presume to lay hands upon nature and transform the works of nature by their own undertakings defile the undefiled. [c] For the things of nature are perfect and full and are not in need of any excision or addition or anything at all. [d]

*2. (Ex. xxii. 21) [e] Why does (Scripture) in admonishing, " Thou shalt not oppress a sojourner," add, " For ye were sojourners in the land of the Egyptians " [f] ?

[a] Book II of the *Quaestiones in Exodum*, which is about three times as long as Book I, probably contains most, if not all, of what were, in the original Greek, Books III-V. See the Introduction.

[b] The whole verse reads in LXX ἐὰν δὲ θυσιαστήριον ἐκ λίθων ποιῇς μοι, οὐκ οἰκοδομήσεις αὐτοὺς τμητούς. τὸ γὰρ ἐγχειρίδιόν σου (Heb. " thy knife ") ἐπιβέβληκας ἐπ' αὐτούς (Heb. " if thou lift against it "), καὶ μεμίανται (Heb. " then thou wilt defile it "). The Greek frag. reads more briefly τί ἐστι " τὸ γὰρ ἐγχειρίδιόν σου " καὶ τὰ ἑξῆς;

[c] So the Greek frag., οἱ τὴν φύσιν παρεγχειρεῖν τολμῶντες καὶ τὰ ἔργα τῆς φύσεως ἐγχειρήμασιν ἰδίοις μεταμορφοῦντες τὰ ἀμίαντα μιαίνουσι.

[d] The Greek frag. reads more briefly τέλεια γὰρ καὶ πλήρη τὰ τῆς φύσεως, προσθήκης οὐδεμιᾶς δεόμενα.

[e] Heb., Ex. xxii. 20.

[f] LXX καὶ προσήλυτον (Heb. gēr originally meant " sojourner " or " guest," " client," etc., later " proselyte " as in the LXX) οὐ κακώσετε οὐδὲ μὴ θλίψετε αὐτόν· ἦτε γὰρ προσήλυτοι ἐν γῇ Αἰγύπτῳ.

(Scripture) first makes it clearly apparent and demonstrable [a] that in reality [b] the sojourner [c] is one who circumcises not his uncircumcision but his desires and sensual pleasures and the other passions of the soul.[d] For in Egypt the Hebrew nation was not circumcised [e] but being mistreated with all (kinds of) mistreatment by the inhabitants in their hatred of strangers, it lived with them in self-restraint and endurance, not by necessity but rather of its own free choice,[f] because it took refuge in God the Saviour, Who sent His beneficent power and delivered from their difficult and hopeless situation those who made supplication (to Him).[g] Therefore (Scripture) adds,[h] " Ye yourselves know the soul of the sojourner." But what is the mind of the sojourner [i] if not [j] alienation from belief in many gods [k] and familiarity with honouring the one

[a] The Greek frag. reads more briefly ἐμφανέστατα παρίστησιν.

[b] The Greek frag. (see next note but one) has nothing corresponding to the Arm. *isk* = " in reality " or the like.

[c] Here, as usually, Philo takes προσήλυτος in the sense of " proselyte."

[d] So the Greek frag. (with one change of word-order), ὅτι προσήλυτός ἐστιν, οὐχ ὁ περιτμηθεὶς τὴν ἀκροβυστίαν ἀλλ' ὁ τὰς ἡδονὰς καὶ τὰς ἐπιθυμίας καὶ τὰ ἄλλα πάθη τῆς ψυχῆς.

[e] So the Greek frag., ἐν Αἰγύπτῳ γὰρ τὸ Ἑβραῖον γένος οὐ περιτέτμητο.

[f] So the Greek frag., κακωθὲν δὲ πάσαις κακώσεσι τῆς παρὰ τῶν ἐγχωρίων περὶ τοὺς ξένους ὠμότητος, ἐγκρατείᾳ καὶ καρτερίᾳ συνέβιον οὐκ ἀνάγκῃ μᾶλλον ἢ ἐθελουσίῳ γνώμῃ.

[g] So the Greek frag., διὰ τὴν ἐπὶ τὸν σωτῆρα θεὸν καταφυγήν, ὃς ἐξ ἀπόρων καὶ ἀμηχάνων ἐπιπέμψας τὴν εὐεργέτιν δύναμιν ἐρρύσατο τοὺς ἱκέτας.

[h] In Ex. xxiii. 9, of which the LXX text reads καὶ προσήλυτον οὐ θλίψετε· ὑμεῖς γὰρ οἴδατε τὴν ψυχὴν τοῦ προσηλύτου· αὐτοὶ γὰρ προσήλυτοι ἦτε ἐν γῇ Αἰγύπτῳ.

[i] So the Greek frag., τίς δὲ προσηλύτου διάνοιά ἐστιν; Note the shift from LXX's ψυχή to Philo's διάνοια.

[j] The words " if not " are omitted in the Greek frag., see next note but one.

[k] Aucher amplifies in rendering, " a voluntate serviendi multis Diis."

God and Father of all ? *ᵃ* In the second place, some call
strangers " newcomers." *ᵇ* But strangers are also those
who by themselves have run to the truth, not *ᶜ* in the same
way as those who made their sojourn in Egypt.*ᵈ* For these
are newcomers to the land,*ᵉ* while those are (newcomers)
to laws and customs.*ᶠ* But the common name of " newcomers " is ascribed to both.*ᵍ*

*3. (Ex. xxii. 22) *ʰ* Why does (Scripture) prohibit mis-
treating every widow and orphan ? *ⁱ*

It *ʲ* does not permit doing wrong to anyone, male or
female, even among strangers.*ᵏ* It does, however, give a
better and special share of thoughtfulness to widows and
orphans,*ˡ* since they are deprived of closely related helpers
and caretakers—the widows of their husbands, and the
orphans of their parents.*ᵐ* It therefore wishes them to

ᵃ The Greek frag. reads ἀλλοτρίωσις τῆς πολυθέου δόξης,
οἰκείωσις δὲ τῆς πρὸς τὸν ἕνα καὶ πατέρα τῶν ὅλων τιμῆς.

ᵇ So the Greek frag., δεύτερον ἐπήλυδας ἔνιοι καλοῦσι τοὺς
ξένους.

ᶜ The negative is omitted in the Greek frag., see next note.

ᵈ The Greek frag. reads ξένοι δὲ καὶ οἱ πρὸς τὴν ἀλήθειαν
αὐτομοληκότες, τὸν αὐτὸν τρόπον τοῖς ἐν Αἰγύπτῳ ξενιτεύσασιν.

ᵉ So the Greek frag., οὗτοι μὲν γὰρ ἐπήλυδες χώρας.

ᶠ So the Greek frag., ἐκεῖνοι δὲ νομίμων καὶ ἐθῶν εἰσι.

ᵍ So the Greek frag., τὸ δὲ ὄνομα κοινὸν ἑκατέρων " ἐπηλύδων "
ὑπογράφεται.   *ʰ* Heb., Ex. xxii. 21.

ⁱ The first of the two Greek fragments of the beginning
and end of this section reads χήραν καὶ ὀρφανὸν ἀπείρηται
κακοῦν: LXX πᾶσαν χήραν καὶ ὀρφανὸν οὐ κακώσετε. Philo
cites the verse and briefly allegorizes it in different fashion in
De Congressu 178-179, see also De Cherubim 50.

ʲ The Greek frag. has " the Law " as subject, see the next
note.

ᵏ So the Greek frag., οὐδένα μέν, οὐδὲ τῶν ἄλλων, οὔτε ἄρρενα
οὔτε θήλειαν, ἀφίησιν ἀδικεῖν ὁ νόμος.

ˡ The Greek frag. reads similarly but more smoothly
ἐξαιρέτου δὲ προνοίας μεταδίδωσιν χήραις καὶ ὀρφανοῖς.

ᵐ So the Greek frag., ἐπειδὴ τοὺς ἀναγκαίους βοηθοὺς καὶ
κηδεμόνας ἀφήρηνται, χῆραι μὲν ἄνδρας, ὀρφανοὶ δὲ γονεῖς.

enjoy their natural partnership and have their deficiencies supplied by those who [a] are in (a state of) abundance.[b] That is the literal meaning.[c] But as for the deeper meaning,[d] such souls [e] as love themselves honour the mind [f] as a husband and as a father,—as a husband perhaps because it sows in them the powers of the senses [g] by which the sense-perceptible object [h] is attained and seized ; and (they honour it) as a father because it is thought to be the parent of disciplines and arts.[i] But those who are free of self-love [j] and hasten to God obtain from above His visitations [k] and care as from a father, and as from a husband (they obtain) the sowing of good thoughts and intentions [l] and words and deeds. But it happens customarily among men that the opposite thing comes about, for when a man comes in contact with a woman, he marks the virgin as a woman.[m] But when souls become divinely inspired,[n] from (being) women they become virgins, throwing off the womanly corruptions which are (found) in sense-perception and passion.[o] Moreover, they follow after and pursue the

---

[a] Arm. *ayk'* is a misprint for *ork'*, the plural of the rel. pron.

[b] So the Greek frag., βούλεται γὰρ τῇ φυσικῇ κοινωνίᾳ χρωμένους, τὰς ἐνδείας ὑπὸ τῶν ἐν περιουσίᾳ ἀναπληροῦσθαι. Here the first Greek frag. ends ; the second begins with the sentence reading " But when souls become divinely inspired, etc."

[c] τὸ ῥητόν.   [d] τὸ πρὸς διάνοιαν.

[e] ψυχαί.   [f] τὸν νοῦν.

[g] Cf. *De Migratione* 3 πατὴρ μὲν ἡμῶν ὁ νοῦς σπείρων . . . τὰς ἀφ' ἑαυτοῦ δυνάμεις.   [h] τὸ αἰσθητόν.

[i] παιδειῶν καὶ τέχνων.   [j] φιλαυτίας.

[k] ἐπισκοπάς *vel sim.*: Aucher " visitationes."

[l] Aucher omits the second noun.

[m] As a woman with sexual experience, cf. *De Cherubim* 50 ἀνθρώπων . . . σύνοδος τὰς παρθένους γυναῖκας ἀποφαίνει.

[n] The second Greek frag. (which begins with this sentence) has προσκολληθῶσι θεῷ, of which the Arm. *astouacazgestk'* (usu. = ἔνθεοι or θεοφόροι) seems to be a free rendering.

[o] So the Greek frag., ἐκ γυναικῶν γίνονται παρθένοι, τὰς μὲν γυναικώδεις ἀποβάλλουσαι φθορὰς τῶν ἐν αἰσθήσει καὶ πάθει.

genuine and unmated virgin, the veritable wisdom of God.[a]
And so, rightly do such minds [b] become widows and are
orphaned of mortal things [c] and acquire for themselves
and have as husband the right law of nature, with which
they live.[d] And (they have) the same (as) father to tell
them with higher thoughtfulness, as though (they were)
his sons, what they ought to do.[e]

*4. (Ex. xxii. 23) [f] What is the meaning of the words,
" Ye shall not with badness mistreat the widow and the
orphan " [g] ?

The word [h] " mistreat " is used properly [i] (in some cases)
and is also used improperly [j] in other cases. (It is used)
properly in reference to deeds of badness which are peculiar
to the soul, and improperly of other cases in which harm
is done to possessions and bodies.[k] Accordingly (Scripture)
did not mention the latter evils, as not being great mis-

---

[a] The Greek frag. reads a little differently τὴν δὲ ἄψαυστον
(ἄψευστον conj. Pitra from the Arm.) καὶ ἀμιγῆ παρθένον, ἀρέσ-
κειαν θεοῦ, μεταδιώκουσι.

[b] One expects " souls " as in the Greek frag., see the next
note but one.

[c] This clause is omitted in the Greek frag.

[d] The Greek frag. reads more briefly κατὰ λόγον οὖν αἱ
τοιαῦται ψυχαὶ χηρεύουσιν, ἄνδρα τὸν τῆς φύσεως ὀρθὸν νόμον
προσσυμβιοῦσιν.

[e] So the Greek frag., καὶ πατέρα τὸν αὐτόν, ἃ χρὴ πράττειν
παραγγέλλοντα καθάπερ ἐγγόνοις μετὰ τῆς ἀνωτάτω κηδεμονίας.

[f] Heb., Ex. xxii. 22.

[g] Philo here paraphrases the lxx text which reads more
fully ἐὰν δὲ κακίᾳ κακώσετε αὐτοὺς (Heb. " him ") καὶ κεκρά-
ξαντες καταβοήσουσι (Heb. " if crying he cries out ") πρὸς
ἐμέ, ἀκοῇ εἰσακούσομαι τῆς φωνῆς αὐτῶν (Heb. " his cry ").

[h] Lit. " name " or " noun."

[i] κυρίως.

[j] καταχρηστικῶς.

[k] The fragmentary paraphrase in Procopius reads καὶ
κακοῦν ἀπαγορεύει οὐ τοσοῦτον τὴν σωματικὴν κάκωσιν ὅσον τὴν
ψυχικήν.

fortunes at all.[a] But knowing that the harm of badness
overturns entire lives by their roots from their foundation,
it first says that one should not be to anyone a teacher of
folly or licentiousness or injustice or anything similar and
of a cursed intention but should destroy the devices [b] of
such things.[c] But one should likemindedly build schools
of thoughts of wisdom and justice and the other virtues [d]
for the improvement of children in order that their natures,
before they have become hard and tough, may be able
easily to receive the shapes and forms of good things.[e]

5. (Ex. xxii. 28a) [f] Why does (Scripture) say, " gods
thou shalt not revile " [g] ?

Do they [h] then still accuse the divine Law of breaking
down the customs of others ? [i] For, behold, not only does
it offer support to those of different opinion [j] by accepting
and honouring those whom they have from the beginning
believed to be gods, but it [k] also muzzles and restrains [l]

[a] Aucher renders less literally, " posterius istud, quia nihil
magnum est malum, vix memoravit."
[b] Aucher " sedes."
[c] Procopius' paraphrase reads more briefly ὀρφανοῖς γὰρ
γινέσθω μηδεὶς ἀφροσύνης ἢ ἀκολασίας διδάσκαλος.
[d] λογισμῶν σοφίας καὶ δικαιοσύνης καὶ τῶν ἄλλων ἀρετῶν διδα-
σκαλεῖα συμφώνως οἰκοδομεῖν.
[e] Procopius' paraphrase reads more briefly ἀλλὰ τῶν
ἐναντίων (sc. διδάσκαλος γινέσθω), ἐν ὅσῳ τὰς ψυχὰς ἔχουσιν ἁπαλὰς
πρὸς τὴν τῶν θείων χαρακτήρων ὑποδοχήν.
[f] Heb., Ex. xxii. 27a.
[g] lxx θεοὺς (Heb. 'ᵉlōhîm = " God " or " gods " or
" judges ") οὐ κακολογήσεις. Philo comments on this half-
verse in De Vita Mosis ii. 203-205 and De Spec. Leg. i. 53,
see Colson's notes on these passages.
[h] i.e. opponents of the Jews.
[i] i.e. of the Gentiles.   [j] τοῖς ἑτεροδόξοις.
[k] The unexpressed subject may be Moses as well as Scripture, here as elsewhere.
[l] Aucher renders the two verbs by the single verb " co-
ercet."

40

its own disciples,[a] not permitting them to revile these with
a loose tongue, for it believes that well-spoken praise [b] is
better. In the second place, those who are in error and
are deluded about their own native [c] gods and because of
custom believe to be inerrant truth what is a falsely created
error, by which even keen and discerning minds are blinded,
are not peaceful toward or reconciled with [d] those who do
not gladly accept their (opinion). And this is the beginning
and origin of wars. But to us the Law has described the
source of peace as a beautiful possession. In the third
place, he who speaks evil (of others) must of necessity
receive the contrary reproach in similar matters. Accordingly, those who have in mind a concern for dignity [e] will
refrain from reviling other gods, in order that the power [f]
of the truly certain and existent (God) [g] may be well spoken
of and praised in the mouths of all. For (thus) we shall
seem not to be hearing but to be speaking, as others use
our voice.[h] For there is no difference between saying
something oneself and inviting others to say it in any way.

*6. (Ex. xxii. 28b) [i] Why, after first saying that one is
not to revile gods, does (Scripture) straightway add, " nor
rulers " [j]?

[a] τοὺς ἑαυτοῦ μαθητάς, i.e. the Jews.
[b] εὔφημον ἔπαινον.   [c] ἐγχωρίους or πατρίους.
[d] Aucher renders more freely, " implacabilem hostilitatem
colunt."
[e] Or " holiness " : Aucher " dignitatis."
[f] δύναμις.
[g] The Arm. lit.= τοῦ ὄντως σαφοῦς καὶ ὄντος. Perhaps the
Arm. translator misread σαφῶς as σαφοῦς ; if so, we should
render, " the truly and clearly existent (God ") ; elsewhere
Philo refers to God as ὁ ὄντως ὤν but never as σαφής. Aucher
renders more briefly, " veri Entis."
[h] i.e. if we cause others to praise God, we shall be praising
Him vicariously.
[i] Heb., Ex. xxii. 27b.
[j] LXX καὶ ἄρχοντας (v.l. ἄρχοντα : Heb. " ruler ") τοῦ λαοῦ
σου οὐ κακῶς ἐρεῖς.

QUESTIONS AND ANSWERS

As the poets say, rulers are closely akin and near in lineage to and of the same seed as the gods, for leaders and rulers are, as these [a] say, able to do good or evil by virtue of their own power. In the second place, it takes thought for all other men in order that they may not incur irremediable punishments.[b] For when rulers hear evil things said (about themselves), they do not punish the speakers by judicial process but unrestrainedly use their power for utter destruction.[c] In the third place, (Scripture) does not seem to legislate about every ruler but hints in many ways that he who is (ruler) of the whole people and belongs to the Hebrew nation has been appointed as a virtuous ruler and leader.[d] For reviling is foreign to a good man while praise is most congenial.[e] For nothing is so conducive to thoughtful care [f] as well-spoken praise.[g]

7. (Ex. xxii. 29, xxiii. 15c) [h] What is the meaning of the

[a] Aucher " ipsi."
[b] Slightly different is the reading of the first Greek frag. of this section, προνοεῖται τῶν ἰδιωτῶν ὡς μὴ περιπίπτοιεν ἀνηκέστοις τιμωρίαις.
[c] So the Greek frag., οἱ γὰρ κακῶς ἀκούσαντες ἄρχοντες τοὺς εἰπόντας οὐ μετὰ δίκης ἀμυνοῦνται· καταχρήσονται δυναστείαις εἰς πανωλεθρίαν.
[d] The Greek frag. reads somewhat differently ἐπεί, φησίν, οὐ περὶ παντὸς ἄρχοντος ἔοικε νομοθετεῖν ἀλλ' ὡσανεὶ τοῦ λαοῦ τοῦδε ἢ ἔθνους ἡγεμόνα σπουδαῖον ὑποτίθεται, διὰ πλειόνων. It adds καταχρηστικῶς δὲ δυνάτους ἢ ἱερεῖς ἢ προφήτας ἢ ἁγίους ἄνδρας ὡς Μωυσέα. " Ἰδοὺ γάρ, ἔθηκά σε θεὸν Φαραώ," ἐλέχθη πρὸς Μωυσῆν.
[e] So the second Greek frag., τῷ ἀγαθῷ ἀνδρὶ βλασφημία μὲν ἀλλότριον, ἔπαινος δὲ οἰκειότατον.
[f] Lit. " thoughtfulness of care." The Arm. translator apparently read πρόνοιαν instead of εὔνοιαν, which is the reading in the Greek fragments.
[g] Slightly different is the reading of the third Greek frag., οὐδὲν οὕτως εὐάγωγον εἰς εὔνοιαν ὡς ἡ τῶν εὐεργετημάτων εὐφημία.
[h] Philo here combines parts of two separate verses.

words, " Thou shalt not appear with empty hands before Me " [a] ?

The literal meaning [b] is this, (namely) that those who approach the shrines [c] of God should come near with full hands, bearing the first-fruits of every living thing in which there is no blemish.[d] But as for the deeper meaning,[e] there is no prohibition,[f] for even though He said, " Thou shalt not appear," still He did not say it by way of prohibition, as is altogether reasonable.[g] For it is impossible for anyone who comes into the sight of God to be empty but (rather must he be) full of every good. For just as one who comes near the light is straightway illumined, so also is filled the entire soul of him to whom God has appeared. A spiritual light, however, is called by other names, (namely) knowledge and wisdom.[h]

8. (Ex. xxii. 30) [i] Why does He command that the off-spring of cattle be left with their mothers for seven days ? [j]

(This is said) in order that there may not be one and the same time for birth and destruction but that the generation of life may keep its due place [k] for some time. In the second place, because the mercy of love abounds in mothers at

[a] LXX (Ex. xxiii. 15c) οὐκ ὀφθήσῃ ἐνώπιον μου κενός (Heb. " And not shall be seen my face empty ").

[b] τὸ ῥητόν.

[c] Or " altars " : Aucher " aram."

[d] Cf. LXX (Ex. xxii. 29 = Heb. xxii. 28) ἀπαρχὰς ἅλωνος καὶ ληνοῦ σου οὐ καθυστερήσεις· τὰ πρωτότοκα τῶν υἱῶν σου δώσεις ἐμοί.

[e] τὸ πρὸς διάνοιαν.

[f] ἀπαγόρευσις.

[g] ὡς πάντως εἰκός vel sim. : Aucher " quovis modo."

[h] ἐπιστήμη καὶ σοφία : Aucher " intelligentia et sapientia."

[i] Heb., Ex. xxii. 29 (cf. Lev. xxii. 27).

[j] LXX οὕτως ποιήσεις τὸν μόσχον σου καὶ τὸ πρόβατόν σου καὶ τὸ ὑποζύγιόν σου· ἑπτὰ ἡμέρας ἔσται ὑπὸ τὴν μητέρα, τῇ δὲ ὀγδόῃ ἡμέρᾳ ἀποδώσῃ μοι αὐτό. Philo comments similarly but more fully on this verse in De Virtutibus 126-130.

[k] τὴν τάξιν : Aucher " ordinem."

43

the very beginning of birth, wherefore their breasts, being filled, flow abundantly and pour out in (the form of) milk unlimited nourishment for desire.[a] For in the course of time love, like everything else, diminishes, but at the very beginning of birth it possesses great strength. Accordingly, He considers it very cruel and senseless to separate (the offspring) from its mother immediately upon birth, while it is still naturally attached and united to her.

*9. (Ex. xxiii. 1a) What is the meaning of the words " Thou shalt not admit a false rumour "[b] ?

Nothing vain is to be admitted whether through hearing or any other sense, for very great harm follows the deception of falsehood.[c] Therefore it has been ordained by some legislators that one should not testify by hearsay, on the ground that what is believed through the eyes is true but through hearing is false.[d]

*10. (Ex. xxiii. 3) Why does (Scripture) say, " To the poor thou shalt not be merciful in judgment "[e] ?

Poverty in itself is in want of mercy for the redress of its need, but when it comes to judgment it uses the law of

---

[a] i.e. as much as their young desire.

[b] LXX Οὐ παραδέξῃ ἀκοὴν ματαίαν (Heb. "empty" or "baseless report "). Philo quotes this half-verse and comments on it briefly in De Confus. Ling. 141 and more fully in De Spec. Leg. iv. 59-61.

[c] Slightly different is the wording of the Greek frag., μάταιόν φησιν οὔτε ἀκοαῖς οὔτε ἄλλῃ τινὶ τῶν αἰσθήσεων προσιτέον· ἐπακολουθοῦσι γὰρ ταῖς ἀπάταις αἱ μέγισται ζημίαι.

[d] So the Greek frag., διὸ καὶ παρ' ἐνίοις νομοθέταις ἀπείρηται μαρτυρεῖν ἀκοῇ, ὡς τὸ μὲν ἀληθὲς ὄψει πιστευόμενον, τὸ δὲ ψεῦδος ἀκοῇ. In the parallel passage, De Spec. Leg. iv. 61, Philo attributes this view to "some of the Greek legislators who copied it from the most sacred stelae of Moses."

[e] LXX καὶ πένητα οὐκ ἐλεήσεις (Heb. "thou shalt not favour ") ἐν κρίσει. Philo quotes this verse and comments on it a little more fully in De Spec. Leg. iv. 72-74.

equality as judge.[a] For justice is divine and incorruptible, wherefore it is well said by some [b] "judgments are of God." [c]

*11. (Ex. xxiii. 4) Why does (Scripture) command one who encounters the straying asses [d] of an enemy to bring them back and give them back ? [e]

It is an excess of gentleness if in addition to not harming an enemy one even tries to be of help.[f] In the second place, it is a prohibition and shaming of greed.[g] For he who is not willing to harm even an enemy, whom else will he wish to harm for his own profit ? [h] In the third place, it removes quarrels and fights from (our) midst, being a

---

[a] So the Greek frag., πενία καθ' ἑαυτὴν μὲν ἐλέου χρῄζει εἰς ἐπανόρθωσιν ἐνδείας, εἰς δὲ κρίσιν ἰοῦσα βραβευτῇ χρῆται τῷ τῆς ἰσότητος νόμῳ.

[b] The Greek frag. reads more intelligibly ἐν ἑτέροις, i.e. in Deut. i. 17.

[c] The Greek frag. reads somewhat differently θεῖον γὰρ ἡ δικαιοσύνη καὶ ἀδέκαστον· ὅθεν καὶ ἐν ἑτέροις εὖ εἴρηται ὅτι " ἡ κρίσις τοῦ θεοῦ δικαία ἐστίν." The wording of the last clause is obviously incorrect, see the preceding note.

[d] The fragment from John of Damascus ap. H. Lewy has ὑποζυγίῳ, see next note.

[e] LXX 'Εὰν δὲ συναντήσῃς τῷ βοῒ τοῦ ἐχθροῦ σου ἢ τῷ ὑποζυγίῳ αὐτοῦ (Heb. " his ass ") πλανωμένοις, ἀποστρέψας ἀποδώσεις αὐτῷ. The fragment from Procopius quotes only the first part of the verse, ending with ἐχθροῦ σου. Philo comments on this verse in De Virtutibus 117-118.

[f] So the two Greek fragments, ἡμερότητος ὑπερβολὴ πρὸς τὸ μὴ βλάπτειν τὸν ἐχθρὸν ἔτι καὶ συνωφελεῖν (v.l. ὠφελεῖν) πειρᾶσθαι.

[g] This sentence is missing from both Greek fragments. Lewy reconstructs the Greek, somewhat freely, I think, as δεύτερον δὲ παραίτησις πλεονεξίας.

[h] So the Greek frag. from John of Damascus (which ends here), ὁ γὰρ μηδ' ἐχθρὸν ζημιοῦν ὑπομένων τίνα τῶν ἄλλων ἐθελήσειεν ἂν βλάπτειν ἐπ' ὠφελείᾳ <ἰδίᾳ>; Procopius reads more briefly τίνα δὲ καὶ ἀδικήσειεν <ἂν> ὁ μηδὲ τὸν ἐχθρὸν ζημιῶν;

protector of peace,[a] whose possessions it depicts and shows
in many ways. Accordingly, it regards the giving back
of the asses as the beginning of offerings of peace and
reconciliation.[b] For he who gives (something) back, performing a work of love, is in some manner made gentle in
soul,[c] while he who receives (it), if he is not completely
ungrateful, puts aside the rancour that seeks revenge.

12. (Ex. xxiii. 5) Why, if one sees the ass of an enemy
fall under a burden, does (Scripture) command one not to
neglect to raise it up with him ?[d]
(This is) a confirmatory addition to the preceding, since
there is much said on this subject which is to be connected
with this, including what was previously said about one
who gives back (something lost).[e] But it must be said in
addition that it shows an extraordinary abundance of
humaneness and gentleness,[f] inasmuch as it exhorts (us)
not only to be useful to an enemy but also to lighten the

---

[a] Procopius reads slightly differently ἔτι δὲ καὶ στάσιν
καθαιρεῖ καὶ δυσμένειαν προκατάρχων εἰρήνης. The next two
sentences in the Procopius fragment do not correspond closely
to the Armenian.

[b] Or " friendship," but cf. De Virtutibus 118.

[c] Aucher " ex animo familiaris demonstratur." The
Greek verb was prob. ἡμεροῦται.

[d] LXX Ἐὰν δὲ ἴδῃς τὸ ὑποζύγιον (Heb. " ass ") τοῦ ἐχθροῦ
σου πεπτωκὸς (Heb. " crouching ") ὑπὸ τὸν γόμον αὐτοῦ, οὐ
παρελεύσῃ αὐτὸ ἀλλὰ συνεγερεῖς αὐτὸ μεθ' αὐτοῦ (Heb. " thou
shalt desist from abandoning it ; thou shalt surely help [?]
with him "). In De Virtutibus 116 Philo paraphrases the
LXX text as follows, κἂν ἐχθρῶν ὑποζύγια ἀχθοφοροῦντα τῷ
βάρει πιεσθέντα προπέσῃ, μὴ παρελθεῖν ἀλλὰ συνεπικουφίσαι καὶ
συνεγεῖραι. In the latter passage Philo deals only with the
literal meaning and not with the symbolism as here.

[e] This is the best sense I can extract from the obscure Arm.
sentence. Aucher's rendering is not too clear either, " in-
tensio additamenti anteriorum est, unde et plura quidem
dicta est adaptare super hoc, ex iis nimirum quae de reddente
sunt dicta."   [f] φιλανθρωπίας καὶ ἡμερότητος.

EXODUS, BOOK II

heaviness of the burden of irrational animals, especially when they have already fallen under the pressure of a very heavy weight. For who would disregard any human being, with whom he has a single natural kinship,[a] when he has been taught by the divine Law and is accustomed not to disregard even a beast? That is the literal meaning.[b] But as for the deeper meaning,[c] the ass is symbolically [d] our body,[e] and (this) is altogether errant and roving. For the sake of bringing profit to its kindred sensual pleasure,[f] it loads itself with much unmixed (wine) and various foods and a variety of dishes and still other drinks and foods in immense profusion. Accordingly, it is necessary for one who is smitten by wisdom [g] to lighten (his) heaviness through the related virtues of frugality and contentedness [h] and to lead the errant (man) into inerrant constancy by accustoming him to give up his anxious pursuit of avarice and, instead, to follow the richness of nature, which is ascendant and self-sufficient.[i]

*13. (Ex. xxiii. 20-21) [j] What is the meaning of the words, " Behold, I am sending My angel [k] before thy face, that he may guard thee on the way, in order that he may lead and bring thee to the land which I have prepared for thee. Give heed and listen and do not disobey. For he

---

[a] μία συγγένεια φύσεως.   [b] τὸ ῥητόν.
[c] τὸ πρὸς διάνοιαν.   [d] συμβολικῶς.
[e] In *De Sacr. Abelis* 112 the ass is said to be a symbol of πόνος, in *De Cherubim* 32 of ἡ ἄλογος προαίρεσις τοῦ βίου, in *De Migratione* 224 of ἡ ἄλογος φύσις, in *De Mut. Nom.* 193 of ἄνοια.   [f] τῇ συγγενικῇ ἡδονῇ.
[g] τὸν ὑπὸ τῆς σοφίας πληχθέντα: Aucher "qui amore sapientiae captus sit."
[h] ταῖς ἀναγκαίαις ἀρεταῖς, ὀλιγοδείᾳ καὶ εὐκολίᾳ. These two virtues are coupled in several other passages in Philo.
[i] ἀνωφερὴς (*vel sim.*) καὶ αὐτάρκης: Aucher "quae feracissima est (*vel*, superiora tendit) et sibi sufficiens."
[j] This section should follow § 15, which deals with Ex. xxiii. 18.
[k] Lit. " messenger," see next note but one.

will not show consideration for thee,[a] for My name is upon him " [b] ?

An angel is an intellectual soul [c] or rather wholly mind,[d] wholly incorporeal, made (to be) a minister of God,[e] and appointed over certain needs and the service of the race of mortals, since it was unable, because of its corruptible nature, to receive the gifts and benefactions extended by God. For it was not capable of bearing the multitude of (His) good (gifts). (Therefore) of necessity was the Logos appointed as judge and mediator,[f] who is called " angel." Him He sets " before the face," there where the place of the eyes and the senses is, in order that by seeing and receiving sense(-impressions) it [g] may follow the leadership of virtue,[h] not unwillingly but willingly. But the entry into the previously prepared land is allegorized [i] in the several (details) of the above-mentioned (statements) in respect of the guarding [j] of the way, (namely) " giving heed," " listening," " not disobeying," " not showing consideration," " setting His name upon him." This, however, must first be examined. Those who incautiously travel a

---

[a] Aucher " non verebitur te," see next note.

[b] lxx καὶ ἰδοὺ ἐγὼ ἀποστέλλω τὸν ἄγγελόν μου (Heb. " my messenger ") πρὸ προσώπου σου ἵνα φυλάξῃ σε ἐν τῇ ὁδῷ ὅπως εἰσαγάγῃ σε εἰς τὴν γῆν (Heb. " place ") ἣν ἡτοίμασά σοι (Heb. om. " for thee "). πρόσεχε σεαυτῷ καὶ εἰσάκουε αὐτοῦ καὶ μὴ ἀπείθει αὐτῷ· οὐ γὰρ μὴ ὑποστείληταί σε (Heb. " he will not suffer thy disobedience "), τὸ γὰρ ὄνομά μού ἐστιν ἐπ' αὐτῷ (Heb. " within him "). Philo cites the first part of this passage in De Agricultura 51, and the entire passage in De Migratione 174 in verbal agreement with the lxx but without extended commentary in either place.

[c] νοερὰ ψυχή : Aucher " spiritus intellectualis." Philo several times speaks of angels as ψυχαί but never, I think, as πνεύματα. On his doctrine of angels see Wolfson, Philo, i. 366-385.   [d] νοῦς : Aucher " intellectus."

[e] γενόμενος ὑπηρέτης θεοῦ.

[f] μεσίτης.

[g] i.e. the human race.   [h] ἀρετῆς.

[i] ἀλληγορεῖται : Aucher " allegorice adaptatur."

[j] Aucher " observationem."

road go astray from the right and genuinely broad road,
and many times turn aside into trackless, impassable and
rough places.[a]   And similar to this is it when souls experience something juvenile and pious,[b] for when one is without
a share of discipline one is borne along like unimpeded
streams where it is unprofitable.[c]   And the second thing
was the entry into the land, (that is) an entry into philosophy,[d] (which is), as it were, a good land and fertile in the
production of fruits, which the divine plants, the virtues,[e]
bear.   Therefore it is proper that he who wishes to enjoy
these fruits should receive training in exercising caution ;
but caution is the supervision of the counselling mind [f]
and readiness to listen.   For just as a lover puts aside all
other things and hastens to his desire, so also does one
who hungers and thirsts for the knowledge of the disciplines and for learning what he does not know put away
his concern for other things and hasten to listen, and by
night and by day he watches the doors of the houses of the
wise.[g]   Thus, to give heed is (referred to) in these (words).
But (next) in order is to listen, and it is naturally mentioned

[a] The first of the two Greek fragments of this section
(which begins here) reads only slightly differently οἱ ἀφυλάκτως ὁδοιποροῦντες διαμαρτάνουσιν τῆς ὀρθῆς καὶ λεωφόρου
ὡς πολλάκις εἰς ἀνοδίας καὶ δυσβάτους καὶ τραχείας ἀτραποὺς
ἐκτρέπεσθαι.

[b] The text is obviously corrupt, see next note.

[c] The Greek frag. (which ends here) reads more intelligibly
τὸ παραπλήσιόν ἐστιν ὅτε καὶ αἱ ψυχαὶ τῶν νέων παιδείας ἀμοιροῦσιν, καθάπερ ῥεῦμα ἀνεπίσχετον ὅπη μὴ λυσιτελὲς ῥεμβεύονται.
Possibly the Arm. translator mistook νέων for the gen. plural
of νεώς " temple."

[d] φιλοσοφίαν.

[e] αἱ ἀρεταί.

[f] ἡ τῆς βουλευτικῆς διανοίας προστασία vel sim. : Aucher
" praesidentia consiliarii (sic) mentis."

[g] The second Greek fragment (which contains only the
second part of this comparison) reads only slightly differently
ὁ πεινῶν καὶ διψῶν ἐπιστήμης καὶ τοῦ μαθεῖν ἃ μὴ οἶδεν, τὰς
ἄλλας μεθιέμενος φροντίδας, ἐπείγεται πρὸς ἀκρόασιν, καὶ νύκτωρ
καὶ μεθ᾽ ἡμέραν θυρωρεῖ τὰς τῶν σοφῶν οἰκίας.

in connexion therewith.[a] For he who listens with the tips
of his ears is able to get (only) a somewhat vague perception
of what is said, while to him who listens carefully the words
enter more clearly and the things heard travel on all the
paths, so that they form his mind [b] with deep impressions,[c]
as if (it were) wax, lest it easily become stupid and (the
impressions) leap away.[d] After this comes (the statement)
that it is not right to disobey. For some men receive
within them the appearances of words and, after receiving
them, [do not] become disobedient [e] but display a quarrel-
some and rebellious nature. Such men He shames,[f] wishing to admonish them by preparing lawful and constant
declarations of good things.[g] But whenever the word of
God is announced, it is altogether good, beautiful and
precious. For to him who does not obey He says, " he [h]
has no respect for thee," and (this is said) most naturally.
For when conviction [i] is established in the soul and per-
ceives it inclining to wickedness, it reproaches (the soul)
and becomes its accuser, and by scolding and threatening,

[a] i.e. in connexion with giving heed.

[b] τὸν νοῦν or τὴν διάνοιαν.

[c] Lit. " forms."

[d] Aucher renders, " ne facile insipidum videatur et foras
resiliat," apparently taking " mind " to be the subject of
both verbs (in spite of the neuter gender of the pred. adj.
" insipidum ").

[e] Either we must eliminate the negative particle or emend
" disobedient " to " obedient." Aucher renders more freely,
" nec tamen revera recipientes, dissentiunt."

[f] δυσωπεῖ.

[g] The meaning is obscure, partly because of the diverse
meanings of the verb (here a ptc.) aṛt'el, which I have
rendered " preparing." Aucher renders, " monere volens,
ut sibi concilient bonorum enarrationes legitimas ac con-
stantes."

[h] i.e. the angel.

[i] ἔλεγχος, cf. e.g. Quod Deus Immut. Sit 135, De Decalogo
87, where ἔλεγχος has the force of " conscience " or inward
" monitor " (as Colson there renders). It is symbolized by
an angel in De Fuga 1-6 and elsewhere.

EXODUS, BOOK II

puts it to shame. For he within whom it is, is apprehended by his own judgment as being altogether foolish. And in contrast to all the counsellors[a] who are in the various cities[b] it is obliged not to show respect or to admonish with fear but with both wisdom and freedom of speech.[c] And a very clear proof of this is that the divine name is called upon the angel. And this is the most sovereign and principal (being) which the heaven and earth and the whole world knows.[d] And he who has so great a power[e] must necessarily be filled with all-powerful[f] wisdom.[g]

*14. (Ex. xxiii. 18a) What is the meaning of the words, " Thou shalt not sacrifice with leaven the blood of the victim "[h] ?

In another passage also[i] He has ordained something similar to this, commanding that upon an altar upon which victims are offered in sacrifice leaven is not to be brought.[j] He indicates through two necessary symbols[k] that one

---

[a] τοὺς συνέδρους.

[b] The context obliges us to correct the Arm. text which reads " and by (or " among ") all the counsellors who are outside in the various cities."

[c] καὶ σοφίᾳ καὶ παρρησίᾳ.

[d] Apparently Philo means that the angel here represents the Logos.

[e] δύναμιν.   [f] Variant " all-free."

[g] Aucher renders more freely, " ut sit sapientia potentissimus (vel, liberrimus)."

[h] LXX οὐ θύσεις ἐπὶ ζύμῃ αἷμα θυμιάματός μου. Philo allegorizes this half-verse, without quoting it literally, in De Spec. Leg. i. 293-295, cf. ii. 182-185.

[i] Lev. ii. 11, where honey is also proscribed.

[j] Somewhat different is the wording of the Greek frag. preserved in three Catenae, ἀντὶ τοῦ οὐ δεῖ ζυμωτὸν παρεῖναι ἐπὶ τῶν θυσιαζομένων ἀλλὰ πάντα τὰ προσαγόμενα εἰς θυσίαν ἤτοι προσφορὰν ἄζυμα δεῖ εἶναι.

[k] Prob. the original reading is preserved in the Catenae, αἰνίττεται δὲ διὰ συμβόλου δύο τὰ ἀναγκαιότατα. Procopius reads more briefly αἰνίττεται δὲ διὰ συμβόλου.

should despise sensual pleasures,[a] for leaven is a sweetener of food but not food (itself).[b] And the other thing (indicated) is that one should not be uplifted in conceit by common [c] belief.[d] For both are impure and hateful, (namely) sensual pleasure and arrogance (or) foolish belief, (both being) the offspring of one mother, illusion.[e] But the blood of the sacrificed victims is a sign of the souls which are consecrated to God. Moreover, it is not right to mix the unmixed.[f]

*15. (Ex. xxiii. 18b) What is the meaning of the words, " The fat of My festival shall not lie [g] until morning " [h] ?

The literal text [i] gives the command that the fat shall be consumed the same day, having become material for the divine fire.[j] But as for the deeper meaning,[k] the nature

---

[a] So Procopius, καταφρονεῖν ἡδονῆς. The Catenae read more fully ἐν μὲν τὸ καταφρονεῖν ἡδονῆς.

[b] So Procopius and the Catenae, ζύμη γὰρ ἥδυσμα τροφῆς, οὐ τροφή.

[c] The Arm. translator mistakenly read κοινῆς instead of κενῆς οἰήσεως " empty belief," see next note.

[d] Procopius καὶ τὸ μὴ δεῖν ὑπὸ κενῆς φυσωμένους οἰήσεως αἴρεσθαι: the Catenae read ἕτερον δὲ τὸ μὴ δεῖν ἐπαίρεσθαι φυσωμένους διὰ κενῆς (v.l. καινῆς) οἰήσεως.

[e] Procopius lacks this sentence. The Catenae read more briefly ἀνίερον γὰρ ἑκάτερον, ἡδονή τε καὶ οἴησις, μητρὸς μιᾶς ἀπάτης ἔγγονα. Philo, like some of the early Christian writers, uses ἀπάτη in the sense of "illusory worldly pleasure."

[f] So Procopius and the Catenae, τὸ δὲ αἷμα τῶν θυσιῶν δεῖγμα ψυχῆς ἐστι σπενδομένης θεῷ· μιγνύναι δὲ τὰ ἄμικτα οὐχ ὅσιον.

[g] Or " sleep," see next note.

[h] LXX οὐδὲ μὴ κοιμηθῇ στέαρ τῆς ἑορτῆς μου ἕως πρωί. There seems to be no other direct comment on this half-verse in Philo's other works but cf. De Spec. Leg. iv. 123-124.

[i] τὸ ῥητόν.

[j] The Catenae read similarly but omitting the subject, κελεύει τὰ στέατα αὐθήμερον ἀναλίσκεσθαι, γινόμενα ὕλην ἱερᾶς φλογός. Procopius has preserved only the words ὕλη τε τῆς ἱερᾶς γινέσθω φλογός.
[k] τὸ πρὸς διάνοιαν.

of fat brings oiliness [a] to the entrails and other (parts), and surrounding these with its fatness, prevents them for ever, when dried, from very quickly dissolving and melting away. [b] For one who has the moisture of fatness receives the moisture as most vital nourishment. Accordingly, He wishes to show through a symbol [c] that every soul which piety fattens with its own mystical and divine piety is sleepless and watchful for the vision of things worthy to be seen. [d] Now this experience is the festival of souls and the greatest of festivals, an occasion of true joy, [e] which not unmixed (wine) but sober wisdom [f] produces. For one of these is the cause of drunkenness and delirium, [g] while the other (is the cause) of soberness and of properly accomplishing all things. And so, if it also happens that some mortal seed has passed, (it is) an unfortunate accident, that is, the sleep of the mind, which will not last long. [h]

*16. (Ex. xxiii. 22) What is the meaning of the words, " If hearing thou wilt hear My voice and thou wilt do all

[a] λίπος, cf. De Vita Mosis ii. 146.
[b] The meaning of the second clause is obscure, chiefly because of the presence of the pass. ptc. " dried." Aucher renders more briefly, " ne arescens celeriter dissolvatur."
[c] διὰ συμβόλου.
[d] Slightly different is the wording of the Greek frag. from the Parallels of John Monachus (ap. Harris, p. 101), first identified by Früchtel, ψυχὴ πᾶσα ἣν εὐσέβεια λιπαίνει τοῖς ἰδίοις ὀργίοις, ἀκοιμήτως ἔχει πρὸς τὰ θεῖα καὶ διανίσταται πρὸς τὴν θέαν τῶν θέας ἀξίων.
[e] Again the Greek frag. (which ends with " joy ") differs slightly, τοῦτο γὰρ τὸ πάθος τῆς ψυχῆς ἐν ἑορτῇ μεγίστῃ καὶ καιρὸς ἀψευδὴς εὐφροσύνης.
[f] νηφάλιος σοφία.   [g] Aucher " petulantiae."
[h] The meaning of the sentence is not clear to me but seems to refer to a nocturnal emission. Aucher, confessing in a footnote that he is not sure of the meaning, renders, " quod si etiam superveniet, id quod transactum est, et aliquod semen mortale, improsperitatis erramentum, id est mentis somnus, non longius durabit."

that I say to thee, I shall be an enemy to thine enemies and I will oppose those who oppose thee " [a] ?

Because some men do not hearken when hearing or, rather, pretend not to have heard, He has specified in this passage, " If hearing ye [b] will hear My voice," (which), it must be supposed, refers to the angel mentioned a little while ago. For the prophet of Him Who speaks is properly an angel. For it is necessary for him who " hearing hears," that is, with firmness [e] receives what is said, to carry out in deed also what is said, for the deed is proof of the word.[f] Now he who is obedient to what is said and carries out in deed what has been ordered by declaration, necessarily acquires his teacher as ally and protector, who, as it seems, is helping his disciple but in truth (is helping) his own ruling doctrines,[g] which his opponents and enemies desire to destroy.[h]

[a] LXX ἐὰν ἀκοῇ ἀκούσητε (v.l. ἀκούσῃς) τῆς φωνῆς μου (Heb. " his voice ") καὶ ποιήσητε πάντα ὅσα ἂν εἴπω σοι, ἐχθρεύσω τοῖς ἐχθροῖς σου καὶ ἀντικείσομαι τοῖς ἀντικειμένοις σοι. Philo paraphrases the verse in De Praemiis 79.

[b] Sic (change from sing. to plural).

[e] In § 13. Most of the present section (from " voice " on) is preserved in the Catenae and paraphrastically in Procopius. The former read, in this sentence, φωνὴν θεοῦ τὸν πρὸ μικροῦ λεχθέντα ἄγγελον ὑπονοητέον μηνύεσθαι.

[d] So the Catenae, τοῦ γὰρ λέγοντος ὁ προφήτης ἄγγελος κυρίως (v.l. κυρίου) ἐστίν. Procopius paraphrases, τὸν προφήτην φασί τινες καὶ τὴν ἐν αὐτῷ τοῦ λαλοῦντος φωνήν, οὗ παρακελεύεται εἰσακούειν. [e] Aucher " constanter."

[f] So the Catenae, ἀνάγκη (l. ἀνάγκη) γὰρ τὸν ἀκοῇ ἀκούοντα, τουτέστι τὸν τὰ λεγόμενα βεβαίως παραδεχόμενον, ἔργοις ἐπιτελεῖν τὰ λεχθέντα· λόγου γὰρ πίστις ἔργον. Procopius has preserved only the words λόγου δὲ πίστις ἔργον.

[g] Aucher " voluntate legis."

[h] So the Catenae, ὁ δὲ καὶ τοῖς εἰρημένοις καταπειθὴς καὶ ἐνεργῶν τὰ ἀκόλουθα, σύμμαχον καὶ ὑπερασπιστὴν ἐξ ἀνάγκης ἔχει τὸν διδάσκαλον, ὅσα μὲν τῷ δοκεῖν, βοηθοῦντα τῷ γνωρίμῳ, τὸ δ' ἀληθὲς τοῖς αὐτοῦ (l. αὑτοῦ) δόγμασι καὶ παραγγέλμασιν, ἅπερ οἱ ἐναντίοι καὶ ἐχθροὶ βούλονται καθαιρεῖν. Procopius reads more briefly ὁ δὲ καὶ πεισθεὶς καὶ πράξας ἕξει πάντως ὑπερασπιστὴν τὸν διδάσκαλον συμμαχοῦντα δι' αὑτοῦ τοῖς ἰδίοις δόγμασιν, ἅπερ οἱ ἐναντίοι βούλονται καθαιρεῖν.

EXODUS, BOOK II

*17. (Ex. xxiii. 24c) What is the meaning of the words,
" Destroying thou shalt destroy and shattering thou shalt
shatter their pillars " [a]?

The " pillars " are symbolically the accepted opinions [b]
which seem to have been established and firmly supported.[c]
But of (these) pillar-like [d] accepted opinions some are
good, and for these it is right to be erect and to have a firm
position, while there are others which are reprehensible,
and of these it is profitable to cause the destruction.[e] And [f]
such are those which folly decrees in opposition to prudence,[g] and intemperance to temperance,[h] and injustice to
justice,[i] and in general whatever it is that evil opposes to
virtue.[j] But the words " Destroying thou shalt destroy
and shattering thou shalt shatter " suggest something
like the following sense.[k] There are some things which

---

[a] LXX καθαιρέσει καθελεῖς (v.l. and Heb. add " them ") καὶ
συντρίβων συντρίψεις τὰς στήλας (A.V. " images ") αὐτῶν.

[b] Aucher " gratae leges," see next note.

[e] So the Greek frag. (preserved in the Catenae and Procopius), στῆλαί εἰσι (Procopius omits the first two words) τὰ
δόγματα συμβολικῶς, ἅπερ ἑστάναι καὶ ἐρηρεῖσθαι δοκεῖ.

[d] Or " posted-up ": Aucher " statuae instar erectarum."
The Arm. translator had difficulty in rendering κατεστηλιτευμένων, see next note.

[e] So the Catenae, τῶν δὲ κατεστηλιτευμένων δογμάτων τὰ
μὲν ἀστεῖά ἐστιν, ἃ καὶ (Procopius omits ἐστιν ἃ καί) θέμις
ἀνακεῖσθαι καὶ βεβαίαν ἔχειν τὴν ἵδρυσιν, τὰ δὲ ἐπίληπτα ὧν τὴν
καθαίρεσιν ποιεῖσθαι λυσιτελές (Procopius τὰ δὲ ἐπίληπτα καθαιρεῖσθαι ὡς μὴ πάλιν ἀναστησόμενα μηδὲ ἁρμοσόμενα—the last
words being a paraphrase of the end of the section).

[f] The following sentence is missing in the Catenae and
Procopius.

[g] ἀφροσύνη . . . φρονήσει.

[h] ἀκολασία . . . σωφροσύνῃ.

[i] ἀδικία . . . δικαιοσύνῃ.

[j] κακία . . . ἀρετῇ.

[k] So the Catenae, τὸ δὲ " καθαιρῶν καθελεῖς " καὶ " συντρίβων
συντρίψεις " τοιοῦτον ὑποβάλλει νοῦν. Procopius (ending with
this sentence) paraphrases, τοιαύτη γὰρ ἔμφασις ἡ τοῦ " καθαιρῶν καθελεῖς " καὶ " συντρίβων συντρίψεις."

55

(people) destroy only to raise them up another time, and shatter as if they would again put them together.[a] But it is His will that those things which are opposed to the good and beautiful, when once they have been destroyed and shattered, shall not again undergo repair but shall always remain destroyed.[b]

*18. (Ex. xxiii. 25b) Why does He say, " I will bless thy bread and water,[c] and I will turn away illnesses from thee " [d] ?

He indicates food and health—food through " bread and water," and health through " turn away illnesses." [e] In the second place, He speaks of the self-control of endurance here in mentioning only the receiving of necessary foods,[f] for bread is a plain food without anything extra, and flowing water [g] is (a similarly plain) drink, and upon these (depends) health. In the third place, He makes mention of both life (in general) and a good life, for bread and water are necessary for living, while freedom from

---

[a] So the Catenae, ἔνιά τινες καθαιροῦσιν ὡς ἀναστήσοντες, καὶ σιντρίβουσιν ὡς αὖθις ἁρμοσόμενοι.

[b] So the Catenae, βούλεται δὲ τὰ καθαιρεθέντα ἅπαξ καὶ συντριβέντα μηκέτι τυχεῖν ἀνορθώσεως ἀλλ' εἰς ἅπαν ἠφανίσθαι τὰ ἐναντία τοῖς ἀγαθοῖς καὶ καλοῖς.

[c] Philo agrees with Heb. against LXX in omitting " and wine " after " bread."

[d] LXX καὶ εὐλογήσω (Heb. " He will bless ") τὸν ἄρτον σου καὶ τὸν οἶνόν σου καὶ τὸ ὕδωρ σου καὶ ἀποστρέψω μαλακίαν ἀφ' ὑμῶν.

[e] So Cat. Lips., τροφὴν καὶ ὑγίειαν αἰνίττεται· τροφὴν μὲν δι' ἄρτου καὶ ὕδατος· ὑγίειαν διὰ τοῦ μαλακίαν ἀποστρέφειν. Procopius condenses, τροφὴν καὶ ὑγίειαν ἐπαγγέλλεται.

[f] So the Catena, δεύτερον, ἐγκράτειαν εἰσηγεῖται, τὴν τῶν ἀναγκαίων μετουσίαν μόνον ἐπειπών. Procopius reads more briefly καὶ τῶν ἀναγκαιοτάτων μόνων μνησθεὶς ἐδίδαξε τὴν ἐγκράτειαν (with this clause the Greek fragments break off, to resume with the sentence beginning " In the fifth place ").

[g] ναματιαῖον ὕδωρ : Aucher " aqua scaturiens."

passion ^a and health (are necessary) for living well. In the fourth place, Scripture ^b seems to declare that plain simplicity in food is the cause of health. For wine-drinking and cookery which are done with insatiability and gluttony, because of their being artificial ^c produce illness and the causes of greater illnesses. But simplicity in necessary foods is productive of health.^d In the fifth place, it teaches us a most worthwhile lesson and one that is in order, showing that neither bread nor water gives nourishment by itself alone,^e but that there are times when they do more harm than good,^f (namely) if the divine Logos does not graciously bestow upon them his helpful powers.^g For this reason, indeed, He says, " I will bless thy bread and thy water," as if they were not sufficient to give nourishment by themselves alone without the loving friendship and care ^h of God.ⁱ

---

^a ἀπάθεια.

^b ἡ γραφή. This is one of the very few passages in the *Quaestiones* in which Philo expressly mentions Scripture rather than God or Moses as authority, although of course the three terms are interchangeable.

^c Aucher " ob abusum expletionis."

^d Aucher inadvertently omits to render this sentence.

^e Slightly different is the text of Catena Lips., πρὸς δὲ τούτοις, μάθημα ἡμᾶς αἰσιώτατον ἀναδιδάσκει, δηλῶν ὅτι οὔτε ἄρτος οὔτε ὕδωρ καθ᾽ ἑαυτὰ τρέφουσιν. Procopius reads more briefly καὶ μάθημα δὲ παρέδωκεν αἰσιώτατον, ὡς οὐδὲν τούτων τρέφει καθ᾽ ἑαυτό.

^f So Cat. Lips., ἀλλ᾽ ἔστιν ὅτε καὶ βλάπτουσι μᾶλλον ἢ ὠφελοῦσιν. Procopius condenses, βλάπτει δὲ μᾶλλον ἢ ὠφελεῖ.

^g So (with the exception of one word) Cat. Lips., ἐὰν μὴ θεῖος λόγος καὶ τούτοις χαρίσηται τὰς ἀφελητικὰς (l. ὠφελητικὰς) δυνάμεις. Procopius paraphrases, μὴ τοῦ θεοῦ δύναμιν ὠφελητικὴν διὰ τῆς εὐλογίας παρέχοντος.

^h Emending Arm. *hogwoy* (= " spirit " or " soul ") to *hogoy* (= " care "): Aucher " sine divina conciliatione cum anima."

ⁱ Cat. Lips. is defective, ὡς οὐχ ἱκανὰ καθ᾽ ἑαυτὰ τρέφειν ἄνευ θείας [noun missing] καὶ ἐπιφροσύνης. The sentence is missing in Procopius.

*19. (Ex. xxiii. 26a) Why does He [a] say, " There shall not be in thee anyone infertile or barren " [b] ?

He [c] places infertility and barrenness among the curses,[d] (and) says that they shall not be (found) among those who act with justice and lawfulness.[e] For (as) a prize to those who keep the divine writing of the Law He offers the more ancient law of immortal nature, which was laid down for procreation and the begetting of sons for the perpetuity of the race.[f] That is the literal meaning.[g] But as for the deeper meaning,[h] no one will find any evil greater than childlessness and infertility of soul.[i] And this is ignorance and lack of education,[j] which make barren the deliberative mind.[k] But fecundity and abundance of children come about through learning and knowledge,[l] so that those who have an abundance of learning have an abundance of children, and those who are learned in the knowledge of good and excellent things [m] have good children. And

---

[a] See below, note c.

[b] ᴌxx οὐκ ἔσται ἄγονος οὐδὲ στεῖρα ἐπὶ τῆς γῆς σου. In De Praemiis 108 Philo quotes freely, οὐδεὶς ἄγονος οὐδὲ στεῖρα γενήσεται.

[c] The context indicates that God is the subject although the Greek frag. supplies Μωυσῆς.

[d] So the Greek frag., ἀγονίαν καὶ στείρωσιν ἐν κατάραις τάττω Μωυσῆς.

[e] So the Greek frag., οὔ φησιν ἔσεσθαι παρὰ τοῖς τὰ δίκαια καὶ νόμιμα δρῶσιν.

[f] So the Greek frag. (which ends with this sentence), ἆθλον γὰρ τοῖς τὸ ἱερὸν γράμμα τοῦ νόμου φυλάττουσι παρέχει τὸν ἀρχαιότερον νόμον τῆς ἀθανάτου φύσεως, ὃς ἐπὶ σπορᾷ καὶ γενέσει τέκνων ἐτέθη πρὸς τὴν τοῦ γένους διαμονήν.

[g] τὸ ῥητόν.

[h] τὸ πρὸς διάνοιαν.

[i] Lit. " of souls "—ψυχῶν.

[j] ἀμαθία καὶ ἀπαιδευσία.

[k] τὸν βουλευτικὸν νοῦν vel sim. : Aucher " consiliarium intellectum."

[l] διὰ μαθήσεως καὶ ἐπιστήμης.

[m] Aucher renders more freely, " qui bonae optimaeque intelligentiae periti sunt."

childless are they whose natures are sluggish and dull and at the same time unlearned.

*20. (Ex. xxiii. 26b) What is the meaning of the words, " The number of thy days I will fill " *a* ?

That it is most excellent and fine that the lives of His worshippers should be reckoned not by months nor by numbers *b* but by days.*c* For they are really of equal value with eternity when taken into account and number,*d* for he who is of no account and has no number is to be altogether condemned.*e* But it is well that an addition has been made to the passage, (namely) " I will fill," because of the intervals empty of thoughtfulness and virtue in the soul of him who wishes to progress.*f* For He wishes him who philosophizes in accordance with Him to be a harmony of all sounds like a musical instrument with no discord or dissonance in any part but with one and the

a LXX τὸν ἀριθμὸν τῶν ἡμερῶν σου ἀναπληρώσω. In *De Praemiis* 111 Philo quotes the half-verse as here except for the personal ending of the verb, which there appears as ἀναπληρώσεις (*v.l.* ἀναπλήσεις).

b The original prob. had " years," as in Procopius, see next note.

c Somewhat different is Procopius' reading, πάγκαλον δέ φασι τὸ μήτε μησὶ μήτε ἐνιαυτοῖς καταριθμεῖσθαι τὸν βίον τῶν ἱκετῶν.

d The Arm. is obviously corrupt, see end of note. Procopius reads more intelligibly τῷ γὰρ ὄντι ἑκάστου σοφοῦ ἡμέρα ἰσότιμός ἐστιν αἰῶνι. Similar is the wording in *De Praemiis* 112 : ὅθεν ἰσότιμον καλῷ (καὶ ὅλῳ conj. Colson) βίῳ σοφοῦ καὶ μίαν ἡμέραν ὑπέλαβεν εἶναι κατορθουμένην. I suspect that Arm. *i hamar ankeal ew i t'iw* " taken into account and number " is a corruption of *hančarakani mi t'iw* (*vel sim.*) " one day of the intelligent (man)."

e Cf. *De Praemiis* 111 ὁ μὲν γὰρ ἀμαθὴς καὶ ἔκνομος " οὔτ' ἐν λόγῳ," φασίν, " οὔτ' ἐν ἀριθμῷ." The sentence is missing in Procopius.

f Slightly briefer is Procopius' text, εὖ δὲ καὶ τὸ " ἀναπληρώσω " διὰ τὰ κενὰ φρονήσεως καὶ ἀρετῆς ἐν ψυχῇ διαστήματα τοῦ προκόπτοντος.

QUESTIONS AND ANSWERS

same consonance and harmony, of will with word and word with deed and of deed with both of these.ᵃ

*21. (Ex. xxiii. 27a) Why does He say, " Fear will I send to go before thee " ᵇ ?

The literal meaning is clear,ᶜ for a strong force to ᵈ terrify the enemy is ᵉ fear,ᶠ by which more (easily) the force of adversaries is taken and conquered.ᵍ But as for the deeper meaning,ʰ there are two reasons why men honour the Deity, (namely) love and fear,ⁱ and love is later, being in the elder ones,ʲ while fear comes earlier,ᵏ so that not ineptly is it said that fear is the leader, for love, which comes after, is also acquired later.ˡ And may it not be

ᵃ Procopius reads more briefly ὃν βούλεται καθάπερ μουσικὸν ὄργανον διὰ πάντων ἡρμόσθαι πρὸς μίαν συμφωνίαν βουλημάτων καὶ λόγων καὶ πράξεων.

ᵇ ʟxx (and the Greek frag. in the Catenae) καὶ τὸν φόβον ἀποστελῶ ἡγούμενόν σου (Heb. " My fear will I send before thee ").   ᶜ τὸ μὲν ῥητὸν ἐμφανές, as in the Catenae.

ᵈ The preposition i " to " or " in " has fallen out of the Arm. text, probably by haplography.

ᵉ Emending Arm. ew " and " to ē " is."

ᶠ So the Catenae, εἰς κατάπληξιν ἐχθρῶν ἰσχυρὰ δύναμις ὁ φόβος.

ᵍ The Catenae and Procopius (whose excerpt begins here) read somewhat differently ; the Catenae have ὑφ' οὗ μᾶλλον ἡ (ἢ Wendland) τῆς τῶν ἀντιπάλων ἐφόδου ῥώμη ἁλίσκεται : Procopius ὑφ' οὗ μᾶλλον ἢ τῆς τῶν ἀντιπάλων ῥώμης οἱ πολέμιοι ἁλίσκονται.

ʰ τὸ δὲ πρὸς διάνοιαν as in the Catenae, which add οὕτως.

ⁱ So the Catenae (for Procopius' condensed paraphrase see below), δυοῖν οὐσῶν αἰτιῶν, ὧν ἕνεκα τὸ θεῖον ἄνθρωποι τιμῶσιν, ἀγάπης καὶ φόβου.

ʲ Presumably meaning " in mature persons," cf. Procopius ⟨ἐν⟩ τοῖς τελείοις. The Catenae read more briefly τὸ μὲν ἀγαπᾶν ἐστιν ὀψίγονον (v.l. ὀψέως).

ᵏ So the Catenae, τὸ δὲ φοβεῖσθαι συνίσταται πρότερον.

ˡ Only slightly different is the reading of the Catenae (which end here), ὥστε οὐκ ἀπὸ σκοποῦ λελέχθαι τὸ ἡγεῖσθαι τὸν φόβον, τῆς ἀγάπης ὕστερον καὶ ὀψὲ προσγενομένης. Procopius condenses the whole sentence, προηγεῖται δὲ τῆς ἀγάπης ὁ φόβος, ἢ τοῖς τελείοις ἐγγίνεται. δι' ἀμφοῖν γὰρ τιμᾶται θεός.

60

that one who fears does so rightly and properly ?[a] For just
as imprudence is younger than prudence,[b] so is fear
(younger) than love, since fear is born in a worthless man,[c]
while love (is born) in a virtuous one.[d]

22. (Ex. xxiii. 27b) What is the meaning of the words,
" I will terrify all the nations into which thou wilt come " [e] ?

The (expression) " I will terrify " in the literal sense [f] is
equivalent to " I will strike with fear," which He earlier
spoke of sending down for the destruction of their adversaries' force,[g] for fear is the cause of weakness.[h] In the
second place, He seems to bear testimony to the surpassing
virtue [i] of the nation [j] in that it would convert [k] not only
its own (members) but also its enemies ; and by " enemies "
I mean not only those who commit acts of war but also
those who are heterodox.[l] But as for the deeper meaning,[m]
this must be said. When there comes into the soul,[n] as
into a land, the prudence [o] of a keen-eyed and seeing
nature,[p] all the Gentile laws which are in it become mad

---

[a] The text is suspect. Aucher renders, " ne forte timere
quoque sit jure digneque."

[b] ἀφροσύνη . . . φρόνησις.

[c] Aucher " in contempto."   [d] ἐν σπουδαίῳ.

[e] LXX καὶ ἐκστήσω (Heb. " I will confuse ") πάντα τὰ ἔθνη
εἰς οὓς σὺ εἰσπορεύῃ εἰς αὐτούς.

[f] πρὸς τὸ ῥητόν.

[g] See the preceding section.   [h] ἀσθενείας.

[i] τὴν ὑπερβάλλουσαν ἀρετήν.

[j] i.e. the Hebrew nation.

[k] Arm. darzouçanel sometimes renders ἐπιστρέφειν, which
seems to have been the verb used in the Greek, although it
is not listed in Leisegang's Index Philonis. Aucher here
renders, " convertat."

[l] τοὺς ἑτεροδόξους.

[m] τὸ πρὸς διάνοιαν.

[n] Lit. " souls "—τὰς ψυχάς.

[o] εὐβουλία.

[p] Philo here, as often elsewhere, alludes to the etymology
of " Israel " as " seeing (God)."

and rage and turn aside *ᵃ* from worthy thoughts, for evil things are unable to dwell and live *ᵇ* together with good ones.

23. (Ex. xxiii. 27c) What is the meaning of the words, " I will make *ᶜ* thine enemies fugitives " *ᵈ* ?

He declares more certainly (and) clearly what was said earlier.*ᵉ* For he who has supervened *ᶠ* makes a beginning of flight. That is the literal meaning.*ᵍ* But as for the deeper meaning,*ʰ* He speaks of acceptable laws,*ⁱ* which are unknown to youths and (which) He Himself *ʲ* knows. For every foolish man is without a home or dwelling and is, as it were, a fugitive, driven from the city of virtue,*ᵏ* which must be thought of as the native place of wise and virtuous souls.*ˡ*

ᵃ Philo plays on the ἐκστήσω of LXX as being the causative of ἐξίστασθαι in the sense of "be beside oneself" and "stand out of the way," *i.e.* "turn aside."

ᵇ Aucher "stare," evidently mistaking *keal* "to live" for *kal* "to stand."

ᶜ Lit. "give," as in the LXX, which reflects Heb. idiom.

ᵈ LXX καὶ δώσω πάντας (a few MSS. om. πάντας) τοὺς ὑπεναντίους σου φυγάδας (Heb. "And I will give all thine enemies to thee a neck "—an idiom meaning "and I will cause all thine enemies to turn their backs to thee "—*i.e.* "to flee from thee").

ᵉ In the preceding verses.

ᶠ The Arm. verb *i veray gal* may render ἐπιγίγνεσθαι (which is, it seems, not used by Philo), but in exactly what sense is not clear. Aucher here renders, "supervenerat."

ᵍ τὸ ῥητόν.

ʰ τὸ πρὸς διάνοιαν.

ⁱ νόμους εὐαρέστους *vel sim.* : Aucher "leges gratas."

ʲ Arm. *ink'n* = αὐτός, but this is evidently a corruption or translator's misreading of ἀστεῖος (see below). The original must have meant "and (which) the wise man knows."

ᵏ ἐκ πόλεως ἀρετῆς, *cf. Leg. All.* iii. 1 πόλις οἰκεία τῶν σοφῶν ἡ ἀρετή.

ˡ πατρὶς ψυχῶν ἀστείων καὶ σπουδαίων. Here, as elsewhere, Arm. *asti* renders ἀστεῖος "wise," not "constant" as Aucher renders.

*24. (Ex. xxiii. 28) Why does He say, "I will send the wasp before thee and I will drive out thine enemies" *a* ?

Wasps fly upon one from nowhere *b* without first being seen, and after wounding with their stings they withdraw ; and they wound the principal parts,*c* the face, the eyes and the head.*d* And the fearful noise made (by them) in the air penetrates *e* the ears. And so, from the very beginning alliance (and) help are not *f* to be cut off, inasmuch as one is to do the enemy much harm through the smallest (animals),*g* especially when God commands, by which *h* even very weak men are innervated *i* and form an army with invincible power.*j* And allegorically it is to be said *k* that the wasp should be considered a symbol of unhoped

---

a Philo here paraphrases the LXX καὶ ἀποστελῶ τὰς σφηκίας (Heb. "the wasp," a collective singular : A.V. "hornets") προτέρας σου καὶ ἐκβαλεῖς (v.l. ἐκβαλῶ : Heb. "it will drive out") τοὺς Ἀμορραίους (Heb. omits "the Amorites") καὶ Εὐαίους καὶ Χαναναίους καὶ τοὺς Χετταίους (v.l. + καὶ τοὺς Φερεζαίους καὶ τοὺς Γεργεσαίους καὶ τοὺς Ἰεβουσαίους) ἀπὸ σοῦ. Procopius cites only the first half of the verse, καὶ ἀποστελῶ τὰς σφηκίας προτέρας σου. In De Praemiis 96 Philo briefly alludes to this verse without quoting LXX or commenting in detail.

b ἐξ ἀφανοῦς, as in Procopius.

c τὰ κυριώτατα (rendered by two Arm. words) : Procopius τὰ καιριώτατα.

d Procopius condenses the sentence, οἱ σφῆκες ἐξ ἀφανοῦς οὐ προειδομένους τιτρώσκουσι τὰ καιριώτατα, κεφαλήν τε καὶ τὰ ἐν αὐτῇ.   *e* Or "wounds."

f One Arm. MS. omits "not."

g The text seems to be corrupt, especially the phrase "from the very beginning." The Arm. glossator paraphrases, "one ought not to reject the help of God even though it be small." Procopius adds, either on his own or some post-Philonic authority, καὶ κατὰ τὸ ῥητὸν οὖν οἶδε θεὸς καὶ διὰ τῶν σμικροτάτων καταγωνίζεσθαι ὡς καὶ σκνιπῶν τε καὶ βατράχων τοὺς Αἰγυπτίους . . . φίλον γὰρ ἀεὶ θεῷ διὰ σμικρῶν περιγίνεσθαι.

h Or perhaps "through Whom."

i νευροῦνται.

j There is no Greek parallel to the second half of this sentence.   *k* ἀλληγορητέον.

QUESTIONS AND ANSWERS

for and unexpected power *a* divinely sent.*b* And when it
inflicts blows with great force from the upper regions, it
does not miss its mark with the blows, and after striking,
it does not suffer any counter-(blow) at all.*c*

*25. (Ex. xxiii. 29) Why does He add the reason why
not all enemies are to be driven out all together at one time
but little by little, (namely) " that the land may not be
made desolate and many animals congregate " *d* ?

The literal sense *e* does not require a long discussion, for
beasts flee from man as from their natural lord, wherefore
they do not enter cities when these are populous ; but if
they become small, (the beasts) move about with the inhabitants.*f* But as for the deeper meaning,*g* if from one
who has just *h* for the first time been introduced (to know-

---

a Aucher " inexpectatae subitaneaeque virtutis."

b Similar is the text of the Catenae (which begins here),
σύμβολον δὲ ὑποληπτέον εἶναι τοὺς σφῆκας ἀνελπίστου δυνάμεως
θείᾳ πομπῇ σταλησομένης. Procopius (resuming here) paraphrases, σημαίνοι δ᾽ ἂν καὶ θείαν πομπὴν ἀνελπίστου δυνάμεως
στελλομένης ἐξ οὐρανοῦ.

c Slightly different and in part corrupt is the text of the
Catenae (the sentence is lacking in Procopius), ἥτις ἀφ᾽ ὑψηλοτέρων κατ᾽ ἄκρον τὸ οὓς ὑποφέρουσα τὰς πληγάς, εὐστοχήσει
πᾶσι ταῖς βλήμασι, καὶ διαθεῖσα οὐδὲν ἀντιπεσεῖται τὸ παράπαν.
Mangey has emended ἀντιπεσεῖται to ἀντιπείσεται. We must
further (on the basis of the Arm.) emend κατ᾽ ἄκρον τὸ οὓς
ὑποφέρουσα to κατὰ κράτος ἐπιφέρουσα.

d LXX οὐκ ἐκβαλῶ αὐτοὺς (v.l., with Heb., adds ἀπὸ προσώπου σου) ἐν ἐνιαυτῷ ἑνί, ἵνα μὴ γένηται ἡ γῆ ἔρημος καὶ πολλὰ
γένηται ἐπὶ σὲ τὰ θηρία τῆς γῆς (Heb. " and the beasts of the
field increase against thee "). Procopius quotes only the
words οὐκ ἐκβαλῶ αὐτοὺς ἐν ἐνιαυτῷ ἑνί.

e τὸ ῥητόν.

f Procopius condenses and paraphrases, τὰ γὰρ θηρία φεύγει
τὰς τῶν πλειόνων ἀνθρώπων οἰκήσεις ὡς ἡγεμονῶν τῇ φύσει καὶ
τὰς ἐρήμους πληροῖ.   *g* τὸ πρὸς διάνοιαν.

h The Arm. reads " not then," but we must correct this
from the Greek, see next note but one.

64

ledge) and is learning you take pains to cut away all his
errors and to cause disciplined knowledge to dwell in him
all at once, you will achieve the opposite of that which ^a
is in your mind.^b For he will not stand up under the removal (of error), if it is done at one time, nor will he hold
the immense stream and flow of teaching,^c but in both
respects, by the cutting away and by the adding, he will
be afflicted and suffer pain and will be carried away.^d But
(if) one quietly and measuredly and little by little removes
ignorance and adds instruction proportionate thereto, it
would admittedly become the cause of profit.^e For not
even a good physician would seek to restore all his health
in one day to one who is ill, knowing that (thereby) he
would do harm rather than good.^f But measuring the

^a Here again we must correct the Arm. which reads οὐ
instead of οὗ.

^b The Catenae (which begin here) read similarly (except
for the two places mentioned in the preceding two notes)
ἐὰν τοῦ ἄρτι πρῶτον εἰσαγομένου καὶ μανθάνοντος σπουδάσῃς,
πᾶσαν τὴν ἀμαθίαν ἐκτεμών, ἀθρόαν ἐπιστήμην εἰσοικίσαι τοὐναντίον οὗ διανοῇ πράξεις. Procopius condenses, ἀλλ' οὐδὲ
τὰς τῶν εἰσαγομένων ψυχὰς ἔστιν ὑφ' ἓν ἀπαλλάττειν ἀγνοίας καὶ
πληροῦν ἐπιστήμης.

^c So the Catenae, οὔτε γὰρ τὴν ἀφαίρεσιν ἑνὶ καιρῷ γινομέ-
νην ὑπομενεῖ, οὔτε τὴν ἄφθονον ῥύμην καὶ φορὰν τῆς διδασκαλίας χωρήσει. Again Procopius paraphrases, οὐ φέρουσι γὰρ
οὔτε τὴν ἐκείνης ἀφαίρεσιν οὔτε τὴν ἄφθονον τῆς διδασκαλίας
φοράν.

^d Aucher "resiliet." In the Catenae the clause reads
similarly except for the last verb ἀλλὰ καθ' ἑκάτερον τό τε
ἐκτεμνόμενον καὶ προστιθέμενον ὀδυνηθεὶς καὶ περιαλγήσας ἀφη-
νιάσει (v.l. ἀπεράσει).

^e So the Catenae, τὸ δὲ ἡσυχῇ καὶ μετρίως ἀφαιρεῖν μὲν κατ'
ὀλίγον (v.l. omits κατ' ὀλίγον) τι τῆς ἀπαιδευσίας, προστιθέναι
δὲ τῆς παιδείας τὸ ἀνάλογον ὠφελείας γένοιτ' ἂν ὁμολογουμένης
αἴτιον.

^f So the Catenae, ὁ δὲ ἀγαθὸς ἰατρὸς οὐ μιᾷ ἡμέρᾳ τῷ νο-
σοῦντι πάντα ἀθρόα τὰ ὑγιεινὰ προσφέρειν (v.l. ἐπιφέρειν) ἂν ἐθελήσειεν, εἰδὼς βλάβην ἐργαζόμενος μᾶλλον ἤπερ ὠφέλειαν (v.l.
ὑγίειαν).

times, he administers the cure at intervals,[a] and by apply-
ing different things at different times he gently brings about
health.[b] But he who is impatient[c] and presumptuous and
insists upon cutting away (ignorance) all at once, and
insists upon adding instruction all at once, increases rather
than lessens the illness.

*26. (Ex. xxiii. 33b) Why does He call the service of
heterodox gods[d] " a stumbling-block "[e]?

Just as those who stumble on whole feet[f] because they
are unable to walk a long way[g] fall short of the end of the
road, having earlier given up, so also the soul, being led
to piety, is prevented from completing (its journey)[h] when
it has earlier come upon the trackless places of impiety.[i]
For these are obstacles and the cause of stumbling, by

[a] Lit. " managing he apportions the cure "; the Arm.
ptc. and verb probably render ἐπιδιανέμει, as in the Greek
frag., see next note.

[b] So the Catenae (which end with this sentence), ἀλλὰ
διαμετρησάμενος τοὺς καιροὺς ἐπιδιανέμει τὰ σωτήρια καὶ ἄλλοτε
ἄλλα προστιθεὶς πρᾴως ὑγίειαν ἐμποιεῖ.

[c] Lit. " trenchant ": Aucher " importunus."

[d] i.e. of the gods of the Gentiles.

[e] LXX ἐὰν γὰρ δουλεύσῃς τοῖς θεοῖς αὐτῶν, οὗτοι ἔσονταί σοι
πρόσκομμα (Heb. " snare ").

[f] i.e. on even feet, see the Greek text (below), in which this
phrase occurs more appropriately in the following clause.

[g] Here again the order of words in the Arm. is to be
corrected from the Greek which places " a long way " in the
clause beginning " fall short."

[h] In the Greek (see next note) it is the road, not the soul,
which leads to piety.

[i] The Greek frag. (from John of Damascus) reads more
smoothly ὥσπερ οἱ προσπταίσαντες, ἀρτίοις βαίνειν ποσὶν ἀδυνατοῦντες, μακρὰν τοῦ κατὰ τὴν ὁδὸν τέλους ὑστερίζουσι προσκάμνοντες (l. προκάμνοντες?), οὕτω καὶ ἡ ψυχὴ τὴν πρὸς εὐσέβειαν
ἄγουσαν ὁδὸν ἀνύειν κωλύεται, προεντυγχάνουσα ταῖς ἀσεβέσιν
ἀνοδίαις. Procopius (covering only this sentence) condenses
and paraphrases, τοῦτο γὰρ παθὼν ὁδοιπόρος προκάμνει, πρὶν εἰς
τὸ τέλος ἐλθεῖν τῆς ὁδοῦ, καὶ ψυχὴ πρὸς θεὸν ὁδεύειν ἐθέλουσα
δυσσεβέσιν ἀνοδίαις τῆς εὐθείας ἀπείργεται.

which the mind is lamed and falls short of the natural road.[a]
Now this road is that which ends in the Father.[b]

27. (Ex. xxiv. 1a) What is the meaning of the words,
" And He said to Moses, Go up, thou and Aaron [c] and
Nadab [d] and Abihu [e] " [f]?

You see indeed that the number of those gathered together for ascending was worthy of God,[g] (namely) the
tetrad,[h] which is the essence [i] of the decad,[j] while seventy [k]
is produced by multiplying seven by ten or ten by seven.[l]
But one should recognize that through the literal meaning [m]
this passage is allegorized.[n] For Moses is the most pure
and God-loving mind,[o] while Aaron is his word, which is

---

[a] So the Greek frag., αὗται γάρ εἰσιν ἐμπόδιοι καὶ προσπταισμάτων αἰτίαι, δι᾽ ὧν κυλλαίνων ὁ νοῦς ὑστερίζει τῆς κατὰ φύσιν
ὁδοῦ.

[b] After " the Father " we should prob. add " of all things "
as in the Greek frag., which reads ἡ δὲ ὁδός ἐστιν ἡ ἐπὶ τὸν
πατέρα τῶν ὅλων τελευτῶσα.

[c] Arm. *Aharon* (as in Heb.).

[d] Arm. *Nabad.*   [e] Arm. *Abioud* (as in lxx).

[f] lxx Καὶ Μωυσῆ εἶπεν, Ἀνάβηθι πρὸς τὸν κύριόν σου, σὺ καὶ
Ἀαρὼν καὶ Ναδὰβ καὶ Ἀβιοὺδ καὶ ἑβδομήκοντα τῶν πρεσβυτέρων Ἰσραήλ. Philo's commentary refers to the seventy
elders, of whom there is no mention in the lemma. In De
Migratione 168 Philo quotes the lxx text except that for
τῶν πρεσβυτέρων he has τῆς γερουσίας.

[g] θεοπρεπῆ.

[h] *i.e.* Moses and his three companions.

[i] οὐσία.

[j] Cf. *De Opif. Mundi* 47 and *De Plantatione* 123, where
four is said to be the source or potentiality of ten, *i.e.* the sum
of 1, 2, 3, 4 = 10.

[k] *i.e.* the seventy elders.

[l] Aucher's rendering adds, after the " seventy," the words
" mysterium cernis " in parenthesis, though there is nothing
corresponding in the Arm.

[m] διὰ τοῦ ῥητοῦ.   [n] ἀλληγορεῖται.

[o] διάνοια or νοῦς. Both terms are used in the parallel, *De
Migratione* 169-170, see notes below.

the unlying interpreter of the truth.[a] And Nadab is
voluntary vision, for (his name) is to be interpreted as
" voluntary." [b] And Abihu is truth from God,[c] for it is
this to which the name refers.[d] Thus you see a soul adorned
with all the ornaments that lead to virtue [e] so as to please
God, (namely) a worthy mind,[f] a true word,[g] one who is
voluntarily pious [h] and one who guards them (like) a barrier
and wall, (namely) help from God.[i] But the power of the
number four will be subordinated to a commander consisting of one,[j] for there are three ornaments of the one
prophetic mind which is acquired by you. The powers of
the seventy elders are honoured with seniority, not by
length of many years but by the ascension of perfect
numbers, which are worthy of honour and are privileged.

*28. (Ex. xxiv. 1b) Why does He say, " they shall wor-
ship the Lord from afar " [k] ?

Just as those who are near a fire are burned, while those

---

[a] Cf. De Migratione 169 Ἀαρών . . . ὁ γεγονὼς λόγος προ-
φητεύων διανοίᾳ.

[b] Cf. De Migratione 169 Ναδὰβ δὲ ἑκούσιος ἑρμηνεύεται ὁ μὴ
ἀνάγκῃ τιμῶν τὸ θεῖον.

[c] Aucher " divinitus veritas."

[d] This far-fetched etymology is apparently based on the
Arm. translator's reading ἀλήθεια instead of βοήθεια " help,"
see below. In De Migratione 169 Abihu is more accurately
etymologized as πατήρ μου. Heb. 'ᵃbîhû lit. = " he is my
father."   [e] ἀρετήν.

[f] Symbolized by Moses.

[g] Symbolized by Aaron.

[h] Symbolized by Nadab.

[i] Symbolized by Abihu.

[j] The Arm. text is not altogether clear. Aucher renders,
" caeterum cum duce militiae quaterno numero ordinetur
virtus unitatis comprehensae."   More intelligible is the
parallel in De Migratione 170, αἵδ' εἰσὶν αἱ τοῦ βασιλεύειν
ἀξίου νοῦ δορυφόροι δυνάμεις.

[k] lxx καὶ προσκυνήσουσιν μακρόθεν τῷ κυρίῳ (Heb. omits
" the Lord ").

who stand apart at a distance measured by a long interval
attain to security, so it is with the soul; whatever soul
comes too near in desiring the vision of God, does not per-
ceive when it is being consumed.[a] But as for that (soul)
which stands far off at a distance, no longer do the tongues
of flame [b] burn it but warming it moderately, they kindle [c]
it with vitality. This [d] is said in reference to the dissolution and rapture of the most perfect and prophetic mind,[e]
for which it is fitting and lawful to enter the dark cloud [f]
and to dwell in the forecourt [g] of the palace of the Father.
Wherefore also there are some animals which move and
dwell in fire, by which others are destroyed, and they are
called " fire-born." [h]

29. (Ex. xxiv. 2) Why does He say, " Moses alone shall
come near to God, and they shall not come near, and the
people shall not go up with them " [i] ?

O most excellent and God-worthy ordinance, that the
prophetic mind [j] alone should approach God and that those

---

[a] The Greek frag. (which extends only to the end of the
sentence) seems to be paraphrastic, οὐχ ὁρᾷς ὅτι τοῦ πυρὸς ἡ
δύναμις τοῖς μὲν ἀφεστηκόσι μεμετρημένον διάστημα παρέχει φῶς
(Arm. = ἀσφάλειαν), κατακαίει δὲ τοὺς ἐγγίζοντας; ὅρα μὴ τοιοῦτόν τι πάθῃς τῇ διανοίᾳ, μή σε ὁ πολὺς πόθος ἀδυνάτου πράγματος
ἀναλώσῃ.

[b] Lit. " sparks (or " effulgences ") of rays " : Aucher
" radiorum splendor."   [c] ζωπυροῦσι.

[d] i.e. the statement about souls that draw near to the fire.

[e] κατὰ τὴν κατάλυσιν καὶ ἀφαίρεσιν τοῦ τελειοτάτου καὶ προφητικοῦ νοῦ: Aucher " secundum dissolutionem et avulsio-
nem perfecti propheticique intellectus."

[f] τὸν γνόφον, cf. De Vita Mosis i. 158 on Ex. xx. 21.

[g] αὐλῇ vel sim.: Aucher " atrio."

[h] πυρίγονα, cf. De Gigantibus 7 et al., and also Aelian,
De Nat. An. 2. 2. 231 on salamanders.

[i] LXX καὶ ἐγγιεῖ Μωυσῆς μόνος πρὸς τὸν θεόν (Heb.
" YHWH "), αὐτοὶ δὲ οὐκ ἐγγιοῦσιν· ὁ δὲ λαὸς οὐ συναναβήσεται
μετ' αὐτῶν (Heb. " with him ").

[j] τὸν προφητικὸν νοῦν.

in second place [a] should go up, making [b] a path to heaven, while those in third place and the turbulent characters of the people [c] should neither go up above nor go up with them but those worthy of beholding should be beholders of the blessed path above. But that "(Moses) alone shall go up " is said most naturally.[d] For when the prophetic mind becomes divinely inspired and filled with God,[e] it becomes like the monad, not being at all mixed with any of those things associated with duality. But he who is resolved into the nature of unity,[f] is said to come near God in a kind of family relation,[g] for having given up and left behind all mortal kinds,[h] he is changed into the divine, so that such men become kin to God and truly divine.

30. (Ex. xxiv. 4b) Why does Moses, rising early in the morning, build an altar below the mountain and twelve stones for the twelve tribes of Israel ? [i]

Either the altar was built of only twelve stones in order that all the tribes of the nation together might in some way [j] be a sacred altar to God, or the twelve stones were set up separately apart from [k] the altar, in order that some, although they might be missing from the daily service,[l] might seem to be there, for the absence of some would be

---

[a] τοὺς δευτέρους.　　　　　　[b] Lit. "cutting."

[c] Aucher "tertios vero populares mores conturbatos."

[d] φυσικώτατα, *i.e.* "most philosophically."

[e] ἐνθουσιᾷ καὶ θεοφορεῖται.

[f] Cf. De Vita Mosis ii. 288 (Moses) μετακληθεὶς ὑπὸ τοῦ πατρός, ὃς αὐτὸν δυάδα ὄντα, σῶμα καὶ ψυχήν, εἰς μονάδος ἀνεστοιχείου φύσιν.

[g] κατὰ συγγενῆ τινα οἰκειότητα: Aucher "cognativa quadam familiaritate."

[h] πάντα θνητὰ γένη.

[i] LXX ὀρθρίσας δὲ Μωυσῆς τὸ πρωὶ ᾠκοδόμησεν θυσιαστήριον ὑπὸ τὸ ὄρος καὶ δώδεκα λίθους (Heb. "pillars"; *v.l.* in LXX adds ἔστησεν after λίθους) εἰς τὰς δώδεκα φυλὰς τοῦ Ἰσραήλ.

[j] τρόπον τινά.

[k] χωρίς.

[l] τῆς καθ' ἡμέραν λειτουργίας vel sim.

filled by the permanent setting up *a* of the twelve stones, which would be a suitable memorial of the tribes, which he wishes always to be present as ministers to the Father.

31. (Ex. xxiv. 5a) Why does he send young men, not the elders ? *b*

Since the elders, numbering seventy, had brought the nation to the foot of the mountain,*c* performing (this) service at the ascent of the prophet, it would have been unsuitable and strange to summon them again to another work when they had already been summoned earlier to the sight,*d* and if he had commanded their contemporaries to offer sacrifice, he would have been held in low esteem by those who were not offering (sacrifice) with them. In the second place, (it was) because the elder generations were a kind of first-fruits and new (offerings), as if performing a bloodless sacrifice, which is more appropriate to elders of advanced age. But as for those who as young men in the flower of their youth were sent to offer sacrifice, because there was much blood in them by reason of their flourishing youth it was profitable *e* for them to offer every offering of sacrifice with blood, as a thankoffering *f* to God and Father, using their youth to lead their desires to piety *g* and not to the madness of unrestrained desires. That is the literal meaning.*h* But as for the deeper meaning,*i* the allwise and God-beloved soul *j* has in itself both

---

a Aucher " constanti erectione."

b lxx καὶ ἐξαπέστειλεν τοὺς νεανίσκους τῶν υἱῶν Ἰσραήλ.

c Aucher renders less accurately, I think, " quoniam senes numerum gentis septuaginta praeseferentes obtulerunt ad radices montis."

d *i.e.* of what was to take place on the mountain.

e λυσιτελές *vel sim.* : Aucher " expediebat."

f εὐχαριστίαν.   *g* τὰς ἐπιθυμίας πρὸς εὐσέβειαν.

h τὸ ῥητόν.   *i* τὸ πρὸς διάνοιαν.

j Arm. *ogi* (= ψυχή) is here exceptionally provided with a plural ending, although it governs a singular verb. Possibly the plural ending here is analogous to that of *mitk* (νοῦς), a *pluralia tantum.* Aucher too renders, " anima."

elderly and youthful principles,[a] all (of them) holy. Now
the elderly ones are used in the contemplation of nature [b]
and of those things which are therein, while those which
are vigorous (are used) for the power [c] of worthy deeds,
so that the life of those who are excellent in these ways,
in both the contemplative and the practical, is publicly
posted and widely famed.[d]

32. (Ex. xxiv. 5b) Why do the young men who were
sent offer whole-burnt-offerings [e] and sacrifice calves as
victims ? [f]

Calves of tender years [g] are offered by the hands of youths
of tender years in order that the sacrifices which are offered
may preserve a correspondence of age [h] with those who
make the offering. Not lambs and not kids (are offered),
for these animals are weaker than calves, whereas he seems
to make the sacrifice from more powerful (animals). Therefore the youths [i] who [j] perform the sacrifice offer sacrifices
of whole-burnt-offerings and salutary offerings [k] in their
prime vigour. The third (kind of offering, namely) the
sin-offering is not (made) inasmuch as that place does not
admit of any transgression at all because of the visible
appearance of the Father. For in that place there was

---

[a] λόγους.　　　　　　　　[b] τῆς φύσεως.
[c] δύναμιν: Aucher " in virili occupatione."
[d] στηλιτεύεται καὶ διαφημίζεται vel sim.
[e] The Arm. oḷjakēzs reflects LXX ὁλοκαυτώματα = Heb.
'ōlôt (A.V. " burnt offerings ").
[f] LXX (abbreviated here) καὶ ἀνήνεγκαν ὁλοκαυτώματα καὶ
ἔθυσαν θυσίαν σωτηρίου (Heb. " covenant-offerings ": A.V.
" peace offerings ") τῷ θεῷ (Heb. " to YHWH ") μοσχάρια
(Heb. " oxen ").
[g] ἀπαλοί.
[h] Variant " equality " or " community."
[i] Lit. " the youth " (collective abstract)—ἡ νεότης.
[j] A different division of words yields the variant " the new
youth " for " the youths who."
[k] τὰ σωτήρια, which is the LXX rendering of Heb. šᵉlāmîm
" covenant-offerings," see above, note f.

not anything to oppose (Him).[a] For when the sun rises, darkness disappears and everything becomes filled with light. Moreover, when God appears or is about to appear, is not every form and substance [b] of sin first to be destroyed and removed ? Accordingly, the two kinds of sacrifice are here the best that can be [c] performed, (namely) the whole-burnt-offering in honour of the unbribable and unbought [d] Father, which is made for no one else but Him Who is honoured, and the salutary offering, which is made for our sake, in return for the fact that good things have happened to us [e] and that we experience and await them. For it is to God Who gives them to the race of mortals that we render the sacrifices of health and salvation and all good things in general.

33. (Ex. xxiv. 6) Why did Moses take half of the blood and pour it into mixing-bowls,[f] and pour half upon [g] the altar ? [h]

He divides the blood in a manner appropriate to its worth,[i] desiring that some of it should be a sacred offering to God and that some should be a sacred unction [j] in place of oil for sanctity and perfect purity, and, if one must speak

[a] A variant omits the negative. Aucher renders, " quae illico ipsi opponebat sese," and as (a free) alternative, " cui illic illud peccatum non poterat sese opponere." The Arm. glossator takes the text to mean " there was no sin there, which is opposed to God."

[b] εἶδος καὶ οὐσία.　　　　[c] Lit. " that are."

[d] The two Arm. adjectives prob. render the single Greek adjective ἀδεκάστου : Aucher " dona vix accipientis."

[e] Aucher renders more freely, " beneficia probavimus."

[f] κρατῆρας, as in lxx, see note h.　　[g] Aucher " circa."

[h] lxx λαβὼν δὲ Μωυσῆς τὸ ἥμισυ τοῦ αἵματος ἐνέχεεν εἰς κρατῆρας· τὸ δὲ ἥμισυ τοῦ αἵματος προσέχεεν πρὸς (v.l. ἐπί : Heb. " upon ") τὸ θυσιαστήριον. Philo cites the lxx text of this verse (omitting Moses' name) in Quis Rer. Div. Heres 182-185 and allegorizes it in somewhat the same manner as here but without Pythagorean number-mysticism.

[i] Aucher " legitimo ordine."　　　　[j] χρίσμα.

the truth, in order that (men) may be inspired [a] to receive
the holy spirit.[b] But the mixing-bowls are symbols
of the mixed and composite nature,[c] which is ours. For
the divine (nature) is pure and unmixed, whereas all such
things as through generation come into existence from
contraries are necessarily receptacles, in part of a good,
in part of a bad form.[d] Accordingly, that which belongs
to the better is assigned to the part of God, for He acquires
this through His simpler and more lucid essence,[e] while
that which belongs to the worse (is assigned) to the race
of mortals. But one should begin with the incorporeal
and intelligible things,[f] which are the measures and models
of sense-perceptible things.[g] Now the principle [h] of all
things arises from numbers, some of which are odd, having
the status of active causes,[i] and some even, (having the
status) of matter.[j] It is therefore necessary to attribute
the idea [k] of the odd (number) to God because of His
connexion [l] with activity,[m] whereas the even (is to be attributed) to the race of mortals because of its familiarity with
suffering and passion.[n] The same (distinction holds) for

---

[a] Prob. ψυχοῦσθαι: Aucher " in spiritum verti."

[b] τὸ ἅγιον πνεῦμα, which is not Philonic usage, though
Philo often speaks of a θεῖον πνεῦμα. Possibly the Arm.
translator has here substituted " holy " for " divine."

[c] τῆς μικτῆς καὶ συνθέτου φύσεως, cf. Quis Rer. Div. Heres
183: Aucher " sibi invicem compactae naturae."

[d] Prob. εἴδους rather than ἰδέας: Aucher " ideae."

[e] Aucher " qui ergo melioris statûs est, partum Dei sortitus
est per simpliciorem lucidioremque essentiam." The parallel
in Quis Rer. Div. Heres 183 and the present context indicate
that it is God's essence which is meant here.

[f] τοῖς ἀσωμάτοις καὶ νοητοῖς. [g] παραδείγματα τῶν αἰσθητῶν.

[h] Or " origin "—ἀρχή. [i] δραστηρίων αἰτίων λόγον ἔχοντες.

[j] Cf. De Opif. Mundi 13 ἄρρεν μὲν γὰρ ἐν τοῖς οὖσι τὸ
περιττόν, τὸ δ' ἄρτιον θῆλυ (where " male " connotes " active,"
and " female " connotes " passive " and " material ").

[k] Or " form." [l] συγγένειαν.

[m] Lit. " doing " or " making."

[n] Aucher renders more briefly, " ob familiaritatem ad
patiendum."

equality and inequality, similarity and dissimilarity, identity and difference, unity and separation.[a] As for equality, similarity, identity and unity, they are to be ordered under the better class, as it were, with God, while the unequal, the dissimilar, the different and the separate (are to be ordered) in the worse (class), of which mortal (nature) has obtained the greater part. It is (possible), however, to see the equivalent of this (distinction) not only in incorporeal and intelligible things but also in sense-perceptible natures. For even in the cosmos heaven itself and everything in heaven are found worthy of the divine and best essence [b] and come near to God and are conse-crated to Him. But that which is sublunary [c] belongs to the more material and denser part and is assigned to the race of mortals. Moreover, in us ourselves the soul [d] con-sists of the rational and the irrational.[e] And the rational, being the better, is consecrated to the better nature, while the irrational, being worse, (is consecrated) to the inferior,[f] which we, the untaught and incontinent and undisciplined,[g] have received. Nevertheless, one who considers the mortal body with good judgment will say that the sovereign head is consecrated to the holy Creator and Father, while (the part) from the breast to the feet belongs to material sub-stance. This (part), therefore, he reckons to the mixing-bowls symbolically,[h] because it is mixed and composite, while he consecrates the pure and unmixed (part) by making it an offering to God.

34. (Ex. xxiv. 7a) What is the meaning of the words, " Taking the book of the covenant, he read to the ears [i] of all the people " [j]?

---

[a] Prob. διαιρέσει.   [b] Or " substance "—οὐσίας.
[c] τὸ μετὰ σελήνην.   [d] ἡ ψυχή.
[e] τοῦ λογικοῦ καὶ τοῦ ἀλόγου.
[f] Lit. " lesser " : Aucher " minori."
[g] i.e. those of us who are untaught, etc.   [h] συμβολικῶς.
[i] So LXX and Heb. literally (A.V. " audience "), see next note.
[j] LXX καὶ λαβὼν τὸ βιβλίον τῆς διαθήκης ἀνέγνω εἰς τὰ ὦτα τοῦ λαοῦ.

QUESTIONS AND ANSWERS

Concerning the divine covenant we have already spoken in detail,[a] so that it is not proper to discuss the subject again at the present time. However, some notice must be taken of (the words) " reading to the ears." Now this takes place without separation and interruption, for the air is not agitated from without as the sound reaches the hearers but (the voice of) the speaker resounds in them without separation or distance [b] like some pure and lucid voice which is extended.[c] And there is no third thing interposed, by the intervention of which the reception [d] becomes less but the sound echoes more surely in an only purer form when the hearers and the word come together without any separation between them. That is the literal meaning.[e] But as for the deeper meaning,[f] since it was impossible for anyone to reach such a multitude of hearers [g] or to come near and speak to their ears,[h] it is necessary to hold the opinion that the teacher and the pupil [i] were there. One of them speaks privately [j] to his disciples [k] without concealing anything, not even things not to be spoken of,[l] and the other is the recipient who offers himself as one worthy of voluntarily being a repository of the divine Law [m] and a guardian of those things which it would not be proper to interpret [n] to the many, whatever may happen.

---

[a] ἡμῖν ἠκρίβωται. Philo here apparently alludes to his (lost) work Περὶ Διαθηκῶν in two books, see *De Mut. Nom.* 53.

[b] Aucher renders more freely, " sed dicentis vox immediate in eas sonans."

[c] Aucher " expansa."   [d] Aucher " perceptio."

[e] τὸ ῥητόν.   [f] τὸ πρὸς διάνοιαν.

[g] Aucher renders more freely, " ut vox unius cujusdam in tantae multitudinis aures perveniret."

[h] Aucher " aut ipse ad singulorum accedens aures loqueretur."

[i] ὁ γνώριμος : Aucher " auditor."

[j] ἰδίως or κατ᾽ ἰδίαν : Aucher " seorsum."

[k] τοῖς μαθηταῖς.   [l] ἀπόρρητα vel sim.

[m] The meaning of the clause is not quite clear : Aucher " praestans se dignum divina traditione legis voluntariae."

[n] ἀποδίδοσθαι : Aucher " referre."

35. (Ex. xxiv. 8a) Why did he take that blood which
(was) in the mixing-bowls *a* and sprinkle (it) over the
people ? *b*

By indicating that the blood of all (was) the same and
that their kinship *c* (was) the same, he wishes to show that
in a certain way *d* they were animated by one idea and
nature,*e* for on many occasions he puts the blood in the
same class as the soul.*f* Even if they are separated from
one another by their bodies, they are nevertheless united
by mind and thought,*g* and they share together the divine
sacrifices and victims, being brought from estrangement
to community *h* and to the concord *i* of distinguished
blood.

36. (Ex. xxiv. 8b) Why does he say further, " Behold
the blood of the covenant which the Lord commanded you
concerning all these words " *j* ?

(He does so) because the blood is a symbol *k* of family
kinship.*l* And the form *m* of kinship is twofold *n* : one is
that among men, which has its origin in ancestors, while
that among souls *o* has its origin in wisdom.*p* Now he did
not mention the kinship of ancestors and offspring, because

---

a See *QE* ii. 33 on Ex. xxiv. 6.

b LXX λαβὼν δὲ Μωυσῆς τὸ αἷμα κατεσκέδασεν τοῦ λαοῦ.

c τὴν συγγένειαν.   *d* τρόπον τινά.

e μιᾷ ψυχοῦσθαι ἰδέᾳ καὶ φύσει.

f ἐν μέρει τῆς ψυχῆς.   *Cf.* Lev. xvii. 14 (*et al.*) " the blood
of it is its life."

g Lit. " by the mind of thoughts " : Aucher " per consilia
mentis."

h ἐξ ἀλλοτριώσεως εἰς κοινωνίαν.

i Or " sincerity " or " singleness " : Aucher " concor-
diam."

j LXX καὶ εἶπεν, Ἰδοὺ τὸ αἷμα τῆς διαθήκης ἧς διέθετο (Heb.
" cut," *i.e.* " made ") κύριος πρὸς ὑμᾶς περὶ πάντων τῶν λόγων
τούτων.   *k* σύμβολον or σημεῖον.

l συγγενικῆς οἰκειότητος.   *m* Or " species "—εἶδος.

n Lit. " of two faces " : Aucher " duplex."

o ψυχῶν.   *p* σοφίαν.

it is also common to irrational animals, but from the other (kind of kinship) as from a root grew wisdom.[a] Now wisdom is the font of words and the voluntary laws [b] which the teacher has proclaimed and taught to lovers of learning as being most necessary, (namely) concord and community.[c] But this cannot be acquired by polytheists,[d] because they put forth variant opinions distinguished for difference and diversity,[e] and they become the cause of quarrelling and fighting. But an harmonious adjustment to one (opinion) is the agreement of all who are ministers and servants of the work.

*37. (Ex. xxiv. 10) What is the meaning of the words, " They saw the place where the God of Israel was standing, and under His feet (was something) like the work of a plinth of sapphire and like the form of the firmament of heaven in purity " [f] ?

All this is, in the first place, most suitable to and worthy of the theologian,[g] for no one will boast of seeing the invisible God, (thus) yielding to arrogance.[h] And holy and

---

[a] The Arm. translator may have misunderstood the Greek here. One expects " but the other (kind of kinship) grew from wisdom as from a root."

[b] τῶν ἑκουσίων νόμων, cf. De Mut. Nom. 26.

[c] ὁμόνοιαν καὶ κοινωνίαν vel sim.   [d] τῶν πολυθέων.

[e] The construction is not wholly clear but Aucher is wrong, I think, in rendering, " quia honoratae huic distinctioni disjunctiores opiniones oppositas faciunt."

[f] LXX καὶ εἶδον τὸν τόπον οὗ εἱστήκει ὁ θεὸς τοῦ Ἰσραήλ· καὶ τὰ ὑπὸ τοὺς πόδας αὐτοῦ ὡσεὶ ἔργον πλίνθου (v.l. λίθου) σαπφείρου καὶ ὥσπερ εἶδος στερεώματος τοῦ οὐρανοῦ (Heb. " and like the very heaven ") τῇ καθαριότητι. Philo quotes the first clause (to Ἰσραήλ) in De Somniis i. 62 and ii. 222, and the rest of the verse in De Confus. Ling. 96 ff., where the mss. of Philo read λίθου for πλίνθου but the commentary (as in this section of the Quaestiones) requires πλίνθου (see also notes below).

[g] τοῦ θεολόγου, i.e. Moses.

[h] The brief Greek frag. (which contains only this clause) reads similarly οὐδεὶς αὐχήσει τὸν ἀόρατον θεὸν ἰδεῖν, εἴξας ἀλαζονείᾳ.

divine is this same place alone in which He is said to appear, for He Himself does not go away or change His position but He sends the powers,[a] which are indicative of His essence.[b] And if it is right (to say so, we may) say that this place is that of His Logos,[c] since He has never given a suspicion of movement but of always standing, for the nature of the Father remains fixed and unchanged [d] and more lucid and simpler [e] than the (number) one which alone is a form of likeness.[f] Now he has represented the unchanged and immutable nature of God (as) the oneness of unity because of His substance.[g] And the whole heaven altogether was under His feet, for its colour indeed was rather like a sapphire. And the " plinth " is a figure [h] of the stars as one group,[i] harmoniously arranged in an order of numbers,

---

[a] τὰς δυνάμεις.

[b] Aucher " essentiam." Although Arm. ēout'iun renders both οὐσία and ὕπαρξις, the context favours the rendering " essence " rather than " existence " in spite of Philo's statement in De Poster. Caini 169 αὗται γὰρ (sc. αἱ δυνάμεις) οὐ τὴν οὐσίαν, τὴν δ' ὕπαρξιν ἐκ τῶν ἀποτελουμένων αὐτῷ παριστᾶσι. Philo here (in QE) seems to mean that God's powers merely indicate His essence but do not make this fully known to man. The rendering " essence " seems preferable to " existence " also because of the Heb. 'eṣem in this verse (see above, note f on p. 78), which means something like " essence."

[c] Arm. banaworout'iun = λογιότης rather than λόγος (Aucher renders, " rationalitatis "), but other passages in Philo, e.g. De Confus. Ling. 96, show that the Logos is meant here.

[d] βεβαία καὶ ἄτρεπτος.   [e] ἁπλουστέρα.

[f] Variant " simpler than (the number) one to which unity is a form of likeness " : Aucher " simplicior unitate, quae unica est forma similitudinis."

[g] The construction and meaning are not wholly clear : Aucher " unam autem unitatis invariabilem immutabilemque naturam Dei propter substantiam indicavit."

[h] The original was πλινθίον or πλινθίς : Aucher " laterculus." I have here rendered it by " figure " rather than " small brick " because Philo seems to be playing on the metaphorical meaning of πλινθίον, " musical scale."

[i] Lit. " at one time " : Aucher " simul."

proportions and progressions,[a] that is, (as) a constant likeness and image of an incorporeal form.[b] For it is a very
holy and lucid sense-perceptible type-form [c] of the intelligible heaven and is a worthy portion of the divine
essence, of which I have spoken earlier.[d] Therefore is it
said, " Like the form of the firmament [e] in purity," for
incorporeal forms are most lucid and pure inasmuch as
they have obtained a share of unmixed essence and of
that which is most simple. Accordingly, he says that the
sense-perceptible heaven, which he calls " firmament," is
distinct from the intelligible form because of its purity.

*38. (Ex. xxiv. 11a) Why does (Scripture) say, " Of the
chosen seeing ones [f] there differed [g] not even one " [h] ?
　　The literal text has a clear interpretation, (namely) that

　[a] ἀριθμῶν καὶ λόγων καὶ ἀναλογιῶν: Aucher " numerorum,
rationum et collationum."

　[b] ἀσωμάτου εἴδους.

　[c] τύπος εἰδῶν.

　[d] Text slightly emended (by removal of superfluous verb
ē " is ") : Aucher " siquidem intelligibilis caeli sensibile hoc
typus est purus et lucidus omnino, illius, quam jampridem
dixi divinam essentiam ac portionem meruisse."

　[e] In the quotation from Scripture in the heading of this
section we read " of the firmament of heaven."

　[f] Philo here, as often elsewhere, substitutes " the seeing
one(s) " for " Israel."

　[g] More literally " was separated ": variant (as in Arm.
O.T.) " was consumed," see next note.

　[h] LXX καὶ τῶν ἐπιλέκτων τοῦ Ἰσραὴλ οὐ διεφώνησεν οὐδὲ εἷς
(Heb. reads quite differently " and upon the nobles of the
Israelites He laid not His hand "). Although the LXX trans-
lators meant διεφώνησεν as " perished," Philo took it to mean
" differed " or " was discordant," as is shown by the rest of
this section and also by the parallel in De Confus. Ling. 56
γένος γάρ ἐσμεν τῶν ἐπιλέκτων τοῦ τὸν θεὸν ὁρῶντος Ἰσραὴλ ὧν
διεφώνησεν οὐδὲ εἷς, ἵνα . . . ὁ κόσμος πᾶς ταῖς ἁρμονίαις μουσι-
κῶς μελῳδῆται. R. Reitzenstein, Die Vorgeschichte der christ-
lichen Taufe (Leipzig, Berlin, 1929), p. 116, concludes too
hastily that Philo here took διεφώνησεν to mean " perished."

all were preserved whole.[a] But as for the deeper meaning, immortal in soul is the chosen race to which has come wisdom [b] and every virtue [c] and, above all, piety, the queen of the virtues.[d] For dissonance from decency [e] and disharmony are death to the soul. Therefore it is well said that " no one differed," (meaning) that as in an all-musical chorus with the blended voices of all [f] one should play music in harmonious measures of modulation and with skilled fingers, seeking to show (this harmony) not so much in sound as in mind.

39. (Ex. xxiv. 11b) What is the meaning of the words, " They appeared to God in the place [g] and they ate and drank " [h] ?

Having attained [i] to the face of the Father, they do not

---

[a] So the Greek frag., τὸ μὲν ῥητὸν διήγημα φανερὰν ἔχει τὴν ἀπόδοσιν ὡς ἀπάντων σώων διατηρηθέντων.

[b] σοφία.　　　　　　　　　　[c] πᾶσα ἀρετή.

[d] The Greek frag. summarizes this sentence and the rest of the section very briefly, τὸ δὲ πρὸς διάνοιαν τὸ πάντας περὶ τὴν εὐσέβειαν συμφώνους εἶναι καὶ ἐν μηδενὶ τῶν ἀγαθῶν διαφωνεῖν. See also Reitzenstein, op. cit. p. 117, note 4.

[e] πρὸς καλοκἀγαθίαν vel sim.: Aucher " ad probitatem."

[f] ἐν παμμούσῳ χορείᾳ καὶ πάντων συμφωνίᾳ.

[g] Aucher " apparuerunt Deo in eo loco." For a possible different rendering see the next note.

[h] LXX καὶ ὤφθησαν ἐν τῷ τόπῳ τοῦ θεοῦ (so Arm. O.T.: Heb. " and they saw God ") καὶ ἔφαγον καὶ ἔπιον. Although the Arm. reflects ὤφθησαν τῷ θεῷ ἐν τῷ τόπῳ (as Aucher and I have rendered), it is possible that, with a change in word-order, it agrees with LXX in reading " they appeared in the place of God," since the Arm. astouacoy may be either genitive or dative. I suspect that the Arm. translator inadvertently wrote " God " after " they appeared," and that Philo originally agreed with the LXX in reading ὤφθησαν ἐν τῷ τόπῳ τοῦ θεοῦ and did not read ὤφθησαν τῷ θεῷ ἐν τῷ τόπῳ, as the Arm. suggests.

[i] The text is slightly uncertain but the variant (hasanin for hanen) does not change the meaning greatly.

remain in any mortal place at all, for all such (places) are profane and polluted, but they send and make a migration ^{a} to a holy and divine place, which is called by another name, Logos.^{b} Being in this (place) through the steward ^{c} they see the Master ^{d} in a lofty and clear manner, envisioning ^{e} God with the keen-sighted eyes of the mind.^{f} But this vision ^{g} is the food of the soul,^{h} and true partaking ^{i} is the cause of a life of immortality.^{j} Wherefore, indeed, is it said, " they ate and drank." For those who are indeed very hungry and thirsty did not fail ^{k} to see God become clearly visible, but like those who, being famished, find an abundance of food, they satisfied their great desire.

*40. (Ex. xxiv. 12a) What is the meaning of the words, " Come up to Me to the mountain and be there " ^{l} ?

This signifies that a holy soul ^{m} is divinized ^{n} by ascending not to the air or to the ether or to heaven (which is) higher than all but to (a region) above the heavens. And

---

^{a} ἀποικίαν.

^{b} A similar idea is expressed in a passage from Procopius cited by R. Reitzenstein, *op. cit.* (see preceding section), p. 117, note 4, τὸ δὲ φαγεῖν ἐκεῖ καὶ πιεῖν τὴν ἀποκειμένην τοῖς εἰς οὐρανὸν ἀνιοῦσιν ὑποσημαίνει τρυφήν.

^{c} διὰ τοῦ οἰκονόμου (or ἐπιτρόπου or διοικητοῦ): Aucher " per dispensatorem," *cf.* Reitzenstein, *op. cit.* p. 119.

^{d} Lit. " leader " or " chief " : Aucher " principalem."

^{e} φανταζόμενοι: Aucher " invisentes." (Incidentally, Aucher's punctuation in the Arm. text differs from that in his Latin rendering.) ^{f} τοῦ νοῦ.

^{g} φαντασία: Aucher " apparentia."

^{h} Lit. " souls "—ψυχῶν. ^{i} κοινωνία.

^{j} Aucher disregards the word-order in rendering, " et vera participatio vitae causa est immortalitatis " instead of " et vera participatio vitae immortalitatis causa est."

^{k} Aucher renders more freely, " non fuerunt prohibiti."

^{l} LXX (καὶ εἶπεν κύριος πρὸς Μωυσῆν) Ἀνάβηθι πρός με εἰς τὸ ὄρος καὶ ἴσθι ἐκεῖ. ^{m} ψυχὴν ἁγίαν.

^{n} Aucher " deificari." Arm. *astouacanal* usu. renders θεοῦσθαι, a word that seems not to occur elsewhere in Philo. Perhaps the original here was θεοφορεῖσθαι.

beyond the world *a* there is no place but God. And He
determines *b* the stability of the removal *c* by saying " be
there," (thus) demonstrating the placelessness *d* and the
unchanging habitation of the divine place. For those who
have a quickly satiated passion for reflexion fly upward for
only a short distance under divine inspiration *e* and then
they immediately return.*f* They do not fly so much as
they are drawn downward, I mean, to the depths of Tar-
tarus.*g* But those who do not return from the holy and
divine city, to which they have migrated, have God as their
chief leader in the migration.*h*

41. (Ex. xxiv. 12b) Why are the commandments written
on " tablets of stone " *i* ?

Tablets and written documents are hand-made things,*j*
and what is written in them is easily destroyed, for in
tablets there is wax, which is easily rubbed away, and in
papyrus-rolls *k* the writing is sometimes spread out *l* and

---

a μετὰ τὸν κόσμον : Aucher " post mundum."
b Lit. " seals " : Aucher " decernit."
c Aucher " constantiam transmigrationis."
d Arm. *anteḷ* lit.= ἄτοπον : Aucher " loco carentem."
e From the reading of the Greek frag. (which begins with
this sentence, see next note) it appears that the Arm. phrase
" fly upward . . . under divine inspiration " takes the ptc.
ἀναπτεροφορηθέντες as a combination of ἀναπτεροῦντες and
θεοφορηθέντες.
f The Greek frag. reads ἐνίοις ἀψίκορος ἐγγίνεται λογισμός,
οἳ πρὸς ὀλίγον ἀναπτεροφορηθέντες αὐτίκα ὑπενόστησαν.
g So the Greek frag., οὐκ ἀναπτάντες μᾶλλον ἢ ὑποσυρέντες
εἰς ταρτάρου, φησίν, ἐσχατίας.
h Aucher " in habitationem constantem." The Greek
frag. reads more briefly εὐδαίμονες δὲ οἱ μὴ παλινδρομοῦντες.
i LXX (καὶ δώσω σοι) τὰ πυξία τὰ λίθινα, τὸν νόμον καὶ τὰς
ἐντολάς (ἃς ἔγραψα νομοθετῆσαι αὐτοῖς).
j χειροποίητα.
k ἐν στήλαις . . . ἐν χαρτιδίοις, cf. *Quod Omnis Probus* 46,
De Spec. Leg. iv. 149 *et al.*
l Aucher " spargitur." Possibly Philo means that the
writing is so erratic or cursive as to be illegible.

sometimes seems obscure.[a] But stones are the work of
nature and are easily converted into tablets ; and also the
forms on polished stone tablets [b] and the writings on them
are permanent and fixed because of the strength of the
material. In the second place, it was not possible for the
divine commandments to remain concealed in any recess
and to avoid meeting those who were eager to see and learn
(them), but (they had) to be published abroad and to be
openly circulated. But those things which were to be
proclaimed abroad were in need of hard material because
of the burning heat of the sun and the falling of rain, so
that later the stone tablets were placed in the ark. In the
third place, the tablets were of stone, for stone signifies
permanence, while a tablet (signifies) impermanence, for
a tablet is written on and erased with ease.[c] And this
is a symbol [d] of the preservation [e] and dissolution of the
law. What is written (is a symbol) of preservation, what
is erased (is a symbol) of dissolution, since for those who
transgress commandments, one would truly say that there
is no law at all.

42. (Ex. xxiv. 12c) Does God write the Law ? [f]
Since God is a legislator [g] in the highest sense of the
term,[h] it is necessary that the best law, which is called the
true Law,[i] should be laid down by Him and be written in
writing, not of hands, for He is not of human form, but at
His command and nod. For if at His word [j] the heaven
and earth and the entire world were created and the whole
of substance received its form from the divine principles

---

[a] ἀμυδρά vel sim. : Aucher " subobscure."
[b] ἐν πλαξί vel sim. : Aucher " in lapidibus."
[c] Aucher " nam tabula tam facile scribitur quam deletur."
[d] σύμβολον.   [e] Or " observance."
[f] LXX τὸν νόμον καὶ τὰς ἐντολὰς ἃς ἔγραψα νομοθετῆσαι αὐτοῖς.
[g] νομοθέτης.
[h] κατὰ τὸν ἀνωτάτω λόγον vel sim. : Aucher " secundum
supremam rationem."
[i] ὁ ἀψευδὴς νόμος : Aucher " infallibilis lex."
[j] Lit. " saying."

(as) fashioners,[a] then when God says that the Law should be written, were not the writings immediately to be obeyed?[b] In the second place, this world is a great city[c] and is a legal one.[d] And it is necessary for it to use the best law of state.[e] And it is fitting that it should have a worthy author[f] of law and legislator,[g] since among men He appointed the contemplative race[h] in the same manner (as the Law) for the world.[i] And rightly does He legislate for this race, also prescribing (its Law) as a law for the world,[j] for the chosen race[k] is a likeness[l] of the world, and its Law (is a likeness of the laws) of the world.

43. (Ex. xxiv. 13) Why does Moses, who has been summoned alone,[m] go up not alone but with Joshua?[n]

[a] ἐκ τῶν θείων λόγων (v.l. = τοῦ θείου λόγου) τῶν συμπλεκτικῶν vel ἁρμοττόντων: Aucher " a verbo divino efficaci."

[b] I render freely, since the Arm. lit. = " were not the writings immediately obedient " (or " ministering "). Evidently the Arm. translator should have written spasaworesçin instead of spasawor linēin. Aucher, too, renders freely, as the context requires, " obsequi debet liber."

[c] Cf. De Spec. Leg. i. 34 τὴν ὡς ἀληθῶς μεγαλόπολιν, τόνδε τὸν κόσμον.   [d] νόμιμος.

[e] πολιτείας.   [f] κτίστης.

[g] Aucher renders less literally, " atque aequum est et conveniens ut sit ei legislator ac legisdator."

[h] i.e. Israel.

[i] The syntax and meaning are not clear. Aucher renders, " et cum hominem (sic) genti contemplativae legem daret, daret quoque ipsi mundo," adding in a footnote " Sic explicavimus locum incertum." The Arm. glossator takes it to mean " gentem Dei videntem (sive, Israel) tamquam legem alteram Deus mundo dedit."

[j] καὶ κοσμικὸν νόμον διαγράφων vel sim.: Aucher " delineans etiam legem mundi."

[k] τὸ ἐκλεκτὸν γένος.   [l] Aucher " forma."

[m] See QE ii. 40 on Ex. xxiv. 12a.

[n] LXX καὶ ἀναστὰς Μωυσῆς καὶ Ἰησοῦς ὁ παρεστηκὼς αὐτῷ (Heb. " his servant ") ἀνέβησαν (Heb. " and Moses went up ") εἰς τὸ ὄρος τοῦ θεοῦ.

85

QUESTIONS AND ANSWERS

The two are potentially [a] one, since no one would say
that those who are of like mind and like sentiments with
one another are the same single (person) except in respect
of another species.[b] For " Joshua " [c] is to be interpreted
as " salvation." [d] But is being saved by God more appropriate [e] to anyone else than the inspired soul, in which
prophecy resounds,[f] since even in (Moses') lifetime he was
over the rulers [g] and at (Moses') death he was his succes-
sor.[h] ? Rightly, therefore, does he go up as an assurance [i] of
two most necessary things : one, of the election of the
contemplative race,[j] and the other, that the Law should
be considered not as an invention of the human mind but
as a divine command and divine words.[k] But perhaps,
according to the unspoken meaning of what is said,[l]
Joshua too was openly summoned (to go) up and was not

---

[a] δυνάμει.

[b] The meaning is not altogether clear : Aucher " etenim
nemo est qui eundem solum dixerit sibi invicem unanimes ac
concordes, verum etiam secundum aliam speciem."

[c] Arm. Yisūs (Heb. Yᵉhôšu'a).

[d] Cf. De Mut. Nom. 121 τὸν Ὡσηὲ μετονομάζει Μωυσῆς εἰς
τὸν Ἰησοῦν, τὸν ποιὸν εἰς ἕξιν μεταχαράττων. Ὡσηὲ μὲν ἑρμηνεύεται ποιὸς οὗτος, Ἰησοῦς δὲ σωτηρία κυρίου, ἕξεως ὄνομα τῆς
ἀρίστης.

[e] μᾶλλον οἰκεῖον.

[f] ἐν ᾗ ἐξηχεῖ ἡ προφητεία : Aucher " et inflatae ipsi pro-
phetiae," in his footnote, " flaveritque in eum prophetia."
Apparently Philo means that Joshua is the sounding-board
of Moses' prophecies.

[g] i.e. of Israel.

[h] Cf. De Virtutibus 68 (on Num. xxvii. 18-23) ὁ δὲ τῆς ...
ἐπιτροπῆς διάδοχος οὗτός ἐστιν αἱρεθεὶς ὑπὸ θεοῦ.

[i] εἰς πίστιν : Aucher " ad fidem faciendam."

[j] i.e. Israel.

[k] Cf. De Decalogo 15 ἐπειδὴ γὰρ ἔδει πίστιν ἐγγενέσθαι ταῖς
διανοίαις περὶ τοῦ μὴ εὑρήματα ἀνθρώπου τοὺς νόμους ἀλλὰ θεοῦ
χρησμοὺς σαφεστάτους εἶναι, πορρωτάτω τῶν πόλεων ἀπήγαγε τὸ
ἔθνος εἰς ἐρήμην κτλ.

[l] κατὰ τὰ ἡσυχασθέντα τῶν εἰρημένων vel sim. : Aucher
" sub silentio intelligendum in dictis."

thought worthy of being called earlier to go up because (God) deemed the prophet *a* worthy of this honour and great prerogative.*b*

44. (Ex. xxiv. 14) Why did he leave Aaron and Hur *c* below with the elder judges ? *d*

Just as a navy,*e* if it has no commander,*f* is in need of commanders from time to time for taking care of and equipping the entire fleet, so also to an infantry force, which has no commander-in-chief, the secondary officers, such as company-commanders and squadron-commanders,*g* being in second place,*h* supply necessary and useful things.*i* And when nations have been reduced to obedience by the great king,*j* he grants them many things for whatever lawful purposes may be fitting, and in the various states appoints those whom it is customary to call satraps.*k* And as the prophet, who was about to go on an ethereal and heavenly journey, was well and rightly concerned about such things, he was careful to leave in his place overseers and supervisors. And (as) a sign of victory for those who were in doubt he offered the just man as an arbitrator

---

a *i.e.* Moses.

b προνομίας. The text seems not to be in good order, but the general meaning seems to be that God left it to be understood that Joshua was to go up with Moses, although originally He specifically commanded only Moses to go up (in Ex. xxiv. 12).

c Arm. *Or.*

d LXX καὶ τοῖς πρεσβυτέροις εἶπεν, Ἡσυχάζετε αὐτοῦ ἕως ἀναστρέψωμεν πρὸς ὑμᾶς· καὶ ἰδοὺ Ἀαρὼν καὶ Ὢρ (Heb. Ḥur) μεθ᾽ ὑμῶν· ἐάν τινι συμβῇ κρίσις, προσπορευέσθωσαν αὐτοῖς.

e στρατῷ ναυτικῷ *vel sim.* : Aucher " navi classicae."

f ναύαρχος.

g λοχαγοὶ καὶ ταξίαρχοι.

h Aucher " praesentes." The text appears to be corrupt.

i For a rather remote parallel to the preceding see *De Decalogo* 14.

j *i.e.* of Persia.

k σατράπας.

of the laws.[a] That is the literal meaning.[b] But as for the
deeper meaning,[c] there are two brothers in one—the mind
and the word.[d] Now Moses, who is called by another
name, mind, has obtained the better part, (namely) God,
whereas the word, which is called Aaron, (has obtained)
the lesser (part, namely) that of man. And the word of an
unrighteous and wicked man is very dark, for even if it
reaches great men,[e] it is obscured.[f] But (the word) of him
who is of the Lord is very lucid,[g] even though there is no
very well adapted instrument [h] in his mouth and tongue.[i]

[a] The meaning of this sentence is far from clear, partly
because of the plurality of senses of the word *arit'*, which
renders such diverse Greek terms as πρόξενος, μεσίτης, πρύτανις,
ὑπόθεσις and ἀφορμή. Aucher renders, " atque victoriae
signum adhibens dubio animo haerentibus, conciliat legitime
justum." Possibly the original of " those who were in
doubt," τοῖς ἀμφιβαλλομένοις, meant " for matters in dispute "
or was a corruption of τοῖς ἀμφισβητουμένοις. At any rate
the " victory " seems to have been a judicial victory, not a
military one as the Arm. glossator explains.

[b] τὸ ῥητόν.   [c] τὸ πρὸς διάνοιαν.

[d] ὁ νοῦς (or ἡ διάνοια) καὶ ὁ λόγος.

[e] Lit. " greatly," but Arm. *meçapes* seems to reflect
μεγάλους corrupted to μεγάλως.

[f] The text is probably not in order : Aucher " verbum
autem vilioris ac improbi obscurius est, quamvis enim
magnifice consecutus fuerit (verbum), obnubilatum est."
The general sense seems to be that ordinary speech or reason
is obscure unless it is illuminated by the light of truth (symbolized by Hur, see the following).

[g] Aucher " Domini vero (verbum) lucidissimum est."
But he ignores the word *oroy*, which is the gen. case of the
rel. pron. If my rendering is correct, Philo means that in
contrast to ordinary or wicked men Aaron, who is the word
of Moses, the man of God, is enlightened. See also next note
but one.   [h] ὄργανον οὐ σφόδρα εὐάρμοστον.

[i] Aucher, construing wrongly, I think, renders, " etsi in
ore sit atque lingua instrumentis haud nimis coaptatis." If
my rendering is correct, Philo means that in Aaron Moses had
a worthy interpreter, even though he (Moses) had a defect of
speech, *cf. Quis Rer. Div. Heres* 4 on Ex. iv. 10.

Indeed [a] it is because of this that he associates Hur, who is to be interpreted as " light," [b] with the wise man,[c] showing through a symbol [d] that the word of the wise man is luminous,[e] for he reveals his beauty not in words but in deeds performed.[f]

*45. (Ex. xxiv. 16a) What is the meaning of the words, " And the glory of God came down upon Mount Sinai " [g] ?

(Scripture) clearly puts to shame those who whether through impiety or through foolishness believe that there are movements of place or of change in the Deity.[h] For, behold, what is said to come down is clearly not the essence of God, which is understood only as to its being, but His glory.[i] And the notion of glory (*doxa*) is twofold.[j] On the one hand, it denotes the existence of the powers, for the armed force of a king is also called " glory." [k] On the other hand, (it denotes) only a belief in and counting on

[a] Arm. *kam* = ἤ, which here seems to be a corruption of ἤ.

[b] *Cf. Leg. All.* iii. 45 στηρίζονται ὑπό τε ᾿Ααρών, τοῦ λόγου, καὶ ῍Ωρ, ὅ ἐστι φῶς. The etymology is based on Philo's fanciful equation of ῍Ωρ with Heb. '*ôr* " light."

[c] τῷ σοφῷ. [d] διὰ συμβόλου. [e] φωτοειδῆ.

[f] ἔργοις ἐνεργουμένοις *vel sim.*: Aucher " in rebus expositis."

[g] LXX καὶ κατέβη (Heb. " dwelt ") ἡ δόξα τοῦ θεοῦ ἐπὶ τὸ ὄρος τὸ Σινά.

[h] So the Greek frag. from the Catenae, ἐναργέστατα δυσωπεῖ τοὺς ἐγγὺς [?] ὑπὸ ἀσεβείας εἴτε ἠλιθιότητος οἰομένους τοπικὰς καὶ μεταβατικὰς κινήσεις εἶναι περὶ τὸ θεῖον. Procopius briefly paraphrases, ἐλέγχει τοὺς οἰομένους μεταβατικὰς δυνάμεις εἶναι περὶ θεόν.

[i] So the Catenae and Procopius, ἰδοὺ γὰρ ἐμφανῶς οὐ (Procopius οὐ γὰρ) τὸν οὐσιώδη θεὸν τὸν κατὰ τὸ εἶναι μόνον ἐπινοούμενον κατεληλυθέναι φησίν, ἀλλὰ τὴν δόξαν αὐτοῦ.

[j] So the Catenae (Procopius omits), Διττὴ δὲ ἡ περὶ τὴν δόξαν ἐκδοχή.

[k] So the Catenae and Procopius, ἡ μὲν παρουσίαν ἐμφαίνουσα τῶν δυνάμεων (Procopius ἢ δυνάμεων παρουσίαν ἐμφαίνων), ἐπεὶ καὶ βασιλέως λέγεται δόξα ἡ στρατιωτικὴ δύναμις (Procopius δύναμις στρατιωτική).

the divine glory,*a* so as to produce in the minds of those who happen to be there an appearance of the coming of God,*b* Who was not there,*c* as though He were coming for the firmest assurance of things about to be legislated.*d* The mountain, moreover, is most suitable to receive the manifestation *e* of God, as the name " Sinai " shows, for when it is translated into our language,*f* it means " inaccessible." *g* Now the divine place is truly inaccessible and unapproachable, for not even the holiest mind is able to ascend such a height to it *h* so as merely to approach and touch it.*i*

*46. (Ex. xxiv. 16b) Why is the mountain covered with

---

a Aucher renders more freely, " altera, quatenus opinionem causat solam putandi videre gloriam divinam." The Catenae read ἡ δὲ τῇ δοκήσει αὐτοῦ μόνου καὶ ὑπολήψει δόξης θείας: Procopius ἢ δόκησιν αὐτὸ μόνον καὶ δόξης θείας ὑπόληψιν.

b So the Catenae, ὡς ἐνειργάσθαι (sic) ταῖς τῶν παρόντων διανοίαις φαντασίαν ἀφίξεως θεοῦ. Procopius paraphrases, ἢ τῶν παρόντων ὡς ἐπὶ τοιούτῳ τὴν φαντασίαν ἐτύπωσεν.

c This clause is missing from the Catenae and Procopius.

d So the Catenae and Procopius (which end here), ὡς ἥκοντος (Procopius adds θεοῦ) εἰς (Procopius πρὸς) βεβαιοτάτην πίστιν τῶν μελλόντων νομοθετεῖσθαι.

e τὴν ἐπιφάνειαν vel sim.: Aucher " apparitionem."

f Aucher renders freely, " aliam linguam."

g ἄβατον vel sim. Philo does not elsewhere etymologize the name " Sinai." I imagine that the present etymology is based upon a fanciful connexion between *Sinai* and Heb. *sᵉnêh* (the " burning bush " of Ex. iii. 2), which is translated βάτος in LXX. In *De Fuga* 161-162 Philo plays on the words βάτος and ἄβατος (-ον) ; commenting on the biblical phrase, ὁ βάτος καίεται, he writes, . . . τὸν γὰρ ἄβατον οὐ πολυπραγμονεῖ χῶρον, θείων ἐνδιαίτημα φύσεων.

h Aucher, construing differently (and failing to recognize a genitive absolute construction), renders, " ita ut neque purissimi intellectûs tanta celsitudo ad eum ascendere queat."

i So the Greek frag. from John of Damascus, ἄβατος καὶ ἀπροσπέλαστος οὕτως ἐστὶν ὁ θεῖος χῶρος, οὐδὲ τῆς καθαρωτάτης διανοίας τοσοῦτον ὕψος προσαναβῆναι δυναμένης ὡς θίξει μόνον ἐπιψαῦσαι.

a cloud for six days, and Moses called above on the seventh day ? [a]

The even [b] number, six, He apportioned both to the creation of the world and to the election of the contemplative nation,[c] wishing to show first of all that He had created both the world and the nation elected for virtue.[d] And in the second place, because He wishes the nation to be ordered and arrayed in the same manner as the whole world so that, as in the latter, it may have a fitting order in accord with the right law and canon of the unchanging, placeless and unmoving nature of God.[e] But the calling above of the prophet is a second birth better than the first.[f] For the latter is mixed with a body and had corruptible parents, while the former is an unmixed and simple soul of the sovereign,[g] being changed from a productive to an unproductive [h] form,[i] which has no mother but only a

---

[a] LXX καὶ ἐκάλυψεν αὐτὸ ἡ νεφέλη ἓξ ἡμέρας καὶ ἐκάλεσεν κύριος (Heb. " He ") τὸν Μωυσῆν τῇ ἡμέρᾳ τῇ ἑβδόμῃ ἐκ μέσου τῆς νεφέλης.   [b] Lit. " equal."

[c] So the Greek frag., τὸν ἴσον ἀριθμὸν ἀπένειμε καὶ τῇ τοῦ κόσμου γενέσει καὶ τῇ τοῦ ὁρατικοῦ γένους ἐκλογῇ, τὴν ἑξάδα. On " the contemplative nation," i.e. Israel, see QE ii. 43 et al.

[d] Somewhat different is the reading of the Greek frag. βουλόμενος ἐπιδεῖξαι ὅτι αὐτὸς καὶ τὸν κόσμον ἐδημιούργησε καὶ τὸ γένος εἵλετο.

[e] κατὰ τὸν ὀρθὸν νόμον καὶ κανόνα τῆς ἀτρέπτου καὶ τόπον μὴ ἐχούσης (vel sim.) καὶ ἀκινήτου φύσεως τῆς τοῦ θεοῦ. This sentence is not found in the Greek fragment.

[f] So the Greek frag., ἡ δὲ ἀνάκλησις τοῦ προφήτου δευτέρα γένεσίς ἐστι τῆς προτέρας ἀμείνων.

[g] Aucher " ista vero incommixta simplexque anima principalis (vel, spiritus principis)." The wording of the original Greek (this sentence and the next are missing from the Greek frag.) was probably " the former is an unmixed and simple sovereign part of the soul," i.e. the mind, since Moses symbolizes the pure mind, and is elsewhere called ὁ καθαρώτατος νοῦς.

[h] Prob. ἄγονον rather than ἀγένητον " unproduced ": Aucher " ingenitam."

[i] εἶδος vel sim.: Aucher takes the noun " animam " to be understood.

91

father, who is (the Father) of all. Wherefore the calling above or, as we have said, the divine birth happened to come about for him in accordance with the ever-virginal nature of the hebdomad.[a] For he is called on the seventh day,[b] in this (respect) differing from the earth-born first moulded man,[c] for the latter came into being from the earth and with a body, while the former (came) from the ether [d] and without a body.[e] Wherefore the most appropriate number, six, was assigned to the earth-born man, while to the one differently born (was assigned) the higher nature of the hebdomad.[f]

*47. (Ex. xxiv. 17) What is the meaning of the words, " The form of the glory of the Lord (was) like a fire burning before the sons of the seeing one " [g] ?

[a] On the ἀειπάρθενος ἑβδομάς or ἑβδόμη of the Pythagoreans see Leg. All. i. 15, De Vita Mosis ii. 210 et al.

[b] Lit. " For he (or " it ") is called the seventh day " (pred. nominative), an obvious error. The Greek frag. reads ἑβδόμη δὲ ἀνακαλεῖται ἡμέρα.

[c] The Greek frag. reads more briefly ταύτῃ διαφέρων τοῦ πρωτοπλάστου. On the creation of the earth-born " moulded " man on the sixth day, and that of the heavenly man, created in God's image on the seventh day, see Leg. All. i. 5, 31, 88 et al.

[d] This detail is omitted in the Greek frag., see next note.

[e] The Greek frag. reads only slightly differently ὅτι ἐκεῖνος μὲν ἐκ τῆς γῆς καὶ μετὰ σώματος συνίστατο· οὗτος δὲ ἄνευ σώματος.

[f] Again the Greek frag. differs slightly, διὸ τῷ μὲν γηγενεῖ ἀριθμὸς οἰκεῖος ἀπενεμήθη ἑξάς· τούτῳ δὲ ἡ ἱερωτάτη φύσις τῆς ἑβδομάδος.

[g] Philo omits one phrase of the biblical text, LXX τὸ δὲ εἶδος τῆς δόξης κυρίου ὡσεὶ πῦρ φλέγον (Heb. " devouring " or " consuming ") ἐπὶ τῆς κορυφῆς τοῦ ὄρους ἐναντίον τῶν υἱῶν Ἰσραήλ. On the substitution of " the seeing one " for " Israel " see the preceding sections. Note, too, that below Philo has in mind the Heb. text " fire consuming " although he quotes the LXX πῦρ φλέγον.

(This is said) because, as has been said before,[a] the glory
of God is the power [b] through which He now appears ; the
form of this power is like a flame or rather, it is not but
appears (to be so) to the spectators,[c] for God showed not
that which pertained to His essence [d] but what He wished
to seem to be to the amazement of the spectators.[e] And
so, (Scripture) adds, " before the sons of the seeing one,"
indicating most clearly that there was an appearance of
flame, not a veritable flame.[f] In the second place,[g] because He showed [h] the mountain (to be) inaccessible and
unapproachable [i] to the people, He extended the appearance of a flame-like fire around it [j] in order that no one,
even if he wished, might be able to come near in disregard
of his own safety.[k] For they are silly and at the same time
frivolous in belief [l] who believe that the fire [m] is the essence

[a] In QE ii. 45.

[b] ἡ δύναμις : Aucher " virtus."

[c] Slightly different is the wording of the Greek frag. from
the Catenae, τὸ δὲ εἶδος τῆς δόξης κυρίου φησὶν ἐμφερέστατον
εἶναι φλογί, μᾶλλον δὲ οὐκ εἶναι ἀλλὰ φαίνεσθαι τοῖς ὁρῶσι.

[d] The Arm. translator here uses two nouns to render
οὐσίαν : Aucher " essentiam."

[e] Here again the wording of the Greek frag. is slightly
different, τοῦ θεοῦ δεικνύντος ὅπερ ἐβούλετο δοκεῖν εἶναι πρὸς τὴν
τῶν θεωμένων κατάπληξιν, μὴ ὢν τοῦτο ὅπερ ἐφαίνετο.

[f] So the Greek frag., ἐπιφέρει γοῦν τὸ " ἐνώπιον τῶν υἱῶν
Ἰσραήλ," ἐνεργέστατα μηνύων ὅτι φαντασία φλογὸς ἦν ἀλλ' οὐ
φλὸξ ἀληθής. Procopius briefly paraphrases the preceding two
sentences, ἐδείκνυε δὲ πῦρ θεός, οὐχ ὅπερ ἦν ἀλλ' ὅπερ ἐβούλετο
δοκεῖν· ὃ δηλῶν ἐπήνεγκεν " ἐνώπιον τῶν υἱῶν Ἰσραήλ."

[g] The following sentences, down to " just as the flame
consumes," are missing from the Greek frag. and Procopius.

[h] One expects " in order that He might show."

[i] Aucher condenses the two adjectives into one, " in-
accessum."

[j] Aucher, construing a little differently, renders, " flammi-
formis ignis apparitionem extendebat circa eum."

[k] Lit. " of his taking care " : Aucher " visitatione."

[l] Aucher " faciles putandi."

[m] I follow Aucher in reading howr " fire " with the margin
of Cod. A rather than hawr " father " with Codd. A and C.

of God when (Scripture) clearly proclaims that it is the form of the glory and power of God which appears but not the truly existing One,[a] and that the fire is not His power but only His glory [b] and that in the opinion of the spectators it appeared to their eyes not to be what it was,[c] because of the reasons mentioned. That is the literal meaning.[d] But as for the deeper meaning,[e] just as the flame consumes all the material that comes its way, so, too, when the thought of God clearly reaches the soul, it destroys all the heterodox thoughts of piety,[f] bringing the whole mind into (a state of) holiness.[h]

48. (Ex. xxiv. 18a) Why does Moses enter into the midst of the cloud ? [i]

He had been called from its midst and therefore he rightly followed the voice.[j] In the second place, it was

---

[a] τὸν ὄντως Ὄντα : Aucher " veri Entis."

[b] Philo seems to mean that God's power was only *like* His glory (symbolized by the flame) but not identical with it, and that neither God's essence nor His power actually appeared.

[c] The syntax of the last clause is not wholly clear to me : Aucher " at videntibus phantastice apparens sicut non est qui est."   [d] τὸ ῥητόν.   [e] τὸ πρὸς διάνοιαν.

[f] The Arm. translator read εὐσεβείας in place of ἀσεβείας, which is the reading of the Greek frag., see below. Aucher tacitly corrects the Arm. by rendering, " omnem cogitationem a pietate alienam."   [g] Lit. " mind of thought(s)."

[h] The Greek frag. from the Catenae reads similarly but more smoothly Ὥσπερ δὲ ἡ φλὸξ πᾶσαν τὴν παραβληθεῖσαν ὕλην ἀναλίσκει, οὕτως, ὅταν ἐπιφοιτήσῃ εἰλικρινὴς τοῦ θεοῦ ἔννοια τῇ ψυχῇ, πάντας τοὺς ἑτεροδόξους ἀσεβείας λογισμοὺς διαφθείρει, καθοσιοῦσα τὴν ὅλην διάνοιαν. Procopius, as before, briefly paraphrases the last sentence, τὸ δὲ σύμβολον ὅτι δαπανητικὸν τὸ θεῖον λογισμῶν ἀσεβῶν, ὡς καὶ τῆς ὕλης τὸ πῦρ.

[i] LXX καὶ εἰσῆλθεν Μωυσῆς εἰς τὸ μέσον τῆς νεφέλης καὶ ἀνέβη εἰς τὸ ὄρος.

[j] i.e. God had called him from the midst of the cloud (a detail not commented on by Philo in *QE* ii. 46 on Ex. xxiv. 16), and therefore it was right for him to follow God's voice into the midst of the same cloud.

natural that a division was made in that part of the cloud by the noise of the speech, and when the two sides had been condensed,[a] it was easy to pass through.

*49. (Ex. xxiv. 18b) Why does Moses remain on the mountain forty days and the same number of nights ?[b]

Concerning the number forty and its place in nature[c] a detailed account was given earlier,[d] so that one need not speak further of this at length. Perhaps, however, it is necessary to add that the migrant generation was about to be condemned and waste away in corruption for forty years in all after receiving many benefactions and showing ingratitude in many ways.[e] And so, he remains there above for the same number of days as these years, reconciling the Father to the nation[f] by prayers and intercessions,[g] especially at the very time when the laws were given by God and there was constructed in words[h] the portable temple, which is called the Tent of Testimony.[i]

---

[a] πυκνωθέντων.

[b] lxx καὶ ἦν ἐκεῖ ἐν τῷ ὄρει τεσσαράκοντα ἡμέρας καὶ τεσσαράκοντα νύκτας. In De Somniis i. 36 and De Vita Mosis ii. 70 Philo alludes to this verse and adds the unscriptural detail that Moses was without food and drink during his forty-day stay on the mountain. [c] πῶς ἐν τῇ φύσει ἔχει.

[d] In QG i. 25, ii. 14, iv. 154.

[e] So (with only slight differences) the Greek frag. from the Catenae, ὅτι ἔμελλε κατάκριτος ἔσεσθαι ἡ ἀποικισθεῖσα γενεὰ καὶ ἐπὶ τεσσαράκοντα ἔτεα φθείρεσθαι· μυρία μὲν εὐεργετηθεῖσα, διὰ μυρίων δὲ ἐπιδειξαμένη τὸ ἀχάριστον. Procopius paraphrases, τεσσαράκοντα δὲ μένει τὰς πάσας ἡμέρας ἐν ὄρει Μωυσῆς ὅσα ἔμελλεν ἔτη τῶν εὐπαθόντων ἡ ἀγνώμων φθείρεσθαι γενεά.

[f] The phrase " to the nation " is omitted in Aucher's rendering.

[g] Procopius condenses, ὑπὲρ ὧν ἐν ἰσαρίθμοις ἡμέραις ἱκέτευε τὸν πατέρα.

[h] The original prob. read " at His word."

[i] ἡ σκηνὴ τοῦ μαρτυρίου, see lxx Ex. xxvi-xl. Procopius again condenses, καὶ μάλιστα παρὰ τοιοῦτον καιρόν, ἐν ᾧ δίδονται νόμοι καὶ φορητὸν ἱερόν, ἡ σκηνή.

QUESTIONS AND ANSWERS

For whom, then, were the laws (given)? Was it, indeed, for those who were to perish? And for whose sake were the oracles [a] (given)? Was it for those who were to be destroyed a little later? [b] It seems to me, however, that someone may say, "Is it possible that [c] he had foreknowledge of the judgment that was to come upon it [d]?" But he who says this should bear in mind that every prophetic soul is divinely inspired [e] and prophesies [f] many future things not so much by reflecting as through divine madness and certainty. [g]

*50. (Ex. xxv. 1-2) Why does He command (them) to take first-offerings [h] from all those of willing heart? [i]

In the present passage [j] (Scripture) uses "heart" instead of [k] "sovereign (mind)." [l] Accordingly, it wishes to introduce the first-offerings (as) the willing dispositions of those

[a] Procopius (see next note) has θυσίαι.

[b] So (except for the word noted) Procopius, Τίσι γὰρ οἱ νόμοι; ἆρά γε τοῖς ἀπολλυμένοις; Ὑπὲρ τίνων δὲ αἱ θυσίαι; ἆρα τῶν μικρὸν ὕστερον φθαρησομένων;

[c] μήποτε vel sim.: Aucher "ne" (though "num" seems to be required).

[d] Here the pronoun apparently refers to the nation. Procopius reads more briefly προῄδει γὰρ ὡς προφήτης τὰ ἐσόμενα. (According to Wendland, Procopius does not make use of Philo beyond this point.)

[e] πᾶσα προφητικὴ ψυχὴ ἐπιθειάζει.

[f] προθεσπίζει: Aucher "praescribit."

[g] Aucher renders less literally, "divino oestro securus."

[h] ἀπαρχάς, as in the LXX, see next note.

[i] LXX Καὶ ἐλάλησεν κύριος πρὸς Μωυσῆν, λέγων, Εἰπὸν τοῖς υἱοῖς Ἰσραὴλ καὶ λάβετε (v.l. ἀναλαβέτωσάν μοι) ἀπαρχὰς παρὰ πάντων οἷς ἂν δόξῃ τῇ καρδίᾳ· καὶ (v.l. omits καί) λήμψεσθε τὰς ἀπαρχάς μου. Philo quotes the LXX text verbatim in Quis Rer. Div. Heres 113 and allegorizes it at some length.

[j] Lit. "now."

[k] i.e. "in the sense of."

[l] Similarly the first Greek frag. (from Cod. Vat. 1553), τὴν καρδίαν ἀντὶ τοῦ ἡγεμονικοῦ παρείληφεν ἡ γραφή.

vho bring them,[a] for the Deity is in need of nothing.[b] But
.e who unwillingly brings an offering is forgotten and
.eceives himself, for even if he offers silver or something
lse, he does not bring first-offerings, in the same way as
.e who unwillingly makes a sacrifice is thought to offer
nsacrificed meat to the fire rather than a (real) sacrifice.[c]

51. (Ex. xxv. 7 [Heb. 8]) What is the meaning of the
vords, "Thou shalt make for Me a sanctuary, and I shall
ppear among you "[d] ?
Clear indeed is the literal meaning,[e] for the shrine is
poken of (as) the archetype of a sort of shrine, (namely, as)
he tent.[f] But as for the deeper meaning,[g] God always
ppears in His work, which is most sacred ; by this I mean
he world.[h] For His beneficent powers [i] are seen and move
round in all its parts, in heaven, earth, water, air and in

[a] Aucher renders differently, " vult ergo primitias volun-
aria indole oblatas introduci." Similar in thought but
lifferent in wording is the (misplaced) last sentence of the
econd Greek frag. (from John Monachus), οὐ γὰρ ἐν ὕλαις
λλ' ἐν εὐσεβεῖ (Mangey's correction of εὐσεβείᾳ) διαθέσει τοῦ
ομίζοντος ἡ ἀληθὴς ἀπαρχή. (Harris is mistaken in thinking
he Greek to be a gloss.)   [b] ἀπροσδεής.

[c] Considerably different is the wording of the Greek frag.,
 μὴ ἐκ προαιρέσεως ἀπαρχῶν θεῷ, καὶ ἂν τὰ μεγάλα (μέταλλα
onj. Harris) πάντα κομίζῃ μετὰ τῶν βασιλικῶν θησαυρῶν, ἀπαρχὰς
ὑ φέρει. In favour of the partial genuineness of the Greek is
he reference to precious metals, stones, etc., in Ex. xxv. 3-7.

[d] LXX καὶ ποιήσεις (Heb. " make "—imperative plural) μοι
γίασμα καὶ ὀφθήσομαι ἐν ὑμῖν.   [e] τὸ ῥητόν.

[f] This is a literal rendering of the Arm., which is evidently
orrupt : Aucher " quoniam templum (Graecus, sanctuarium
el sacellum, ἱερόν) dicitur templi prototypus quidam taber-
aculum." The original may have been " for the tent (of
estimony, see above, QE ii. 49) is spoken of in a certain sense
s an archetypal shrine," see next note but one.

[g] τὸ πρὸς διάνοιαν.

[h] Cf. De Plantatione 50 τὸ τὸν κόσμον εὐτρεπῆ καὶ ἕτοιμον
ισθητὸν οἶκον εἶναι θεοῦ . . . τὸ ἁγίασμα, οἷον ἁγίων ἀπαύγασμα,
ίμημα ἀρχετύπου.   [i] αἱ εὐεργετικαὶ δυνάμεις.

what is in these. For the Saviour *a* is beneficent and kind,*b* and He wishes to except the rational race *c* from all living creatures. He therefore honours them with an even ampler gift, a great benefaction in which all kinds of good things are found, and He graciously grants *d* His appearance, if only there be a suitable place, purified with holiness and every (kind of) purity. For if, O mind,*e* thou dost not prepare thyself of thyself, excising desires, pleasures, griefs, fears, follies,*f* injustices and related evils,*g* and dost (not) change and adapt thyself to the vision of holiness, thou wilt end thy life in blindness, unable to see the intelligible sun.*h* If, however, thou art worthily initiated *i* and canst be consecrated *j* to God and in a certain sense *k* become an animate *l* shrine of the Father, (then) instead of having closed eyes,*m* thou wilt see the First (Cause) *n* and in wakefulness thou wilt cease from the deep sleep in which thou hast been held. Then will appear to thee that manifest One,*o* Who causes incorporeal rays *p* to shine for thee,

---

a ὁ σωτήρ.

b Slightly emending the text (in which the second adjective has the article). Aucher renders more literally, " propitius est salvator et benefactor."

c τὸ λογικὸν γένος, *i.e.* Israel, or perhaps, pious men in general.　　　　　　　　　　　　*d* χαρίζεται.

e ὦ νοῦ or διάνοια : Aucher " O anime."

f Before " follies " the Arm. repeats the participle " excising."

g ἐκτέμνων ἐπιθυμίας, ἡδονάς, λύπας, φόβους, ἀφροσύνας, ἀδικίας καὶ τὰ συγγενῆ κακά.

h τὸν νοητὸν ἥλιον, *i.e.* the divine light, *cf. De Spec. Leg.* iv. 231 *et al.*　　　　*i* ἐὰν δ' ἀξίας τελεσθῇς τελετάς *vel sim.*

j Or " initiated " (*bis*): Aucher " consecrari."

k τρόπον τινά.

l Or " spiritual "—ἔμψυχον or πνευματικόν : Aucher " animatum (*vel*, spirituale)."

m ἀντὶ τοῦ καταμύειν *vel sim.*

n Variant " the first (things) " ; Aucher " primum."

o ὁ ἐπιφανής *vel sim.*: Aucher " visibilis," adding in a footnote " *vel*, qui appariturus est *aut* mirabilis ille."

p ἀσωμάτους αὐγάς.

and grants visions of the unambiguous and indescribable
things of nature *a* and the abundant sources of other good
things. For the beginning and end of happiness is to be
able to see God. But this cannot happen to him who has
not made his soul, as I said before, a sanctuary and altogether a shrine of God.

52. (Ex. xxv. 8 [Heb. 9]) What is the meaning of the
words, " Thou shalt make, according to all that I shall
show thee on the mountain, the patterns of the tent and
the vessels " *b* ?

That every sense-perceptible likeness has (as) its origin
an intelligible pattern in nature (Scripture) has declared
in many other passages as well as in the present one.*c*
Excellently, moreover, has it presented (as) the teacher
of incorporeal and archetypal things *d* not one who is be-
gotten and created but the unbegotten and uncreated
God.*e* For it was indeed proper and fitting to reveal to an
intelligent man the forms *f* of intelligible things and the
measures of all things in accordance with which the world

---

a Aucher renders more freely, " datis etiam visionibus
naturae inexpectatis ac inenarrabilibus."

b LXX καὶ ποιήσεις μοι (Heb. omits the first three words)
κατὰ πάντα ὅσα (*v.l.* + ἐγώ) δεικνύω σοι ἐν τῷ ὄρει (Heb. omits
" on the mountain "), τὸ παράδειγμα (*v.l. hic et infra* ὑπόδειγμα)
τῆς σκηνῆς καὶ τὸ παράδειγμα πάντων τῶν σκευῶν αὐτῆς οὕτως
ποιήσεις (Heb. " ye shall make "). Philo alludes to this verse
in *De Vita Mosis* ii. 74-75.

c Cf. *De Vita Mosis* ii. 74 ἔδει καθάπερ ἀπ᾽ ἀρχετύπου
γραφῆς καὶ νοητῶν παραδειγμάτων αἰσθητὰ μιμήματα ἀπεικονισθῆναι.

d διδάσκαλον ἀσωμάτων καὶ ἀρχετύπων : Aucher " magis-
trum incorporeorum et a principio existentium."

e τὸν ἀγέννητον καὶ ἀγένητον θεόν. Aucher inadvertently
writes " patrem " instead of " Deum." The same thought
is differently expressed in *De Vita Mosis* ii. 74 σκηνήν . . .
ἧς τὴν κατασκευὴν θεσφάτοις λογίοις ἐπὶ τοῦ ὄρους Μωυσῆς
ἀνεδιδάσκετο.

f Or " ideas "—εἴδη or ἰδέας.

99

was made.[a] For these reasons also the prophet [b] alone was
called and taken above, in order not to deprive the race
of mortals of an incorruptible vision [c] and not to spread
abroad and publish to the multitude these divine and holy
essences.[d] And he was taken up to a high mountain, ascent
to which was vouchsafed to no others. And a dense and
thick cloud covered the whole place, hindering reception [e]
through these places, not as if the nature of invisible things
could be seen by corporeal eyes but because the multi-
symbolism [f] of intelligible things is described through the
clear vision of the eyes, (namely) how one who learns by
seeing rather figuratively [g] can, by attributing certain
forms to certain symbols, achieve a correct [h] apprehension
of them.[i]

53. (Ex. xxv. 9 [Heb. 10]) Why is the ark of " undecaying wood " [j] ?

[a] Aucher, construing differently, renders, " quoniam conveniens utique erat ut intelligens referret ideas intellectualium
mensurasque universorum, ad quarum formam mundus
factus fuit." In support of the rendering which makes " the
intelligent man " (Moses) the indirect object of the infinitive
" to reveal," one can cite the parallel in *De Vita Mosis* ii. 75
προσῆκον γὰρ ἦν τῷ ὡς ἀληθῶς ἀρχιερεῖ καὶ τὴν τοῦ ἱεροῦ κατασκευὴν ἐπιτραπῆναι κτλ.

[b] ὁ προφήτης.

[c] Aucher " facie."

[d] οὐσίας.

[e] Aucher " perceptionem."

[f] Lit. " much symbol " : Aucher " multum signum."

[g] τροπικώτερον *vel sim.* : Aucher " utcumque typice."

[h] The two Arm. adjectives prob. render the single Greek
adjective ὀρθήν.

[i] Aucher " potest secundum symbolum aliquam formam
adaptando, directe et apposite eorum rationem attingere."

[j] LXX καὶ ποιήσεις κιβωτὸν μαρτυρίου ἐκ ξύλων ἀσήπτων:
Heb. " and make (imperative plural) an ark of *šiṭṭîm*
(" acacia ") wood." Both LXX and Heb. proceed to give the
dimensions of the ark, to which Philo does not refer here,
but see *De Vita Mosis* ii. 96.

In the same manner in which the head is the principal
(part) of living creatures is the ark (the principal kind) of
divine vessels, wherefore it has merited the best and holiest
places, being placed alone and by itself within the inner
sanctuary,[a] wherefore also it was natural that the material
of which it was made should by some necessity [b] be unlikely
to decay and be corrupted,[c] since the Law, of which it was
the repository,[d] was also incorruptible. In the second place,
the sanctuary [e] and all the order of things arranged in it
were ordained not for a limited time but for an infinite
age.[f] For this reason the artificer, (namely) the divine
Logos,[g] chose the most lawful [h] material, especially that
which could remain permanently with it.[i] That is the
literal meaning.[j] But this is the deeper meaning.[k] In
reality nothing terrestrial is undecaying or incorruptible.
Accordingly, when (Scripture) says " undecaying wood,"
it alludes symbolically [l] to the parts of the world attached
to one another, of which it consists and is compacted and
which hold fast to one another. To me it seems that (this
property is found) also in the rational virtues of the soul,[m]
each of which happens to be unwithered and unaging and
incorruptible.

---

[a] ἐν τῷ ἀδύτῳ.   [b] ἀνάγκῃ τινί.

[c] Both Arm. adjectives are compounded with *džowar*=
Gr. δυσ-: Aucher " imputridam ac incorruptibilem."

[d] ἀποθήκη *vel sim.*

[e] τὸ ἱερόν, *i.e.* " the tent of testimony."

[f] οὐ πρὸς ὡρισμένον χρόνον ἀλλ' ἄπειρον αἰῶνα *vel sim.*

[g] ὁ τεχνίτης, ὁ θεῖος λόγος.

[h] Aucher " magis convenientem." Arm. *ōrinawor* usu.=
νόμιμος, but here the context calls for a different adjective in
the original.

[i] *i.e.* with the Law.   [j] τὸ ῥητόν.

[k] τὸ πρὸς διάνοιαν.

[l] συμβολικῶς.

[m] Or " in the virtues of the rational soul(s) "—the original
may have been either ἐν ταῖς λογικαῖς τῶν ψυχῶν ἀρεταῖς or ἐν
ταῖς τῶν λογικῶν ψυχῶν ἀρεταῖς (Arm. adjectives are not in-
flected in agreement with their nouns) : Aucher " in rationa-
libus animi virtutibus."

QUESTIONS AND ANSWERS

54. (Ex. xxv. 10a [Heb. 11a]) Why does he overlay (the ark) with pure gold within, and with gold without ? [a]

Others falsify the external appearance with deceit, while they leave the inside concealed and without care or attention. Moreover, they adorn the outside with variegated adornment for the sake of magnificence or to cause astonishment among spectators. But the divine (and) holy Moses adorns the inside before the outside with due adornment, (namely) with gold, the prime material and the most precious of all, and furthermore with gold that is pure, cleansed and refined for purity of substance. That is the literal meaning.[b] But this is the deeper meaning.[c] In nature there is a species[d] which is invisible and one which is visible. The invisible and unseen one consists of incorporeal things,[e] and this (species) is in the intelligible world.[f] But the visible one is made of bodies, and this is the sense-perceptible world.[g] These two (species) are the inner and the outer. The one who created them made the incorporeal inner (species) and the corporeal outer (species) undecaying and incorruptible,[h] and, in addition, also seemly and noble[i] and precious. Accordingly, the precious gold is allegorically used[j] of the human structure and,

---

[a] LXX καὶ καταχρυσώσεις αὐτὴν χρυσίῳ καθαρῷ ἔξωθεν καὶ ἔσωθεν (v.l. ἔσωθεν καὶ ἔξωθεν : Heb. " within and without ") χρυσώσεις αὐτήν. Philo obviously took the text to mean that pure gold was used inside the ark and ordinary gold outside. In parallel allusions to this verse, although he follows the reading ἔσωθεν καὶ ἔξωθεν as here, he does not stress the difference between inside and outside, see De Ebrietate 85, De Mut. Nom. 43-44, and De Vita Mosis ii. 95, where he says, ἡ δὲ κιβωτός . . . κεχρυσωμένη πολυτελῶς ἔνδοθέν τε καὶ ἔξωθεν.

[b] τὸ ῥητόν.   [c] τὸ πρὸς διάνοιαν.
[d] εἶδος.   [e] ἐξ ἀσωμάτων.
[f] ἐν τῷ νοητῷ κόσμῳ.   [g] ὁ αἰσθητὸς κόσμος.
[h] The syntax is not altogether clear : Aucher " interna, incorporea ; et externa, corporea ; quas qui fecit, imputridas effecit " (sc. " species ").

[i] The two Arm. adjectives prob. render the single Greek adj. σεμνός.   [j] ἀλληγορεῖται.

102

as is proper, of the soul.[a] But this is invisible and with every virtue, as with gold, it adorns the dispositions [b] and the movements of the visible body. For that way of life [c] is perfect [d] which consists of two (kinds of things), of a pure mind,[e] which is invisible, and of irreproachable and blameless deeds, of which there are many spectators.

*55. (Ex. xxv. 10b [Heb. 11b]) What is the " wreathed wave " which He commands (them) to construct round the ark ? [f]

By the " wave " He indicates [g] the stars, for they circle and roll around, some in the same way as [h] the whole heaven, and others with a particular motion which has been assigned to them as peculiarly their own.[i] For in the same way as a rotating axle does not change its position and, as it goes around by itself, does not move away, so also does the heaven revolve without change of place. In the second place, the " wreathed wave " is similar to the corruption of the soul [j] and the body, for the mind [k] keeps turning in different directions and does not possess stability, and the body, which is always flowing like a stream at (various) stages [l] and with the (various) illnesses that over-

---

[a] Again the syntax is not clear: Aucher " sicut oportet esse animam."

[b] τὰς ἕξεις : Aucher " habitus."

[c] βίος or διαγωγή.   [d] τέλειος.

[e] νοῦ or διανοίας.

[f] LXX καὶ ποιήσεις αὐτῇ κυμάτια στρεπτὰ χρυσᾶ (Heb. " wreath of gold "): A.V. " crown of gold ") κύκλῳ.

[g] αἰνίττεται.

[h] Lit. " by themselves together with." Evidently the Arm. translator read κατὰ ἑαυτά instead of κατὰ τὰ αὐτά as does the Greek frag., see next note.

[i] The Greek frag. from John Monachus (the first of two belonging to this section) reads only slightly differently Οἱ ἀστέρες στρέφονται καὶ εἰλοῦνται κύκλον· οἱ μὲν κατὰ τὰ αὐτὰ τῷ σύμπαντι οὐρανῷ, οἱ δὲ καὶ κινήσεσιν ἰδίαις ⟨ἃς⟩ ἔλαχον ἐξαιρέτοις.   [j] τῆς ψυχῆς.

[k] ὁ νοῦς or ἡ διάνοια.   [l] ἡλικίας.

take it, is wont to undergo change. In the third place, the course of human life is to be likened to a broad sea (which) experiences storms and rolling disturbances of all kinds in accordance with (varying) fortunes.[a] For nothing on earth is stable but (everything) vacillates this way and that and is tossed about like a ship sailing the sea against contrary winds.[b]

56. (Ex. xxv. 11 [Heb. 12]) Why does he fit four rings to [c] the ark, two on one side and two on the other side ? [d]

It so happens that there are two sides in existing things,[e] one the intelligible and one the sense-perceptible (side),[f] each of which (in turn) is sealed with two seals.[g] For there are two sections of the intelligible (side), one being a sign of immortal things, and one a sign of mortal things. The sense-perceptible (side), moreover, is divided into two (parts), one of which is light and of an upward-tending

[a] One Arm. ms. has "not good fortunes," the other "good fortunes." The Greek frag. (see rest of note) prob. has the correct reading. The second Greek frag. (preserved in three different sources : Dam. Par., Anon. Flor. Cod. Barocc. and Cod. Reg.) reads similarly ὁ τῶν ἀνθρώπων βίος, ὁμοιούμενος πελάγει, κυματώσεις καὶ στροφὰς παντοίας προσεπιδέχεται (v.ll. προσδέχεται, προσενδέχεται) κατά τε εὐπραγίας καὶ κακοπραγίας (Cod. Barocc. om. καὶ κακοπραγίας).

[b] The Greek frag. agrees closely, ἵδρυται γὰρ οὐδὲν τῶν γηγενῶν ἀλλ' ὧδε καὶ ἐκεῖσε διαφέρεται, οἷα σκάφος θαλαττεῦον ὑπ' ἐναντίων πνευμάτων (Dam. Par. πραγμάτων).

[c] Lit. "upon."

[d] LXX καὶ ἐλάσεις αὐτῇ τέσσαρας δακτυλίους χρυσοῦς καὶ ἐπιθήσεις ἐπὶ τὰ τέσσαρα κλίτη (Heb. "feet" or "corners") δύο δακτυλίους ἐπὶ τὸ κλίτος τὸ ἕν, καὶ δύο δακτυλίους ἐπὶ τὸ κλίτος τὸ δεύτερον (v.l. ἕτερον).

[e] Lit. "in the ears," which cannot be the reading of the Greek original. Evidently the Arm. translator read ὠσί instead of (original) οὖσι.

[f] τὸ μὲν νοητόν, τὸ δ' αἰσθητόν.

[g] Philo says "sealed" because of the LXX δακτυλίους, which can mean "seal-rings."

104

substance,ᵃ to which the air and ether belong, and the other heavy and extending downward, to which earth and water belong. In the second place, some take the two sides (to represent) the equinoxes,ᵇ of which the four seasons are divisions. There are two warm and fair ᶜ (seasons), summer and autumn; and two are cold, winter and spring. These ᵈ have the status ᵉ of perfect and stable acts ᶠ in the sense-perceptible world, while (they have that) of signs and hints ᵍ in the intelligible (world).

57. (Ex. xxv. 12 [Heb. 13]) What were the " bearing-poles," which were of " undecaying wood " ʰ ?

(This statement) indicates two divine principles ⁱ : one, the pillar and base and stability ʲ of the intelligible world,ᵏ and the other (those) of the sense-perceptible,ˡ on which, as if on a foundation, it ᵐ is set up with stability. For each of these bears its own arrangement ⁿ ; although it is very heavy, the heaviness is, as it were, very light. The principles,ᵒ moreover, are undecaying, since they are the utterances of God.

ᵃ Aucher " naturae."
ᵇ τὰς ἰσημερίας, here taken to include the solstices as subdivisions.
ᶜ Lit. " ethereal " : Aucher " pro sereno."
ᵈ i.e. the two sets of rings.
ᵉ Or " reckoning "—λόγον : Aucher " calculum."
ᶠ Or " works "—ἔργων : Aucher " operum."
ᵍ αἰνιγμάτων vel sim., i.e. symbols.
ʰ ʟxx ποιήσεις δὲ ἀναφορεῖς ἐκ ξύλων ἀσήπτων (v.l. ξύλα ἄσηπτα) καὶ καταχρυσώσεις αὐτὰ χρυσίῳ : Heb. " and thou shalt make staves of šiṭṭim (acacia)-wood, and overlay them with gold."
ⁱ λόγους : Aucher " verba," in footnote, " vel, . . . ratio-nes."
ʲ Aucher " columnam ac fulcrum constantiae."
ᵏ τοῦ νοητοῦ κόσμου.   ˡ τοῦ αἰσθητοῦ.
ᵐ i.e. each of the two worlds.
ⁿ κόσμον or διακόσμησιν : Aucher " ornamentum."
ᵒ οἱ λόγοι : Aucher " verba."

QUESTIONS AND ANSWERS

58. (Ex. xxv. 13 [Heb. 14]) Why are the bearing-poles fitted to the rings for lifting the ark ? [a]

There are two principles [b] of the two worlds,[c] which (Scripture) calls " bearing-poles." Being attached to seals,[d] they show the fated and necessary order of events,[e] which is the harmonious nexus [f] of things integrating single (events) into order.   Accordingly, in the visible world they [g] are a likeness and form, but in the intelligible (world they are) signs and archetypes of rank and orders of things which progress and retrogress in accordance with the consistent order of nature.[h]

59. (Ex. xxv. 15 [Heb. 16]) What is the meaning of the words, " Thou shalt put into the ark the testimony which I shall give thee " [i] ?

Now since the ark is a symbol of the incorporeal world,[j] and it is necessary that this world be a sign of the laws [k] which He has called " testimonies," rightly and fittingly has He said that in word they should be placed in the ark

---

[a] LXX καὶ εἰσάξεις τοὺς ἀναφορεῖς εἰς τοὺς δακτυλίους τοὺς ἐν τοῖς κλίτεσι τῆς κιβωτοῦ αἴρειν τὴν κιβωτὸν ἐν αὐτοῖς.

[b] λόγοι.

[c] i.e. the intelligible and the sense-perceptible worlds.

[d] Here again, as in QE ii. 56, Philo plays on the LXX word δακτυλίους, which can mean " seal-rings."

[e] Slightly emending the Arm. text, which has " events of orders."   The original was something like τὴν εἱμαρμένην καὶ ἀναγκαίαν τάξιν τῶν συμβαινόντων.   Aucher renders more briefly, " praescriptum ac necessarium eventum."

[f] εἱρμός.

[g] Although the verb is singular, the context requires a plural pronoun to be supplied, referring to the two bearing-poles.

[h] κατὰ τὰς τῆς φύσεως ἀκολουθίας vel sim.: Aucher " secundum naturae concinnationem."

[i] LXX καὶ ἐμβαλεῖς εἰς τὴν κιβωτὸν τὰ μαρτύρια ἃ ἂν δῶ σοι. Philo briefly alludes to this verse in De Vita Mosis ii. 97 εἰς γὰρ ταύτην κατατίθεται τὰ χρησθέντα λόγια.

[j] σύμβολον τοῦ ἀσωμάτου κόσμου.   [k] τῶν νόμων.

106

but in deed *a* in the intelligible world *b* in order that it *c* may be attached to them *d* in all its parts and extend (throughout).*e*

60. (Ex. xxv. 16a [Heb. 17a]) What is the " mercy-seat " *f* and why did He call it a " cover " *g* ?

The " mercy-seat " is mentioned as a symbol of the propitious and beneficent power.*h* And it is called " cover " because it stands over and is established over the intelligible world.*i* But since the perfect form *j* is above, rightly is the propitious power (said to be) up above, since all things are established and stand firm upon it.

61. (Ex. xxv. 16b [Heb. 17b]) Why does the mercy-seat have only length and breadth but not depth ? *k*

---

a λόγῳ μέν . . . ἔργῳ δέ. *b* ἐν τῷ νοητῷ κόσμῳ.

c *i.e.* the intelligible world.

d *i.e.* the laws.

e Aucher renders less accurately, I think, " ut cunctis suis partibus illic jacens perseverabit."

f Lit. " propitiatory (instrument) "= LXX ἱλαστήριον, see next note ; " mercy-seat " is here used because it is the familiar A.V. term.

g LXX καὶ ποιήσεις ἱλαστήριον ἐπίθεμα χρυσίου καθαροῦ. The two Greek nouns render the single Heb. noun *kapprōret*, which means both " cover " and " propitiation " or " atonement." It seems to have been a gold plate fastened to the top of the ark and serving as a floor for the Cherubim, as Philo assumes in *De Vita Mosis* ii. 97 τὸ δ' ἐπίθεμα τὸ προσαγορευόμενον ἱλαστήριον βάσις ἐστὶ πτηνῶν δυοῖν, see also *De Fuga* 100.

h τῆς ἵλεω καὶ εὐεργετικῆς δυνάμεως σύμβολον.

i διὰ τοῦ στῆναι αὐτὸ καὶ ἱδρύεσθαι ὑπὲρ τοῦ νοητοῦ κόσμου *vel sim.* Aucher renders, " quia superpositus est firmiter intelligibilis mundus," but in a footnote he gives an alternative and better rendering, " *vel*, super intelligibilem mundum positum est." *j* Prob. εἶδος : Aucher " visione."

k *i.e.* why does Scripture give only two of its dimensions? LXX δύο πήχεων καὶ ἥμισους τὸ μῆκος, καὶ πήχεος καὶ ἥμισους τὸ πλάτος. In *De Vita Mosis* ii. 96, Philo allegorizes this question somewhat differently, see last note on this section.

QUESTIONS AND ANSWERS

A magnitude lacking depth and seen only in length and breadth is called a " surface " [a] by geometricians. And the " surface " [b] of the Existent One [c] is seen also through other powers,[d] especially through the propitious and beneficent ones.[e] But those who receive good, immediately thereupon see the Benefactor appear before their eyes together with His virgin daughters, the graces.[f]

*62. (Ex. xxv. 17a [Heb. 18a]) What are the cherubim ? [g] (" Cherubim ") is to be interpreted as " great recognition," in other words,[h] " knowledge poured out in abundance." [i] But they are symbols of the two powers, the

---

[a] ἐπιφάνεια.

[b] Philo plays on the double meaning of ἐπιφάνεια as " surface " and " (divine) manifestation."   [c] τοῦ Ὄντος.

[d] Lit. " other virtues and powers," but the two Arm. nouns prob. render the single Greek noun δυνάμεων : Aucher " per alias virtutes."

[e] διὰ τῆς ἵλεω καὶ εὐεργετικῆς, see the preceding section.

[f] i.e. acts of divine grace. The " virgin graces " of God are also mentioned in De Poster. Caini 32. The general idea of this section is partially paralleled in De Vita Mosis ii. 96 ὅπερ ἔοικεν εἶναι σύμβολον φυσικώτερον μὲν τῆς ἵλεω τοῦ θεοῦ δυνάμεως, ἠθικώτερον δὲ διανοίας πάλιν, ἵλεω δ᾽ ἑαυτῇ, τὴν πρὸς ὕψος ἄλογον αἴρουσαν καὶ φυσῶσαν οἴησιν ἀτυφίας ἔρωτι σὺν ἐπιστήμῃ στέλλειν καὶ καθαιρεῖν ἀξιούσης.

[g] lxx καὶ ποιήσεις δύο χερουβείμ (v.l. χερουβείν : Heb. kᵉrūbîm). Philo allegorizes the cherubim of the ark in De Vita Mosis ii. 97-100, and the cherubim of the Garden of Eden in De Cherubim 21-29. The whole of the present section has been preserved in Greek (in Cod. Vat. 379).

[h] Lit. " names."

[i] The Greek frag. reads more smoothly τὰ χερουβὶμ ἑρμηνεύεται μὲν ἐπίγνωσις πολλή, ἢ ἐν ἑτέροις ὄνομα ἐπιστήμη πλουσία καὶ κεχυμένη, cf. De Vita Mosis ii. 97 χερουβὶμ ὡς δ᾽ ἂν Ἕλληνες εἴποιεν ἐπίγνωσις καὶ ἐπιστήμη πολλή. According to Edmund Stein, Die allegorische Exegese des Philo aus Alexandreia (Giessen, 1924), p. 52, Philo's fanciful etymology is based on the combination of the two Heb. words hakkîr " to recognize " and bîn " knowledge," but the second word may be rabbîm " much," " many."

EXODUS, BOOK II

creative and the royal.[a] The creative (power), however, is the elder according to (our) thinking,[b] for though the powers around God are of the same age, still the creative (power) is thought of before the royal one.[c] For one is king not of that which does not exist, but of that which already exists.[d] And the creative (power) has been given the name " God " in the sacred [e] Scriptures, for the ancients [f] spoke of creating as " placing," [g] while the royal (power) is called " Lord," since " Lord of all " is (the name) consecrated to the king.[h]

*63. (Ex. xxv. 17b [Heb. 18b]) Why is the chasing of gold ? [i]

Gold is a symbol of a precious substance,[j] while the

[a] So the Greek frag. (except that it adds " of the Existent One " to " powers "), σύμβολα δέ ἐστι δυεῖν τοῦ Ὄντος δυνάμεων ποιητικῆς τε καὶ βασιλικῆς, see also De Vita Mosis ii. 99. On these two chief divine attributes see QG ii. 51, iv. 2, De Cherubim 27 et al.

[b] So the Greek frag., πρεσβυτέρα δὲ ἡ ποιητικὴ τῆς βασιλικῆς κατ' ἐπίνοιαν.

[c] The Greek frag. reads slightly more fully ἰσήλικες γὰρ αἵ γε περὶ τὸν θεὸν ἅπασαι δυνάμεις, ἀλλὰ προεπινοεῖται πως ἡ ποιητικὴ τῆς βασιλικῆς.

[d] So the Greek frag., βασιλεὺς γάρ τις οὐχὶ τοῦ μὴ ὄντος ἀλλὰ τοῦ γεγονότος.

[e] Lit. " sacred and divine," but the two Arm. adjectives prob. render the single Greek adjective ἱεροῖς, as in the Greek frag.

[f] i.e. the ancient Greeks.

[g] So the Greek frag., ὄνομα δὲ ἔλαχεν ἐν τοῖς ἱεροῖς γράμμασιν ἡ μὲν ποιητικὴ θεός, τὸ γὰρ ποιῆσαι θεῖναι ἔλεγον οἱ παλαιοί. Philo makes the same etymological connexion between θεός and θεῖναι in De Vita Mosis ii. 99 et al.

[h] The Greek frag. reads only slightly differently ἡ δὲ βασιλικὴ κύριος, ἐπειδὴ τὸ κῦρος ἁπάντων ἀνακεῖται τῷ βασιλεῖ.

[i] So the Greek frag., Διατί χρυσοῦ τορευτά : LXX (καὶ ποιήσεις δύο χερουβεὶμ) χρυσᾶ τορευτά (v.l. χρυσοτορευτά).

[j] The Greek frag. has the superlative form of the adjective, ὁ μὲν χρυσὸς σύμβολον τῆς τιμιωτάτης οὐσίας.

109

chasing (is a symbol) of an artful and skilled nature.[a] For it was proper that the chief powers of the Existent One should be ideas of ideas and partake of a substance that is most pure and unmixed and most precious and, in addition, most skilful.[b]

*64. (Ex. xxv. 17c-18 [Heb. 18c-19]) Why did He fit the cherubim to the two sides of the altar ?[c]

(This indicates that) the bounds of the whole heaven and the world are fortified by the two highest guards, one being that (power) by which God created all things, and the other that by which He is ruler of existing things.[d] For (each power) was destined to look out for (the world) as its most proper and related possession, the creative (power seeing to it) that the things made by it should not be destroyed,[e] and the royal power that nothing be in excess, mediating the victory by law as a sign of equality,

[a] So the Greek frag., ἡ δὲ τορεία τῆς ἐντέχνου καὶ ἐπιστημο-νικῆς φύσεως.

[b] The Greek frag. differs only slightly, ἔδει γὰρ τὰς πρώτας τοῦ Ὄντος δυνάμεις ἰδέας ἰδεῶν ὑπαρχούσας καὶ τῆς καθαρωτάτης καὶ ἀμιγοῦς καὶ τιμαλφεστάτης καὶ προσέτι τῆς ἐπιστημονικωτάτης φύσεως μεταλαχεῖν.

[c] Apparently the Arm. translator has erred in using seḷan " altar " instead of haštaran " mercy-seat." The Greek frag. reads Διατί ἐπ' ἀμφοτέρων τῶν κλιτῶν τοῦ ἱλαστηρίου τὰ χερουβὶμ ἥρμοττε : LXX καὶ ἐπιθήσεις αὐτὰ ἐξ ἀμφοτέρων τῶν κλιτῶν τοῦ ἱλαστηρίου· ποιηθήσονται χερουβ εἷς ἐκ τοῦ κλίτους τούτου καὶ χερουβ εἷς ἐκ τοῦ κλίτους τοῦ δευτέρου τοῦ ἱλαστηρίου· καὶ ποιήσεις τοὺς δύο χερουβεὶμ ἐπὶ τὰ δύο κλίτη.

[d] So the Greek frag., τοὺς ὅρους τοῦ παντὸς οὐρανοῦ καὶ κόσμου δυσὶ ταῖς ἀνωτάτω φρουραῖς ὠχυρῶσθαι, τῇ τε καθ' ἣν ἐποίει τὰ ὅλα θεός, καὶ τῇ καθ' ἣν ἄρχει τῶν γεγονότων. On the cherubim as symbols of the two highest divine attributes, corresponding to the names " God " and " Lord," see above, QE ii. 62, notes.

[e] So the Greek frag., ἔμελλε γὰρ ὡς οἰκειοτάτου καὶ συγ-γενεστάτου κτήματος προκήδεσθαι, ἡ μὲν ποιητικὴ ἵνα μὴ λυθείη τὰ πρὸς αὐτῆς γενόμενα.

110

by which things eternally endure.[a] For through excess
and inequality (come) occasions for war, the destroyers of
existing things.[b] But good order and equality are the
seeds of peace and the causes of salvation and perpetual
survival.[c]

*65. (Ex. xxv. 19a [Heb. 20a]) Why does He say that
the cherubim shall extend their wings to overshadow (the
mercy-seat) ?[d]

All the powers of God are winged. striving for and desiring the path upward to the Father.[e] And that, like
wings, they overshadow the parts of the universe indicates that the world is protected by guards, (namely) by
the two powers (already) mentioned,[f] the creative and the
royal.[g]

*66. (Ex. xxv. 19b [Heb. 20b]) Why do the faces of the

[a] Here apparently the Arm. translator has clumsily rendered the original which, according to the Greek frag., read
ἡ δὲ βασιλικὴ ὅπως μηδὲν μήτε πλεονεκτῇ μήτε πλεονεκτῆται,
νόμῳ βραβευόμενα τῷ τῆς ἰσότητος, ὑφ' ἧς τὰ πράγματα διαιω-
νίζεται.

[b] Here again the Greek frag. reads more smoothly πλεονεξία μὲν γὰρ καὶ ἀνισότης ὁρμητήρια πολέμου, λυτικὰ τῶν ὄντων.

[c] So the Greek frag., τὸ δὲ εὔνομον καὶ τὸ ἴσον εἰρήνης σπέρματα, σωτηρίας αἴτια καὶ τῆς εἰσάπαν διαμονῆς.

[d] So the Greek frag., Διατί φησιν " ἐκτείνει τὰς πτέρυγας τὰ
χερουβὶμ ἵνα συσκιάζῃ"; LXX ἔσονται οἱ χερουβὶμ ἐκτείνοντες τὰς
πτέρυγας ἐπάνωθεν, συσκιάζοντες ἐν ταῖς πτέρυξιν αὐτῶν ἐπὶ τοῦ
ἱλαστηρίου.

[e] So the Greek frag., αἱ μὲν τοῦ θεοῦ πᾶσαι δυνάμεις πτεροφυοῦσι, τῆς ἄνω πρὸς τὸν πατέρα ὁδοῦ γλιχόμεναί τε καὶ ἐφ-
ιέμεναι.

[f] See above, QE ii. 62 and notes.

[g] Only slightly different is the wording of the Greek frag.,
συσκιάζουσι δὲ οἷα πτέρυξι τὰ τοῦ παντὸς μέρη· αἰνίττεται δὲ ὡς
ὁ κόσμος σκέπαις καὶ φυλακτηρίοις φρουρεῖται, δυσὶ ταῖς εἰρημέναις
δυνάμεσι τῇ τε ποιητικῇ καὶ βασιλικῇ.

cherubim look at each other, and both (look) at the mercy-seat ?[a]

Most excellent in a way and seemly is the form of what is said,[b] for it was proper that the powers, the creative and the royal,[c] should look in the direction of each other, beholding their own beauty and at the same time both conspiring together for the advantage of created things.[d] In the second place, since God is one (and is) both Creator and King,[e] rightly did they receive divided power.[f] For they were indeed usefully divided in order that one might create and the other rule, for they are distinct.[g] And they were joined together in another way by the eternal attachment of names to one another,[h] in order that the creative (power) might be a spectator of[i] the royal, and the royal

[a] So the Greek frag., Διατί τὰ πρόσωπα τῶν χερουβὶμ εἰς ἄλληλα ἐκνεύει καὶ ἄμφω πρὸς τὸ ἱλαστήριον; LXX καὶ τὰ πρόσωπα αὐτῶν εἰς ἄλληλα· εἰς τὸ ἱλαστήριον ἔσονται τὰ πρόσωπα τῶν χερουβείν. In De Cherubim 25 Philo paraphrases Scripture as follows, καὶ γὰρ ἀντιπρόσωπά φησιν εἶναι νεύοντα πρὸς τὸ ἱλαστήριον πτεροῖς, ἐπειδὴ καὶ ταῦτα ἀντικρὺ μέν ἐστιν ἀλλήλων, and he adds the brief comment νένευκε δὲ ἐπὶ γῆν τὸ μέσον τοῦ παντός, ᾧ καὶ διακρίνεται.

[b] So the Greek frag., παγκάλη τίς ἐστι καὶ θεοπρεπὴς ἡ τῶν λεχθέντων εἰκών.

[c] See the preceding sections.

[d] So the Greek frag., ἔδει γὰρ τὰς δυνάμεις, τήν τε ποιητικήν καὶ βασιλικήν, εἰς ἀλληγορίαν (l. cum edd. ἀλλήλας) ἀφορᾶν, τὰ σφῶν κάλλη κατανοούσας καὶ ἅμα πρὸς τὴν ὠφέλειαν τῶν γεγονότων συμπνεούσας.

[e] So the Greek frag., δεύτερον ἐπειδὴ ὁ θεός, εἷς ὤν, καὶ ποιητής ἐστι καὶ βασιλεύς.

[f] Here the Arm. translator either had a different text or misunderstood the original. The Greek frag. reads εἰκότως αἱ διαστᾶσαι δυνάμεις πάλιν ἕνωσιν ἔλαβον, "rightly did the divided powers again receive unity."

[g] So the Greek frag. (except for the pronoun added at the end), καὶ γὰρ διέστησαν ὠφελίμως ἵνα ἡ μὲν ποιῇ, ἡ δὲ ἄρχῃ· διαφέρει γὰρ ἑκάτερον.

[h] So the Greek frag. (except for the phrase "to one another" added in the Arm.), καὶ ἡρμόσθησαν ἑτέρῳ τρόπῳ κατὰ τὴν τῶν ὀνομάτων ἀΐδιον προσβολήν.

[i] Greek frag. (see next note) "might hold to."

of the creative.^a For both rightly look at each other and
at the mercy-seat,^b for if God were not propitious to those
things which exist together,^c He would not have made
anything through the creative (power) nor would He have
been a lawgiver ^d through the royal (power).^e

*67. (Ex. xxv. 21a [Heb. 22a]) What is the meaning
of the words, " I shall be made known to thee from
there " ^f ?

The most lucid and most prophetic mind receives the
knowledge and science of the Existent One not from the
Existent One Himself, for it will not contain His greatness,
but from His chief and ministering ^g powers.^h And it is
admirable ⁱ that from these His splendour should reach
the soul in order that through the secondary splendour ^j

^a The Greek frag. differs in the verb, ὅπως καὶ ἡ ποιητικὴ
τῆς βασιλικῆς καὶ ἡ βασιλικὴ τῆς ποιητικῆς ἔχηται.
^b Again the Greek frag. differs slightly (omitting " at each
other and "), ἀμφότεραι γὰρ συννεύουσιν εἰς τὸ ἱλαστήριον εἰκότως.
^c The Arm. translator evidently read τοῖς συνοῦσιν, instead
of τοῖς νῦν οὖσιν, as in the Greek frag. (see next note but
one).
^d Aucher " neque disposuisset."
^e The Greek frag. differs slightly (see also note c), εἰ μὴ
γὰρ ἦν τοῖς οὖσιν ἵλεως ὁ θεός, οὔτ᾽ ἂν εἰργάσθη τι διὰ τῆς
ποιητικῆς οὔτ᾽ ἂν εὐνομήθη διὰ τῆς βασιλικῆς.
^f So the Greek frag., τί ἐστι ''γνωσθήσομαί σοι ἐκεῖθεν'';
LXX καὶ γνωσθήσομαί σοι ἐκεῖθεν (Heb. " there ").
^g The Greek frag. reads more concretely " body-guard,"
see next note.
^h So (except for the word mentioned in the preceding note)
the Greek frag., γνῶσιν καὶ ἐπιστήμην ὁ εἰλικρινέστατος καὶ
προφητικώτατος νοῦς λαμβάνει τοῦ "Οντος οὐκ ἀπ᾽ αὐτοῦ τοῦ
"Οντος, οὐ γὰρ χωρήσει τὸ μέγεθος, ἀλλ᾽ ἀπὸ τῶν πρώτων αὐτοῦ
καὶ δορυφόρων δυνάμεων.
ⁱ Lit. " loved," but this prob. renders the same word as in
the Greek frag., ἀγαπητόν.
^j The Arm. translator uses the same word to render
φέγγους here as he used to render αὐγάς above, see next note.

113

it may be able to behold the more splendid (splendour).[a]

*68. (Ex. xxv. 21b [Heb. 22b]) What is the meaning of the words, " I will speak to thee [b] above from [c] the mercy-seat, between the two [d] cherubim " [e] ?

By this He shows first of all that the Deity is above the propitious and the creative and every (other) power.[f] Next, (He shows) that He speaks rightly [g] in the midst of the creative (power).[h] And this the mind conceives somewhat as follows.[i] The divine Logos, inasmuch as it is

---

[a] So the Greek frag., καὶ ἀγαπητὸν ἐκεῖθεν εἰς τὴν ψυχὴν φέρεσθαι τὰς αὐγὰς ἵνα δύνηται διὰ τοῦ δευτέρου φέγγους τὸ πρεσβύτερον καὶ αὐγοειδέστερον θεάσασθαι.

[b] The Greek frag. omits " to thee," which is found in LXX and Heb. and in other passages of Philo, see below.

[c] *i.e.* " from above."

[d] The Greek frag. omits " two," which is found in LXX and Heb. and in other passages of Philo, see next note.

[e] The Greek frag. reads slightly more briefly τί ἐστι· " λαλήσω ἄνωθεν τοῦ ἱλαστηρίου ἀνὰ μέσον τῶν χερουβίμ "; LXX καὶ λαλήσω σοι ἄνωθεν τοῦ ἱλαστηρίου ἀνὰ μέσον τῶν δύο χερουβεὶν τῶν ὄντων ἐπὶ τῆς κιβωτοῦ τοῦ μαρτυρίου καὶ (*v.l.* omits καί with Heb.) κατὰ πάντα ὅσα ἂν ἐντείλωμαί σοι πρὸς τοὺς υἱοὺς Ἰσραήλ. In *Quis Rer. Div. Heres* 166 and *De Fuga* 101 Philo quotes part of the LXX in the same wording as here, and comments more briefly than here. On the symbolism of the cherubim see the preceding sections in *QE* ii.

[f] So the Greek frag., ἐμφαίνει διὰ τοῦτο (*l.* τούτου) πρῶτον μὲν ὅτι καὶ τῆς ἴλεω καὶ τῆς ποιητικῆς καὶ πάσης δυνάμεως ὑπεράνω τὸ θεῖόν ἐστι."

[g] Aucher " quasi." The word, which is missing in the Greek frag., is perhaps the Armenian translator's device for conveying the force of the superlative ending in μεσαίτατον, see next note.

[h] The Arm. text is apparently defective. The Greek frag. reads more intelligibly ἔπειτα ὅτι λαλεῖ κατὰ τὸ μεσαίτατον τῆς τε ποιητικῆς καὶ βασιλικῆς.

[i] So the Greek frag., τοῦτο δὲ τοιοῦτον ὑπολαμβάνει νοῦς.

EXODUS, BOOK II

appropriately *a* in the middle, leaves nothing in nature empty,*b* but fills all things and becomes a mediator and arbitrator for the two sides which seem to be divided from each other, bringing about friendship and concord,*c* for it is always the cause of community and the artisan of peace.*d* Now the particular features of the ark have been spoken of,*e* but we must also summarily resume and review for the sake of finding out what things these are symbols of.*f* Now these symbols are the ark and the ordinances stored in it and the mercy-seat upon it and, upon the mercy-seat, the cherubim, as they are called in the Chaldaean *g* tongue, and directly above them, in their midst, the voice and the Logos and, above it, the Speaker.*h* And so, if one can accurately view and understand *i* the natures of these, it seems to me that one should renounce all the other things that are eagerly sought after, being captivated by their godlike beauty.*j* But let us consider what

---

a Or " chances to be " : Aucher " est conveniente."

b The Greek frag. reads slightly more briefly ὁ τοῦ θεοῦ λόγος μέσος ὢν οὐδὲν ἐν τῇ φύσει καταλείπει κενόν.

c The Greek frag. reads similarly but a little more smoothly τὰ ὅλα πληρῶν καὶ μεσιτεύει καὶ διαιτᾷ τοῖς παρ' ἑκατέρα διεστάναι δοκοῦσι, φιλίαν καὶ ὁμόνοιαν ἐργαζόμενος.

d The Greek frag. reads more briefly ἀεὶ γὰρ κοινωνίας αἴτιος καὶ δημιουργός (Grossmann add. εἰρήνης).

e So the Greek frag., τὰ μὲν οὖν περὶ τὴν κιβωτὸν κατὰ μέρος εἴρηται.

f So the Greek frag., δεῖ δὲ συλλήβδην ἄνωθεν ἀναλαβόντα τοῦ γνωρίσαι χάριν τίνων ταῦτά ἐστι σύμβολα διεξελθεῖν.

g *i.e.* Hebrew.

h So the Greek frag., ἦν δὲ ταῦτα συμβολικά· κιβωτὸς καὶ τὰ ἐν αὐτῇ θησαυριζόμενα νόμιμα καὶ ἐπὶ ταύτης τὸ ἱλαστήριον καὶ τὰ ἐπὶ τοῦ ἱλαστηρίου Χαλδαίων γλώττῃ λεγόμενα χερουβίμ, ὑπὲρ δὲ τούτων κατὰ τὸ μέσον φωνὴ καὶ λόγος καὶ ὑπεράνω ὁ λέγων.

i The Greek frag. omits " and understand," see next note.

j Aucher, taking the participle, here rendered " being captivated," to agree with " all the other things " rather than with the impersonal subject of the verb " should renounce " (infinitive in the Arm. text), renders, " caetera omnia quaecumque aemulationem merent deiformi pulchritudine circum-

115

each (of these things) is like.[a] In the first place (there is)
He Who is elder than the one and the monad and the beginning.[b] Then (comes) the Logos of the Existent One,
the truly [c] seminal substance of existing things.[d] And
from the divine Logos,[e] as from a spring, there divide and
break forth two powers.[f] One is the creative (power),
through which the Artificer placed [g] and ordered all things;
this is named " God." [h] And (the other is) the royal
(power), since through it the Creator rules over created
things [i]; this is called " Lord." [j] And from these two

data." The Greek frag. agrees closely with the Arm. as
rendered above (except for the omission mentioned in note *i*
on p. 115), εἰ δέ τις ἀκριβῶς δυνηθείη κατανοῆσαι τὰς τούτων
φύσεις, δοκεῖ μοι πᾶσι τοῖς ἄλλοις ἀποτάξασθαι ὅσα ζηλωτά,
κάλλεσι θεοειδεστάτοις περιληφθείς.

[a] So the Greek frag., σκοπῶμεν δέ ἕκαστον οἷόν ἐστι.

[b] So the Greek frag., τὸ πρῶτον ὁ καὶ ἑνὸς καὶ μονάδος καὶ
ἀρχῆς πρεσβύτερος.

[c] The adverb (= Gr. ὄντως) is missing in the Greek frag.,
and may reflect a mistaken repetition of ὄντος or ὄντων in the
Arm. translator's Greek text, see next note.

[d] So the Greek frag. (except for the omission mentioned
in the preceding note), ἔπειτα ὁ τοῦ Ὄντος λόγος, ἡ σπερματικὴ
τῶν ὄντων οὐσία.

[e] The Arm. *yēn* (= ἐκ τοῦ ὄντος) is prob. a corruption of
the usual contraction, *ayin*, of the adjective *astouacayin*
" divine." Aucher renders, " ex ente vero Verbo," adding
in a footnote the theological comment " Judaeus noster
Philo Entem fassus est ipsum Verbum, sicut Patrem suum,
etc."

[f] The Greek frag. reads slightly more briefly ἀπὸ δέ τοῦ
θείου λόγου, καθάπερ ἀπὸ πηγῆς, σχίζονται δύο (αἱ δύο edd.)
δυνάμεις.

[g] *i.e.* " created." Philo uses ἔθηκε for the sake of explaining the etymology of θεός, the name of the creative power, see
QE ii. 62 notes.

[h] So the Greek frag., ἡ μέν ποιητική, καθ᾽ ἥν ἔθηκε τά πάντα
καὶ διεκόσμησεν ὁ τεχνίτης, αὕτη θεός ὀνομάζεται.

[i] Variant " He rules over things created by the Creator."

[j] So the Greek frag., ἡ δέ βασιλική, καθ᾽ ἥν ἄρχει τῶν γεγονότων ὁ δημιουργός, αὕτη καλεῖται κύριος.

powers have grown the others.[a] For by the side of the creative (power) there grows the propitious, of which the name is " beneficent," while (beside) the royal (power there grows) the legislative, of which the apt name is " punitive." [b] And below these and beside them (is) the ark ; and the ark is a symbol of the intelligible world.[c] And the ark symbolically contains all things established in the innermost sanctuary, (namely) the incorporeal world and the ordinances which He has called " testimonies " (and) the legislative and punitive powers (and) the mercy-seat [d] (and) the propitious and beneficent (powers and), up above, the creative (power), which is the source [e] of the propitious and beneficent (powers), and the royal (power), which is the root of the punitive and legislative (powers).[f] But there appears [g] as being in their midst the divine Logos and, above the Logos, the Speaker.[h] And the

[a] So (except for omission of the article before "others") the Greek frag., ἀπὸ δὲ τούτων τῶν δυεῖν δυνάμεων ἐκπεφύκασιν ἕτεραι.

[b] So the Greek frag., παραβλαστάνει γὰρ τῇ μὲν ποιητικῇ ἡ ἵλεως, ἧς ὄνομα εὐεργέτις, τῇ δὲ βασιλικῇ ἡ νομοθετική, ὄνομα δὲ εὐθύβολον ἡ κολαστήριος.

[c] So the Greek frag., ὑπὸ δὲ ταύτας καὶ περὶ ταύτας ἡ κιβωτός· ἔστι δὲ κιβωτὸς κόσμου νοητοῦ σύμβολον.

[d] Arm. haštakan " propitious " is an obvious miswriting of haštaȥan " mercy-seat."

[e] The Greek frag. has πίστις, an obvious corruption of πηγή (so the Arm.), which occurs in the same connexion earlier in this section.

[f] So (with the exception of the word mentioned in the preceding note) the Greek frag., ἔχει δὲ τὰ πάντα ἱδρυμένα ἐν τοῖς ἐσωτάτοις ἁγίοις συμβολικῶς ἡ κιβωτός, τὸν ἀσώματον κόσμον, τὰ νόμιμα ἃ κέκληκε μαρτύρια, τὴν νομοθετικὴν καὶ κολαστήριον δύναμιν, τὸ ἱλαστήριον, τὴν ἵλεω καὶ εὐεργέτιν, τὰς ὑπεράνω τήν τε ποιητικήν, ἥτις ἐστὶ πίστις (l. πηγή) τῆς ἵλεω καὶ εὐεργέτιδος, καὶ τὴν βασιλικήν, ἥτις ἐστὶ ῥίζα τῆς κολαστηρίου καὶ νομοθετικῆς.

[g] Arm. aṛaweleal ē " there is multiplied " is evidently a corruption of ereweli ē " there appears," as in the Greek frag., see next note.

[h] So the Greek frag., ὑπεμφαίνεται δὲ μέσος ὢν ὁ θεῖος λόγος, ἀνωτέρω δὲ τοῦ λόγου ὁ λέγων. Philo here repeats an earlier part of this section.

number of the things here enumerated amounts to [a] seven, (namely) the intelligible world and the two [b] related powers, the punitive and beneficent [c]; and the two other ones preceding these, the creative and the royal, have greater kinship to the Artificer than what is created [d]; and the sixth is the Logos,[e] and the seventh is the Speaker.[f] But if you make the beginning [g] from the upper end, (you will find) [h] the Speaker first, and the Logos second, and the creative power third, and the ruling (power) fourth, and then, below the creative, the beneficent (power) fifth, and, below the royal, the punitive (power) sixth, and the world of ideas seventh.[i]

[a] Lit. "is filled up," see the next note but one.

[b] The Arm. lit. = δι' οὗ, an obvious error for δύο, as in the Greek frag.

[c] So the Greek frag., ἔστι δὲ καὶ ὁ τῶν κατειλεγμένων ἀριθμὸς ἑβδομάδι συμπληρούμενος νοητὸς κόσμος, καὶ δυνάμεις δύο συγγενεῖς ἥ τε κολαστήριος καὶ εὐεργέτις.

[d] Here we must emend the Arm. on the basis of the clearly better readings of the Greek frag., καὶ ἕτεραι πρὸ τούτων δύο ἥ τε ποιητικὴ καὶ ἡ βασιλική, συγγένειαν ἔχουσαι μᾶλλον πρὸς τὸν δημιουργὸν ἢ τὸ γεγονός. The Arm. lit. = συγγένειαν ἔχει μᾶλλον ὁ δημιουργὸς καὶ τὸ γένος, which makes no sense.

[e] Here again we must correct the Arm. from the Greek frag., which reads καὶ ἕκτος ὁ λόγος. The Arm. = καὶ ἕκαστος ὁ λόγος, which is meaningless.

[f] So the Greek frag., καὶ ἕβδομος ὁ λέγων. With this list of seven cosmic symbols compare the list of ten cosmic parts in QG iv. 110.

[g] The Armenian translator appears to have read καταρχήν instead of καταρίθμησιν, as in the Greek frag., see next note but one.

[h] The Arm. lacks a verb to govern the following nouns, which are in the accusative case.

[i] So (except for the two variants mentioned in the preceding two notes) the Greek frag., ἐὰν δὲ ἄνωθεν τὴν καταρίθμησιν ποιῇ, εὑρήσεις τὸν μὲν λέγοντα πρῶτον, τὸν δὲ λόγον δεύτερον, τρίτην δὲ τὴν ποιητικὴν δύναμιν, τετάρτην δὲ τὴν ἀρχήν, εἶτα δὲ ὑπὸ μὲν τῇ ποιητικῇ πέμπτην τὴν εὐεργέτιν, ὑπὸ δὲ τῇ βασιλικῇ ἕκτην τὴν κολαστήριον, ἕβδομον δὲ τὸν ἐκ τῶν ἰδεῶν κόσμον.

69. (Ex. xxv. 22 [Heb. 23]) What is " the table " and why is it " of pure gold " [a] ?

Having spoken symbolically of incorporeal things,[b] when He was discoursing divinely [c] about the ark in the inner sanctuary,[d] He now begins to speak of those things which are in sense-perception,[e] rightly and appropriately beginning with the table. Since the table is a vessel [f] for food and (since) nothing intelligible [g] is given food but only those who have been allotted the nature of corporeality, He makes the table a symbol of sense-perceptible and body-like substance.[h] Not only that but also because the table indicates a kind of communion [i] among those who receive a common share [j] of salt and sacrifices. For (this) leads to loving one's fellow [k] for one's own sake.[l] But there is nothing anywhere so lovable as the parts of the world made from their own substance.[m] For one who is about to eat and to be made glad by the Father, (Who is) the begetter of these (foods), is taught from above to give in exchange

---

[a] LXX καὶ ποιήσεις τράπεζαν χρυσῆν (v.l. omits χρυσῆν) χρυσίου καθαροῦ, δύο πήχεων τὸ μῆκος καὶ πήχεος τὸ εὖρος καὶ πήχεος καὶ ἡμίσους τὸ ὕψος. Instead of " a table of gold " Heb. has " a table of šittim (acacia)-wood," but adds " and thou shalt overlay it with pure gold."

[b] περὶ ἀσωμάτων διαλεξάμενος συμβολικῶς.

[c] ἐθεολόγει.   [d] ἐν τοῖς ἀδύτοις.

[e] ἐν τῇ αἰσθήσει (v.l. ἐν ταῖς αἰσθήσεσι).

[f] σκεῦος : Aucher " receptaculum."

[g] νοητόν.

[h] αἰσθητῆς καὶ σωματοειδοῦς οὐσίας.

[i] κοινωνίαν τινά.

[j] Here the Arm. uses a different word for κοινωνίαν.

[k] Lit. " one's like."

[l] The syntax and meaning are not clear : Aucher " siquidem est adducens similem in dilectionem propter (vel, per) se."

[m] This sentence is also obscure. Aucher in a footnote cites the interpretation of the Arm. glossator, who takes " their own " to mean " one another's," and thinks that Philo is referring to the changing of the four elements into one another.

119

QUESTIONS AND ANSWERS

and return the benefit as if to brothers by the same father
and the same mother.[a] Moreover, the table was of pure
gold because the entire substance of the world was of the
tested and chosen part, for everything, whatever it was by
its own substance and nature, was about to receive even
greater perfection.[b]

70. (Ex. xxv. 23 [Heb. 24]) Why are there " wreathed
waves " around the table ?[c]

The corporeal substance[d] of all things undergoes turning[e] and change[f] for the genesis of the parts of which the
world was constituted.

71.[g] (Ex. xxv. 28 [Heb. 29]) Why are there, upon the
table, cups and censers and libation-bowls and ladles ?[h]

---

[a] The Arm. glossator takes this sentence to mean that the
elements of the world have been taught to give parts of themselves to one another in gratitude to the divine powers from
which their substance is derived.

[b] τελειότητα.

[c] LXX καὶ ποιήσεις αὐτῇ στρεπτὰ κυμάτια χρυσᾶ (v.l. στρεπτὸν
κυμάτιον χρυσοῦν): Heb. " And thou shalt make for it a
wreath (A.V. " crown ") of gold around." See above, QE
ii. 55 (= Ex. xxv. 10) on the " wreathed waves " around the
ark.

[d] ἡ σωματικὴ οὐσία.

[e] στροφήν.

[f] Aucher renders both nouns by the single word " mutationem," but this obscures Philo's point, which is that the
" turning " (i.e. twisting) of the " wreathed waves " symbolizes the changing of the elements into one another,
mentioned in the preceding section.

[g] The four verses of Scripture here passed over in silence
speak of the gold rings to be made for holding the staves by
which the table is to be carried, see above, QE ii. 56 (= Ex.
xxv. 11) on the gold rings made for the ark.

[h] LXX καὶ ποιήσεις τὰ τρύβλια αὐτῆς καὶ τὰς θυίσκας καὶ τὰ
σπόνδια (sic) καὶ τοὺς κυάθους, ἐν οἷς σπείσεις ἐν αὐτοῖς· χρυσίου
καθαροῦ ποιήσεις αὐτά.

The cups were symbols of foods, and the ladles of banqueting, since unmixed wine [a] is measured by them, and the censers are vessels of incense, and the libation-bowls are for wine which is poured as a libation. Accordingly, through the food and the unmixed wine (Scripture) indicates [b] the graciousness [c] of the greatness and munificence of God, Who gives not only necessities [d] but also whatever pertains to the abundant and ample enjoyment of munificence. And through the incense and libation (Scripture indicates) the pleasure of those to whom good things happen. For those who are nourished by visible food [e] in the form of allegory [f] also say that every soul desirous of moral excellence [g] is a libation, that is if one first pours out and dedicates one's virtue [h] to God. [i] And this is an act desirable and agreeable [j] and pleasing to the heart of the Father, just as is the most sweet-smelling incense by its fragrance.

72. (Ex. xxv. 29 [Heb. 30]) Why does He say, " Thou shalt place upon the table bread before Me continually " [k] ?
The loaves of bread [l] are symbolical of necessary foods,

[a] τὸ ἄκρατον.
[b] αἰνίττεται.
[c] τὰς χάριτας.
[d] τὰ ἀναγκαῖα.
[e] Aucher " constantibus cibis."
[f] ἀλληγορίας.
[g] καλοκἀγαθίας : Aucher " probitatis."
[h] ἀρετήν.
[i] Aucher, construing slightly differently, renders, " libamen est, profundens dedicansque virtutem Deo." A similar idea is expressed by Philo in Quis Rer. Div. Heres 184 τῆς ψυχῆς τὸ μὲν ἀμιγὲς καὶ ἄκρατον μέρος ὁ ἀκραιφνέστατος νοῦς ἐστιν, ὅς . . . ὅλος εἰς ἱερὰν σπονδὴν ἀναστοιχειωθεὶς ἀνταποδίδοται.
[j] Lit. " to the mind."
[k] LXX καὶ ἐπιθήσεις ἐπὶ τὴν τράπεζαν ἄρτους ἐνωπίους (Heb. ' bread of face " : A.V. " showbread ") ἐναντίον μου διὰ παντός. Philo refers to the showbread briefly in De Congressu 168, De Vita Mosis ii. 104 and De Spec. Leg. ii. 161.
[l] Lit. " the bread."

without which there is no life ; and the power [a] of rulers
and peasants [b] by the ordering of God (consists) in the
necessities of nature, (namely) in food and drink. Wherefore He adds, " before Me continually thou shalt place the
loaves of bread," for " continually " means that the gift
of food is continual and uninterrupted, while " before "
(means) that it is pleasing and agreeable to God both to
be gracious [c] and to receive gratitude.[d]

73. (Ex. xxv. 30a [Heb. 31a]) Why is the lampstand
" turned " (and) of pure gold " [e] ?

The lampstand is a symbol of the purest substance,
(namely) the heaven.[f] For this reason it is said later [g] that
it was made of one (piece of) gold. For the other parts of
the world were wholly made through the four elements,
earth, water, air, and fire, but the heaven of (only) one,
(this being) a superior form,[h] which the moderns [i] call
" the quintessence." [j] And rightly has (heaven) been

[a] Variant " equality."
[b] Or " commoners " : Aucher " villicorum."
[c] χαρίζεσθαι.
[d] εὐχαριστίαν.
[e] LXX καὶ ποιήσεις λυχνίαν (Heb. m⁰nôrāh : A.V. " candle-
stick ") ἐκ χρυσίου καθαροῦ, τορευτὴν (v.l. τορνευτὴν, which
seems to have been Philo's reading, see below) ποιήσεις τὴν
λυχνίαν. The cosmic symbolism of the lampstand is also
dealt with in De Vita Mosis ii. 102-103, cf. Josephus, Ant.
iii. 182 and B.J. v. 217.
[f] σύμβολον τῆς καθαρωτάτης οὐσίας τοῦ οὐρανοῦ.
[g] At the end of this verse, see the following section.
[h] εἴδους.
[i] οἱ νεώτεροι, perhaps the Aristotelians, but see next
note.
[j] Or " fifth substance," τὴν πέμπτην οὐσίαν. Curiously
enough, in Quis Rer. Div. Heres 283 Philo acribes the notion
of the quintessence to " the ancients," πέμπτη γάρ, ὡς ὁ τῶν
ἀρχαίων λόγος, ἔστω τις οὐσία κυκλοφορητική, τῶν τεττάρων κατὰ
τὸ κρεῖττον διαφέρουσα, ἐξ ἧς οἵ τε ἀστέρες καὶ ὁ σύμπας οὐρανὸς
ἔδοξε γεγενῆσθαι.

likened to the lampstand in so far as it is altogether full
of light-bearing stars. And rightly does He describe it ^a as
" turned," for the heaven was made and illuminated ^b by
a certain turner's art ^c in accordance with periodic cycles,^d
each of which is accurately and clearly ^e turned,^f and the
natures of the stars are all described by divine skill.^g

74. (Ex. xxv. 30b [Heb. 31b]) Why is it that the shaft
and the branches and the bowls ^h (and) the knops and the
lilies were all " of that " ⁱ ?

(Since) the theologian ^j was all-wise," ^k he clearly knew
in his wisdom that the heaven itself is a harmony and union
and bond ^l of all those things which are in heaven, just as
the limbs which are arranged in the body are all adapted
(to one another) and grow together.^m

^a i.e. the lampstand.
^b Or " adorned " : Aucher " illustratum."
^c Prob. τορευτικῇ τινι τέχνη rather than τορευτικῇ τινι
τέχνῃ " by a certain chaser's art," although LXX and Heb.
refer to chasing or embossing (A.V. " beaten work ") rather
than lathe-turning.
^d The Arm. apparently uses two nouns to render περιόδους.
^e The latter adverb also means " accurately." Aucher
renders both adverbs by the single word " accurate."
^f τορνοῦται.
^g θεία ἐπιστήμη.
^h Lit. " holders " but here reflecting LXX κρατῆρες. Below,
in QE ii. 76, a different Arm. word is used, meaning " water-
jar."
ⁱ LXX ὁ καυλὸς αὐτῆς καὶ οἱ καλαμίσκοι καὶ οἱ κρατῆρες καὶ οἱ
σφαιρωτῆρες καὶ τὰ κρίνα (Heb. " flowers ") ἐξ αὐτῆς ἔσται.
Apparently Philo took ἐξ αὐτῆς to mean " all of a piece " or
the like.
^j ὁ θεολόγος, i.e. Moses.
^k πάνσοφος, an adjective elsewhere applied by Philo to
the patriarchs as well as Moses.
^l Aucher renders the three Arm. nouns by only two,
' conjunctio colligatioque."
^m Aucher " sicut connexa in corpore membra coaptata
sunt naturaliter."

75. (Ex. xxvi. 31 [Heb. 32]) What were the six branches which went out from either side, three equally [a]? [b]

Since it is not in a straight line but obliquely [c] that the zodiac [d] lies over and glancingly comes near the summer and winter solstices,[e] He says that the approach [f] to them is from the side, (and) the middle place is that of the sun.[g] But to the other (planets) He distributed three positions [h] on the two sides; in the superior (group) [i] are Saturn,[j] Jupiter [k] and Mars,[l] while in the inner (group) [m] are Mercury,[n] Venus [o] and the moon.[p]

[a] *i.e.* in two identical sets of three. The form of the lampstand (*menorah*) may be schematically represented as

[b] LXX ἓξ δὲ καλαμίσκοι ἐκπορευόμενοι ἐκ πλαγίων, τρεῖς καλαμίσκοι τῆς λυχνίας ἐκ τοῦ κλίτους αὐτῆς τοῦ ἑνός, καὶ τρεῖς καλαμίσκοι τῆς λυχνίας ἐκ τοῦ κλίτους τοῦ δευτέρου. Philo comments on the two "triads" of branches in *De Congressu* 8, where they represent the two chief attributes of God, see also below, *QE* ii. 78, 79 on Ex. xxv. 37.

[c] οὐκ εὐθυβόλως ἀλλὰ πλαγίως.

[d] ὁ ζωοφόρος (κύκλος), *cf. De Opif. Mundi* 112.

[e] Aucher " quoniam zodiacus non recte sed oblique jacet juxta tropica aestatis et hiemis." Philo is apparently referring to the obliquity of the ecliptic.

[f] ἀγωγή or φορά : Aucher " inductio."

[g] The general sense is that the light on the central shaft of the lampstand represents the sun, while the side-lights represent the planets.   [h] τάξεις : Aucher " ordines."

[i] The " superior " or " outer " planets are those whose orbits are farther from the sun than is the earth's.

[j] Arm. *ereveli*, lit. " visible " or " bright "=Gr. φαίνων.

[k] Arm. *lousnt'ag*, lit. " light-crowned "=Gr. φαέθων.

[l] Arm. *hrawor*, lit. " fiery "=Gr. πυρόεις.

[m] Aucher " inferius " (possibly a misprint for " interius "). The " inferior " or " inner " planets are those whose orbits are nearer the sun than is the earth's.

[n] Arm. *p'aylol*, lit. " coruscating "=Gr. στίλβων.

[o] Arm. *arousek*, lit. " dawn-bearer "=Gr. φωσφόρος.

[p] The ancients counted the moon (and sun) among the seven planets.

76. (Ex. xxv. 32 [Heb. 33]) Why are there, on each of the three branches, bowls *a* modelled into the form of nuts and knops and lilies ? *b*

At each season of the year the sun completes (its course) through three zodiacal signs,*c* which He has called " mixing-bowls," since three powers,*d* distinct and separate from one another, undergo a unified mixing to make up the time of one year. For example, the spring (consists of) Aries,*e* Taurus,*f* Gemini *g* ; and, again, in the summer (we have) Cancer,*h* Leo,*i* Virgo *j* ; and in the autumn, Libra,*k* Scorpio,*l* Sagittarius *m* ; and in the winter, Capricorn,*n* Aquarius,*o* Pisces.*p* And He likens the form and nature of the zodiacal signs to those of a nut, perhaps because a nut first sends out a bud *q* and afterwards flowers. It seems that (this comparison is made) also because harmonious sounds are set in motion, for I am not unaware that the name of the nut is mentioned in (the festival of) Heralds,*r* for its shell is wont to make a sound of rattling.

---

a Lit. " water-jars," but here = κρατῆρες, see above, *QE* ii. 74 note *h*.

b LXX καὶ τρεῖς κρατῆρες ἐκτετυπωμένοι καρυΐσκους (Heb. *m*^e*šuqqādîm* " almond-shaped " [?]) ἐν τῷ καλαμίσκῳ σφαιρωτὴρ καὶ κρίνον (Heb. " flower ")· οὕτως τοῖς ἓξ καλαμίσκοις τοῖς ἐκπορευομένοις ἐκ τῆς λυχνίας.   *c* ζῳδίων.

d δυνάμεις : Aucher " virtutes."

e Arm. *xoy* " ram."   *f* Arm. *çoul* " bull."

g Arm. *erkaworeakkʻ* " twins."

h Arm. *xeçgeti* " crab."

i Arm. *ariuc* " lion."

j Arm. *koys* " virgin."

k Arm. *louc* " yoke."

l Arm. *karič* " scorpion."

m Arm. *aleļnaωor* " archer."

n Arm. *ayceļjiurn* " goat-horn."

o Arm. *jrhos* " water-pourer."

p Arm. *zkounkʻ* " fishes."

q βλαστόν.

r Since no such festival seems to be known, one may suppose that the Arm. translator mistook Καρνατείαις for a noun derived from κηρύττειν " to herald," and that Philo actually

125

And (the bowls) are modelled in the form of spheres,[a] since whatever is in heaven is wholly spherical, being given a perfect form just as is the world.[b] And the lily (is mentioned), perhaps because of its whiteness—since it is luminous,[c] and the stars, moreover, are brilliant—perhaps also because there are radiant axes around a lily [d]—since each of the stars gives off radiance. The statement [e] also contains a description of character.[f] The lily has a certain contrariety to other flowers, for (of these) some send out buds in winter, and (some) in spring, but the lily (buds) with the coming of summer, when other (flowers) wither. And (it is) a symbol [g] of the distinction between the human and the divine, and between profane or polluted and holy sacrifices, and between the imperfect and the perfect. For (other flowers) blossom when they are irrigated by streams of water, but the lily (blossoms) with the dog-star and after the dog-star, when the sun is flaming-hot. Wherefore some prophet says that the contemplative nation [h] shall blossom like the lily,[i] indicating [j] that it does not enjoy

---

referred to the festival of Artemis Karyatis, celebrated at Karyai on the border of Arcadia and Laconia, where Artemis was associated with a nut-tree, cf. Lactantius on Statius, *Theb.* iv. 225 (cited by M. P. Nilsson, *Griechische Feste von religiöser Bedeutung*, Leipzig, 1906, p. 196).

[a] LXX σφαιρωτῆρες (A.V. " knops ").

[b] ὁ κόσμος.

[c] φωτοειδές.

[d] Or " they are circling axes of lily-like radiance ": Aucher " propter axes splendoris instar lilium circumdantes."

[e] ὁ λόγος.

[f] ἠθοποιΐαν.

[g] σύμβολον.

[h] τὸ ὁρατικὸν (or θεωρητικὸν) γένος, *i.e.* Israel, so referred to in several other passages of Philo.

[i] Hosea xiv. 5, LXX ἔσομαι ὡς δρόσος τῷ Ἰσραήλ, ἀνθήσει ὡς κρίνον καὶ βαλεῖ τὰς ῥίζας αὐτοῦ ὡς ὁ Λίβανος. Philo quotes from Hosea three times, from Isaiah four times, from Jeremiah three times, from Ezekiel twice, from Zechariah once, and in only one passage does he refer to the prophet (Jeremiah) by name. [j] αἰνιττόμενος.

prosperity at the same time (as other nations) but that at the time when others have passed their prime, (Israel) begins (to flower) without the things it ought to have as inducements,[a] for its flowering without water, when the sun is flaming, is not to be compared with what is usual.[b]

77. (Ex. xxv. 33-36 [Heb. 34-36]) Why are there four (mixing-)bowls on the lampstand ?[c]

Each branch constitutes[d] one season of the year through three zodiacal signs,[e] as has been said,[f] while the lampstand (represents) the seasons of the year, which are four. Now these undergo a certain mixing to produce a year, for a year is nothing else than the completion of four seasons, of which it is mixed and consists. For the nature[g] of the seasons is not unmixed and inharmonious but has a harmony of mixture and a community[h] of interchanging (elements). For the completion of the preceding (season) happens to be the beginning of that which follows it.

78. (Ex. xxv. 37a) Why are there seven lamps on the lampstand ?[i]

It is clear to all that the seven lamps are symbols[j] of

---

[a] Lit. " without convenient things and persuasions " ; Aucher " sine convenientibus expectatisque mediis."

[b] Aucher, in a footnote, renders, " sive, praeter opinionem est, vel, vix credi potest."

[c] LXX καὶ ἐν τῇ λυχνίᾳ τέσσαρες κρατῆρες ἐκτετυπωμένοι καρυΐσκους . . . καὶ ἐν τῇ λυχνίᾳ τέσσαρες κρατῆρες ἐκτετυπωμένοι καρυΐσκους (sic : many LXX MSS. and Heb. omit the repeated half-verse). These four " bowls " (i.e. ornaments shaped like almond-blossoms) were distinct from the " bowls " placed at the ends of the six branches and on top of the central shaft to hold the lamps.

[d] Lit. " completes " : Aucher " perficit."

[e] ζῳδίων.   [f] In QE ii. 76.

[g] ἡ φύσις.   [h] κοινωνίαν.

[i] LXX καὶ ποιήσεις τοὺς λύχνους αὐτῆς ἑπτά.

[j] σύμβολα.

127

the planets, for the holy hebdomad belongs to those things reckoned as divine.[a] And the movement and revolution of these through the zodiacal signs [b] are the causes, for sublunary beings,[c] of all those things which are wont to take place in the embrace of concord,[d] in the air, in the water, on the earth and in all mixtures [e] from animals to plants.[f]

79. (Ex. xxv. 37b) Why does He say that the lampstand shall give light " from one side " [g] ?

The planets do not travel around all parts and sides of the celestial sphere but only in one part, in the south, for their motion is, as it were, near our zone,[h] whence the

[a] Text slightly emended : Aucher " septenario numero in connumerationem cum divinorum sacro calculo conscriptorum." For the thought cf. Quis Rer. Div. Heres 225 ἐπίγειον οὖν βουληθεὶς ἀρχετύπου τῆς κατ' οὐρανὸν σφαίρας ἑπταφεγγοῦς μίμημα παρ' ἡμῖν ὁ τεχνίτης γενέσθαι πάγκαλον ἔργον προσέταξε τὴν λυχνίαν δημιουργηθῆναι, but in the latter passage Philo also makes the lampstand a symbol of the soul.

[b] ζῳδίων.

[c] τοῖς μετὰ σελήνην.

[d] Aucher " causa . . . conciliandi in osculum concordiae."

[e] Aucher " temperamentis."

[f] Text slightly emended, reading minč (=ἕως) instead of mišt (=ἀεί): Aucher " animalium plantarumque semper."

[g] Aucher " ex una regione ": LXX καὶ ἐπιθήσεις τοὺς λύχνους (v.l. adds αὐτῆς), καὶ φανοῦσιν ἐκ τοῦ ἑνὸς προσώπου (v.l. adds αὐτῆς): Heb. " and thou shalt make its lamps seven. and they shall put up its lamps and cause it to give light over against its face." Philo understands the last obscure phrase to mean that the lampstand was to be placed in one part (the south) of the tabernacle, see next note.

[h] Aucher notes that his text represents a conflation of the two MSS. in this sentence, but he does not give their separate readings. For the thought cf. De Vita Mosis ii. 102 τὴν δὲ λυχνίαν ἐν τοῖς νοτίοις, δι' ἧς αἰνίττεται τὰς τῶν φωσφόρων κινήσεις ἀστέρων· ἥλιος γὰρ καὶ σελήνη καὶ οἱ ἄλλοι πολὺ τῶν βορείων ἀφεστῶτες νοτίους ποιοῦνται τὰς περιπολήσεις.

128

shadow *a* falls not on the southern but on the northern side. For this reason He has said not ineptly that the lampstand shall give light from one part, indicating (thereby) that the revolution of the planets is in the southern regions.

80. (Ex. xxv. 38) What are the " uplifters " *b* of the ampstand, and the " bases " *c* ?

The " uplifters " are so named from " lifting up," *d* for the oil, which kindles the light, is lifted upon the lamps,' while to the light-bearing stars all their light happens to be brought from the celestial sphere.' For just as whatever is luminous in the eyes is irrigated *g* by the soul, for souls are most luminous, so is the radiance of light in the stars wont to receive its illumination from the most pure ether.*h*

a Cast by the noon-day sun in the northern hemisphere.

b Aucher " tegmina ": Arm. *verarkouk'* usu. = ἀναβολαί, περιβόλαια and the like : LXX ἐπαρυστῆρα " vessels for pouring (oil) " : Old Lat. " suffusorium " : Heb. *malqāḥêhā* " its snuffers " (A.V. " tongs ") : Arm. O.T. *bazamkakals* = ἐπαρυστῆρας. Apparently Philo read ἐπαρυστῆρα and fancifully took it to be connected with ἐπαίρειν " to lift up " as well as ἐπαρύειν " to draw a liquid from above." It should be noted, moreover, that in the papyri ἀρυστήρ means " dipping-pail " or the like, such as was used in irrigation-machines, *cf.* Claire Préaux in *Chronique d'Égypte,* xxv. (1950), p. 352.

c LXX τὰ ὑποθέματα : Heb. *maḥtôtêhā* " its coal-pans " (A.V. " snuff dishes ") : Arm. O.T. *neçouks* = τὰ ὑποθέματα.

d Aucher renders freely, " Tegmina seu Anabola nomen sortita sunt ab ἀναβάλλειν, *supermittere.*"

e Aucher " eoquod sicut lucernis ad lumen excitandum oleum supermittitur."

f See above, *QE* ii. 78, on the cosmic symbolism of the lamps.

g ἄρδεται (with a play on ἐπαρύειν), *cf. Leg. All.* i. 28 πηγῆς δὲ τρόπον ἄρδει τὰς αἰσθήσεις ὁ νοῦς.

h ἐκ τοῦ καθαρωτάτου αἰθέρος.

81. (Ex. xxv. 39) Why did He assign to the lampstand the weight of " a talent of pure gold " *a* ?

The ark, the table and the censers He described by giving their dimensions but in the case of the lampstand He does not mention the dimensions but indicates the weight,*b* for the reason that, as I said a little while ago,*c* it is a symbol *d* of the whole heaven. Now heaven, (being) a sphere,*e* is unprovided with work-tools and unequal measures,*f* being adapted to the rule of equality *g* in accordance with its figure and the rest of its nature.*h* But it does have weight, since everything ponderable is after it.*i* For nothing sublunary *j* (stands) by itself, but everything small or large is wont to be elastic,*k* as if (affected) by the wonderful artificer, the invisible Logos in heaven.*l* And the talent

---

a LXX πάντα τὰ σκεύη ταῦτα τάλαντον (Heb. *kikkār*) χρυσίου καθαροῦ.

b τὴν ὁλκήν.

c In *QE* ii. 73-80.

d σύμβολον.

e σφαίρα.

f The Arm. lit. = ὀργανικῶν σκευῶν καὶ ἀνίσων μέτρων ἀμέτοχός ἐστι but is apparently a misunderstanding of the Greek. The original may have been ὀργάνων καὶ ἀνισοτήτων, as Prof. L. A. Post suggests, citing Plato, *Tim.* 33.

g ἰσότητος κανόνι, as in *De Aeternitate Mundi* 108.

h κατὰ τὸ σχῆμα καὶ κατὰ τὴν ἄλλην φύσιν *vel sim.*: Aucher " secundum figuram et diversam naturam."

i Apparently this means that the weight of objects on earth is determined by the weight of heaven.

j μετὰ σελήνην.

k Lit. " sinew-stretching "—νευροτενές. Prof. Post thinks that this refers to the commutation of the four elements, as in Stoic doctrine ; he cites Dio Chrysostom, *Or.* xxxvi. 50-53.

l Syntax and meaning not clear : Aucher " sed omne quidquam pusillum ac magnum, tamquam ab admirabili artifice secundum caeli rationem invisibilem, vigorem praeferre consuevit." The Arm. glossator, cited in Aucher's footnote, paraphrases, " sicut oculorum delusores mira quaedam apparentia figurant, sic et luminaria invisibiliter demutant elementa mundi : nec non Verbum divinum prae manibus gerens universum, sicut auriga habenas."

EXODUS, BOOK II

is likened to unity (because) the heaven is one and is not like anything else in its shape or powers.[a] For the four elements [b] have a kinship [c] to one another both in substance and in their movement [d]—in substance when they are transformed into one another, and in their movement in that fire and air are confined to a rectilinear motion upwards from the centre, while water and earth (move) downwards from the centre.[e] But heaven moves not in a straight line but in a circle, having a figure that is equal on all sides and most perfect. May it not be, then, since the parts of the earth, according to those who study astrology,[f] are said to measure sixty,[g] that He appointed the talent (to be) its form, for the talent consists of sixty minas?

82. (Ex. xxv. 40) What is the meaning of the words, "Thou shalt make (them) according to the pattern which has been shown to thee on the mountain" [h]?

[a] δυνάμεις : Aucher " vires."

[b] στοιχεῖα.

[c] συγγένειαν or possibly οἰκείωσιν, cf. F. C. Robbins in Loeb Ptolemy, Tetrabiblos, p. 65 n. 3.

[d] καὶ κατ' οὐσίαν καὶ κατὰ περιφοράν (?).

[e] Arm. kēt = both κέντρον and στιγμή : Aucher " centro," adding in a footnote, " proprie punctum sonat." For the upward movement of the two lighter elements and the downward movement of the two heavier elements (ἡ ὁδὸς ἄνω and ἡ ὁδὸς κάτω) see, among other passages in Philo, De Aeternitate Mundi 110.

[f] κατὰ τοὺς τῇ μαθηματικῇ σχολάζοντας, here meaning philosophical astronomers like Plato in the Timaeus.

[g] Cf. QG iv. 164, where, however, Philo speaks of the sixty parts of the cosmos rather than of the earth.

[h] LXX ὅρα ποιήσεις (v.l. + πάντα) κατὰ τὸν τύπον (Heb. " their form ") τὸν δεδειγμένον (Heb. " which thou art shown ") ἐν τῷ ὄρει. The verse is quoted in Leg. All. iii. 102 in slightly different wording κατὰ τὸ παράδειγμα τὸ δεδειγμένον σοι ἐν τῷ ὄρει πάντα ποιήσεις. There Philo quotes it to show that Moses was the artificer of the archetypes, while Bezaleel was the artificer of the objects made in accordance with these.

131

QUESTIONS AND ANSWERS

Through the " pattern " He again indicates [a] the incorporeal heaven, the archetype of the sense-perceptible,[b] for it [c] is a visible pattern and impression [d] and measure. He testifies to these things by saying " See," [e] (thereby) admonishing (us) to keep the vision of the soul sleepless [f] and ever wakeful in order to see incorporeal forms,[g] since, if it were (merely a question of) seeing the sense-perceptible with the eyes of the body, it is clear that no (divine) command would be needed for this.

83. (Ex. xxvi. 1a) What is the tabernacle ? [h]
Having first of all alluded to the incorporeal and intelligible world [i] by means of the ark, and the substance of the sense-perceptible (world) [j] by means of the table, and heaven by means of the lampstand,[k] He begins to represent [l] in order those things which are sublunary,[m] (namely) air, water, fire and earth, making the tabernacle represent their nature and substance. For the tabernacle

---

[a] αἰνίττεται.

[b] τὸν ἀσώματον οὐρανόν, ἀρχέτυπον τοῦ αἰσθητοῦ.

[c] i.e. heaven.

[d] i.e. seal-impression—σφραγίς: Aucher " signum."

[e] It is not necessary to suppose that the word "see" has accidentally been omitted from the lemma of this section, since Philo occasionally takes it for granted that his readers will be able to supply for themselves words omitted from the verses he quotes.

[f] Cf. De Vita Mosis i. 289 τοῖς τῆς ψυχῆς ἀκοιμήτοις ὄμμασι.

[g] εἴδη or ἰδέας : Aucher " species."

[h] LXX καὶ τὴν σκηνὴν ποιήσεις κτλ. Philo refers to the cosmic symbolism of the tabernacle in De Congressu 116-117, cf. De Vita Mosis ii. 74-88. In several other passages, e.g. Leg. All. iii. 46 and Quis Rer. Div. Heres 112, he makes the tabernacle a symbol of wisdom or virtue.

[i] αἰνιξάμενος πρῶτον τὸν ἀσώματον καὶ νοητὸν κόσμον.

[j] τὴν τοῦ αἰσθητοῦ οὐσίαν.

[k] See QE ii. 53-81 on Ex. xxv. 9-40.

[l] ἀπεικονίζεσθαι vel sim.: Aucher " describere." The same verb, nmaneçouçanel, is used at the end of the sentence.

[m] τὰ μετὰ σελήνην.

is a portable temple ^{a} of God and not a stationary or fixed
one. And (similarly) those things which are below heaven ^{b}
are mutable and changeable, while heaven alone is unchangeable and self-consistent ^{c} and similar to itself. But
this statement ^{d} also reveals a certain delineation of character.^{e} Since they were passing through a wilderness
where there were no courts ^{f} or houses but (only) tabernacles,^{g} which were made for necessary purposes (such
as) giving the help of warmth against the cold, he ^{h} thought
it right that there should be a most holy temple to the
Father and Creator of all things. Moreover, he showed
that the divine name, which is in need of nothing,^{i} dwelt
together, so far as one might believe, with those who were
in need of a tabernacle, to receive piety and worthy holiness.^{j} Now, as for those who saw the structure of the
divine tabernacle likened to their own dwelling,^{k} what
would they have been likely to do ^{l} other than to bow down
in return for what was done ^{m} and bless the Overseer and

---

^{a} φορητὸν ἱερόν, as it is called in De Vita Mosis ii. 73.

^{b} Lit. " behind heaven "—τὰ μετ' (instead of ὑπ') οὐρανόν,
apparently on the analogy of τὰ μετὰ σελήνην.

^{c} καθ' ἑαυτόν: Aucher " stante per se."

^{d} λόγος. ^{e} ἠθοποιΐαν τινά.

^{f} Aucher " porticus." The same Arm. word (srah) is used
to render LXX αὐλαίας " curtains " in the next section. Here
it prob. renders αὐλαί, cf. De Congressu 116.

^{g} σκηναί. ^{h} Presumably Moses.

^{i} ἀπροσδεές.

^{j} The syntax is uncertain, and the sense is obscure. More
intelligible is the corresponding passage in De Vita Mosis ii.
73 (Colson's translation), " But, as they were still wandering
in the desert and had as yet no settled habitation, it suited
them to have a portable sanctuary, so that during their
journeys and encampments they might bring their sacrifices
to it and perform all their other religious duties, not lacking
anything which dwellers in cities should have."

^{k} Variant " nature." ^{l} τί ἔμελλον πράττειν vel sim.

^{m} The meaning of the prepositional phrase is not clear:
Aucher renders freely, " pro viribus suis (vel, propter similitudinem visam)."

QUESTIONS AND ANSWERS

Guardian and Curator of His power ? [a]   And familiar [b]
to God is His power, O ministers ! [c]

84. (Ex. xxvi. 1b) Why does the tabernacle have 10 [d]
curtains ? [e]

Many a time has much been said about the number ten
in other places,[f] which for those who wish to prolong the
discussion it would be easy to transfer here. But brevity
of speech is liked by us, and it is timely and sufficient that
whatever has been said be remembered.[g]

*85. (Ex. xxvi. 1c) Why are the curtains (made) of
woven linen and of hyacinth and of purple and of woven
scarlet ? [h]

What is spoken about is the workmanship of the
(materials) woven together, which are four in number and
are symbols of the four elements,[i] earth, water, air and
fire, of which sublunary things [j] are made, while the

---

[a] τὸν ἔφορον καὶ ἐπίτροπον καὶ ἐπιμελητὴν αὐτοῦ δυνάμεως vel
sim.

[b] Or " peculiar," as Prof. Post suggests.

[c] Or " worshippers."

[d] Written as a numeral letter.

[e] LXX καὶ τὴν σκηνὴν ποιήσεις δέκα αὐλαίας κτλ. Philo comments on the ten curtains as symbols of the perfect number
in De Congressu 116 and De Vita Mosis ii. 84.

[f] For various passages on the decad in Philo's writings
(including the Quaestiones) see Staehle, pp. 53-58.

[g] The exact sense of the clause is not clear. Aucher
renders more smoothly but more freely, " et quod olim
dictum fuit, satis juvat ad memoriam."

[h] LXX ἐκ βύσσου κεκλωσμένης καὶ ὑακίνθου καὶ πορφύρας καὶ
κοκκίνου κεκλωσμένου. The interpretation of the four colours
(linen being equated with white by Philo) is also found in
De Congressu 116-117 and De Vita Mosis ii. 84-88. There
is also a brief paraphrase of this passage in Theodoret's
Quaestiones in Exodum (Migne, 248 D).

[i] Cf. De Congressu 117 ἃ τῶν τεττάρων στοιχείων σύμβολά
ἐστιν.   [j] τὰ ὑπὸ σελήνην.

EXODUS, BOOK II

celestial sphere *a* (is made) of a special substance,*b* of the very most excellent things which have been brought together.*c* For (Scripture) indicates *d* the earth by " linen," for linen *e* is earthly and from the earth ; and water by " purple," since water is the producer of this *f* ; and air by " hyacinth," for the air is black *g* and has no illumination in itself, wherefore it is illuminated by another light *h* ; and fire by " scarlet," for its colour is fiery.*i* And so he *j* thought it right that the divine temple of the Creator of all things should be woven *k* of such and so many things as the world was made of, (being) the universal temple *l* which (existed) before the holy temple.*m*

86. (Ex. xxvi. 1d, 3) Why does He say in addition, " Work of weaving thou shalt make the curtains which are woven together with one another " *n* ?

---

a τῆς κατ' οὐρανὸν σφαίρας.

b ἐξ ἐξαιρέτου οὐσίας : Aucher " ex separata substantia."

c Aucher renders less literally, " optimisque rebus constante " (for " constantibus "). *d* αἰνίττεται.

e Here the Arm. renders βύσσος by *vouš*, whereas elsewhere in this section he uses the word *behez*.

f Philo explains this more fully in *De Congressu* 117 τὸ γὰρ τῆς βαφῆς αἴτιον ἐκ θαλάττης, ἡ ὁμωνυμοῦσα κόγχη (prob. the murex).

g So *De Congressu* 117 and *De Vita Mosis* ii. 88 μέλας γὰρ οὗτος φύσει. By " black " Philo means " dark blue."

h This further explanation is omitted in the parallels.

i πυροειδής *vel sim.*, *cf. De Congressu* 117 ἐμφερέστατον γὰρ φλογί : *De Vita Mosis* ii. 88 διότι φοινικοῦν (" bright red," not " purple ") ἑκάτερον. *j* Moses.

k *i.e.* constructed. *l* τὸ πανίερον.

m *Cf. De Vita Mosis* ii. 88 ἣν γὰρ ἀναγκαῖον ἱερὸν χειροποίητον κατασκευάζοντας τῷ πατρὶ καὶ ἡγεμόνι τοῦ παντὸς τὰς ὁμοίας λαβεῖν οὐσίας αἷς τὸ ὅλον ἐδημιούργει.

n Philo here combines the last clause of vs. 1 and vs. 3, and paraphrases : LXX χερουβεὶμ ἐργασίᾳ ὑφάντου ποιήσεις αὐτὰς (*sc.* τὰς αὐλαίας) . . . πέντε δὲ αὐλαῖαι ἔσονται ἐξ ἀλλήλων ἐχόμεναι ἡ ἑτέρα ἐκ τῆς ἑτέρας καὶ πέντε αὐλαῖαι ἔσονται συνεχόμεναι ἑτέρα τῇ ἑτέρᾳ.

135

QUESTIONS AND ANSWERS

It *a* has such a nature as to be perfected *b* (as) one out of many. Such too is the substance of the world,*c* for it was mixed of the four elements,*d* and these were, after a fashion,*e* woven together *f* with one another to produce one completely worked texture.*g*

87. (Ex. xxvi. 2) Why was the length of (each) curtain 28 *h* cubits, and the breath 4 (cubits) ? *i*

The doctrine *j* of the number four is divine and holy and most apt (and) has been allotted the proper praise pertaining to numbers.*k* But at the present time the natural virtue *l* of the number 28 must be set down. Now it is the first perfect number equal to its parts,*m* and it has the matter of its substance from three,*n* and especially for this

---

a *i.e.* the tabernacle, see *QE* ii. 88.
b τελειοῦσθαι.   *c* ἡ τοῦ κόσμου οὐσία.
d ἐκ τῶν τεττάρων στοιχείων.
e τρόπον τινά.
f Aucher " contextus est," apparently taking " world " to be the implied subject of the verb instead of " elements " as the context demands (neut. pl. subj. with sing. verb).
g The Arm.=πρὸς ἑνὸς ὑφάσματος τελεσιουργουμένου γένεσιν *vel sim.* : Aucher " ad unius staminis perfecti productionem."
h This and the following numbers, unless they are otherwise rendered, are numeral letters in the Arm. text.
i LXX μῆκος τῆς αὐλαίας τῆς μιᾶς ὀκτὼ καὶ εἴκοσι πήχεων, καὶ εὖρος τεσσάρων πήχεων ἡ αὐλαία ἡ μία ἔσται· μέτρον τὸ αὐτὸ ἔσται πάσαις ταῖς αὐλαίαις. There are parallels to this section in *De Vita Mosis* ii. 84 and *De Spec. Leg.* ii. 40, *cf. De Opif. Mundi* 101.   *j* ὁ λόγος.
k The meaning is not wholly clear : Aucher " eoquod numerorum condignam benedictionem sortitus fuerit," adding in a footnote " *vel*, in sermone nostro de numeris laudem propriam."
l ἡ φυσικὴ ἀρετή, *i.e.* the philosophical force.
m *i.e.* equal to the sum of its factors, $1+2+4+7+14=28$; *cf. De Vita Mosis* ii. 84 τὸν ὀκτὼ καὶ εἴκοσι ἀριθμὸν τέλειον ἴσον τοῖς ἑαυτοῦ μέρεσι.
n Possibly this means that 28 is a cubic number, $1 \times 4 \times 7$ or $2 \times 2 \times 7$.

136

reason is it concordant with the first six,[a] for six is the first
(digit) equal to its parts.[b] Accordingly, this number has
one good (quality). And it has still another essence [c]
through the number seven, since it is composed of units
which go singly from one to seven, as follows : 1, 2, 3, 4, 5,
6, 7, making 28. And the third (property) is that it multi-
plies the number seven, being four times seven or seven
times four. Now the number four is also related in
species [d] to the number seven, and there is nothing more
perfect.[e] By these numbers the theologian [f] says the tabernacle was erected, making the length of the ten curtains
twenty-eight cubits (each) and the total two hundred and
eighty, while the (total) breadth was forty.[g] And the
power [h] which the number forty brings to living beings [i]
has already been spoken of.[j] As for the number two
hundred and eighty, it is forty multiplied by seven, and
the number seven is dedicated to God.

88. (Ex. xxvi. 6) Why does He say, " And the tabernacle
shall be one " ? [k]

Someone may say, " But, Master Theologian,[l] who does
not know that many are not one, especially since you [m]
have already said,[n] ' The tabernacle shall be made of ten
curtains ' but not ' the tabernacles ' ? " May it not be,
therefore, that the tabernacle's being " one " is a firmer

---

[a] *i.e.* the digit six.
[b] *i.e.* to the sum of its factors, $1 + 2 + 3 = 6$.
[c] οὐσίαν, possibly a corruption of φύσιν.
[d] συγγενὴς εἴδει.
[e] *i.e.* than the number seven.
[f] ὁ θεολόγος, *i.e.* Moses.
[g] Each of the ten curtains being four cubits broad.
[h] ἡ δύναμις.
[i] τοῖς οὖσι.
[j] In *QG* iv. 154.
[k] LXX (end of verse) καὶ ἔσται ἡ σκηνὴ μία.
[l] ὦ κύριε ὁ θεολόγος, *i.e.* Moses.
[m] Speaking in God's name.
[n] See *QE* ii. 84 on Ex. xxvi. 1.

seal indicating [a] the unities of sublunary things ? [b] For even though earth is distinct from water, and water from air, and air from fire, and fire from each of these, nevertheless all are adapted to one determined form.[c] For it is natural that the matter [d] which was perfected out of so many things should be one, especially since the interchange of the elements [e] with one another clearly demonstrates their common nature.[f]

89.[g] (Ex. xxvi. 28) What is the meaning of the words, " The middle bar between the pillars shall reach from one side to the other side " [h] ?

Above this straight line of the single walls there is a bar between the twenty pillars to take firmer hold of their joining.[i] For by " the bar " He indicates [j] the Logos [k] ascribed to necessity,[l] which in heaven above tends toward

---

[a] The Arm. = σφραγὶς βεβαιοτέρα αἰνιττομένη vel sim., meaning " confirms the impression given by (earlier) indications " or the like.

[b] τῶν ὑπὸ σελήνην.

[c] εἰς ἓν ὡρισμένον εἶδος.

[d] τὴν ὕλην.

[e] τῶν στοιχείων.

[f] τὴν κοινωνίαν : Aucher " communionem."

[g] Ex. xxvi. 7-27, on which Philo does not comment here, describes the covering and framework of the Tabernacle.

[h] LXX καὶ ὁ μοχλὸς ὁ μέσος ἀνὰ μέσον τῶν στύλων (Heb. " frame ": A.V. " boards ") διἴκνείσθω ἀπὸ τοῦ ἑνὸς κλίτους εἰς τὸ ἕτερον κλίτος. Philo seems to allude to this verse in De Vita Mosis ii. 77-79.

[i] The syntax and meaning are uncertain, but cf. De Vita Mosis ii. 78 " for the length (of the tabernacle) the craftsman set up forty pillars, half of them, twenty, on each side, leaving no interval between, but fitting and joining each to the next in order that it might present the appearance of a single wall."

[j] αἰνίττεται.

[k] Aucher " rationem." Arm. ban here prob. means the cosmic Logos rather than the individual reason, cf. QE ii. 90.

[l] So Aucher, " necessitati adscriptam " (the margins of the Arm. mss. have " Fate " for " necessity "), but the meaning escapes me.

heavenly things. For by these *a* everything is held together as by an indissoluble bond.

90.*b* (Ex. xxvi. 30) What is the meaning of the words, "Thou shalt erect *c* the tabernacle according to the pattern shown to thee on the mountain " *d* ?

Again He indicates *e* the paradigmatic essences of the ideas *f* by saying " according to the appearance *g* which was shown to thee on the mountain." But the prophet *h* did not see any corporeal thing there but all incorporeals.*i* And it is said that the tabernacle is to be erected directly before (their) faces,*j* for sublunary things *k* have been granted a lower place *l* but are again raised above and elevated and established and set up upon the divine Logos,*m* for the divine Logoi *n* are the foundations and bars *o* of the security *p* of all things. Do you not see that earth and

---

a Aucher " per istam (*i.e.* rationem)," but the pron. is plural.

b A similarly framed question is asked in *QE* ii. 82 on Ex. xxv. 40.

c Reading *yarousçes* with Codd. A, C : marginal variant *arasçes* " thou shalt make."

d LXX καὶ ἀναστήσεις τὴν σκηνὴν κατὰ τὸ εἶδος τὸ δεδειγμένον σοι (Heb. " which thou wast shown ") ἐν τῷ ὄρει.

e αἰνίττεται.

f τὰς παραδειγματικὰς οὐσίας τὰς τῶν ἰδεῶν *vel sim.* : Aucher " indicativas essentias specierum."

g Arm. *tesil* = εἶδος, ἰδέα, ὄψις, etc. : Aucher " visionem." Note that in the Question a different word (*orinak*) is used.

h ὁ προφήτης, *i.e.* Moses.

i πάντα ἀσώματα.

j κατέναντι ἐκ προσώπου *vel sim.* : Aucher " directe . . . in conspectu."

k τὰ ὑπὸ σελήνην.

l Lit. " part."

m Aucher, construing slightly differently, renders, " elevata fundataque super divinum verbum erectum."

n Or " words " : Aucher " verba."

o μοχλοί, *cf. QE* ii. 89.

p Aucher " constantiae."

water, inasmuch as they are in the midst of all air and fire,
with the heaven surrounding (them), are not firmly fixed
by anything at all other than their holding to each other,
as the divine Logos binds them with all-wise art and most
perfect adaptation ? [a]

91. (Ex. xxvi. 31a) What is " the veil " [b] ?

By the veil the inside (of the tabernacle) is set off and
separated from the things outside, for the inside is holy
and truly divine,[c] while the outside, though it is also holy,
does not attain the same nature or a similar one. Moreover,
it indicates [d] the changeable parts of the world which are
sublunary [e] and undergo changes of direction,[f] and the
heavenly (region) which is without transient events [g] and
is unchanging. And (it shows) how they are set off and
separated from one another, for the ethereal and airy
substance is, as it were, a covering.[h]

92. (Ex. xxvi. 31b) Why does He command that the veil
be made " of hyacinth and of purple and of scarlet and of
woven linen " [i] ?

---

[a] συνδέοντος αὐτὰ τοῦ θείου λόγου πανσόφῳ τέχνῃ καὶ τελειο-
τάτῃ ἁρμονίᾳ vel sim. For the thought see Wolfson, Philo.
i. p. 338.   [b] LXX καὶ ποιήσεις καταπέτασμα.

[c] ὄντως θεῖον.   [d] αἰνίττεται.   [e] ὑπὸ σελήνην.

[f] Lit. " turnings "—στροφάς or τροπάς : Aucher " varia-
tionem."   [g] Aucher " caret casu."

[h] ὑπὸ τῆς αἰθερίας καὶ ἀερίας οὐσίας ὡς καλύμματος vel sim. :
Aucher " mediante aetherea aereaque essentia." While Arm.
aragast can mean " partition " or the like as well as " covering," the latter seems to be indicated by the partial parallel
in De Vita Mosis ii. 101 πρόναον εἰργόμενον δυσὶν ὑφάσμασι,
τῷ μὲν ἔνδον ὃ καλεῖται καταπέτασμα, τῷ δ' ἐκτὸς ὃ προσαγορεύεται
κάλυμμα.

[i] LXX καὶ ποιήσεις καταπέτασμα ἐξ ὑακίνθου καὶ πορφύρας
καὶ κοκκίνου κεκλωσμένου καὶ βύσσου νενησμένης· ἔργον ὑφαντὸν
ποιήσεις αὐτὸ χερουβείμ. Here, as in QE ii. 85 on Ex. xxvi. 1,
Philo omits any reference to the woven designs of cherubim.

Just as He commands the ten curtains of the tabernacle to be woven of four mixtures, so also (He commands) the veil (to be made). For the curtains are veils in a certain sense,[a] (although they are) not above the entrance but throughout the whole tabernacle. And these, as I have said,[b] are tokens and symbols [c] of the four elements.[d]

93. (Ex. xxvi. 32a) Why does He command the veil to be placed above four pillars at the end of the tabernacle ? [e]

The four columns [f] are made solid,[g] but in the tabernacle everything is a symbol of corporeal things,[h] while incorporeal things stand above the tetrad.[i] The point [j] is ordered in accordance with the monad, and the line in accordance with the dyad, and the surface in accordance with the triad, while the solid [k] (is ordered) in accordance

---

[a] τρόπον τινά or, as in *De Vita Mosis* ii. 87, σχεδόν.

[b] In *QE* ii. 85.

[c] The two Arm. words prob. render the single word σύμβολα.

[d] τῶν τεττάρων στοιχείων.

[e] LXX καὶ ἐπιθήσεις αὐτὸ ἐπὶ τεσσάρων στύλων ἀσήπτων κεχρυσωμένων χρυσίῳ. By " at the end of the tabernacle " Philo means the inner sanctuary at the western end of the tabernacle.

[f] The Arm. translator here uses a different word from that rendered " pillars " in the Question.

[g] Prob. στερεοῦνται, anticipating the reference to the solid (τὸ στερεόν) below : Aucher " firmatae sunt."

[h] σύμβολον σωμάτων.

[i] This may mean that the objects in the inner sanctuary, concealed by the veil over the four columns, are symbols of the heavenly and incorporeal bodies (see the preceding sections) which stand over corporeal and sublunary bodies composed of the four elements.

[j] The Arm. text reads *nšanaki* " of a symbol " but this word is obviously meaningless here. Either the Arm. translator's eye must have fallen upon the word σύμβολον in the preceding sentence or he must have misread or misinterpreted στίγμα as σημεῖον. Aucher renders, " signum (puncti)."

[k] τὸ στερεόν.

with the tetrad, upon which stands the substance of incorporeal things.[a] Or by solidly drawing the progressions [b]
after the intelligible,[c] you will lead to the sense-perceptible
form,[d] as [e] all the visible columns of the tabernacle altogether amount to fifty, omitting the two hidden in the
corners. And their power is that of a right-angled triangle.[f]

94. (Ex. xxvi. 33b) What is the meaning of the words,
" Thou shalt set apart [g] the veil between the Holy of
Holies " [h] ?

I have said [i] that the simple holy [j] (parts of the tabernacle) are classified with the sense-perceptible heaven,[k]

[a] ἡ τῶν ἀσωμάτων οὐσία.

[b] ἀναβάσεις (?) : Aucher " egressum."

[c] μετὰ τὸ νοητόν.

[d] εἰς τὸ αἰσθητὸν εἶδος. The meaning of the clause escapes
me. [e] Aucher " ita ut."

[f] Cf. De Vita Mosis ii. 79-80, " Thus the whole number of
pillars visible in the tabernacle, leaving out the two in the
corners hidden from view, amounted to fifty-five. . . . But if
you choose to exclude the five in the propylaeum . . . there
will be the most sacred number fifty, the square of the sides
of the right-angled triangle, the original source from which
the universe springs." As Colson notes, " $50 = 3^2 + 4^2 + 5^2$,
and 3, 4, 5 are the sides of the primary form of the right-
angled triangle." Cf. also De Spec. Leg. ii. 176.

[g] Aucher " facias dividere," see next note. The Arm.
translator seems to have omitted the words " the holy (place) "
and " after " between," as the present text is obviously
defective.

[h] LXX καὶ διοριεῖ (v.l. διοριεῖς) καταπέτασμα ὑμῖν ἀνὰ μέσον
τοῦ ἁγίου καὶ ἀνὰ μέσον τοῦ ἁγίου τῶν ἁγίων. Philo briefly
alludes to the veil separating (ὅπως διακρίνηται) the Holy of
Holies from the " holy place " (the longer chamber of the
tabernacle) in De Mut. Nom. 43, 192. The preceding clause
in Ex. xxvi. 33 states that the ark is to be placed " within the
veil," i.e. in the Holy of Holies. [i] In QE ii. 91.

[j] τὰ ἁπλᾶ ἅγια, i.e. the " holy place," contrasted with the
Holy of Holies.

[k] τάττεται κατὰ τὸν αἰσθητὸν οὐρανόν.

whereas the inner (parts), which are called the Holy of
Holies, (are classified) with the intelligible world.[a] The
incorporeal world is set off and separated from the visible
one by the mediating Logos [b] as by a veil. But may it not
be that this Logos is the tetrad, through which the corporeal
solid [c] comes into being ? [d] For this [e] is classified with the
invisible intelligible things,[f] while the other (part of the
tabernacle) [g] is divided into three [h] and is connected with
sense-perceptible things, so that there is between them
something (at once) invisible and visible of substance.

95. (Ex. xxvi. 35) Why does He command the table and
the lampstand to be placed " outside the veil " ? [i]

I have shown earlier [j] that by the table He indicates
sense-perceptible substance, and by the lampstand, the
sense-perceptible heaven.[k] And they are placed [l] outside
the veil because the things in the inner recess [m] are invisible
and intelligible,[n] whereas those which are more external
are visible and sense-perceptible.

---

[a] κατὰ τὸν νοητὸν κόσμον.

[b] ὑπὸ τοῦ μεθορίου λόγου, cf. Quis Rer. Div. Heres 205.

[c] τὸ σωματικὸν στερεόν.

[d] See the preceding section.

[e] i.e. the Holy of Holies.

[f] τὰ ἀόρατα νοητά.

[g] i.e. the " holy place."

[h] Prob., as the Arm. glossator explains, the table of showbread, the lampstand and the altar of incense.

[i] LXX καὶ θήσεις τὴν τράπεζαν ἔξωθεν τοῦ καταπετάσματος,
καὶ τὴν λυχνίαν ἀπέναντι τῆς τραπέζης ἐπὶ μέρους τῆς σκηνῆς τὸ
πρὸς νότον· καὶ τὴν τράπεζαν θήσεις ἐπὶ μέρους τῆς σκηνῆς (Heb.
om. " of the tabernacle ") τὸ πρὸς βορρᾶν.

[j] In QE ii. 69 and 73.

[k] αἰνίττεται . . . τὴν αἰσθητὴν οὐσίαν καί . . . τὸν αἰσθητὸν
οὐρανόν.

[l] The Arm. verb is sing.

[m] ἐν τοῖς ἐσωτέροις μυχοῖς vel sim., i.e. in the inner sanctuary
or Holy of Holies.

[n] ἀόρατα καὶ νοητά.

96. (Ex. xxvi. 36) Why does He call the outer (hanging) [a] ' a covering " and not " a veil," as in the case of the inner one ? [b]

Since those things which are within (the sanctuary) incline toward the nature of incorporeal things,[c] which is winged and upward-tending, their substance [d] stands near to God. Now the veil is brought in (as derived) from " spreading wings." [e] In the second place, moreover, it has propinquity to the sense-perceptible things outside,[f] and is rightly (called) " a covering," for the sense-perceptible hardly ever tends toward flying upward, since it is indeed less winged than incorporeal things, and in the same manner as that which is covered,[g] it has an unclear comprehension.[h] And may (this) not be because every-

---

[a] *i.e.* the hanging at the entrance to the sanctuary or " holy place " contrasted with the hanging at the entrance to the Holy of Holies. In *De Vita Mosis* ii. 87 Philo calls the former κάλυμμα, while LXX calls it ἐπίσπαστρον and uses κάλυμμα for the hanging at the entrance to the court of the tabernacle. The Heb., however, uses the same word, *māsāk*, for the hanging at the entrance to the tabernacle as well as for that at the entrance to the court (Ex. xxvii. 16). The various lists may be seen in this scheme :

1. Hanging at Entrance to Holy of Holies

| Heb. *pārōket* | LXX καταπέτασμα | Philo καταπέτασμα |

2. Hanging at Entrance to Tabernacle

| Heb. *māsāk* | LXX ἐπίσπαστρον | Philo (*De Vita Mosis*) κάλυμμα |

3. Hanging at Entrance to Court

| Heb. *māsāk* | LXX κάλυμμα | Philo (*De Vita Mosis*) ποικίλον ὕφασμα |

[b] LXX καὶ ποιήσεις ἐπίσπαστρον (*v.l.*, following Heb., adds τῇ θύρᾳ τῆς σκηνῆς) ἐξ ὑακίνθου κτλ.
[c] πρὸς τὴν φύσιν τὴν τῶν ἀσωμάτων.   [d] ἡ οὐσία.
[e] Philo plays on the resemblance between καταπέτασμα and καταπετᾶσθαι *vel sim.*
[f] τοῖς ἔξωθεν αἰσθητοῖς.   [g] Or " concealed."
[h] ἄδηλον κατάληψιν, *i.e.* it is not clearly apprehended.

thing sense-perceptible is experienced [a] through sense-perception, and sense-perception is unstable and related to false belief,[b] while the intelligible (is related) to reason,[c] and the mind [d] is inerrant and a friend of knowledge ? [e]

97. (Ex. xxvi. 37) Why is the " covering " placed upon five columns ? [f]

Most excellently and carefully [g] has He assigned the pentad to the second covering [h] since this part (of the tabernacle) looks toward sense-perceptible substance.[i] For the pentad is the number of the senses.[j] But to the former and inner (hanging [k] He has assigned) the tetrad, as I have said,[l] because it touches incorporeal things,[m] and incorporeal things come to an end with the tetrad.[n]

98. (Ex. xxvii. 1a) Why does He call the altar *thysias-tērion* ? [o]

---

[a] Lit. " receives experience ": Aucher " probationem (*vel*, experimentum) habet."   [b] ἀβεβαία καὶ ψευδεῖ δόξῃ συγγενής.

[c] λογισμῷ : Aucher " consiliis."   [d] ὁ νοῦς or ἡ διάνοια.

[e] φίλος ἐπιστήμης : Aucher " intelligentiae amantissimus."

[f] LXX καὶ ποιήσεις τῷ καταπετάσματι πέντε στύλους κτλ. The word καταπέτασμα in this verse refers to the same hanging as that called ἐπίσπαστρον in the preceding verse, see the notes to *QE* ii. 96. In *De Vita Mosis* ii. 82 Philo refers to the bronze bases of these columns as symbols of the five senses. For other Philonic references to the symbolism of the pentad see Staehle, pp. 31-32.   [g] παγκάλως καὶ ἐπιμελῶς.

[h] *i.e.* the hanging at the entrance to the tabernacle, contrasted with the veil (mentioned in the last sentence of this section) at the entrance to the Holy of Holies.

[i] τὴν αἰσθητὴν οὐσίαν.

[j] *Cf. De Vita Mosis* ii. 81 ἡ πεντὰς αἰσθήσεων ἀριθμός ἐστιν.

[k] *i.e.* the veil, see note [h].

[l] In *QE* ii. 93.   [m] τῶν ἀσωμάτων.

[n] This prob. means that the tetrad is the boundary between the ethereal and the sublunary regions, see *QE* ii. 93, 94.

[o] LXX καὶ ποιήσεις θυσιαστήριον ἐκ ξύλων ἀσήπτων κτλ. On the symbolism of this altar see *De Vita Mosis* ii. 106 and *De Spec. Leg.* i. 274.

QUESTIONS AND ANSWERS

Only this altar does not consume victims but preserves them.[a] For the flesh is consumed by fire but the holiness of the sacrifice remains, for sacrifice is not flesh but the pure and unstained life of a holy (person).[b]

*99. (Ex. xxvii. 1b) Why was the altar quadrangular,[c] and its length five cubits and its breadth equal ? [d]

(This is) because it is made for sense-perceptible and bloody (sacrifices), and the pentad is the number of the sense-perceptible class,[e] as I have said.[f] In the second place, it has equal length and breadth because all the sacrificial victims which are offered by the heart of a pious mind [g] ought to be equal, whether one offers a hundred bulls or brings (merely) roasted wheat. For the Deity does not like wealth nor does He turn away from poverty.[h] In the third place, the quadrangle [i] is a symbol of the fact that he who offers a sacrifice should stand firm in all respects [j] and in no way be deficient or lame in soul but with

---

[a] Philo fancifully etymologizes θυσιαστήριον as a compound of θυσίας " sacrificial victims " and τηρεῖν " to preserve," cf. De Vita Mosis ii. 106 τὸν δ' ἐν ὑπαίθρῳ βωμὸν εἴωθε καλεῖν θυσιαστήριον ὡσανεὶ τηρητικὸν καὶ φυλακτικὸν ὄντα θυσιῶν τὸν ἀναλωτικόν.

[b] Cf. ibid. αἰνιττόμενος οὐ τὰ μέλη καὶ τὰ μέρη τῶν ἱερουργουμένων, ἅπερ δαπανᾶσθαι πυρὶ πέφυκεν, ἀλλὰ τὴν προαίρεσιν τοῦ προσφέροντος.

[c] i.e. with a square top.

[d] lxx πέντε πήχεων τὸ μῆκος καὶ πέντε πήχεων τὸ εὖρος· τετράγωνον ἔσται τὸ θυσιαστήριον κτλ.

[e] τοῦ αἰσθητοῦ γένους : Aucher " sensibilis generationis " (l. " generis ").

[f] In QE ii. 97.

[g] The Arm. lit. = ὑπὸ καρδίας νοῦ (or διανοίας) εὐσεβοῦς.

[h] So the Greek frag. (which begins and ends with this sentence), οὔτε πλοῦτον ἀσπάζεται τὸ θεῖον οὔτε πενίαν ἀποστρέφεται.

[i] Or " square."

[j] βέβαιον παντελῶς vel sim. : Aucher " constanter omnino."

sound and full reason should make a thank-offering of
those things which belong to a sound life.[a]

100. (Ex. xxvii. 1c) Why is the height of the altar three
cubits ?[b]

The literal meaning [c] (refers to) the service of the several
priests, that they may easily be able to perform their office
by standing on a firm base, hiding their bellies and the
things within their bellies, because of that many-headed
beast, desire,[d] and the farther [e] (part) around the heart,
because of anger, the counsellor [f] of evil,[g] that it may be [h]
superior to the head. And the head is the temple of the
mind,[i] in which firmly dwell thoughts [j] and the ministering
senses.[k] But as for the deeper meaning,[l] the triad is a
three-tiered, dense and full number,[m] having no emptiness
but filling up whatever is drawn apart [n] in the dyad. And

[a] Aucher renders the last clause somewhat freely, I think,
"sed integro plenoque consilio, recte tendente ad gratiarum
actionem."

[b] λxx καὶ τριῶν πήχεων τὸ ὕψος αὐτοῦ.   [c] τὸ ῥητόν.

[d] διὰ τὸ πολυκέφαλον θηρίον, τὴν ἐπιθυμίαν, cf. De Somniis
ii. 14, where ἡδονή is compared with "the many-headed
hydra" (cf. Plato, Rep. 588 c). In the present passage Philo
seems to mean that the altar is just high enough to conceal
the lower part of the priest's body.

[e] Lit. "farthest."

[f] The Arm. uses two words for "counsellor."

[g] Aucher "malum consiliarium."

[h] Apparently the original was "may not be."

[i] τοῦ νοῦ.   [j] λογισμοί: Aucher "consilia."

[k] αἱ ὑπηρέτιδες αἰσθήσεις, cf. De Vita Mosis ii. 81 αἴσθησις
. . . ἀνακάμπτει πρὸς νοῦν ὑπηρέτις οὖσα . . . αὐτοῦ.

[l] τὸ πρὸς διάνοιαν.

[m] τρίβολος (?) καὶ πυκνὸς καὶ πλήρης ἀριθμός: Aucher omits
the first adjective (ptc. in Arm.) in rendering, "condensus
plenusque numerus." For other mystical explanations of
the number 3 see Staehle, pp. 25-26.

[n] Aucher "discerptum." I suspect that the Arm. translator has here misinterpreted διαστατόν "having dimensions"
as "torn apart" or has confused διαστατόν with διάσπαστον.

QUESTIONS AND ANSWERS

so He symbolically indicates [a] the height of the soul which
sacrifices, thinking it right that this should be utterly and
completely [b] crowded and full, not having in itself any
desert-emptiness which might admit some evil or act of
passion.[c] But bear in mind that when the dimensions of
the altar are multiplied, (namely) five by five by three, the
number seventy-five is produced, concerning which something has been said before.[d]

101. (Ex. xxvii. 2) Why does the altar have horns not
attached from above [e] but united (to it) ? [f]

(This is) because it is not proper to sacrifice any of those
(animals) which do not have horns, neither those which are
offerings nor anything else.[g] Accordingly, those which
are to be offered as sacrifices are the following three (kinds):
the sheep, the ox and the goat. But beside these there are
seven other (kinds permitted) for food : gazelle, deer, wild
goat, buffalo, white-rumped antelope, oryx and giraffe [h] ;

---

[a] συμβολικῶς αἰνίττεται.

[b] πᾶσαν διὰ πάντων. [c] πάθους.

[d] This may be a reference to Philo's lost book Περὶ Ἀριθμῶν,
since there seems to be no reference to the number 75 either
in the *Quaestiones* or in the extant Greek works of Philo.

[e] Aucher " supercusa."

[f] lxx καὶ ποιήσεις τὰ κέρατα ἐπὶ τῶν τεσσάρων γωνιῶν· ἐξ
αὐτοῦ ἔσται τὰ κέρατα, καὶ καλύψεις αὐτὰ χαλκῷ. Philo stresses
the words ἐξ αὐτοῦ and takes them to mean that the horns, as
it were, grow out of the altar, see the last sentence of this
section.

[g] The syntax of the last clause is not clear : Aucher " nec
sacrificare neque alio modo offerre."

[h] δορκάς, ἔλαφος, τραγέλαφος, βούβαλος, πύγαργος, ὄρυξ,
καμηλοπάρδαλις. This list is based upon Deut. xiv. 5, which
names the same animals in slightly different order. In *De
Spec. Leg.* iv. 105 Philo gives a list of ten kinds of animals
(quadrupeds) permitted as food, consisting of the above seven
plus the three kinds mentioned above (also in Deut. xiv. 4)
as sacrificial animals, or rather the young males, the lamb,
calf and kid.

148

each of these has horns. For He wishes to specify ª those (animals to be used) for food, for even though they are not to be offered as sacrifices, still they are similar to those which are to be sacrificed. Wherefore those who use them for need ᵇ will not offer anything opposed to or unworthy of or alien to a sacrifice. In the second place, the horns (of the altar) incline and face toward the four sides of the world, toward the east, toward the west, toward the south and toward the Dipper,ᶜ for it is proper that those who are in all parts (of the world) should all altogether bring their first-fruits and new (offerings) to this one altar, and sacrifice victims to God, the Father of the world. In the third place, (this is said) symbolically,ᵈ for in place of defensive weapons He has given a crop of horns to animals which grow horns. Just as the (animals) to be sacrificed, (namely) the ram, the ox and the goat,ᵉ repel their enemies with their horns, so also did He wish to rebuke the impious ᶠ who presume to offer sacrifices, by teaching that the divine Logos ᵍ opposes and repels the enemies of truth, goring every soul as if with horns and showing up in their nakedness its unclean and unworthy deeds, which a little while before it had been concealing. For these reasons the horns are not to be placed upon (the altar) from outside but by His command are to be united to the altar itself to extend it,ʰ since sacrificial animals have their horns growing out of themselves.

102. (Ex. xxvii. 3) Why does He command all the vessels of the altar to be made of bronze ? ⁱ

ª Aucher " distinguere."
ᵇ Aucher inadvertently omits the words " for need " in his rendering.　　ᶜ *i.e.* the north.　　ᵈ συμβολικῶς.
ᵉ Or " the calf and the kid " : Aucher " taurus et hircus." Philo uses the name of the young animal interchangeably with that of the full-grown animal.
ᶠ τοὺς ἀσεβεῖς.
ᵍ ὁ θεῖος λόγος : Aucher " divinum verbum."
ʰ See note *f* on p. 148.
ⁱ LXX (end of verse) καὶ πάντα τὰ σκεύη αὐτοῦ ποιήσεις χαλκᾶ.

The altar is an altar of bloody offerings,[a] for men give
thanks both by sacrificing victims and (by making) offerings
of first fruits; and they offer new (portions) of grain
together with fine flour,[b] and offerings of wine with oil,
in which the fine flour is dipped and mixed,[c] and with a
basket of fruit. And all these are of the species [d] of bronze
and iron.[e] For gold belongs to incorporeal and intelligible
things,[f] while silver belongs to the sense-perceptible
heaven,[g] but second bronze [h] belongs to things of earth,
where wars are made. For among the ancients bronze
was the material of weapons of war. Homer indeed shows
this in (his poem about) the Trojan war, introducing
(characters) who used weapons of bronze before there was
iron.

103. (Ex. xxvii. 20) ‘ Why did He command that the

[a] θυσιαστήριον ἐναίμων. Here the Arm. uses two different
words for " altar," seḷan and bagin, both of which sometimes
render βωμός, sometimes θυσιαστήριον; in addition, seḷan
sometimes renders τράπεζα. In Philo's passages on the altar
of the Tabernacle in QE ii. 98 ff. the Arm. translator uses bagin
as the more generic term, and seḷan to designate the altar of
the Tabernacle.

[b] σεμιδάλει.

[c] Aucher " cui farina tincta immiscetur."

[d] τοῦ γένους.

[e] The Arm. glossator comments, " from where fruits are
produced, (namely) the earth, from there come iron and
bronze."

[f] ἐν ἀσωμάτοις καὶ νοητοῖς. On the cosmic symbolism of
gold see QE ii. 69, 73.

[g] κατὰ τὸν αἰσθητὸν οὐρανόν.

[h] I suspect that erkrord, the Arm. word for " second," is
here a scribal error for erkat‘ " iron." The original was
probably " bronze and iron." The Arm. glossator adds
" bronze is second to iron."

[i] The verses of Ex. xxvii (4-19) not commented on by
Philo in this work describe the fittings of the altar and hang-
ings of the pillars and gate of the tabernacle's court.

oil in the lamps be (made) from olives and without sediment ? [a]

He has ordained that it is not proper to bring near to the holy (place) anything foreign,[b] for He has considered as foreign the manufacture of oil [c] of other kinds, (namely) from sesame, from the date, from the nut or the like. Therefore, as the name shows,[d] the (oil made) from olives is appropriate and natural.[e] For the name *elaion* is given to every species (of oil), this being derived from *elaia*, and this conveys the true sense.[f] In the second place, every other (kind), although adulterated [g] with a mixture of other (ingredients) and crushed, is put into the class of olive-oil, whereas olive-oil is distinct by itself, for the olive, when pressed, distils (oil), just as the fruit of the vine makes wine without any admixture. Excellent, moreover, is (His saying) " without sediment " and that the preparation is to be of pure and refined material, for it was fitting and appropriate that everything in the holy (place) should be luminous and shining, especially the oil prepared for the light, since it was of a very pure substance and, in a way,[h] without sediment. For what among existing things can be found more refined and luminous than light ? What is more, it illuminates other things, but first of all itself. There you have the literal meaning.[i] But the symbolical meaning [j] of light is wisdom,[k] through which all things

---

[a] LXX καὶ σὺ σύνταξον τοῖς υἱοῖς Ἰσραήλ, καὶ λαβέτωσάν σοι ἔλαιον ἐξ ἐλαιῶν ἄτρυγον καθαρὸν (Heb. " pure olive-oil ") κεκομμένον εἰς φῶς καῦσαι ἵνα κάηται λύχνος διὰ παντός.

[b] The negative seems to be misplaced in the Arm. which reads lit. " anything foreign not has He ordained that it is proper, etc." : Aucher " alienum quidquam non ordinavit, etc." [c] τὴν ἐλαιουργίαν.

[d] ἔλαιον " oil " from ἐλαία " olive," as Philo explains in the next sentence. [e] οἰκεῖον καὶ κατὰ φύσιν.

[f] ὁ πρὸς ἀλήθειαν κυριολογεῖται.

[g] Arm. *pitaçeal* " being in need " is prob. to be emended to *pitakaçeal* " being adulterated " : Aucher " studiose usurpata."

[h] τρόπον τινά : Aucher " quasi."

[i] τὸ ῥητόν.   [j] τὸ συμβολικόν.   [k] σοφία.

QUESTIONS AND ANSWERS

in nature are known,[a] while olive-oil is the material and
preparation of wisdom. Such are numbers, geometry,
musical art, school studies,[b] the pursuit of philosophy[c]
and, in first place, the discipline of the virtuous man,[d] and
these have nothing like sediment in them.

104. (Ex. xxvii. 21c)[e] Why does He command that the
lamps burn " from evening until morning "[f] ?
(He does so) not in order that they may provide light for
those who are within (the holy place)—for who was in the
holy (place) within the veil ?[g]—no one at all remained
within—, but because the lamps are symbols of the light-
bearing stars.[h] Now the stars shine from evening until
morning, serving in the necessary service of the whole
world.[i] And He thought it fitting to make the lamps bear
a resemblance to the chorus of heavenly stars from evening
until morning.[j]

*105. (Ex. xxvii. 21b)[k] Why does He command Aaron
and his sons to light the lamps ?[l]

[a] πάντα γιγνώσκεται ὅσα ἐν τῇ φύσει ἐστί.
[b] τὰ ἐγκύκλια, cf. QG iii. 19, 21.
[c] ἡ τῆς φιλοσοφίας σπουδή.
[d] ἡ τοῦ σπουδαίου παιδεία vel sim.: Aucher " honesta dis-
ciplina."
[e] According to the order of the three parts of vs. 21 in
LXX and Heb., § 104 should come after § 105, and the latter
after § 106.
[f] LXX καύσει . . . ἀφ᾽ ἑσπέρας ἕως πρωῒ ἐναντίον κυρίου.
[g] i.e. within the Holy of Holies, see below, § 106.
[h] τῶν φωσφόρων ἀστέρων εἰσὶν οἱ λύχνοι σύμβολα.
[i] τὴν ἀναγκαίαν ὑπηρεσίαν τὴν τοῦ παντὸς κόσμου. Philo uses
the phrase ἀναγκαία ὑπηρεσία in De Sacr. Abelis 98 and Quod
Omnis Probus 142.
[j] The above is one of three allegorical explanations of the
verse given in De Spec. Leg. i. 296-298.
[k] This section belongs after § 106 and before § 104, see
note e above.
[l] LXX καύσει (Heb. " shall put in order ") αὐτὸν ᾿Ααρὼν καὶ
οἱ υἱοὶ αὐτοῦ.

152

He represented [a] Aaron as one possessed by God and by the prophetic spirit,[b] (thereby) rebuking and shaming [c] the indolence [d] of the high priests after him, who because of negligence entrusted the performance of the holy service to second and third (assistants),[e] since they themselves did not feel inexpressible pleasure in carrying out all (forms) of the ministerial service. For there is nothing more delightful or pleasant or seemly or noble [f] than to be a servant to God, which surpasses the greatest kingship.[g] And it seems to me that the early kings were at the same time high priests who by their acts showed that those who rule over others should themselves be servants in ministering to God.[h]

106. (Ex. xxvii. 21a) [i] Why does He say that they shall

[a] Lit. " accepted " : Aucher " suscepit." Apparently the Arm. translator has confused παραδεικνύναι with παραδέχεσθαι.

[b] ἐνθουσιῶντα (or ἐπιθειάζοντα) καὶ μετὰ τοῦ προφητικοῦ πνεύματος.

[c] Aucher renders the two participles by the single word " reprehendens."

[d] τὸν ὄκνον: Aucher " negligentiam."

[e] Cf. Wolfson, Philo, ii. p. 344 " The reference is undoubtedly to the actual practice in the Temple of Jerusalem, as Philo himself observed it there, of assigning the task of lighting the perpetual lamp to one of the subordinate priests by means of lots." Wolfson cites Mishnah, Tamid iii. 1, 9 and Yoma ii. 3.

[f] The four Arm. adjectives are prob. doublets of the two Greek ones, see next note.

[g] The Greek frag., which begins here, reads slightly more briefly οὐδὲν οὔτε ἥδιον οὔτε σεμνότερον ἢ θεῷ δουλεύειν, ὃ καὶ τὴν μεγίστην βασιλείαν ὑπερβάλλει.

[h] Slightly different (see end of this note) is the reading of the last part of the Greek frag., καί μοι δοκοῦσιν οἱ πρῶτοι βασιλεῖς ἅμα καὶ ἀρχιερεῖς γενέσθαι, δηλοῦντες ἔργοις ὅτι χρὴ τοὺς τῶν ἄλλων δεσπόζοντας δουλεύειν τοῖς λατρεύουσι θεῷ. The Arm. translator apparently read δουλεύειν λατρεύοντας.

[i] This section should come before § 105 and § 104, see notes to the latter.

153

light the lamps " outside the veil which is over the covenant " ? [a]

May it not be because the things within (the veil) were incorporeal and intelligible [b] and had no need of sense-perceptible light,[c] for they were themselves their own light and more luminous stars than those which are seen ? But the one within the veil He calls " of testimony," [d] symbolically indicating [e] that the covenant of God is the only true one, and that those which (men) write in testaments [f] are permanent and secure in themselves and are similar.[g] And this is the measure of all things in common, the ideas and intelligible forms.[h] Now external things are also secure but still not in the same way, since they have a sense-perceptible and changeable nature and do not have

---

[a] LXX ἐν τῇ σκηνῇ τοῦ μαρτυρίου (Heb. " of meeting ") ἔξωθεν τοῦ καταπετάσματος τοῦ ἐπὶ τῆς διαθήκης (" the testimony ") καύσει κτλ. Scripture here refers to the veil between " the holy place " and the Holy of Holies in which " the ark of testimony " (i.e. the covenant) stood. In De Spec. Leg. i. 296 Philo, in dealing with this verse, speaks of the lampstand being " within " (εἴσω) the veil. If the text there is sound, it would seem that he thinks of two lampstands, one within the veil, the other outside, but see below, note d.

[b] ἀσώματα καὶ νοητά.   [c] αἰσθητοῦ φωτός.

[d] The syntax and meaning are obscure : Aucher " quod autem internum velum testamonii vocat." Among other things it is not clear whether Philo here refers to another lampstand within the veil or to the ark within the veil. That he refers to the veil as a " veil of testimony " seems rather doubtful.

[e] συμβολικῶς αἰνιττόμενος.

[f] The word διαθήκη has in Scripture the meaning " covenant " as well as the secular meaning " testament."

[g] i.e. similar to the covenant associated with the ark in the Holy of Holies.

[h] The last two nouns are nom. plurals but their syntactic relation to the preceding nouns is not clear. The general idea, however, seems to be that all the parts of the world are kept in order by a sort of covenant, which is the work of the Logos, see, e.g., QE ii. 90.

permanence in themselves as do incorporeal things, and
they make use of external bonds, some of which are in
themselves altogether eternal, but others only dissolve
during long periods.

*107. (Ex. xxviii. 2) Why does He say that they shall
make a sacred stole ^a for the high priest " for honour and
glory ^b " ^c ?

These statements are (made) about the radiant and
sumptuous ankle-length stole,^d not about the linen (garment),^e for the latter is made not " for honour and glory "
but for still greater and more perfect honour and glory.
For he ^f wears it when he enters the innermost Holy of
Holies, whereas (he wears) the ankle-length (garment)
when he performs the service outside in the manner of
the sense-perceptible world ^g before man, among whom
precious things ^h are considered matters of glory. But
those things which are in truth (glorious), being unkempt
and unbeautified and adorned (only) by nature, are
honoured by the Father. But may it not be that " honour "
is to be distinguished from " glory " ? For glory is the

---

^a Philo here as elsewhere (*e.g. De Ebrietate* 85) uses στολή
in the generic sense of " garment," as does LXX.

^b Farther on in this section Philo interprets τιμή as
" price " rather than " honour," and δόξα as " opinion "
rather than " glory."

^c LXX καὶ ποιήσεις στολὴν ἁγίαν Ἀαρὼν τῷ ἀδελφῷ σου εἰς
τιμὴν καὶ δόξαν. Philo treats the cosmic symbolism of the
high priest's garments at some length (and somewhat differently) in *De Vita Mosis* ii. 109-135 and *De Spec. Leg.* i. 84-
97.

^d *i.e.* the robe which Philo calls ὑποδύτης in *De Vita Mosis*
ii. 109, and ποδήρης χιτών in *De Spec. Leg.* i. 85, cf. Ex. xxviii.
4 where LXX has ποδήρη χιτῶνα κοσυμβωτόν.

^e *i.e.* the χιτὼν λινοῦς, cf. *De Spec. Leg.* i. 84.

^f *i.e.* the high priest.

^g κατὰ τὸν αἰσθητὸν κόσμον (possibly, however, κόσμον
here = " array ").

^h τίμια, meaning both " honoured " and " expensive."

being praised by men, while honour is the being received
among those who are truly [a] most honourable ; and most
honourable are divine matters,[b] so that when the high
priest is arrayed in the ankle-length (garment), there is
a participation [c] in two things, (namely) in proud dignity
before God,[d] and in a favourable reception [e] among men.
That is the literal meaning.[f] But this is the deeper meaning.[g] The ankle-length (garment) is a symbol [h] of that
which is woven of many and various things. But " glory,"[i]
as the ancient saying has it, is false opinion, and insecure
opinion is by itself alone incomplete.[j] But if opinion is
mixed with truth, it becomes true opinion,[k] being converted to honourableness.[l] Accordingly, He wishes to
show that the life of the wicked man belongs to opinion,
being dominated by and dependent upon [m] false opinion,
while (the life) of the wise man and true high priest [n] is
honourable because it is productive of truth, by which he
changes and adapts falsehood to his better nature.[o]

---

[a] ὄντως.

[b] θεῖα πράγματα vel sim.

[c] κοινωνία.

[d] Aucher " venerationis apud Deum gloriosae." The exact
meaning is not clear, partly because the Arm. adj. ꭓꭉoꭓtali,
here rendered " proud," usually means " boastful " or
" arrogant," partly because the force of the prep. aꭉ, here
rendered " before," is uncertain. However, the original of
the last three words was prob. τῆς περὶ θεὸν σεμνότητος.

[e] Aucher " securae susceptionis."

[f] τὸ ῥητόν.

[g] τὸ πρὸς διάνοιαν.

[h] σύμβολον.

[i] δόξα, here meaning " opinion."

[j] The Greek frag., consisting of only one sentence, reads
more briefly δόξα, ὡς ὁ παλαιὸς λόγος, ψευδής ἐστι ὑπόληψις καὶ
δόκησις ἀβέβαιος.

[k] ἀληθὴς δόξα (or ὑπόληψις) : Aucher " certa opinio."

[l] τιμιότητα : Aucher " honorabile (vel, pretiosum)."

[m] Aucher " pendens ac prehendens."

[n] τοῦ σοφοῦ καὶ ὄντως ἀρχιερέως.

[o] εἰς τὴν βελτίονα φύσιν vel sim.

108. (Ex. xxviii. 7) *a* Why are the two shoulder-pieces,*b* which are joined together, attached in two parts ? *c*

The shoulder-pieces *d* designate serious labours,*e* for they are a part of the sacred garment, and sacred things are serious.*f* And there are two *g* forms of labour : one is the desire of pleasing *h* God, and of piety *i* ; the other is being beneficent to men, which is called kindness and love of man.*j* He therefore exhorts (us) to devote ourselves to every labour and to put our shoulders to it.*k* The theologian *l* wishes (these) two things to be known in order that what has been said in another place *m* may be confirmed by deeds, (namely) " With God thou wast strong

a In vss. 3-6 (on which see *De Vita Mosis* ii. 111-126, of which *QE* ii. 108 is only a partial parallel) Scripture names the high priest's garments and specifies the colours of the ephod.

b *i.e.* of the ephod. LXX uses the word ἐπωμίς both of the ephod and of each shoulder-piece, while Heb. uses a different word for the latter (kātēph, lit. " shoulder "). Philo seems to be following Heb. in *De Vita Mosis* ii. 111-112, where he calls the ephod ἐπωμίς, and the shoulder-pieces ἀκρώμια, see below, note *d*.

c LXX δύο ἐπωμίδες συνέχουσαι ἔσονται αὐτῷ ἑτέρα τὴν ἑτέραν, ἐπὶ τοῖς δυσὶ μέρεσιν (Heb. " ends " : A.V. " edges ") ἐξηρτισμέναι.

d Since the Arm. noun grapank', a plural form, is followed by the verb in the singular number, it is probable that it renders the Greek neuter plural ἀκρώμια, see above, note *b*.

e Prob. ἔργα σπουδαῖα : Aucher " labores honestos."

f The two Arm. adjectives used here prob. render the single Greek adj. σπουδαῖα : Aucher " honesta et studium merentia."

g Lit. " two twofold."

h Or " serving " : Aucher " placitum."

i εὐσεβείας.

j χρηστότης καὶ φιλανθρωπία.

k A play on ἐπωμίς and ἐπ' ὤμοις φέρειν vel sim., cf. De Vita Mosis ii. 130 τὸν γὰρ ὦμον ἐνεργείας καὶ πράξεως ποιεῖται σύμβολον.

l ὁ θεολόγος, *i.e.* Moses.

m *i.e.* of Scripture.

and with men thou shalt have power." [a] But of the two
shoulder-pieces one must be on the right, and the other
on the left. Now the one on the right was given its place
for the sake of pleasing God—a labour worthy of zeal,
while that on the left (was given its place) for the sake of
helpfulness to men and for kindness of thought concerning
them. [b]

109. (Ex. xxviii. 9-12) What are the two emerald stones,
in which are inscribed the names of the twelve patriarchs ? [c]

In each of them are six impressions, [d] of the two hemispheres, [e] of that above the earth and of that below the
earth. As evidence of this statement there are three
things to cite. One is their shape, for the stones are round,
just as the hemispheres are. The second is their colour,
for the emerald is similar to the heaven in colour. The
third is the number (of the names) engraved in them, for
in each of the hemispheres there happen to be six zodiacal
signs, [f] some of them above the earth, and some below the
earth, (and) the halves of the zodiac [g] give light. And
rightly did He call the inscribing " impressions," [h] for all
the immobile stars in the zodiac are types and type-

---

[a] Gen. xxxii. 29 (explaining the name " Israel "), ἐνίσχυσας
μετὰ θεοῦ καὶ μετὰ ἀνθρώπων δυνατός (Heb. " thou hast striven
with God and with men, and thou hast prevailed ").

[b] Aucher " et suavitatem apud istos opinionis (vel, aesti-
mationis)."

[c] LXX καὶ λήμψῃ τοὺς δύο λίθους, λίθους σμαράγδου (A.V.
" two onyx stones "), καὶ γλύψεις ἐν αὐτοῖς τὰ ὀνόματα τῶν
υἱῶν Ἰσραήλ. ἐξ ὀνόματα ἐπὶ τὸν λίθον τὸν ἕνα καὶ τὰ ἐξ ὀνόματα
τὰ λοιπὰ ἐπὶ τὸν λίθον τὸν δεύτερον . . . γλύμμα σφραγῖδος δια-
γλύψεις τοὺς δύο λίθους, κτλ.

[d] σφραγῖδες : Aucher " sigilli."

[e] τῶν δυοῖν ἡμισφαιρίων, symbolized by the two sets of six
names. The threefold cosmic symbolism of the two stones
is discussed by Philo in De Vita Mosis ii. 122-123 and more
briefly in Quis Rer. Div. Heres 176.

[f] ζώδια.   [g] τοῦ ζωοφόρου.

[h] Referring to LXX γλύμμα σφραγῖδος.

EXODUS, BOOK II

impressions,[a] while the sublunary (bodies) [b] are in movement.

110. (Ex. xxviii. 15) [c] What is the Logeion,[d] and why does He call it " of judgments," and why is the Logeion made after the texture of the shoulder-piece [e] ? [f]

As its very name shows, it is a symbol of *logos*.[g] And *logos* is double (in meaning) ; one (meaning) is that found in natural thoughts,[h] and the other is " utterance." [i] And it is the principle [j] of judgments, since everything is determined and distinguished by *logos*—intelligible things [k] by that (*logos*) which is in natural thoughts, and sounds by (the *logos* of) differentiated speech.[l] Most

---

[a] The Arm. lit.=τύποι καὶ τυπωθεῖσαι σφραγῖδες : Aucher " normae ac typi sunt ut sigilli."   [b] τὰ μετὰ σελήνην.

[c] In vss. 13-14, passed over here, Scripture mentions the gold clasps (A.V. " ouches ") and gold chains attached to the high priest's garment.

[d] So Philo elsewhere (see below) spells LXX λόγιον.

[e] *i.e.* the ephod ; the Arm. translator has taken LXX ἐπωμίς in the sense of " shoulder-piece " (of the ephod) instead of the ephod itself, see *QE* ii. 108, note b.

[f] LXX καὶ ποιήσεις λόγιον τῶν κρίσεων (Heb. " ornament (?) of judgment " ; A.V. " breastplate of judgment "), ἔργον ποικιλτοῦ, κατὰ τὸν ῥυθμὸν (Heb. " work " or " workmanship ") τῆς ἐπωμίδος (Heb. " ephod ") ποιήσεις αὐτό· ἐκ χρυσίου καὶ ὑακίνθου, κτλ. Philo allegorizes the Logeion similarly in *De Vita Mosis* ii. 112-115, 127-130, *cf. De Spec. Leg.* i. 87-88 (see also *QE* ii. 112-114).

[g] λόγου σύμβολον, *cf. De Spec. Leg.* i. 88 καλεῖται λογεῖον ἐτύμως ἐπειδὴ τὰ ἐν οὐρανῷ πάντα λόγοις καὶ ἀναλογίαις δεδημιούργηται.

[h] ἐν τοῖς τῆς φύσεως λογισμοῖς *vel sim.* ; Aucher " in naturae consiliis." In *De Vita Mosis* ii. 128 Philo speaks of ὁ τῆς φύσεως λόγος. The reference is to the λόγος ἐνδιάθετος, as the Stoics called thinking or reason.

[i] Another Stoic term, the λόγος προφορικός or speech, often referred to by Philo. Both terms occur in the parallel, *De Vita Mosis* ii. 129.

[j] λόγος again : Aucher " verbum."   [k] τὰ νοητά.

[l] Aucher " vocalia autem sermone privato."

159

excellently, moreover, is its workmanship said to be " after the texture of the shoulder-piece," for one ought to form and adorn one's words by deeds (as if) fitting them together,[a] for everything without workmanship [b] is imperfect and lame.

111. (Ex. xxviii. 16) Why is the Logeion [c] square and twofold and a span [d] in length and a span in breadth ? [e]

The Logeion is twofold, in the first place because it has two *logoi* [f] ; one, which has the force of a spring, is in natural thoughts, and the other, (namely) utterance, is an effluence thereof.[g] And the latter is twofold, inclining partly to truth and partly to falsehood. And in the second place, (it is twofold) because the mind sees two (kinds of object), divine and mortal. And the voice [h] attempts to be adorned by these two,[i] in interpreting both of them. And the Logeion is square symbolically,[j] for the *logos* should be stable and immobile in all respects and not

---

[a] Aucher " texendo." Philo means that words and deeds are to be fitted together like threads in a texture.

[b] Lit. " working."

[c] *i.e.* the high priest's " breastplate of judgment," see *QE* ii. 110.

[d] Arm. *tʻiz* renders both σπιθαμή (as here in LXX) and παλαστή, which is one-third of the σπιθαμή, see notes b and c on p. 161.

[e] LXX τετράγωνον ἔσται, διπλοῦν· σπιθαμῆς τὸ μῆκος αὐτοῦ καὶ σπιθαμῆς τὸ εὖρος. The symbolism of the breastplate is discussed by Philo, in part as here, in *De Vita Mosis* ii. 127-130.

[f] *i.e.* the λόγος ἐνδιάθετος (reason) and the λόγος προφορικός (speech), see next note.

[g] Cf. *De Vita Mosis* ii. 127 ὁ μὲν οἷά τις πηγή, ὁ δὲ γεγονὼς ἀπ' ἐκείνου ῥέων. The phrase " in natural thoughts " corresponds to ὁ τῆς φύσεως λόγος in *De Vita Mosis* ii. 127-129. *cf. QE* ii. 110.　　　　　　　　　　　[h] Or " speech."

[i] Aucher " et vox his duabus exornari nititur." The sense is not clear, but the original prob. meant that speech attempts to be in harmony with nature and the mind.

[j] συμβολικῶς.

waver,[a] whether in thought or in interpreting by tongue
and mouth. And its length is a span and its breadth a
span [b] for the reason that the span is a sixth part of a
cubit,[c] for the cubit is of six spans, so that it is one-sixth
in length and breadth. And this symbol gives this kind
of appearance.[d] And the mind [e] is one and is a uniter of
different intelligibles,[f] as if a harmony of these same things.
And the uttered *logos* [g] is one, and again is similarly the
uniter of different intelligibles, (namely) of letters into
syllables, of syllables into words, and of many words into
compositions and long discourses.[h] For what is vastly and
diffusely extended in these is held together by natural
bonds.[i] And the mind too has length and breadth, for
it is extended and prolonged to all intelligibles in apprehension, just as speech [j] (has) both (dimensions), for this
too is amplified in length and breadth in accordance with
the words uttered.[k]

---

[a] *Cf. De Vita Mosis* ii. 128 σχῆμα δ' ἀπένειμεν ὁ τεχνίτης
τετράγωνον τῷ λογείῳ, πάνυ καλῶς αἰνιττόμενος ὡς χρὴ καὶ τὸν
τῆς φύσεως λόγον καὶ τὸν τοῦ ἀνθρώπου βεβηκέναι πάντῃ καὶ κατὰ
μηδ' ὁτιοῦν κραδαίνεσθαι.

[b] Arm. k'il, like t'iz (see note d on p. 160), renders both
σπιθαμή and παλαστή.

[c] Philo must here be using σπιθαμή as the equivalent of
παλαστή, unless he is following a system of measurement
different from the one used by other Greek writers. The
latter commonly reckons the cubit (πῆχυς) as = six palms
(παλασταί) and twenty-four fingers (δάκτυλοι), whereas the
span (σπιθαμή) = twelve fingers. Thus it is the palm, not the
span, which is one-sixth of a cubit.

[d] Aucher " symbolum autem hujusmodi praestat argu-
mentum." The sense is not clear.   [e] ὁ νοῦς.

[f] ἑνωτικὸς διαφόρων νοητῶν.

[g] ὁ προφορικὸς λόγος.

[h] στοιχείων . . . συλλαβῶν . . . λέξεων εἰς συνθέσεις καὶ
μακρολογίας.

[i] φυσικοῖς ἁρμόττεται δεσμοῖς : Aucher " per naturalia
adaptatur ligamina."   [j] λόγος.

[k] κατὰ τοὺς προφορικοὺς λόγους *vel sim.* Aucher renders
freely, " secundum sermonum varietatem atque vastitatem."

161

QUESTIONS AND ANSWERS

112. (Ex. xxviii. 17-20a) Why is there on the Logeion [a] a texture [b] of four rows, and in each row are three (precious) stones placed ? [c]

The four rows are an indication of the four seasons of the year,[d] each of which consists of an element.[e] And the three stones are symbolically [f] three months, into which each season is divided.[g] For the zodiac consists of twelve constellations [h] divided into four (seasons) of the year, through which the sun revolves and produces the seasons of the year through the three constellations.[i] And there is a " texture " since all the seasons happen to hasten to one end, inasmuch as the fullness of all (the seasons), which are woven together, is summed up [j] in the year. The passage also contains a certain description of character.[k] Each of the four virtues [l] consists of an element of three things,[m] (namely) habit, the thing had and having,[n] just as is the case with the senses,[o] for example, sight and the

---

[a] *i.e.* the high priest's " breastplate of judgment," see QE ii. 110.

[b] ὕφασμα, as in LXX (see next note) = Heb. " setting."

[c] LXX καὶ καθυφανεῖς ἐν αὐτῷ ὕφασμα κατάλιθον τετράστιχον, κτλ. (there follow the names of the twelve precious stones, three in each of the four rows). The passage is cited in *Leg. All.* i. 81-82, and explained partly as here, *i.e.* as symbolical of the zodiac, in *De Fuga* 184-185 and *De Vita Mosis* ii. 124-126.   [d] μήνυμα τῶν τεττάρων ἐτησίων ὡρῶν.

[e] ὧν ἑκάστη ⟨sc. ὥρα⟩ ἐκ στοιχείου συνέστη vel sim. : Aucher " quorum singula ⟨sc. tempora⟩ singula elementa sortita sunt." The " element " here refers to a moral element, see below.   [f] συμβολικῶς.

[g] Slightly emending the Arm. text, which reads " which are divided into the several seasons " and is so rendered by Aucher.   [h] ὁ γὰρ ζῳοφόρος συνέστη ἐκ δώδεκα ζῳδίων.

[i] *i.e.* of each season.

[j] κεφαλαιοῦται vel sim. : Aucher " reducitur."

[k] ἠθοποιίαν τινά, cf. QE ii. 76.

[l] ἀρετῶν.   [m] *i.e.* has three aspects.

[n] ἕξεως (in the sense of " state of being ") καὶ τοῦ ἐχομένου καὶ τοῦ ἔχειν : Aucher " habitudine, habendo et habere."

[o] αἱ αἰσθήσεις.

162

EXODUS, BOOK II

thing seen and seeing, and again, audition and the thing heard and hearing. And similarly (there is) knowledge [a] and the thing known and knowing, just as (there is) moderation [b] and the thing moderated and moderating. And again (there is) courage [c] and the thing courageously done and having courage, which is more commonly called " being manly." [d] The same applies to justice [e] and the just act and having justice, which is called " acting justly." [f]

113. (Ex. xxviii. 20b) Why is each of the rows [g] covered and bound with gold ? [h]

Thus it is with the four rows which make up [i] the annual seasons in the zodiac. [j] Each (row) has ether [k] around it, setting off the three [l] and, again, bringing them together

[a] Arm. *gitout'iun* usu. = γνῶσις or ἐπιστήμη, but here perhaps φρόνησις, which Philo usually includes among the four cardinal virtues, as enumerated by Plato and the Stoics. Aucher here renders, " scientia."

[b] σωφροσύνη. [c] ἀνδρεία.

[d] Perhaps ἀνδραγαθίζεσθαι : Aucher " fortificari."

[e] δικαιοσύνη.

[f] δικαιοπραγεῖν : Aucher " justificari (δικαιοπραγία, actio justa)."

[g] *i.e.* the four rows of precious stones in the high priest's " breastplate of judgment " (Logeion), each of which contained three stones.

[h] LXX περικεκαλυμμένα (*v.l.* περικεκλωσμένα) χρυσίῳ καὶ συνδεδεμένα ἐν (*v.l.* om. ἐν) χρυσίῳ, ἔστωσαν κατὰ στίχον αὐτῶν. Heb. reads more briefly " they shall be woven (*i.e.* " attached ") with gold to their settings."

[i] Lit. " complete ": Aucher " perficiunt."

[j] τὰς ἐτησίους ὥρας ἐν τῷ ζῳδιακῷ ⟨κύκλῳ⟩, *cf. De Vita Mosis* ii. 124-126, *QE* ii. 112 notes. [k] αἰθέρα.

[l] Aucher amplifies slightly in rendering, " distinguentem tres alios." " The three " seems to mean three constellations. Perhaps, however, it means the three divisions of the year, *cf. QG* iii. 3, where Philo counts the two equinoxes as one to make up, with the two solstices, " three cycles " of the sun each year.

163

with one another. For not only do those stars adhere to one another which are near the termination,[a] when a season terminates and the following one begins, but, as I have said, there is between them an intervening space and interval of clear and pure ether, which surrounds [b] the three and binds (them) with gold, in the likeness of which the ether is represented because of its precious substance.[c]

114. (Ex. xxviiii. 21) Why are the stones [d] named after the phylarchs,[e] having seal-engravings of their names ? [f]

Because the twelve stones are representations of the twelve animals which are in the zodiac,[g] and are a symbol [h] of the twelve phylarchs, whose names He cuts and engraves in them, wishing to make them stars [i] and, in a certain sense,[j] to apportion one constellation [k] to each, or rather (to make) each patriarch [l] himself become a constellation (and) heavenly image in order that the tribal leaders and patriarchs may not go about on the earth like mortals but

---

[a] πέρας *vel sim.* : Aucher " terminum." Here it seems to mean one of the seasonal divisions such as a solstice or equinox.

[b] Correcting the Arm. which lit.=" has around itself," see above.

[c] διὰ τὴν τιμίαν (*vel sim.*) οὐσίαν : Aucher " propter nobilem essentiam."

[d] *i.e.* the twelve precious stones of the high priest's breast-plate (the Logeion), representing the twelve tribes of Israel.

[e] ἐπώνυμοι τῶν φυλάρχων.

[f] LXX καὶ οἱ λίθοι ἔστωσαν ἐκ τῶν ὀνομάτων τῶν υἱῶν Ἰσραὴλ δέκα δύο (*v.l.* δώδεκα) κατὰ τὰ ὀνόματα (*v.l.* τὰς γενέσεις) αὐτῶν· γλυφαὶ σφραγίδων ἕκαστος (*v.l.* ἑκάστου) κατὰ τὸ ὄνομα ἔστωσαν εἰς δέκα δύο (*v.l.* δώδεκα) φυλάς.

[g] τῶν ἐν τῷ ζῳοφόρῳ.   [h] σύμβολον.

[i] ἀστροποιεῖν *vid.* (the Arm. is a factitive-denominative verb derived from *astl* = ἄστρον) : Aucher " stellas reddere."

[j] τρόπον τινά : Aucher " quasi."

[k] ζῴδιον : Aucher " signum."

[l] πατριάρχην.

become heavenly plants [a] and move about in the ether, being firmly established there. And He says that their names are "seals," [c] (that is) something unchangeable and unalterable, which always remains in the same likeness. For just as the seal, while stamping many substances with its designs, itself remains imperishable [d] and unchangeable and, while giving a share of its own possession of designs to many other (substances), is not at all affected by anything, [e] so also has He seen fit to immortalize each of the patriarchs as (an ideal) form [f] and make him eternal, so as not to be affected by any accident but, while changing and moving, to be confirmed in the virtues [g] which are similar to the tribe [h] and are apportioned to the (various) ranks of the nation.

115. (Ex. xxviii. 26b [Heb. 30b]) [i] Why is the Logeion, [j] on which were the names, [k] upon the breast of the high priest when he enters the sanctuary ? [l]

The breast is the place of the heart, and it is there that

[a] Cf. *Quod Deterius* 85 φυτὸν οὐράνιον ὁ θεὸς ἄνθρωπον εἰργάσατο.   [b] ἐν αἰθέρι.
[c] σφραγῖδες.   [d] ἄφθαρτος.
[e] *i.e.* is not affected by the material upon which it is pressed.
[f] ἀθανατίζειν . . . ὡς εἶδος (or ἰδέαν): Aucher " tamquam formam immortalitate donare."   [g] τὰς ἀρετάς.
[h] Aucher " quae imitantur tribum."
[i] This section belongs after § 116 according to the order of Scripture.
[j] The high priest's breastplate, see *QE* ii. 110 ff.
[k] Of the twelve tribes, engraved on the precious stones of the breastplate.
[l] LXX καὶ ἔσται ἐπὶ τοῦ στήθους (Heb. " heart ") Ἀαρὼν ὅταν εἰσπορεύηται εἰς τὸ ἅγιον ἐναντίον κυρίου (Heb. " in his entering before YHWH ") καὶ οἴσει Ἀαρὼν τὰς κρίσεις (Heb. " the judgment ") τῶν υἱῶν Ἰσραὴλ ἐπὶ τοῦ στήθους (Heb. " his heart ") ἐναντίον κυρίου διὰ παντός. Philo quotes this passage in part in *Leg. All.* iii. 118-119 (reading εἰσέρχηται for εἰσπορεύηται).

anger *a* dwells, and anger especially has need of the controlling and directing reason.*b* For when it *c* is left without a controller and director, it is borne hither and thither in confusion and tossed about as though by stormy waves, and overturns the entire soul like a ship without ballast,*d* the body being overturned with it. Moreover, it is with care and cautiousness that He says not that the Logeion is to be upon his breast always but (only) when he enters the sanctuary. For the sanctuary is the place of piety and holiness and every virtue,*e* and when the mind *f* reaches this, it altogether acquires perfect reason,*g* which controls and directs and seizes the reins so as to restrain the passions,*h* especially anger,*i* which is wont to be refractory toward it.

116. (Ex. xxviii. 26a [Heb. 30a]) *j* Why are the Revelation and Truth *k* placed upon the Logeion ? *l*

Because the reason *m* in it is twofold, one residing in thought, and the other uttered and revealed.*n* And

---

a θυμός.

b Aucher " rationis regentis et temporantis," *cf. Leg. All.* iii. 118 ἡνίοχον καὶ κυβερνήτην . . . τὸν λόγον.

c *i.e.* the heart.

d ἀνερμάτιστον : Aucher " basi carentem."

e θεοσεβείας καὶ ἁγιότητος καὶ πάσης ἀρετῆς.

f ὁ νοῦς or ἡ διάνοια.   *g* τέλειον λόγον.   *h* τὰ πάθη.

i Aucher " cupiditates," but Arm. *srtmtout'iun* = θυμός, not ἐπιθυμία.

j According to the order of Scripture this section should come before § 115.

k These abstract nouns denote the Urim and Thummim, the oracular device attached to the high priest's breastplate. Philo usually calls them δήλωσις καὶ ἀλήθεια, following LXX, but sometimes σαφήνεια καὶ ἀλήθεια. For other references to them see *Leg. All.* iii. 132, 140, *De Vita Mosis* ii. 113, 128-129 and *De Spec. Leg.* iv. 69.

l LXX καὶ ἐπιθήσεις ἐπὶ τὸ λόγιον τῆς κρίσεως τὴν δήλωσιν καὶ τὴν ἀλήθειαν.   *m* ὁ λόγος.

n *i.e.* the λόγος ἐνδιάθετος (reflexion) and the λόγος προφορικός (utterance), see next note.

rightly did He apportion the two virtues, (one) to each of them, (namely) truth to that (form of reason) which is in thought, and revelation to that which is uttered.[a] For the mind of the virtuous man ought not to consider anything to be more appropriate or more related [b] to it than truth,[c] which one must with all power endeavour to find, while speech has no greater necessity than to reveal (things) clearly by making plain in clear speech what is signified.[d]

*117. (Ex. xxviii. 27 [Heb. 31]) Why is the double [e] hyacinthine stole [f] called " undergarment " [g] ? [h]

They say that since the hyacinthine stole is a symbol [i] of the air, because the air is almost black,[j] it was rightly called " undergarment," since it was under [k] the garment which was upon his breast,[l] for the air is placed below heaven and the ether.[m] But I wonder at and am struck with

---

[a] Cf. De Vita Mosis ii. 129 δυσὶ λόγοις τοῖς καθ' ἕκαστον ἡμῶν, τῷ τε προφορικῷ καὶ ἐνδιαθέτῳ, δύο ἀρετὰς ἀπένειμεν οἰκείας, τῷ μὲν προφορικῷ δήλωσιν, τῷ δὲ κατὰ διάνοιαν ἀλήθειαν.

[b] οἰκειότερον ἢ συγγενέστερον.

[c] Philo phrases the same idea somewhat differently in De Vita Mosis ii. 129 ἁρμόζει γὰρ διανοίᾳ μὲν μηδὲν παραδέχεσθαι ψεῦδος.

[d] Aucher renders less accurately, I think, " quam evidenter declarare revelata artificioso apparatu."

[e] Or " second " : Aucher " duplex " (in footnote, " aliis torta "), see QE ii. 119.

[f] Aucher " tunica," but see QE ii. 107, notes a and d.

[g] ὑποδύτης.

[h] LXX καὶ ποιήσεις ὑποδύτην ποδήρη (Heb. " the robe of the ephod ") ὅλον ὑακίνθινον. Philo alludes to this garment in De Vita Mosis ii. 110 and to its cosmic symbolism in De Spec. Leg. i. 95, cf. De Fuga 110.

[i] σύμβολον.

[j] Aucher " subniger." Philo means that it is dark blue, see QE ii. 85, note g.   [k] Lit. " stood after."

[l] i.e. the ephod, to which the " breastplate of judgment " or Logeion was attached, see the preceding sections.

[m] Cf. De Spec. Leg. i. 94 ὁ ἀὴρ μέλας ὢν τὴν μετ' οὐρανὸν δευτέραν τάξιν κεκλήρωται.

QUESTIONS AND ANSWERS

admiration by the theologian's *a* allegorizing of his philosophical beliefs.*b* For he has likened the whole heaven
to the breast, wherefore in his statements he has orna-
mented the breast of the high priest with the two emerald *c*
stones which stand on his shoulders,*d* and with the twelve
stones on the Logeion, arranged in four rows of three.
Now, (he indicates) the air by the second hyacinthine stole
(called) " undergarment," and by the other parts *e* he
indicates *f* earth and water. [" But where, O theologian,"
someone may say, " is the head of the world ? Teach us,
for you have brought us as far as the breast, which you
have shown to be a likeness of heaven." To me it seems
that he would reply to this with silence, for it is plain to
those who are not foolish but are wont to help their minds
with well ordered (thoughts). If, however, there is anyone
heavy of understanding, let him listen. The head of all
things is the eternal Logos of the eternal God,*g* under
which, as if it were his feet or other limbs, is placed the
whole world, over which He passes and firmly stands.*h*
Now it is not because Christ is Lord that He passes and
sits over the world, for His seat is with His Father and God,
but because for its perfect fullness the world is in need of
the care and superintendence of the best ordered dispensation, and for its own complete piety, of the Divine Logos,
just as living creatures (need) a head, without which it is
impossible to live.] *i*

a τὸν θεολόγον, *i.e.* Moses.
b τῆς φιλοσοφίας ἀλληγοροῦντα τὰ δόγματα vel sim. : Aucher
" una cum philosophia allegorice usum sententia."
c Aucher inadvertently omits rendering of " emerald."
d See *QE* ii. 109 on Ex. xxviii. 9-12.
e *i.e.* the flowers and bells of the robe, see *De Vita Mosis*
ii. 120   *f* αἰνίττεται.
g λόγος αἰώνιος (or ἀΐδιος) τοῦ αἰωνίου θεοῦ.
h Aucher " super quem transiens constanter stat."
i How much of the last part of this section (from " But
where, O theologian ") is the work of a Christian scribe is not
clear. The whole passage has here been bracketed to warn
the reader that some part of it, perhaps all, has been revised
by Christian hands.

168

*118. (Ex. xxviii. 28 [Heb. 32]) Why does the opening [a] in the middle of this very same ankle-length garment have a hem [b] " that it may not be ruptured " ? [c]

Of the elements [d] some are by nature heavy, (such as) earth and water, and others are by nature light, (such as) air and fire. Accordingly, from the beginning the air, which had heaviness, was placed near water. [e] And because of the contrariety of heavy to light there was fear that one (element) might suffer rupture [f] from the other, and the world might be imperfect in harmony and unity if this obstacle were present. For that reason there was need of an opening [g] suitable to the middle region, that is, of the divine Logos as a mediator, [h] for this is the strongest and most stable bond [i] of all things, in order that it might bind and weave together [j] the parts of the universe and their contraries, and by the use of force bring into unity and communion and loving embrace those things which have many irreconcilable differences by their natures. Moreover, this passage also presents a description of character, [k]

---

[a] Lit. " that near the mouth " : Aucher (following LXX) " peristomium."

[b] Aucher " gyrum."

[c] LXX καὶ ἔσται τὸ περιστόμιον ἐξ αὐτοῦ μέσον ᾦαν ἔχον κύκλῳ τοῦ περιστομίου, ἔργον ὑφάντου, τὴν συμβολὴν συνυφασμένην ἐξ αὐτοῦ ἵνα μὴ ῥαγῇ : Heb. " and the mouth of its top shall be in its middle, a hem shall be around its mouth, the work of the weaver ; like a breastplate it shall be to it that it may not be torn."

[d] τῶν στοιχείων.

[e] The original must have meant that air, the heavier of the two light elements, was placed next to water, the lighter of the two heavy elements.

[f] ῥῆξιν, based on LXX μὴ ῥαγῇ : Aucher " ne laedatur unum ab altero."

[g] Lit. " mouth " : Aucher " peristomium (sive, oreficium)."

[h] μεσίτου τινός, τοῦ θείου λόγου.   [i] δεσμός.

[j] Lit. " and mix together by weaving." The cosmic weaving reflects the mythology of Plato's *Timaeus*, see below.

[k] ἠθοποιίαν.

for the hem is a hard and dense woven work [a] and very compact,[b] and he thought it proper that the opening should be in it in the middle. Now the mouth [c] is an organ of two things, (namely) of food and speech.[d] As Plato says, it has the entrance of mortal things into itself, (namely) food, while speech is the exit of immortal things.[e] And both (functions) must be practised in such a way that they do not suffer a rupture,[f] which is what happens to gluttons and babblers, for out of loquacity they rupture, in a sense, that which ought to be kept quiet, and [g] they pour into the ears (of others) [h] things not fit to be heard.[i] And those who are intent upon wine-bibbing and overindulgence break out into belchings and burst with insatiable fullness. And he admonishes those who philosophize with him [j] to place restraints upon the belly and the tongue.

119. (Ex. xxviii. 29 [Heb. 33]) Why does He command that in the lowest part of this undergarment there shall be

---

[a] ὕφασμα. In *De Spec. Leg.* i. 86 Philo describes the ephod, worn over the ankle-length robe of the high priest, as ὕφασμα θωρακοειδές. It is not clear how he thought of the ephod as related to the " opening " and " hem."

[b] Or " compressed " : Aucher " rigidus."

[c] Philo plays on the resemblance between περιστόμιον and στόμα. [d] λόγου.

[e] *Cf. De Opif. Mundi* 119 στόματι δι᾽ οὗ γίνεται θνητῶν μέν, ὡς ἔφη Πλάτων, εἴσοδος, ἔξοδος δ᾽ ἀφθάρτων, a paraphrase of *Timaeus* 75 D-E εἴσοδον τῶν ἀναγκαίων ... τὴν δ᾽ ἔξοδον τῶν ἀρίστων.

[f] Aucher renders less accurately, I think, " et utrique obsequendum est (*vel*, ambo observanda sunt) ne laceratur (*sic*)."

[g] The Arm. has a superfluous indef. pronoun = τινες.

[h] Lit. " pour into the inside," but the Arm. translator obviously misread εἰς ὦτα (see next note) as ἐσώτατα.

[i] Similarly the brief Greek frag., οἱ λάλοι, τὰ ὀφείλοντα ἡσυχάζεσθαι ῥηγνύντες, τρόπον τινὰ ὑπὸ γλωσσαλγίας προχέουσιν εἰς ὦτα ἀκοῆς οὐκ ἄξια.

[j] *i.e.* Moses : Aucher " hac in parte."

EXODUS, BOOK II

pomegranate-shaped (tassels) as if from flowering pomegranates ? *a*

That the undergarment was a double hyacinthine (robe)
and in the likeness of air has been shown.*b* And as water
is lower than air, the pomegranate-shaped (tassel) was
rightly (placed) in the lowest part of the undergarment,
as was the flower of the pomegranate, which is (so) called
from " flowing " and " being liquid." *c* Now, as for that
which is primarily in (the class of) flowing liquids, what else
indeed would it be but water ?

120. (Ex. xxviii. 30 [Heb. 34]) Why does He place a bell
(and) flower *d* around (the hem) beside the pomegranate-
shaped (tassel) ? *e*

---

a LXX καὶ ποιήσεις ἐπὶ τὸ λῶμα τοῦ ὑποδύτου κάτωθεν ὡσεὶ
ἐξανθούσης ῥόας ῥοΐσκους ἐξ ὑακίνθου καὶ πορφύρας καὶ κοκκίνου
διανενησμένου καὶ βύσσου κεκλωσμένης ἐπὶ τοῦ λώματος τοῦ ὑποδύτου κύκλῳ· τὸ αὐτὸ εἶδος ῥοΐσκους χρυσοῦς καὶ κώδωνας ἀνὰ
μέσον τούτων περικύκλῳ : Heb. " and thou shalt make upon
its hem pomegranates of blue and purple and scarlet, upon
its hem round about, and bells of gold between them round
about." For parallels to Philo's allegorical comment see *De
Migratione* 103, *De Vita Mosis* ii. 119 and *De Spec. Leg.*
i. 93.

b In *QE* ii. 117, where, however, it is not clear whether
Philo means a " second " or a " double " hyacinthine garment.

c Philo plays on the resemblance between ῥόα " pomegranate " and ῥεῖν " to flow," or ῥύσις " flowing," cf. *De Vita
Mosis* ii. 119 οἱ δὲ ῥοΐσκοι ⟨σύμβολον⟩ ὕδατος, παρὰ τὴν ῥύσιν
λεχθέντες εὐθυβόλως.

d Lit. " flowering bell " but Philo treats bell and flower
separately in his commentary and in the parallels. See also
LXX, next note.

e LXX παρὰ ῥοΐσκον χρυσοῦν κώδωνα καὶ ἄνθινον ἐπὶ τοῦ
λώματος τοῦ ὑποδύτου κύκλῳ : Heb. " a gold bell and a pomegranate, a gold bell and a pomegranate (*sic, bis*) upon the
hem of the robe round about." Philo allegorizes this verse
similarly (see below) in *De Migratione* 103, *De Vita Mosis*
ii. 119 and *De Spec. Leg.* i. 93.

171

In the earlier (passages) [a] He has represented heaven
by the shoulder-piece [b] and the (object) on the breast,
which He has called " pectoral," [c] and (has represented)
the lower region, [d] (namely) the air, by the double hyacinthine (robe), [e] and then water, which is below the air, by
the symbol [f] of the pomegranate-shaped (tassel).   Now,
however, He mentions the flowers in addition to the pomegranate-shaped (tassels), and by them He indicates [g] the
earth, since everything flowers and grows from the earth. [h]
But the bell has an intermediate position between the
pomegranate-shaped (tassel) and the flower, and indicates
the harmony and community of the elements. [i]   For if
there had not been produced in the world the harmonious
blending into a symphony of antiphonal voices as if of a
choir sounding as one, it would not have received its full
perfection. [j]   But since there are four elements, [k] He has
spoken very circumspectly [l] in distinguishing and separating the bell from fire and air, for the movement of the soul
is only from itself, as is generally agreed, especially by the
philosophers of the Stoa.   But it [m] has united earth with
water, for earth and water are themselves the body of the

---

[a] Aucher " imprimis."

[b] ἐπωμίδος, see QE ii. 110.

[c] περιστήθιον.

[d] Lit. " the following (region)."

[e] See the preceding three sections.

[f] συμβόλου.

[g] αἰνιττόμενος.

[h] Cf. De Vita Mosis ii. 119 τὰ μὲν ἄνθινα σύμβολον γῆς,
ἀνθεῖ γὰρ καὶ βλαστάνει πάντα ἐκ ταύτης.

[i] In De Migratione 103 the bells symbolize the sense of
hearing, in De Vita Mosis ii. 119 they symbolize the harmony
of earth and water, in De Spec. Leg. i. 93 they symbolize the
harmony of the parts of the world (ἁρμονίαν καὶ συμφωνίαν καὶ
συνήχησιν τῶν τοῦ κόσμου μερῶν).   In the present passage
Philo combines the three kinds of symbolism.

[j] τελεσιουργίαν : Aucher " perfectionem."

[k] στοιχεῖα.

[l] Aucher " accurate."

[m] i.e. the bell as a symbol of the unity of earth and water.

world.[a] Now, the body itself is inanimate and unmoving,[b] and it was in need of that Logos,[c] which, by the art of music,[d] adapted and reformed it into a harmony and one-ness of all things.[e]

121. (Ex. xxviii. 32a [Heb. 36a]) What is " the leaf [f] of pure gold " ? [g]
The leaf has a fine [h] construction and also lacks depth, and so it appears to be a surface.[i] Now, a surface is in-corporeal.[j] And may it not be that it is called " leaf " from " flying," [k] so that it may be a symbol of incorporeal and intelligible forms of substance ? [l] That which is always borne upward becomes winged and never turns toward a downward course. Wherefore He has also called it " pure," as being unmixed and luminous, for sense-perceptible things [m] are mixtures which are brought to-gether from many things. For the forms which weave

---

[a] τὸ τοῦ κόσμου σῶμα.   [b] ἄψυχον καὶ ἀκίνητον.

[c] Aucher " rationis illius."

[d] τῇ μουσικῇ τέχνῃ.

[e] Aucher renders more briefly, " in harmoniam reduceret illud pro concordia universorum."

[f] i.e. the plate (πέταλον) on the forehead of the high priest.

[g] LXX καὶ ποιήσεις πέταλον χρυσοῦν καθαρόν. Philo briefly discusses its symbolism in De Migratione 103 and De Vita Mosis ii. 114-116.

[h] i.e. thin or light : Aucher " subtilem." But note that in De Vita Mosis ii. 114 Philo says that it " is wrought into the form of a crown."

[i] ἐπιφάνεια.   [j] ἀσώματος.

[k] Philo plays on the resemblance between πέταλον " leaf " and πέτεσθαι " to fly."

[l] σύμβολον ἀσωμάτων καὶ νοητῶν ἰδεῶν οὐσίας. Although Arm. niut‛ usu. = ὕλη, I have rendered the last word as if the original were οὐσίας rather than ὕλης " of matter," since the former is not only required by the context but is also con-firmed by the parallel in QE ii. 124, where the Arm. trans-lator uses goyout‛iun = οὐσία.

[m] τὰ αἰσθητά.

together things not (previously joined) with one another [a] also have purity, being like a lamb.[b]

122. (Ex. xxviii. 32b [Heb. 36b]) Why does He say, " Thou shalt express [c] in it [d] the expression of a seal-impression, ' Holiness to the Lord ' " [e] ?

It pleases Him that the incorporeal and intelligible substance [f] should be unimpressed by itself and without shape but be formed and shaped like a seal-impression by the Logos of the eternally Existent One.[g] Excellently, therefore, has He represented the seal-impression as an " expression," [h] for there are expressed in them in part [i] the forms which the patterns [j] had. But the divine Logos, which is established over all things, is immaterial,[k] being, as it were, not impressed upon them but expressed,[l] for

[a] Aucher renders more literally, " quae non sunt invicem."

[b] The sense escapes me. Perhaps the last phrase " being like a lamb " is a scribal addition.

[c] i.e. " engrave " or the like. I have rendered literally in order to make clearer Philo's allegorical interpretation.

[d] i.e. in the gold plate worn on the high priest's forehead.

[e] LXX καὶ ἐκτυπώσεις ἐν αὐτῷ ἐκτύπωμα σφραγῖδος ἁγίασμα κυρίου (v.l. κυρίῳ : Heb. " to ẎHWH "). Philo briefly discusses this half-verse in De Migratione 103 (reading κυρίῳ) and De Vita Mosis ii. 114-115, 132, where he deals with the mystical number of the letters of the Tetragrammaton.

[f] τὴν ἀσώματον καὶ νοητὴν οὐσίαν, cf. QE ii. 121, note l.

[g] τῷ τοῦ ἀεὶ (vel sim.) Ὄντος λόγῳ. The idea is more clearly and fully expressed in De Migratione 103 ἐκείνη μὲν ἡ σφραγὶς ἰδέα ἐστὶν ἰδεῶν καθ' ἣν ὁ θεὸς ἐτύπωσε τὸν κόσμον, ἀσώματος δήπου καὶ νοητή.

[h] ἐκτύπωμα.

[i] The original prob. referred to the various parts of the cosmos.

[j] οἱ τύποι, i.e. the archetypes.

[k] ἄυλος.

[l] οὐκ ἐντυπωθεὶς ἀλλ' ἐκτυπωθείς, but contrast De Vita Mosis ii. 132 τῶν τεττάρων αἱ γλυφαὶ γραμμάτων ἐνεσφραγίσθησαν. Philo has slightly modified his allegorical interpretation to make it conform more closely to the literal meaning.

174

it is external to all substances and to all corporeal and
incorporeal elements.[a]

123. (Ex. xxviii. 33a [Heb. 37a]) Why is the leaf [b] placed
over the double hyacinthine (robe) ? [c]

Because the double hyacinthine (robe) is almost black,[d]
and black is the colour of ink and is opaque. But the
forms [e] are not visible, and the leaf presents a symbol [f]
of the forms, since it is the substance of the invisible and
intelligible.[g]

124. (Ex. xxviii. 33b-34 [Heb. 37b-38]) Why is the leaf [h]
(placed) upon the forehead of the high priest but not upon
his head ? [i]

The head is an assemblage of hair, skin and bones, while
the place of the brain [j] is in the front of the head. Now,
the theologians [k] say that the sovereign part (of the mind) [l]

[a] Aucher " quae excellet omnes materias corporeas et
incorporeas."

[b] i.e. the gold plate (πέταλον) on the high priest's forehead.

[c] LXX καὶ ἐπιθήσεις αὐτὸ (sc. τὸν πέταλον) ἐπὶ ὑακίνθου κεκλωσμένης (Heb. " braid of blue "), κτλ. On the problem of the
" double " hyacinthine robe see QE ii. 117, notes.

[d] i.e. dark blue, see QE ii. 85, 117.

[e] αἱ ἰδέαι or τὰ εἴδη.

[f] σύμβολον.

[g] τοῦ ἀοράτου καὶ νοητοῦ οὐσία ἐστίν, cf. QE ii. 121.

[h] i.e. the gold plate (πέταλον).

[i] LXX καὶ ἔσται ἐπὶ τῆς μίτρας· κατὰ πρόσωπον τῆς μίτρας
ἔσται. καὶ ἔσται ἐπὶ τοῦ μετώπου 'Ααρών, κτλ. Contrast De
Migratione 103, where Philo says that the gold plate is on
the high priest's head, ἐπὶ μὲν τῆς κεφαλῆς. Here, as in some
of the preceding sections, Philo's allegorical interpretation is
based upon a more literal reading of Scripture than are the
interpretations in his fuller and earlier commentary on the
Pentateuch.

[j] τοῦ ἐγκεφάλου.

[k] οἱ θεολόγοι, i.e. the Greek philosophers.

[l] τὸ ἡγεμονικόν.

175

has its settled habitation [a] in the brain.[b] For this reason it was in the front of [c] the principal and sovereign (part) of the soul, to which the mind and the reason [d] have been allotted, that the leaf was placed (as) a symbol of intelligible substance [e] (and as) [f] a likeness of the divine Logos and (as) an expressed seal-impression,[g] (namely) the form of forms.[h]

[a] Lit. " constancy of habitation " : Aucher " constantem habitationem."

[b] Philo sometimes follows Aristotle and the Stoics in locating the mind in the heart, but more often follows Plato in locating it in the brain, as, *e.g.*, in *QG* i. 5, ii. 5, *QE* ii. 100. See, for the various passages, Helmut Schmidt, *Die Anthropologie Philons von Alexandreia* (Würzburg, 1933), pp. 51, 143.

[c] Lit. " before " : Aucher " in regione."

[d] ὁ νοῦς (or ἡ διάνοια) καὶ ὁ λόγος.

[e] σύμβολον νοητῆς οὐσίας, cf. *QE* ii. 121, note *l*.

[f] Aucher inserts " praeseferens."

[g] ἐκτυπωθεῖσα σφραγίς, cf. *QE* ii. 122.

[h] ἰδέα ἰδεῶν, cf. *De Migratione* 103, *QE* ii. 122.

APPENDIX A

APPENDIX A

GREEK FRAGMENTS OF THE QUAESTIONES

Although Philo's *Quaestiones in Genesin et Exodum* has survived as a whole (or in large part) only in the ancient Armenian version, the original Greek text of parts of about two hundred sections has been preserved in the works of some of the Church Fathers like John of Damascus or Byzantine chroniclers like Leo Grammaticus or antiquarians like Johannes Lydus or the anonymous authors of catenae arranged in the order of Scriptural verses. A number of these fragments (some of them being rather paraphrastic than literal) were collected by Mangey in his edition of Philo's works published in 1742. Since that time other scholars have added to their number. While it may be expected that future research will discover more fragments of the *Quaestiones* as well as of other lost works of Philo, it still seems worth while at the present time to bring together the fragments of the *Quaestiones* which have been collected by various scholars and published in half a dozen separate works. It should be noted in passing that Dr. Ludwig Früchtel of Ansbach, Germany, to whom we owe the identification of several fragments (published by Harris) formerly unlocated in the *Quaestiones*, proposes to bring out a more complete collection of the fragments of Philo's various lost works and has, as he informed me in 1949, already located a few more hitherto unidentified fragments of the *Quaestiones*.

The fragments (or paraphrases) reproduced from the various modern collections listed below are here given without an English translation, partly because the differences between them and the Armenian have already been mentioned in the footnotes to the translation of that version, and partly because many of the fragments are such free quotations of the original that it might be misleading to translate them

179

APPENDIX A, GREEK FRAGMENTS

and thus make them appear to be of equal weight with the translation of the Armenian version.

The six modern works from which the Greek texts are reproduced are herewith listed in order of publication.

Harris, J. Rendel, *Fragments of Philo Judaeus.* Cambridge, 1886 (includes fragments earlier published by Mangey, Mai, Pitra and Tischendorf).

Wendland, Paul, *Neu entdeckte Fragmente Philos.* Berlin, 1891 (consists mostly of selections from Procopius, including those published earlier by Mai).

Praechter, Karl, " Unbeachtete Philonfragmente," *Archiv für Geschichte der Philosophie,* N.F. 9 (1896), 415-426 (gives nine fragments from Leo Grammaticus and Pseudo-Polydeuces with parallels in other Byzantine chroniclers).

Staehle, Karl, *Die Zahlenmystik bei Philon von Alexandreia.* Leipzig-Berlin, 1931 (gives about a dozen fragments from Johannes Lydus).

Lewy, Hans, *Neue Philontexte in der Ueberarbeitung des Ambrosius* mit einem Anhang : *Neu gefundene griechische Philonfragmente.* Berlin, 1932 (gives about a dozen fragments from the *Sacra Parallela* of John of Damascus and the Catenae).

Früchtel, Ludwig, " Griechische Fragmente zu Philons Quaestiones in Genesin et in Exodum," *Zeitschrift für die alttestamentliche Wissenschaft,* N.F. 14 (1937), 108-115 (locates several fragments listed by Harris as " unidentified ").

Three of Harris' " unidentified " fragments have been located by Emile Bréhier, *Les Idées philosophiques et religieuses de Philon d'Alexandrie,* 2nd ed., Paris, 1925.

The reader is asked to overlook some inconsistencies in abbreviations, forms of citation, etc., in the following pages. They are largely due to the fact that I have in most cases followed the style set by the modern authorities listed above.

GENESIS, BOOK I

1. (Gen. ii. 4) Διὰ τί τὴν κοσμοποιίαν ἐπιλογιζόμενος φησὶ
Μωϋσῆς· " αὕτη ἡ βίβλος γενέσεως οὐρανοῦ καὶ γῆς, ὅτε ἐγένετο ";
Τὸ μὲν " ὅτε ἐγένετο " ἀόριστον[a] ἔοικε χρόνον ἐμφαίνειν· τοῦτο
δ' ἐστὶν ἔλεγχος δυσωπῶν τοὺς συγκεφαλαιουμένους ἀριθμὸν ἐτῶν,
ἀφ' οὗ τὸν κόσμον οἴονται γενέσθαι· τὸ δὲ " αὕτη ἡ βίβλος γενέσεως " ἤτοι δεικτικόν ἐστι τοῦ ὑποκειμένου τεύχους, ὃ τὴν κοσμοποιίαν περιέχει· ⟨ἐν ἐκείνῳ γὰρ⟩ ἡ ἀναφορὰ τῶν εἰρημένων περὶ
τῆς κοσμοποιίας πρὸς τὰ ἐπ' ἀληθείας γεγονότα.

Lewy, p. 55, from *Sacra Parallela* of John of Damascus,
Cod. Hierosolymitanus S. Sep. fol. 124ʳ and Cod. Con-
stantinopolitanus Metochion 274, ἐκ τῶν ἐν Γενέσει ζητημάτων.

17. (Gen. ii. 18)
Φίλους ἡγητέον τοὺς βοηθεῖν καὶ ἀντωφελεῖν ἐθέλοντας καὶ ἂν
μὴ δύνωνται. φιλία γὰρ ⟨οὐκ⟩ ἐν τῷ χρειώδει μᾶλλον ἢ κράσει
καὶ συμφωνίᾳ βεβαίῳ τῶν ἠθῶν, ὡς ἕκαστον τῶν συνελθόντων εἰς
φιλικὴν κοινωνίαν τὸ Πυθαγόρειον ῥῆμα ἐπιφθέγξασθαι, ὅτι " ἆρά
ἐστι φίλος ἕτερον ὡς ἐγώ."

Harris, p. 12, from Dam. Par. 788 (Cod. Rupef. f. 275)
ἐκ τοῦ αʹ τῶν ἐν Γενέσει ζητημάτων. " The first sentence (with
change to the singular number) in Maximus (ii. 548) and
Anton Melissa, col. 849."

20. (Gen. ii. 19)
Ἀνδρὸς δὲ ἐπιστημονικωτάτου καὶ φρονήσει διαφέροντος οἰκειότατον τοῦτο τὸ ἔργον· οὐ σοφῷ μόνον ἀλλὰ καὶ τῷ πρώτῳ γηγενεῖ[b]
τῶν ὀνομάτων ἡ θέσις· ἔδει γὰρ ἡγεμόνα μὲν τοῦ ἀνθρωπείου,
βασιλέα δὲ τῶν γηγενῶν πάντων καὶ τοῦτο λαχεῖν γέρας ἐξαίρετον

---

[a] ἀόριστον ex Arm. Lewy : ἄριστον codd.
[b] γηγενεῖ ex Arm. Harris : εὐγενεῖ codd.

181

APPENDIX A, GREEK FRAGMENTS

ἵνα, ὥσπερ πρῶτος ᾔδει τὰ ζῷα, καὶ πρῶτος ἀξιωθῇ τῆς ἐπὶ πᾶσιν ἀρχῆς καὶ πρῶτος εἰσηγητὴς καὶ εὑρετὴς γένηται τῶν ἐπωνυμιῶν. Ἄτοπον γὰρ ἦν ἀνώνυμα αὐτὰ καταλειφθέντα ὑπό τινος νεωτέρου προσονομασθῆναι ἐπὶ καταλύσει τῆς τοῦ πρεσβυτέρου τιμῆς τε καὶ εὐκλείας.

Harris, pp. 12-13, from Dam. Par. 748 (Cod. Rupef. f. 21 b) " with reference to the questions on Genesis."

21. (Gen. ii. 19) Ἤγαγεν ὁ θεὸς τὰ ζῷα πρὸς τὸν Ἀδάμ, ἰδεῖν τί καλέσει αὐτά.

Οὐ γὰρ ἐνδυάζει θεός· ἀλλ' ἐπειδὴ νοῦν ἔδωκε τῷ ἀνθρώπῳ τῷ πρωτογενεῖ καὶ σπουδαίῳ καθ' ὃ ἐπιστημονικὸς ὢν πέφυκε λογίζεσθαι, καθάπερ ὑφηγητὴς γνώριμον κινεῖ πρὸς ἐπίδειξιν οἰκείαν καὶ ἀφορᾷ τὰ ἄριστα αὐτοῦ τῆς ψυχῆς ἔγγονα. Φανερῶς δὲ πάλιν καὶ διὰ τούτου πᾶν τὸ ἑκούσιον καὶ ἐφ' ἡμῖν διατυποῖ, τοὺς πάντα κατ' ἀνάγκην εἶναι λέγοντας δυσωπῶν. Ἡ ἐπεὶ ἔμελλον οἱ ἄνθρωποι χρῆσθαι, διὰ τοῦτο ἄνθρωπον αὐτὰ θέσθαι προσέταττεν.

Harris, p. 13, from Dam. Par. p. 748 (Cod. Rupef. f. 21 b), ἐκ τῶν ἐν Γενέσει ζητουμένων.

24. (Gen. ii. 21)

Ὁ ὕπνος κατὰ τὸν προφήτην ἔκστασίς ἐστιν, οὐχὶ κατὰ μανίαν, ἀλλὰ κατὰ τὴν τῶν αἰσθήσεων ὕφεσιν καὶ τὴν ἀναχώρησιν τοῦ λογισμοῦ. Τότε γὰρ αἱ μὲν αἰσθήσεις ἐξίστανται τῶν αἰσθητῶν,[a] ὁ δὲ οὐκέτι νευροσπαστῶν οὐδὲ παρέχων κίνησιν αὐταῖς ἠρεμεῖ, αἱ δὲ τὰς ἐνεργείας ἀποτετμημέναι τῷ διεζεῦχθαι τῶν αἰσθητῶν ἀκίνητοι καὶ ἀργαὶ ὑπεκλέλυνται.

Harris, pp. 13-14, from Joh. Monachus (Mangey ii. 667 = Cod. Rupef. f. 265), and Cod. Reg. 923, f. 342 b.

27. (Gen. ii. 21)

Ἀποικίαν στέλλεται γυνὴ τὴν ἀπὸ γονέων πρὸς τὸν ἄνδρα· διὸ προσήκει τὸν μὲν ὑποδεξάμενον ἀντιλαβεῖν τὴν τῶν δεδωκότων εὔνοιαν, τὴν δὲ μετελθοῦσαν, ἣν τοῖς σπείρασι τιμὴν παρεῖχε, τῷ λαβόντι διδόναι· παρακαταθήκην γὰρ ἀνὴρ ἐγχειρίζεται γυναῖκα παρὰ γονέων, γυνὴ δὲ τὸν ἄνδρα παρὰ τῶν νόμων.

Lewy, p. 55, from Dam. Par. Rec. Rupef. f. 243ᵛ, Φίλωνος.

[a] Post αἰσθητῶν verba καὶ ὁ λογισμὸς ἀναχωρεῖ ἐκ τῶν αἰσθήσεων ex Arm. suppl. Harris.

182

GENESIS, BOOK I

28. (Gen. ii. 23)

Ὡς προφήτης φησίν, οὔτε γεγονέναι ἐκ συνομιλίας οὔτε ἐκ
γυναικός, ὡς οἱ μετέπειτα, ἀλλά τινα φύσιν ἐν μεθορίῳ καθάπερ
ἀπὸ ἀμπέλου κληματίδος ἀφαιρεθείσης εἰς ἑτέρας ἀμπέλου γένεσιν.

Harris, p. 14, from Dam. Par. 748 (Cod. Rupef. f. 21 b),
ἐκ τῶν ἐν Γενέσει ζητουμένων.

29. (Gen. ii. 24) Διό φησιν· " Ἕνεκεν τούτου καταλείψει
ἄνθρωπος τὸν πατέρα καὶ τὴν μητέρα αὐτοῦ καὶ προσκολληθήσεται
πρὸς τὴν γυναῖκα αὐτοῦ· καὶ ἔσονται δύο εἰς σάρκα μίαν ";
. . . τὸ εὐαφέστατον καὶ αἰσθητικώτατον, ἐν ᾧ καὶ τὸ ἀλγεῖν
καὶ τὸ ἥδεσθαι.

Harris, p. 14, from Dam. Par. 748 (Mangey ii. 654=Cod.
Rupef. f. 21 b), ἐκ τῶν ἐν Γενέσει ζητουμένων.

31. (Gen. iii. 1)

Φρόνιμος δὲ ἐκλήθη ὁ ὄφις ὅτι τὸ λογικὸν ζῷον τὸν ἄνθρωπον
καὶ τῶν ἄλλων ἀγχινοίᾳ διαφέροντα ἐξαπατᾶν ἔμελλεν.

Praechter, p. 420, from Ps.-Polydeuces, pp. 30, 25–32, 1
(cf. Theod. Mel. p. 7, 31-32, Cedr. p. 10, 10-12).

32. (Gen. iii. 1)

Ἆρα δὲ καὶ ὁ ὄφις τῷ κατὰ προφορὰν λόγῳ ἐχρήσατο; οὐ
πάντως, ἀλλ' οἱ πρωτόπλαστοι ἅτε κακίας ὄντες ἀμιγεῖς ἀκρι-
βεστάτας εἶχον τὰς αἰσθήσεις καὶ πολὺ τῶν ἡμετέρων διαλλατ-
τούσας ὥστε τὴν ἀκοὴν αὐτῶν πάσης ὑπάρχειν φωνῆς ἀκουστικήν.

Praechter, pp. 416-417, from Ps.-Polydeuces, p. 32, 8-12
(cf. Sym. Log. p. 910, 16-20, Theod. Mel. p. 8, 4-8, Cedr. p. 10,
12-16).

41. (Gen. iii. 7)

Ὡς γὰρ ἡδὺς ὁ καρπὸς τῆς συκῆς, τραχὺ καὶ πικρότατον τὸ
φύλλον, οὕτως πᾶσα ἁμαρτία ἐν τῇ πράξει δείκνυται ἡδεῖα, μετὰ
δὲ ταῦτα ὀδύνην παρέχει τῷ πεπραχότι.

Praechter, p. 417, from Ps.-Polydeuces, p. 36, 13-16 (cf.
Sym. Log. pp. 911, 28–912, 2, Theod. Mel. p. 9, 10-13, Cedr.
p. 14, 19-21—" stark verflacht ").

51. (Gen. iii. 19) Τί ἐστιν " ἕως τοῦ ἐπιστρέψαι σε εἰς τὴν γῆν ἐξ ἧς ἐλήφθης"; οὐ γὰρ ἐκ γῆς διεπλάσθη μόνον ὁ ἄνθρωπος ἀλλὰ καὶ θείου πνεύματος.

Ἐπειδὴ δὲ οὐ διέμεινεν ἀδιάστροφος, προστάξεως θείας ἠλόγηκε καὶ τοῦ κρείττονος μέρους ἀποτεμνόμενος οὐρανομίμητον πολιτείαν ὅλον αὐτὸν προσένειμε τῇ γῇ. Εἰ μὲν γὰρ ἀρετῆς, ἥτις ἀθανατίζει, ἐραστὴς ἐγένετο, πάντως ἂν ἐλάμβανε κλῆρον τὸν οὐρανόν· ἐπειδὴ δὲ ἡδονὴν ἐζήτησε, δι' ἧς ψυχικὸς θάνατος ἐπιγίνεται, τῇ γῇ προσενεμήθη.

Harris, p. 15, from Dam. Par. 748 (Cod. Rupef. f. 20 b), ἐκ τῶν ἐν Γενέσει ζητουμένων.

55. (Gen. iii. 22)

Οὔτε ἐνδυασμὸς οὔτε φθόνος περὶ θεόν· χρῆται δὲ πολλάκις ὀνόμασιν ἐνδυαστικοῖς ἢ διανοητικοῖς κατ' ἀναφορὰν ἐπὶ τὸ "ὡς ἄνθρωπος" κεφάλαιον. Διττὰ γάρ, ὡς πολλάκις ἔφην, ἐστὶν τὰ ἀνωτάτω κεφάλαια· τὸ μὲν "οὐκ ὡς ἄνθρωπος ὁ θεός," τὸ δὲ "ὡς ἄνθρωπος παιδεύει τὸν υἱόν." Τὸ μὲν πρότερον ἐξουσίας, τὸ δὲ δεύτερον παιδείας καὶ εἰσαγωγῆς ἐστιν.

Harris, p. 15, from Parallels of Joh. Monachus (Mangey ii. 669 = Cod. Rupef.), ἐκ τῶν αὐτῶν = ἐκ τοῦ β' τῶν ἐν Γενέσει ζητημάτων.

"Ἄλλος δέ φησιν ὡς οὐκ ἐνδοιάζει τὸ θεῖον κἂν ἐνδοιαστικοῖς ὀνόμασι χρῆται. Διττὰ γάρ ἐστι τὰ ἀνωτάτω κεφάλαια, τὸ μὲν "οὐχ ὡς ἄνθρωπος ὁ θεός," τὸ δὲ "ὡς ἄνθρωπος παιδεύει τὸν υἱόν, οὕτως κύριος ὁ θεὸς παιδεύσει σε." Τὸ μὲν οὖν πρότερον ἐξουσίας ἐστί, τὸ δὲ δεύτερον παιδείας καὶ ἐξαγωγῆς, ἵνα καὶ τὸ ἑκούσιον παρεισέλθῃ. Τὸ γὰρ "μήποτε" οὐκ ἔστιν ἐπαμφοτερισμὸς τοῦ θεοῦ ἀλλ' ἀναφορὰ πρὸς ἄνθρωπον τὸν ἐπαμφοτεριστὴν τῇ φύσει καὶ μήνυμα τοῦ περὶ ἐκείνου πάθους· ὅταν γὰρ προσπέσῃ τινὸς φαντασία, τρία εὐθὺς ἐπιγίνεται, ἀφορμὴ ἐκ τοῦ φανέντος, ὁρμὴ πρὸς τὸ φανέν, τρίτον ἐνδοιασμὸς ἀμφικλινῆς ἀντισπωμένης τῆς ψυχῆς, εἶθ' αἱρετέον εἴτε μή. Πρὸς δὴ τοῦτο τὸ τρίτον τὸ "μήποτε" ἀναφέρεται.

Wendland, pp. 36-37, from Procopius 225 в.

59. (Gen. iv. 2)

Ὅρα δὲ πῶς ἐν μὲν τῇ γενέσει τὸν Κάϊν προέταξε κατὰ τάξιν

τὴν χρονικήν, ἐν δὲ τοῖς ἐπιτηδεύμασι προτάττει τὸν δίκαιον· τὰ γὰρ ἔμψυχα τῶν ἀψύχων τῷ τῆς φύσεως λόγῳ διαφέρει, καὶ ἡ ποιμαντικὴ προοιμιάζεται τὴν ἑαυτοῦ τε καὶ ἄλλων ἀρχήν. Οὐκ ἐρρήθη δὲ γεωργὸς ὁ Κάϊν, ἀλλ' ἐργαζόμενος τὴν γῆν. Οὐ γὰρ ἦν ἀστεῖος κατὰ τὸν Νῶε, ὅστις γεωργός, οὐκ ἐργάτης εἴρηται.

Wendland, p. 37, from Procopius 233 D, ". . . aber Pr. oder sein Gewährsmann benutzt vielleicht am Schluss ein verlorenes Stück der Quaest."

60. (Gen. iv. 34)

Ὅρα τοίνυν φιλαύτου καὶ φιλοθέου διαφοράν· ὁ μὲν μεθ' ἡμέρας ἀλλ' οὐκ εὐθὺς καὶ ἀπὸ τῶν καρπῶν, ἀλλ' οὐκ ἀπὸ τῶν πρώτων καὶ τούτων ἐστὶ διανομεὺς πρὸς θεόν· τοιαύτη γὰρ ἡ θυσία· ὁ δὲ τὰ πρωτότοκα μηδὲν μελλήσας καθιεροῖ καὶ τοῦ προσενεχθέντος παντὸς παραχωρεῖ τῷ θεῷ· ἐπεῖδε[a] γὰρ ὁ θεὸς ἐπὶ τοῖς δώροις αὐτοῦ· δωρητικός, οὐ διανομεὺς γεγονώς. Ὅρα δὲ καὶ ὅτι ὅσον ἐκ τῆς τάξεως ἀρξάμενον πρώτον, τοῦ Κάϊν δευτέρου μέμνηται λέγων· " ἐπεῖδεν ὁ θεὸς ἐπὶ Ἄβελ, ἐπὶ δὲ Κάϊν καὶ ταῖς θυσίαις αὐτοῦ οὐ προσέσχεν."

Wendland, p. 38, from Procopius 236 A.

Οὕτως οἶμαι τὰ πρωτότοκα καθιερῶν ὁ Ἄβελ[b] φιλόθεον μᾶλλον ἢ φίλαυτον τὴν ἑαυτοῦ συνίστησι προαίρεσιν. Ἑαυτῷ δὲ ὁ Κάϊν ἀπονέμων τὰ γεννήματα καὶ τῶν δευτερίων[c] ἀσεβῶς τὸν θεὸν ἀξιῶν τῷ καὶ μεθ' ἡμέρας ἀλλὰ μὴ εὐθέως προσενεγκεῖν φίλαυτος μᾶλλον ἢ φιλόθεος ἐξελέγχεται.

Praechter, p. 418, from Leo Grammaticus, pp. 244, 34–245, 21 (cf. Theod. Mel., pp. 11, 18–12, 13, Ps.-Polydeuces, pp. 44, 8–46, 11).

61. (Gen. iv. 4-5)

Οὕτως οὐχ ἡ τάξις τὸ πρωτεῖον ἀλλ' ἡ γνώμη χαρίζεται.
Wendland, p. 38, from Procopius 236 A.

[a] ἐπεῖδε Wendland : ἐπειδὴ codd.
[b] καθιερῶν ὁ Ἄβελ edd. : καθιερῶν(τα) τὸν Ἄβελ codd. : καθιέρωσεν Ἄβελ Sym. Log., Cod. Vind. 91.
[c] δευτερείων corr. Praechter.

APPENDIX A, GREEK FRAGMENTS

62. (Gen. iv. 4-5)

Ζητῶν τίνι διαφέρει δῶρον θυσίας, εὑρίσκω ὅτι ὁ μὲν θύων ἐπιδιαιρεῖ, τὸ μὲν αἷμα τῷ βωμῷ προχέων, τὰ δὲ κρέα οἴκαδε κομίζων· ὁ δὲ δωρούμενος ὅλον ἔοικε παραχωρεῖν τῷ λαμβάνοντι· ὁ μὲν οὖν φίλαυτος διανομεὺς οἷος ὁ Κάϊν, ὁ δὲ φιλόθεος δωρεῖται οἷον[a] ὁ Ἄβελ.

Harris, p. 15, from Cramer, Catena in Heb., p. 580 (Cod. Paris, 238).

Διαφέρει δὲ δῶρον θυσίας, ὅτι ὁ μὲν θύων ἐπιδιαιρεῖ τὸ μὲν αἷμα τῷ βωμῷ προσχέων, τὰ δὲ κρέα οἴκαδε κομίζων, ὁ δὲ δωρούμενος ὅλου[b] ἔοικε παραχωρεῖν τῷ λαμβάνοντι.

Wendland, p. 38, from Procopius 237 в (cf. Gennadius, Cat. Lips. 108).

Ἔοικε γὰρ ἐπιδιαιρεῖν ὁ θύων καὶ τὸ μὲν αἷμα τῷ θυσιαστηρίῳ προχέειν,[c] τὰ δὲ κρέα οἴκαδε ἀποκομίζειν,[d] ὁ δὲ δωρούμενος πάντῃ[e] τῷ λαμβάνοντι παραχωρεῖ τὸ δῶρον.

Praechter, p. 418, from Leo Grammaticus, pp. 244, 34–245, 21 (cf. Theod. Mel. pp. 11, 18–12, 13, Ps. - Polydeuces, pp. 44, 8–46, 11).

64. (Gen. iv. 7)

(a) Ὀρθὴ δὲ διαίρεσις καὶ τομή[f] οὐδὲν ἕτερόν ἐστιν ἢ τάξις καθ' ἣν ὁ κόσμος δεδημιούργηται. Καὶ ταύτην δεῖ κατὰ πάντα τοῦ βίου μιμεῖσθαι τὰ πράγματα καὶ μάλιστα ἐν χαρίτων ἀμοιβαῖς.

Wendland, p. 39, from Procopius 237 d.

(b) Τὸ μὲν οὖν εὐχαριστεῖν τῷ θεῷ καθ' ἑαυτὸ[g] ὀρθῶς ἔχον ἐστί, τὸ δὲ μήτε πρώτῳ μήτε ἐκ τῶν πρώτων ἀπαρχόμενον ψεκτόν. Οὐ γὰρ δεῖ τὰ μὲν πρεσβεῖα τὴν γένεσιν ἑαυτῇ, τὰ δὲ δεύτερα τῷ ἀγενήτῳ προσ

Τὸ εὐχαριστεῖν θεῷ καθ' ἑαυτὸ ὀρθῶς ἔχον ἐστί· τὸ δὲ μήτε πρῶτον μήτε ἐκ τῶν πρώτων ἀπαρχόμενον ψεκτόν. Οὐ γὰρ δεῖ τὰ μὲν πρεσβεῖα ἐν τῇ γενέσει τιθέναι,[h] τὰ δὲ δεύτερα τῷ δωρησαμένῳ θεῷ προσ

[a] δωρητικὸς οἷος con. Harris.   [b] ὅλον Mai.
[c] προσχέων Theod. Mel. et Cod. Vat. 163.
[d] κομίζειν Ps.-Polydeuces.
[e] edd. : παντὶ codd.
[f] τομή Wendland : τὸ μὴ codd.
[g] ἑαυτὸ Wendland : ἑαυτὸν codd.
[h] ἑαυτῷ τιθέναι con. Harris.

νέμειν, ὅπερ ἐξ ἀληθείας οὐκ
ἔστιν εὐχαριστεῖν.
Wendland, p. 39, from
Procopius 237 D (continuing
frag. (a)).

φέρειν. Ἥδε ἐστὶν ἐπίληπτος
διαίρεσις, ἀταξίαν τινὰ τάξεως
εἰσηγουμένη.
Harris, p. 16, from Joh.
Monachus (Mangey ii. 668 =
Cod. Rupef. f. 269 b).

65. (Gen. iv. 7)

Τὸ μὴ ἁμαρτάνειν μηδὲν τὸ
παράπαν μέγιστον ἀγαθόν· τὸ
ἁμαρτάνοντα ἐντραπῆναι συγ-
γενὲς ἐκείνου, νεώτερον, ὡς ἄν
τις εἴποι, παρὰ πρεσβύτερον.
Εἰσὶ γὰρ οἱ ἐπὶ ἁμαρτανομένοις
ὡς ἐπὶ κατορθώμασιν ἀγαλλό-
μενοι δυσίατον, μᾶλλον δὲ ἀνία-
τον νόσον ἔχοντες.
Harris, p. 16, from Dam.
Par. 751 (= Cod. Rupef. f.
46 b), ἐκ τῶν ἐν Γενέσει ζητουμένων.

Μέγιστον μὲν γὰρ ἀγαθὸν τὸ
μηδὲν ἁμαρτεῖν, δεύτερον δὲ τὸ
ἐντραπῆναι τοῖς ἁμαρτήμασιν·
ὁ δὲ διὰ τὴν ἀτιμίαν, οὐ τὴν
ἁμαρτίαν λελύπητο.
Wendland, p. 39, from
Procopius 237 D.

66. (Gen. iv. 7)

Οἷς ἀντιλέγοντες ἕτεροι οὐ περὶ τοῦ θεοσεβοῦς λέγειν φασίν, ἀλλὰ
περὶ τοῦ πραχθέντος ἔργου. Φησὶ γὰρ αὐτῷ ὅτι τούτου τοῦ ἀσεβή-
ματος ἡ ἀποστροφὴ καὶ ἡ ἀναφορὰ πρὸς σέ ἐστιν, ἵνα τὸ ἑκούσιον
παραστήσῃ· " καὶ σύ," φησίν, " ἄρξεις αὐτοῦ," πρῶτος γὰρ
ἀσεβεῖν ἦρξεν[a]· ἔπεται δὲ ὡς κρηπῖδι τῇ ἀσεβείᾳ καὶ τὰ λοιπὰ
πλημμελήματα ὡς ἔξαρχον καὶ ἡγεμόνα παντὸς ἀδικήματος
ἑκουσίου τοῦτον[b] εἶναι.
Wendland, p. 40, from Procopius 240 B.

68. (Gen. iv. 9) Πυνθάνεται θεός· ποῦ Ἄβελ ὁ ἀδελφός σου;

Οὐχ ὡς ἀγνοῶν· τοιγαροῦν ἀρνούμενον ἤλεγξεν· ἀλλ' ἐπισκοπῆς
πρὸς ἰατρείαν αὐτὸν ἀξιῶν καὶ ἐφιστῶν αὐτὸν τῷ μεγέθει τοῦ
πλημμελήματος καὶ πρόφασιν μετανοίας διδοὺς καὶ δεικνὺς δι' ὅλης
τῆς νομοθεσίας ὡς παρ' ἡμᾶς ἐστι τἀδικήματα· ὁ μὲν γὰρ ἄκων
πράξας ὁμολογεῖ συγγνώμην αἰτῶν, ὁ δὲ ἑκὼν ἀρνεῖται.
Wendland, pp. 40-41, from Procopius 240 D (" Das philo-

---

[a] ἦρξας ex Arm. con. Wendland. [b] τοῦτο Cod. Aug.

nische Original ist zum Teil erhalten in Barberinus VI 8 f. 82 unter dem falschen Titel φίλωνος ἐπισκόπου : οὐχ ὡς ἀγνοῶν τοιγαροῦν τὸν ἀρνούμενον bis διδοὺς ohne Abweichungen vom Texte des Pr.").

69. (Gen. iv. 9) Ὡς δὲ τῆς μετανοίας ἠλλάξατο τὴν ἀναίδειαν εἰπὼν ἀγνοεῖν καὶ μὴ φύλαξ εἶναι τοῦ ἀδελφοῦ.

Καίτοι τεττάρων ὄντων ἀνθρώπων, οὓς εἰκὸς ἦν μηδὲ πόρρω λίαν ἀλλήλων καθίσασθαι, καὶ παντὸς μᾶλλον τὸν ἀδελφὸν φυλάττειν ὀφείλοντος, ἔτι δὲ καὶ ἄθεον δεικνύντος ὑπόληψιν τῷ μὴ νομίζειν πάντα τὸν θεῖον ἐφορᾶν ὀφθαλμόν.

Wendland, p. 41, from Procopius 241 A.

70. (Gen. iv. 10)

Τί δ' ἐστιν " φωνὴ αἵματος τοῦ ἀδελφοῦ σου βοᾷ πρός με ἐκ τῆς γῆς ";

Δογματικώτατόν ἐστιν· τὸ γὰρ θεῖον ὁσίων μὲν ὑπακούει, κἂν τελευτήσωσι, ζῆν αὐτοὺς ὑπολαμβάνον τὴν ἀσώματον ζωήν, εὐχὰς δὲ φαύλων ἀποστρέφεται, κἂν εὐεξίᾳ χρήσωνται, νομίζον αὐτοὺς τὸν ἀληθῆ βίον τεθνάναι, τὸ σῶμα οἷον τύμβον περιφέροντας, ᾧ τὴν πανάθλιον ψυχὴν ἐγκατώρυξαν.

Lewy, p. 55, from Dam. Par., Cod. Len. f. 27ᵛ, Φίλωνος Ἑβραίου (cf. Cod. Barb. f. 82ᵛ, Cod. Mosqu. 124ʳ).

Δικαίων γὰρ ἐπακούει (sc. ὁ θεός), κἂν τελευτήσαντες ὦσιν, ἀδίκων δὲ καὶ αὐτὰς ἀποστρέφεται τὰς εὐχάς· τοὺς μὲν γὰρ καὶ τεθνεῶτας νενόμικε ζῆν, τοὺς δὲ καὶ ζῶντας τὴν ἀληθῆ κέκρικε τεθνηκέναι ζωήν.

Praechter, p. 419, from Leo Grammaticus, p. 245, 27-30 (cf. Theod. Mel. p. 12, 18-20, Ps.-Polydeuces, p. 46, 15-17).

Φησὶν ὁ θεός· " φωνὴ αἵματος τοῦ ἀδελφοῦ σου βοᾷ πρός με."

Δυνατὸν δέ καὶ τὸ αἷμα ἀντὶ τῆς ψυχῆς ἐνταῦθα εἰρῆσθαι, καὶ ἔστι δογματικώτατον· τὸ γὰρ θεῖον ὁσίων μὲν ὑπακούει, κἂν τελευτήσωσι, ζῆν αὐτοὺς ὑπολαμβάνον τὴν ἀθάνατον ζωήν, εὐχὰς δὲ φαύλων ἀποστρέφεται, κἂν εὐεξίᾳ χρήσωνται, νομίζον αὐτοὺς τὸν ἀληθῆ βίον τεθνάναι.

Wendland, p. 41, from Procopius 241 A.

GENESIS, BOOK I

72. (Gen. iv. 12)

Λόγιον δέ, φασίν, ἐστὶ καὶ τοῦτο καθολικώτατον· παντὶ γὰρ φαύλῳ τῶν κακῶν τὸ μὲν ἤδη πρόσεστι, τὰ δὲ μέλλει· τὰ μὲν οὖν μέλλοντα φόβους, τὰ δὲ παρόντα λύπας ἐργάζεται.[a]

Wendland, pp. 41-42, from Procopius 241 D (" Das philonische Original ist erhalten in Barb. VI 8 f. 83 ").

73. (Gen. iv. 13)

Οὐκ ἔστι συμφορὰ μείζων ἢ τὸ ἀφεθῆναι καὶ καταλειφθῆναι ὑπὸ θεοῦ.

Wendland, p. 42, from Procopius 243 B.

74. (Gen. iv. 14) Τίνα δὲ δέδοικεν ὁ Κάϊν μηδενὸς ὄντος πλὴν αὐτοῦ καὶ τῶν γονέων;

Προσεδόκα δέ, φασί, καὶ τὴν ἐκ τῶν μερῶν τοῦ κόσμου ἐπίθεσιν ἅπερ ἐπ᾽ ὠφελείᾳ γενόμενα[b] οὐδὲν ἧττον ἀμύνεται τοὺς πονηρούς, εἶτα καὶ τὴν ἀπὸ τῶν θηρίων καὶ ἑρπετῶν ἐπιβουλήν, ἅπερ ἡ φύσις ἐπὶ τιμωρίᾳ τῶν ἀδίκων ἐγέννησεν.[c] Ἴσως δὲ καὶ τὴν ἀπὸ τῶν γονέων τίσιν ὑπονοεῖ, οἷς κοινὸν πένθος προσέβαλεν ἀγνοοῦσι τὸν θάνατον.

Wendland, p. 42, from Procopius 245 A.

76. (Gen. iv. 15)

Τὸ μὲν γὰρ τελευτῆσαι τῶν ἐν τῷ βίῳ πονηρῶν ἐπάγει τὴν κατάπαυσιν· τὸ δὲ ζῆν ἐν φόβῳ καὶ λύπῃ μορίους ἐπάγει τοὺς σὺν αἰσθήσει[d] θανάτους.

Praechter, p. 419, from Leo Grammaticus, p. 246, 11-13 (cf. Theod. Mel. p. 13, 10-12).

77. (Gen. iv. 23)

Ὁ μὲν Κάϊν,[e] ἐπειδὴ τὸ μέγεθος τοῦ ἄγους ἡγνόησε, τοῦ μηδέποτε περιπεσεῖν θανάτῳ, τιμωρίας δίδωσιν ἁπλουστέρας. Ὁ

---

[a] ἀπεργάζεται Cod. Barb.
[b] γενόμενα Wendland : γινόμενα codd.
[c] τίνα . . . ἐγέννησεν, cf. Cat. Lips. 112, Ἀδήλου.
[d] συναισθήσει Theod. Mel. : ἐν συνεσθήσει Sym. Log., Cod. Vind. : ἐν αἰσθήσει con. Praechter.
[e] add. ἴσως Cod. Reg.

APPENDIX A, GREEK FRAGMENTS

δὲ μιμητὴς ἐκείνου, μὴ δυνάμενος εἰς τὴν αὐτὴν[a] ἀπολογίαν τῆς ἀγνοίας συμφυγεῖν,[b] δεκαπλᾶς[c] εἰκότως ὑπομένει δίκας. . . . Διὰ τοῦτο " ἐκ δὲ Λάμεχ ἑβδομηκοντάκις ἑπτά "· διὰ τὴν εἰρημένην αἰτίαν, καθ' ἣν ὁ δεύτερος ἁμαρτὼν καὶ μὴ σωφρονισθεὶς τῇ τοῦ προηδικηκότος τιμωρίᾳ τήν τε ἐκείνου παντελῶς ἀναδέχεται ἁπλουστέραν οὖσαν, καθάπερ ἐν ἀριθμοῖς αἱ μονάδες ἔχουσι, καὶ πολυπλασιωτέραν,[d] ὁμοιουμένην ταῖς ἐν ἀριθμοῖς δεκάσιν. ἦν γνωσιμαχῶν Λάμεχ καθ' ἑαυτοῦ.[e]

Harris, p. 17, from Dam. Par. 776 (Cod. Rupef. and Cod. Reg. 923, f. 356 b).

79. (Gen. iv. 26)
Ἐλπίς ἐστι προπάθειά τις χαρᾶς[f] πρὸ χαρᾶς, ἀγαθῶν οὖσα προσδοκία.

Harris, p. 17, from Anton Melissa (*Patr. Gr.* 136, col. 789).

81. (Gen. v. 3)
Καὶ τὸ μὲν ἐκ Κάϊν γένος μέχρι τούτου μνήμης τῆς ἐν βίβλοις ἠξίωται, τοῦ δὲ[g] ἀριθμοῦ τῶν πατέρων[h] ἀποκεκήρυκται, ἵνα μηδὲ τοῖς πρώτοις εἴη συνταττόμενος μηδὲ τῶν ἑξῆς ἀφηγουμένοις,[i] διὰ δὲ τὸ τῆς προαιρέσεως ἄγριον ὥσπερ ἐπὶ τὴν ἄλογον ἐκ τῆς λογικῆς φύσεως ἐξῴρισται.

Praechter, pp. 419-420, from Ps.-Polydeuces, p. 54, 9-14 (*cf.* Leo Grammaticus, p. 246, 26-29, Theod. Mel. p. 13, 24-27).

85. (Gen. v. 23-24)
Ἤδη τινὲς ἀψίκοροι γευσάμενοι καλοκἀγαθίας καὶ ἐλπίδα παρασχόντες ὑγιείας εἰς τὴν αὐτὴν ἐπανέστρεψαν νόσον.

Harris, p. 17, from Dam. Par. 784 (" apparently as ἐκ τῶν ἐν Ἐξόδῳ ζητημάτων, an easy confusion ").

[a] αὐτὴν om. Cod. Reg.   [b] καταφυγεῖν Cod. Rupef.
[c] διπλᾶς Cod. Rupef.
[d] τιμωρίᾳ . . . πολυπλασιωτέραν] τιμωρίᾳ οὐ μόνον τῇ ἐκείνου παντελῶς ἀναδέχεσθαι ἀλλὰ καὶ πολὺ πλειοτέραν Cod. Reg.
[e] ἦν . . . ἑαυτοῦ susp. Harris.
[f] Harris : χαρᾷ codd.
[g] τοῦ δὲ Praechter cum par. : καὶ τοῦ Ps.-Polydeuces.
[h] πρώτων Sym. Log. et Leo Grammaticus.
[i] ἀφηγούμενος mal. Praechter cum Sym. Log. et Leo. Grammatico.

190

GENESIS, BOOK I

89. (Gen. vi. 1)

'Αεὶ φθάνουσι τὴν δίκην αἱ τοῦ θεοῦ χάριτες. Ἔργον γὰρ αὐτῷ προηγούμενον τὸ εὐεργετεῖν, τὸ δὲ κολάζειν ἑπόμενον. Φιλεῖ δέ, ὅταν μέλλῃ μεγάλα συνίστασθαι κακά, μεγάλων καὶ πολλῶν ἀγαθῶν ἀφθονία προγενέσθαι.

Harris, p. 18, from Joh. Monachus (Mangey ii. 670), ἐκ τῶν ἐν Ἐξόδῳ ζητουμένων.

92. (Gen. vi. 4)

Πνευματικαὶ τῶν ἀγγέλων οὐσίαι· εἰκάζονται δὲ πολλάκις ἀνθρώπων ἰδέαις, πρὸς τὰς ὑποκειμένας χρείας μεταμορφούμενοι.

Harris, p. 18, from Dam. Par. 309, 772, ἐκ τοῦ α' τῶν ἐν Γενέσει ζητουμένων.

93. (Gen. vi. 6)

Ἔνιοι νομίζουσι μεταμέλειαν ἐμφαίνεσθαι περὶ τὸ θεῖον διὰ τῶν ὀνομάτων· οὐκ εὖ δὲ ὑπονοοῦσι. χωρὶς γὰρ τοῦ μὴ τρέπεσθαι τὸ θεῖον, οὔτε τὸ " ἐνεθυμήθη " οὔτε τὸ " ἐνενόησεν " δηλωτικὰ μεταμελείας ἐστίν—τὸ δὲ θεῖον ἄτρεπτον—ἀλλ' ἀκραιφνοῦς λογισμοῦ περιεσκεμμένου τὴν αἰτίαν, ἧς ἕνεκα ἐποίησεν τὸν ἄνθρωπον ἐπὶ τῆς γῆς.

Harris, p. 18, from Joh. Monachus (Mangey ii. 669), ἐκ τῶν β' τῶν ἐν Γενέσει ζητημάτων.

94. (Gen. vi. 7)

Διὰ τί ἄνθρωπον ἀπειλῶν ἀπαλεῖψαι καὶ τὰ ἄλογα προσδιαφθείρει;

Διότι οὐ προηγουμένως δι' ἑαυτὰ γέγονε τὰ ἄλογα ἀλλὰ χάριν ἀνθρώπων καὶ τῆς τούτων ὑπηρεσίας, ὧν διαφθειρομένων εἰκότως καὶ ἐκείνα συνδιαφθείρεται, μηκέτι ὄντων δι' οὓς γέγονε. [Ἐκ τούτου δῆλον ὅτι διὰ τὸν ἄνθρωπον πάντα τὰ

Διὰ τί ἀπειλῶν τὸν ἄνθρωπον ἀπαλείψειν[a] καὶ τὰ ἄλογα[b] προσδιαφθείρει;

Ὅτι οὐ προηγουμένως δι' ἑαυτὰ γέγονεν τὰ ἄλογα ἀλλὰ χάριν ἀνθρώπων καὶ τῆς τούτων ὑπηρεσίας, ὧν διαφθειρομένων εἰκότως κἀκεῖνα συνδιαφθείρεται, μηκέτ' ὄντων τῶν δι' οὓς γέγονε, συμμετροῦντος τοῦ θεοῦ τὸν ἀριθμὸν τῶν σωθησομένων

---

[a] e Cod. Barb. Wendland : ἀπαλεῖψαι vulg.
[b] λοιπὰ Mai, Aug.

191

APPENDIX A, GREEK FRAGMENTS

ζῷα ἐγένετο· διὸ καὶ ἀπολλυ-
μένου τοῦ δεσπότου συναπόλ-
λυται καὶ αὐτά, συμμετροῦντος
τοῦ θεοῦ τὸν ἀριθμὸν τῶν σωθησομένων ζῴων πρὸς τὴν
χρείαν τῶν φυλαχθησομένων
ἀνθρώπων ὥσπερ οὖν καὶ ἀπ'
ἀρχῆς δύο δύο ἔκτισεν.]ᵃ
Harris, pp. 18-19, from
Cat. Ined. Cod. Reg. 1825
(Mangey ii. 675), and Cat.
Mus. Britt. Cod. Burney 34,
f. 35, Φίλωνος Ἑβραίου, cf.
Cat. Lips. 1, col. 141, " where
it is attributed to Procopius."

ἀνθρώπων, ὥσπερ οὖν καὶ ἀπ'
ἀρχῆς δύο δύο ἔκτισεν.
Wendland, p. 47, from
Procopius 272 в (cf. Theo-
doret, Quaest. in Gen. 1,
Chrys. Cat. Lips. 142).

95. (Gen. vi. 7)
Ὅτι δὲ τῆς κακίας κολαζομένης ἡ ἀρετὴ διασῴζεται Νῶε
δεδήλωκεν.
Wendland, pp. 49-50, from Procopius 292 ᴀ.

96. (Gen. vi. 8) . . . ὃς λέγεται χάριν εὑρεῖν παρὰ τῷ θεῷ.
Ὡς τῶν ἄλλων δι' ἀχαριστίαν ἀπολωλότων· οὐ γὰρ ὡς χάριν
λαβὼν ἐκ θεοῦ—κοινὸν γὰρ τοῦτο πάντων ἀνθρώπων—ἀλλ' ἐπεὶ
μόνος εὐχάριστος διεφάνη. Ἔδει δὲ καὶ χάριτος ἀξιωθῆναι θείας
τὸν τοῦ νέου γένους κατάρξαντα· μεγίστης γὰρ χάριτος ἀρχὴν καὶ
τέλος ἀνθρώπων γενέσθαι. Διὸ καὶ ἀπὸ τῶν ἀρετῶν αὐτὸν
γενεαλογεῖ· τοῦ γὰρ σπουδαίου τὸ πρὸς ἀλήθειαν γένος ἐστὶν ἀρετή.
Πρὸς ὃν καί φησι· " καιρὸς παντὸς ἀνθρώπου ἥκει ἐναντίον ἐμοῦ."
Ὄντως γὰρ οὐδὲν ὡς ἀδικία πρὸς τὸν θεὸν ἐναντίον.
Wendland, p. 50, from Procopius 292 ᴀ.

99. (Gen. vi. 12)
Καλῶς δὲ καὶ σάρκα κινουμένην λέγει τὴν ἐν φθορᾷ· κινεῖ γὰρ
τὰς ἡδονὰς ἡ σὰρξ καὶ κινεῖται ὑπὸ τῶν ἡδονῶν, ἥτις κίνησις αἰτία
γίνεται φθορᾶς ταῖς ψυχαῖς ὡς ἡ ἐγκράτεια σωτηρίας.
Wendland, pp. 55-56, from Procopius 269 ᴅ.

ᵃ Ἐκ τούτου . . . ἔκτισεν] e Cod. Barb. vi. 8 add. Wendland.

192

100. (Gen. vi. 13)

(a) Οὐδὲν ἐναντίον καὶ μαχόμενον ταῖς ὁσιωτάταις τοῦ θεοῦ δυνάμεσίν ἐστιν οὕτως ὡς ἀδικία.

Harris, p. 70 (identified by Früchtel), from Dam. Par. 787 (Cod. Rupef. f. 238), ἐκ τοῦ β′ τῶν ἐν Γενέσει ζητημάτων.

(b) Ὁ καιρὸς παρὰ τοῖς φαυλοτέροις νομίζεται εἶναι θεὸς τὸν ὄντα ὄντως παρακαλυπτομένοις . . . καὶ θεοπλαστούντων καὶ ἐξ ἐναντίας τιθέντων τῷ ἀληθεῖ θεῷ τὸ λέγειν τὸν καιρὸν αἴτιον τῶν ἐν τῷ βίῳ πραγμάτων εἶναι. Τοῖς γὰρ εὐσεβέσιν οὐ καιρὸν ἀλλὰ θεὸν παρ' οὗ καὶ οἱ καιροὶ καὶ οἱ χρόνοι· πλὴν αἴτιον οὐ πάντων ἀλλὰ μόνων ἀγαθῶν καὶ τῶν κατ' ἀρετήν· ὡς γὰρ ἀμέτοχος κακίας, οὕτω καὶ ἀναίτιος.

Harris, p. 19, from Cod. Rupef. f. 193, Φίλωνος περὶ κοσμοποιίας. "The last sentence also in Pitra (Anal. Sacr. ii. 307), from Cod. Coislin. 276, f. 238, and again in Rupef. 222 b."

Ἐπάγει δὲ καὶ τὸ τῆς ἐναντιώσεως αἴτιον τὸ πλησθῆναι τὴν γῆν ἀδικίας. Καὶ ἐπεὶ θεὸς ὁ καιρὸς παρὰ τοῖς φαύλοις νομίζεται, δείκνυσιν ὡς καιρῶν καὶ χρόνων αὐτὸς ποιητὴς καὶ τούτοις ὅρον ἐντίθησιν, ὥστε καὶ ἀλλαχοῦ φησιν· " ἀφέστηκεν ὁ καιρὸς ἀπ' αὐτῶν, ὁ δὲ κύριος ἐν ἡμῖν."[a] Τὸ δὲ " καιρὸς ἥκει " σημαίνει τὴν οἱονεὶ συμπλήρωσιν τῶν ἡμαρτημένων, μεθ' ἣν ὁ τῆς δίκης καιρός.

Wendland, pp. 50-51, from Procopius 292 A (Wendland adds a passage as " vielleicht . . . auch aus Philo," but this seems doubtful).

[a] Num. xiv. 9.

193

GENESIS, BOOK II

5. (Gen. v. 15)

(a) Ὅτι ὁ τριάκοντα ἀριθμὸς φυσικώτατός ἐστιν, ὃ γὰρ ἐν μονάσι τριάς, τοῦτο ἐν δεκάσι τριακοντάς. . . . Συνέστηκεν ἐκ τεσσάρων τῶν ἀπὸ μονάδος ἑξῆς τετραγώνων α΄ δ΄ θ΄ ιϛ΄.

Staehle, p. 63, from Joh. Lydus, p. 55, 10-13.

(b) Δυνατὸν ἐν τριακοστῷ ἔτει αὐτὸν ἄνθρωπον πάππον γενέσθαι· ἡβᾶν μὲν περὶ τὴν τεσσερεσκαιδεκάτην ἡλικίαν, ἐν ᾗ σπείρει, τὸ δὲ σπαρὲν ἐντὸς ἐνιαυτοῦ γενόμενον, πάλιν πεντεκαιδεκάτῳ ἔτει τὸ ὅμοιον ἑαυτῷ γεννᾶν.

Harris, p. 20, from Dam. Par. 314.

9. (Gen. vi. 17)
Cf. QG i. 94.

10. (Gen. vi. 18)
Ἄνθρωποι μὲν κληρονομοῦνται ὅταν μηκέτι ὦσιν ἀλλὰ τεθνῶσιν,[a] ὁ δὲ θεὸς ἀΐδιος ὢν μεταδίδωσι τοῦ κλήρου τοῖς σοφοῖς [ζῶν ἀεὶ][b] εὐφραινόμενος αὐτῇ τῇ περιουσίᾳ.[c]

Lewy, p. 56, from Dam. Par. Cod. Rupef. f. 136ᵛ, Φίλωνος.

11. (Gen. vii. 1)

(a) Πρῶτον ἐναργὴς πίστις ὅτι δι᾽ ἕνα ἄνδρα δίκαιον καὶ ὅσιον πολλοὶ ἄνθρωποι σώζονται. Δεύτερον ἐπαινεῖ τὸν δίκαιον ἄνδρα ὡς μὴ μόνον ἑαυτῷ περιπεποιηκότα ἀρετήν, ἀλλὰ καὶ παντὶ τῷ οἴκῳ, δι᾽ ἣν αἰτίαν καὶ σωτηρίας ἀξιοῦνται. Παγκάλως δὲ τουτὶ προσετέθη ὅτι " σε εἶδον δίκαιον ἐνώπιον ἐμοῦ." Ἑτέρως γὰρ

---

[a] ἀλλὰ τεθνῶσιν ex Arm. et Ambros. ins. Lewy.
[b] ζῶν ἀεὶ (ex marg. ad ἀΐδιος) recte secl. Lewy.
[c] αὐτῇ τῇ περιουσίᾳ] αὐτῶν τῇ κτίσει ex Arm. con. Lewy.

GENESIS, BOOK II

ἄνθρωποι δοκιμάζουσι τοὺς βίους καὶ ἑτέρως τὸ θεῖον, οἱ μὲν ἐκ
τῶν φανερῶν, ὁ δὲ ἐκ τῶν κατὰ ψυχὴν ἀοράτων λογισμῶν.

Wendland, p. 48, from Procopius 280 в-c, Cod. Barb.
vi. 8, f. 101.

(b) Καὶ τὸ " ἐν τῇ γενεᾷ ταύτῃ," ἵνα μήτε τὰς πρότερον κατα-
κρίνειν δοκῇ μήτε τὰς αὖθις ἀπογινώσκειν.

Wendland, p. 52, from Procopius 293 в.

12. (Gen. vii. 2-3)

(a) Ὁ γὰρ κατ᾽ αὐτὴν ἀριθμὸς ἀμιγής ἐστι καὶ ἀμήτωρ, μήτε
γεννῶν μήτε γεννώμενος ὡς ἕκαστος τῶν ἐν τῇ δεκάδι ἀριθμῶν.
Ὅθεν καὶ οἱ Πυθαγόρειοι Ἀθηνᾷ τὴν ἑπτάδα ἀνατίθενται.

Staehle, p. 36, from Joh. Lydus, p. 43, 2-5.

(b) Ὥστε ὁ δύο ἀριθμὸς οὐ καθαρός, πρῶτον μὲν ὅτι κενός ἐστι
καὶ οὐ ναστός, τὸ δὲ μὴ πλῆρες οὐ καθαρόν . . . ἀρχὴ δὲ ἀπειρίας
καὶ ἀνισότητος, ἀπειρίας μὲν διὰ τὴν ὕλην, ἀνισότητος δὲ διὰ τοὺς
ἑτερομήκεις. . . . Ὅθεν οἱ παλαιοὶ ὡς ὕλην καὶ ἑτερότητα τὴν
δυάδα παραλαμβάνουσι.

Staehle, p. 23, from Joh. Lydus, p. 24, 7-12.

(c) Ἡ ἐν τῷ φαύλῳ κακία διδυμοτοκεῖ. Διχόνους γὰρ <καὶ>
ἐπαμφοτερὴς ὁ ἄφρων, τὰ ἄμικτα μιγνύς, καὶ φύρων καὶ συγχέων
τὰ διακρίνεσθαι δυνάμενα, τοιαῦτα ἐν ψυχῇ χρώματα ἐπιφέρων,
οἷάπερ ὁ λεπρὸς ἐν τῷ σώματι, μιαίνων καὶ τοὺς ὑγιεῖς λογισμοὺς
ἀπὸ τῶν θανατούντων ἅμα καὶ φωνώντων.

Harris, p. 20, from Joh. Monachus (Mangey ii. 663 = Cod.
Rupef. f. 125 and 138 b).

(d) . . . Τὸ[a] τὴν ἡμετέραν τοῦ σώματος οὐσίαν γεώδη ὑπ-
άρχουσαν μὴ εἰσάπαν περιοραθῆναι χρὴ πνευματικῆς καὶ σῳζούσης
ἐπιμελείας[b]· οἰνοφλυγίαις μὲν γὰρ καὶ ὀψοφαγίαις καὶ λαγνείαις
καὶ συνόλως ὑγρῷ καὶ διαρρέοντι βίῳ χρώμενοι νεκροφορούμεν
σὺν τῇ ψυχῇ καὶ τὸ σῶμα, ἐὰν δὲ ἀποστραφῶμεν τῶν παθῶν τὸν
βομβυσμόν, ζωηφορούμεν καθ᾽ ἑκάτερον.[c]

Lewy, p. 57, from Dam. Par. Cod. Const. f. 501ᵛ, Φίλωνος
(" mit christlicher Tendenz überarbeitet ").

[a] ἠθικώτατον γὰρ τὸ ex Arm. con. Lewy.
[b] περιοραθῆναι ὥσπερ ζῴων ἔρημον ex Arm. con. Lewy.
[c] ἐὰν δὲ ὁ θεὸς ἐλεήσας ἀποστρέψῃ τῶν παθῶν τὸν κατακλυσμὸν
καὶ ξηρὰν ἀπεργάσηται τὴν ψυχήν, ἄρξεται ζῳογονεῖν καὶ ψυχοῦν
τὸ σῶμα καθαρωτέρᾳ ψυχῇ, ἧς ἡ σοφία κυβερνήτης ἐστίν ex Arm.
con. Lewy.

195

APPENDIX A, GREEK FRAGMENTS

13. (Gen. vii. 4, 10)

Μεθ' ἑπτὰ δὲ τοῦ εἰσελθεῖν ἡμέρας ὁ κατακλυσμὸς γίνεται, τοῦ φιλανθρώπου θεοῦ διδόντος αὐτοῖς ἀναχώρησιν εἰς μετάνοιαν ἁμαρτημάτων ὁρῶσιν αὐτόχρημα πλήρη τὴν κιβωτὸν ἀντίμιμον γῆς· καὶ τὸ ἐπιεικὲς δείκνυται τοῦ θεοῦ τὴν πολυετῆ μοχθηρίαν τῶν ἀνθρώπων ἐπιλυομένου τοῖς μετανοοῦσιν ἡμέραις ὀλίγαις. Ἔστι δὲ ὁ ἑπτὰ ἀριθμὸς ὑπόμνημα τῆς τοῦ κόσμου γενέσεως, ἐναργῶς δηλοῦντος τοῦ θεοῦ ὅτι αὐτός εἰμι καὶ τότε κοσμοποιῶν καὶ τὰ μὴ ὄντα ἄγων εἰς τὸ εἶναι καὶ τὰ νῦν ὄντα διαφθείρων. Ἀλλὰ τοῦ μὲν αἴτιον ἀγαθότης ἐμή, τοῦ δὲ τῶν εὐεργετηθέντων ἀσέβεια.

Wendland, p. 53, from Procopius 296 B.

Διὰ τί μετὰ τὸ εἰσελθεῖν ἑπτὰ ἡμέραι διαγίνονται, μεθ' ἃς ὁ κατακλυσμός;

Πρῶτον ἀναχώρησιν δίδωσιν ὁ ἵλεως εἰς μετάνοιαν ἁμαρτημάτων, ἵνα θεασάμενοι τὴν κιβωτὸν ἀντίμιμον γῆς ἕνεκα τοῦ καιροῦ γενομένην καὶ τὰ τῶν ζῴων γένη ταμιεύουσαν, ὧν ἔφερεν ἡ γῆ τὰ κατὰ μέρος εἴδη, πιστεύσωσι μὲν τῷ περὶ τοῦ κατακλυσμοῦ κηρύγματι τὴν διαφθορὰν εὐλαβηθέντες, καθέλωσι δὲ ἀσέβειαν καὶ κακίαν ἅπασαν. Δεύτερον τὴν ὑπερβολὴν τῆς ἐπιεικείας τοῦ σωτῆρος καὶ εὐεργέτου παρίστησιν ἐναργῶς τὸ λόγιον τὴν πολυετῆ μοχθηρίαν τῶν ἀνθρώπων ἐπιλυομένου τοῖς μετανοοῦσιν ἡμέραις ὀλίγαις.

Wendland, p. 53, from Cat. Barb. vi. 8, f. 103ᵛ, Φίλωνος ἐπισκόπου.

14. (Gen. vii. 4, 12)

Ὅθεν καὶ Ἄρτεμις λέγεται ἀπὸ τοῦ ἀρτίου καὶ ὑλικοῦ ἀριθμοῦ (sc. δευτέρα ἡμέρα). Τὸ γὰρ ἄρτιον μέσον διασπᾶται διαιρουμένου τοῦ ἑνός. Μόνος δὲ ἀδιαίρετος ὁ περιττός. Ὁ μὲν γὰρ ἄρρην ἀριθμός . . . τετράγωνος, αὐγὴ καὶ φῶς ἐξ ἰσότητος πλευρῶν συνεστώς, ὁ δὲ θῆλυς ἑτερομήκης, νύκτα καὶ σκότον ἔχων διὰ τὴν ἀνισότητα. Ὁ δὲ ἑτερομήκης τὴν μὲν ἐλάττονα πλευρὰν ἐλάττονα ἔχει ἑνί, τὴν δὲ μείζω περιττοτέραν ἑνί.

Staehle, p. 23, from Joh. Lydus, pp. 23, 21-24, 7.

15. (Gen. vii. 4)

(a) Τί ἐστι· "ἐξαλείψω πᾶσαν τὴν ἐξανάστασιν ἣν ἐποίησα ἀπὸ προσώπου τῆς γῆς";

196

Τί φασι οὐκ " ἀπὸ τῆς γῆς " ἀλλ᾽ " ἀπὸ τοῦ προσώπου τῆς γῆς "; τουτέστι τῆς ἐπιφανείας ἵνα ἐν τῷ βάθει ἡ ζωτικὴ δύναμις τῶν σπερμάτων ὅλων οὖσα φυλάττηται σῶα καὶ ἀπαθὴς παντὸς τοῦ βλάπτειν δυναμένου· τῆς γὰρ ἰδίας προθέσεως οὐκ ἐπιλέλησται ὁ ποιητής· ἀλλὰ τὰ μὲν ἄνω καὶ κατ᾽ αὐτὴν τὴν ἐπιφάνειαν κινούμενα φθείρει, τὰς δὲ ῥίζας βυθίους[a] ἐᾷ πρὸς γένεσιν ἄλλων.

Harris, p. 21, from Cat. Burney, f. 35 b and Cat. Lips. 1, col. 144, Φίλωνος ἐπισκόπου.

Πᾶσαν δὲ τὴν ἀνάστασιν οὐκ ἀπὸ γῆς ἐξαλείψειν ἀλλ᾽ " ἀπὸ προσώπου," λέγει, " τῆς γῆς," τοῦτ᾽ ἔστι τῆς ἐπιφανείας, ἵνα ἐν τῷ βάθει ἡ ζωτικὴ δύναμις τῶν σπερμάτων ὅλων φυλάττηται.

Τὰς γὰρ ῥίζας βυθίους ἐᾷ πρὸς γένεσιν ἄλλων.

Wendland, p. 54, from Procopius 296 c.

(b) Θεοπρεπῶς γὰρ τὸ " ἐξαλείψω " ὥσπερ τῶν ἀπαλειφομένων τὰ μὲν γράμματα ἀπαλείφονται, αἱ δέλτοι δὲ διαμένουσιν· ἡ μὲν γὰρ ἀσεβὴς γενεὰ ἐξήλειπται, τὸ δὲ κατὰ διαδοχὴν τῆς οὐσίας γένος διετηρήθη, ὡς δίκαιον.

Harris, p. 21 (= Pitra, Anal. Sacr. ii. 313), from Cod. Vat. 748, f. 23 and Cod. Vat. 1657, f. 23.

Θεοπρεπῶς γὰρ τὸ " ἐξαλείψω " γέγραπται. Συμβαίνει γὰρ ἐπὶ τῶν ⟨ἀπ⟩αλειφομένων τὰ μὲν γράμματα ἀφανίζεσθαι, τὰς δὲ δέλτους ἢ βίβλους διαμένειν. Ἐξ οὗ παρίστησιν ὅτι τὴν μὲν ἐπιπολάζουσαν γένεσιν διὰ τὴν ἀσέβειαν ἀπαλείψει δίκην γραμμάτων, τὴν δὲ χώραν καὶ τὴν οὐσίαν τοῦ γένους τῶν ἀνθρώπων διαφυλάξει πρὸς τὴν αὖθις σποράν.

Wendland, p. 54, from Cat. Barb. vi. 8, f. 105.

" Ἀπαλείψω " δέ φησιν, ἐπεὶ καὶ τῶν ἀπαλειφομένων τὰ γράμματα μὲν ἀφανίζεται, αἱ δέλτοι δὲ διαμένουσιν· ὅθεν ἐκτρίβων τὴν ἀσεβῆ γενεὰν τῆς οὐσίας τοῦ γένους ἐφείσατο.

Wendland, p. 54, from Procopius 296 c.

___

[a] βυθίας Cat. Lips.

197

(c) Διὸ καὶ " τὴν ἀνάστασίν " φησιν· ἀναστάσει δὲ ἀντίπαλον καθαίρεσις, τὸ δὲ καθαιρεθὲν οὐκ εἰς ἅπαν ἀπόλλυται.

Wendland, p. 54, from Procopius 296 c.

16. (Gen. vii. 5)

Ἔπαινος δὲ τοῦ δικαίου τὸ πάντα ποιῆσαι τὰ προσταχθέντα, δεύτερον τὸ ἐντέλλεσθαι μᾶλλον ἐθέλειν ἢ κελεύειν αὐτῷ τὸν θεόν· ἐντέλλονται μὲν γὰρ φίλοι, κελεύουσι δὲ δεσπόται· ὑπερβάλλει γὰρ ἐπὶ θεοῦ τὸ πρῶτον, εἰ καὶ μέγα τὸ δεύτερον.

Wendland, p. 55, from Procopius 296 c.

Μέγας ἔπαινος τοῦ δικαίου ὅτι τὰ προσταχθέντα πάντα ἐπετέλεσεν ἰσχυρογνώμονι λογισμῷ καὶ θεοφιλεῖ διανοίᾳ· δεύτερον δὲ ὅτι οὐκ ἐθέλει κελεύειν αὐτῷ μᾶλλον ἢ ἐντέλλεσθαι. Κελεύουσι μὲν γὰρ καὶ προστάττουσι δούλοις δεσπόται, ἐντέλλονται δὲ φίλοι. Θαυμαστὴ μὲν οὖν δωρεὰ καὶ τὸ ταχθῆναι τὴν ἐν δούλοις θεράπουσι παρὰ τοῦ θεοῦ τάξιν, ὑπερβολὴ δὲ εὐεργεσίας ἐστὶ τὸ καὶ φίλον γενηθῆναι γενητὸν ἀγενήτῳ.

Wendland, p. 55, from Cat. Barb. vi. 8, f. 101, Φίλωνος ἐπισκόπου.

17. (Gen. vii. 11)

Κατὰ τὸν τῆς ἰσημερίας καιρὸν ἐπισκήπτει ὁ κατακλυσμὸς ἐν ᾗ καὶ τὸν τοῦ γένους ἀρχηγέτην διαπεπλάσθαι φασίν· ὁ δὲ ἕβδομος μὴν λέγεται καὶ πρῶτος καθ᾽ ἑτέραν καὶ ἑτέραν[a] ἐπιβολήν· διὸ καὶ ἡ

Πλησίον δὲ τοῦ τῆς ἰσημερίας καιροῦ γέγονεν ὁ κατακλυσμὸς ἐν τῇ πάντων αὐξήσει καὶ γενέσει τῶν ζῴων φοβερωτέραν τὴν ἀπειλὴν ἐπάγοντος τοῦ θεοῦ τῆς ἀσεβείας εἰς ἔλεγχον. Τότε δὲ καὶ γε-

Εὔλογον γὰρ καὶ τὸν τοῦ ἀνθρώπων γένους ἀρχηγέτην[b] Ἀδὰμ διαπεπλάσθαι τῷ καιρῷ τῆς ἐαρινῆς ἰσημερίας.[c] Ἰσημερία δ᾽ ἐαρινὴ γίνεται καὶ τῷ ἑβδόμῳ μηνί· ὁ δ᾽ αὐτὸς λέγεται καὶ πρῶτος καθ᾽ ἑτέραν

[a] καθ᾽ ἑτέρας καὶ ἑτέρας Cod. Burney.

[b] ἢ γενάρχην ἢ πατέρα ἢ ὅπως δεῖ καλεῖν τὸν πρεσβύτατον ἐκεῖνον ex Arm. add. Lewy.

[c] ὅτ᾽ ἦν κατάπλεως ἡ γῆ φυτῶν ex Arm. add. Lewy.

τοῦ Νῶε πρόσοδος ἐξομοιοῦται τῷ πρώτῳ γηγενεῖ ὡς ἀρχὴ συστάσεως δευτέρου κόσμου.

Harris, p. 22, from Cod. Burney, f. 36 a, Φίλωνος, and Cat. Lips. 1, col. 149.

γονέναι τὴν δημιουργίαν εἰκὸς καὶ πεπλάσθαι τὸν ἄνθρωπον. Τῷ οὖν Ἀδὰμ ἐξομοιοῦται καὶ Νῶε, γενεᾶς ἀνθρώπων δευτέρας ἀρχόμενος.

Wendland, p. 55, from Procopius 296 D.

καὶ ἑτέραν ἐπιβολήν. Ἐπεὶ οὖν[a] ἀρχὴ γίνεται δευτέρας ἀνθρώπων σπορᾶς, ἐξομοιοῦται τῷ πρώτῳ γηγενεῖ.[b]

Lewy, p. 57, from Cat. Barb. vi. 8, f. 106[v] and Cat. Mosq. f. 157[v], Φίλωνος.

26. (Gen. viii. 1) Πῶς δὲ "τοῦ Νῶε μνησθεὶς ὁ θεὸς καὶ κτηνῶν καὶ θηρίων," γυναικὸς ἢ τέκνων οὐ μέμνηται;

Ὅπου συμφωνία πάντων, ὀνομάτων οὐ χρεία πολλῶν· σὺν δὲ τῷ πρώτῳ καὶ τὸν οἶκον ἀνάγκη συνυπακούεσθαι.

Wendland, p. 56, from Procopius 296 D.

28. (Gen. viii. 1) Καὶ "ἐπήγαγε," φησί, "πνεῦμα εἰς τὴν γῆν καὶ κεκόπακε τὸ ὕδωρ."

Οὐκ ἀνέμῳ[c] ὕδωρ μειοῦται, κυμαίνει δὲ[d] καὶ ταράττεται· πάλαι γὰρ ἂν τὰ μέγιστα τῶν πελαγῶν ἐξανάλωτο. Πνεῦμα τοίνυν τὸ θεῖόν φησιν, ᾧ δὴ πάντα καὶ γίνεται καὶ λωφᾷ· οὐκ ἦν γὰρ εὔλογον ὕδωρ τοσοῦτον ἀνέμῳ παυθῆναι, ἀοράτῳ δὲ καὶ θείᾳ δυνάμει.[e]

Wendland, p. 56, from Procopius 296 D, with variants of Cat. Lips. p. 148, Ἀδήλου.

29. (Gen. viii. 2)

Δῆλον δέ ἐστιν ὡς ταῖς μὲν πρώταις μ' ἡμέραις ἄληκτος[f] ἡ τῆς ῥύμης τῶν ὑδάτων ὑπῆρχε φορά, ταῖς δὲ ἄλλαις ρ' καὶ ν' ἔχουσα

---

[a] καὶ Νῶε μετὰ τὴν τοῦ κατακλυσμοῦ φθορὰν πρώτη τοῦ γένους ex Arm. add. Lewy.

[b] καθ' ὅσον δυνατόν ex Arm. add. Lewy.

[c] ἀνέμοις Cat. Lips.

[d] κυμαίνεται Cat. Lips.

[e] πάλαι . . . δυνάμει] ἀλλὰ τοῦτο ἦν τὸ τοῦ θεοῦ πνεῦμα, ὃ ἐξ ἀρχῆς ἐπεφέρετο ἐπάνω τοῦ ὕδατος Cat. Lips.

[f] Wendland : ἄλεκτος codd.

199

APPENDIX A, GREEK FRAGMENTS

πράως οὐκέτι πρὸς αὔξησιν, πρὸς διαμονὴν δὲ τῆς ἀνακαλύψεως[a] καὶ τοῦ ὕψους συνεβάλλετο· " μεθ' ἡμέρας " γάρ φησιν, " ρν' ἐπικαλυφθῆναι τάς τε πηγὰς καὶ τοὺς καταράκτας "· ἐνήργουν ἄρα πρὸ τῆς ἐπισχέσεως. Μετὰ ν' δὲ καὶ ρ' ἡμέρας ἠλαττοῦτο τὸ ὕδωρ· ἆρα τὰς προειρημένας, ἐν αἷς ὑψοῦτο τὸ ὕδωρ ἢ μετὰ τοσαύτας ἑτέρας οὐκ εὔδηλον.

Wendland, pp. 56-57, from Procopius 296 D.

34. (Gen. viii. 6)

Αἱ αἰσθήσεις θυρίσιν ἐοίκασι. Διὰ γὰρ τούτων ὡσανεὶ θυρίδων ἐπεισέρχεται τῷ νῷ ἡ κατάληψις τῶν αἰσθητῶν· καὶ πάλιν ὁ νοῦς ἐκκύπτει δι' αὐτῶν. Μέρος δέ ἐστι τῶν θυρίδων, λέγω δὴ τῶν αἰσθήσεων, ἡ ὅρασις, ἐπεὶ καὶ ψυχῆς μάλιστα συγγενής, ὅτιπερ καὶ τῷ καλλίστῳ τῶν ὄντων φωτὶ οἰκεία, καὶ ὑπηρέτης τῶν θείων. Ἥτις καὶ τὴν εἰς φιλοσοφίαν ὁδὸν ἔτεμε τὴν πρώτην. Θεασάμενος γὰρ ἡλίου κίνησιν καὶ σελήνης καὶ τὰς τῶν ἀστέρων περιόδους καὶ τὴν ἀπλανῆ περιφορὰν τοῦ σύμπαντος οὐρανοῦ καὶ τὴν παντὸς τοῦ λόγου κρείττονα τάξιν τε καὶ ἁρμονίαν καὶ τὸν τοῦ κόσμου μόνου ἀψευδέστατον κοσμοποιόν, διήγγελλε τῷ ἡγεμόνι λογισμῷ ἃ εἶδεν. Ὁ δὲ ἐν ὄμματι ὀξυδερκεστέρῳ θεασάμενος καὶ παραδειγματικὰ εἴδη τούτων[b] ἀνωτέρω καὶ τὸν ἁπάντων αἴτιον, εὐθὺς εἰς ἔννοιαν ἦλθε θεοῦ καὶ γενέσεως καὶ προνοίας, λογισάμενος ὅτι ὅλη φύσις οὐκ αὐτοματισθεῖσα γέγονεν,[c] ἀλλ' ἀνάγκη ποιητὴν εἶναι καὶ πατέρα, κυβερνήτην τε καὶ ἡνίοχον, ὃς καὶ πεποίηκε καὶ ποιήματα αὐτοῦ σώζει.[d]

Harris, pp. 22-23, from Joh. Monachus (Mangey ii. 665 = Cod. Rupef. f. 221), ἐκ τοῦ Περὶ κοσμοποιίας. The two variants in the footnotes, printed by Harris on p. 70 among " unidentified fragments " and located by Früchtel, also come from Joh. Monachus (Mangey ii. 669), ἐκ τοῦ α' τῶν ἐν Γεν. ζητημ.

[a] ἀναλύσεως Cod. Aug.
[b] παραδειγματικὰ . . . τούτων con. Mangey : παραδείγματι καὶ εἴδει διὰ τούτων codd.
[c] ὅτι . . . γέγονεν] ἀμήχανον ἁρμονίαν καὶ τάξιν καὶ λόγον καὶ ἀναλογίαν καὶ τοσαύτην συμφωνίαν καὶ τῷ ὄντι εὐδαιμονίαν ἀπαυτοματισθεῖσαν γενέσθαι Joh. Monach. in alio loco.
[d] ἀλλ' . . . σώζει] ἀνάγκη γὰρ εἶναι ποιητὴν καὶ πατέρα, κυβερνήτην τε καὶ ἡνίοχον, ὃς γεγέννηκεν καὶ γεννηθέντα σώζει Joh. Monach. in alio loco.

GENESIS, BOOK II

39. (Gen. viii. 9)

Σύμβολα δὲ κακίας καὶ ἀρετῆς ὅ τε κόραξ καὶ ἡ περιστερά. Εἰ
γὰρ αὕτη δευτέρα ἐξελθοῦσα οὐχ εὗρεν ἀνάπαυσιν, πῶς ὁ κόραξ;
Οὐδὲ γὰρ τὸ ζῷόν ἐστιν ὑδρόβιον. Ἀλλὰ γὰρ ἡ κακία τοῖς κυ-
μαίνουσιν ἐφήδεται, ἡ δὲ ἀρετὴ τούτων ἀποπηδᾷ πρὸς τὴν πρώτην
δυσχεράνασα θέαν, ἀνάπαυσιν καὶ βάσιν ἐν τούτοις οὐχ ἔχουσα.
Wendland, pp. 57-58, from Procopius 297 c (*cf.* Cat. Lips.
150, Ἀδήλου).

41. (Gen. viii. 10)

Ὁ καλὸς καὶ ἀγαθὸς τοῦ διδασκάλου τρόπος καὶ ἂν ἐν ἀρχῇ
σκληραύχενας ἴδῃ φύσει, οὐκ ἀπογινώσκει τὴν ἀμείνω μεταβολὴν
ἀλλ' ὥσπερ ἀγαθὸς ἰατρὸς οὐκ εὐθὺς ἐπιφέρει τὴν θεραπείαν ἅμα
τῷ κατασκῆψαι τὴν νόσον ἀλλ' ἀναχώρησιν τῇ φύσει δοὺς ἵνα
προανατέμνῃ τὴν εἰς σωτηρίαν ὁδόν, τηνικαῦτα χρῆται τοῖς ὑγιεινοῖς
καὶ σωτηρίοις φαρμάκοις, οὕτω καὶ σπουδαῖος λόγοις κατὰ φιλοσοφίαν καὶ δόγμασιν.
Harris, p. 100, from Cod. Rupef. f. 137 (located by Früchtel).

47. (Gen. viii. 14)

Ἡ μὲν οὖν ἀρχὴ τοῦ κατακλυσμοῦ γέγονεν ἑβδόμῃ καὶ εἰκάδι
τῆς ἐαρινῆς ἰσημερίας, ἡ δὲ μείωσις ἑβδόμῳ μετὰ ταύτην μηνὶ τῇ
μετοπωρινῇ ἰσημερίᾳ, ἑβδόμῃ καὶ εἰκάδι τοῦ μηνός. Οὗτος γὰρ
πέρας μὲν τῆς πρώτης ἰσημερίας, ἀρχὴ δὲ τῆς δευτέρας, ὥσπερ
ὁ ἀπὸ τούτου ἕβδομος πέρας τῆς δευτέρας, ἀρχὴ δὲ τῆς πρώτης,
ἐν ᾧ καὶ τοῦ κόσμου ἡ γένεσις.
Wendland, p. 57, from Procopius 296 D.

48. (Gen. viii. 15-16)

Εὐλαβὴς ὢν ὁ Νῶε ἀκόλουθον ἡγήσατο μετὰ τὸ κοπάσαι τὸ
ὕδωρ ἀναμεῖναι τὴν τοῦ θεοῦ πρόσταξιν ἵν', ὥσπερ χρησμοῖς
εἰσελήλυθεν εἰς τὴν κιβωτόν, χρησμοῖς πάλιν ὑπεξέλθῃ, εἶπεν γὰρ
κύριος ὁ θεὸς τῷ Νῶε· " ἔξελθε σὺ καὶ ἡ γυνή σου " καὶ τὰ ἑξῆς.
Wendland, p. 58, from Procopius *ap.* Cat. Barb. vi. 8, f. 108,
Φίλωνος ἐπισκόπου.

54. (Gen. viii. 21)

(a) Ἡ πρότασις ἐμφαίνει μεταμέλειαν, ἀνοίκειον πάθος θείας
δυνάμεως. Ἀνθρώποις μὲν γὰρ ἀσθενεῖς αἱ γνῶμαι καὶ ἀβέβαιοι,
ὡς τὰ πράγματα πολλῆς γέμοντα ἀδηλότητος. Θεῷ δὲ οὐδὲν
ἄδηλον, οὐδὲν ἀκατάληπτον· ἰσχυρογνωμονέστατος γὰρ καὶ βε-

βαιότατος. Πῶς οὖν τῆς αὐτῆς ὑπούσης αἰτίας, ἐπιστάμενος ἐξ ἀρχῆς ὅτι ἔγκειται ἡ διάνοια τοῦ ἀνθρώπου ἐπιμελῶς ἐπὶ τὰ πονηρὰ ἐκ νεότητος, πρῶτον μὲν ἔφθειρεν τὸ γένος κατακλυσμῷ, μετὰ δὲ ταῦτά φησιν μηκέτι διαφθείρειν, καίτοι διαμενούσης ἐν τῇ ψυχῇ τῆς αὐτῆς κακίας; Λεκτέον οὖν ὅτι πᾶσα ἡ τοιάδε τῶν λόγων ἰδέα περιέχεται ἐν τοῖς νόμοις πρὸς μάθησιν καὶ ὠφέλειαν διδασκαλίας μᾶλλον ἢ πρὸς τὴν φύσιν τῆς ἀληθείας. Διττῶν γὰρ ὄντων κεφαλαίων ἃ κεῖται διὰ πάσης τῆς νομοθεσίας· ἑνὸς μὲν καθ' ὃ λέγεται, " οὐχ ὡς ἄνθρωπος ὁ θεός "· ἑτέρου δὲ καθ' ὃ " ὡς ἄνθρωπος " παιδεύειν λέγεται υἱόν. Τὸ μὲν πρότερον τῆς ἀληθείας ἐστίν· ὄντως γὰρ ὁ θεὸς οὐχ ὡς ἄνθρωπος ἀλλ' οὐδὲ ὡς ἥλιος οὐδὲ ὡς οὐρανὸς οὐδὲ ὡς κόσμος αἰσθητὸς ἢ νοητὸς ἀλλ' ὡς θεός, εἰ καὶ τοῦτο θέμις εἰπεῖν. Ὁμοιότητα γὰρ ἢ σύγκρισιν ἢ παραβολὴν οὐκ ἐπιδέχεται τὸ μακάριον ἐκεῖνο, μᾶλλον δὲ μακαριότητος αὐτῆς ὑπεράνω. Τὸ δὲ ὕστερον τῆς διδασκαλίας καὶ ὑφηγήσεως, τὸ " ὡς ἄνθρωπος," ἕνεκα τοῦ παιδεῦσαι τοὺς γηγενεῖς ἡμᾶς ἵνα μὴ τὰς ὀργὰς καὶ τὰς τιμωρίας μέχρι παντὸς ἀποτείνωμεν ἀσπόνδως καὶ ἀσυμβάτως ἔχοντες.

Harris, pp. 23-24, from Pitra, *Anal. Sacr.* ii. 304 (*e* Cod. Coislin. 276, f. 220 b), Φίλωνος ἐκ τοῦ Περὶ κοσμοποιίας γ´ κεφαλαίου (also in Cod. Rupef. f. 205 b, Φίλωνος, " with much variation ").

(*b*) Τὸ οὖν " διενοήθη " ἐπὶ θεοῦ οὐ[a] κυριολογεῖται, τοῦ τὴν γνώμην καὶ τὴν διάνοιαν βεβαιοτάτου.

Harris, p. 24, from same source as Frag. (a) above.

(*c*) Ἡ τυχοῦσα τῆς κακίας γένεσις δουλοῖ τὸν λογισμὸν καὶ ἂν μήπω τέλειον αὐτῆς ἐκφυτήσῃ τὸ γέννημα. Ἴσον γὰρ ἐστι τῷ κατὰ τὴν παροιμίαν λεγομένῳ " πλίνθον πλύνειν ἢ δικτύῳ ὕδωρ κομίζειν " τὸ κακίαν ἐξελεῖν ἀνθρώπου ψυχῆς. Ὅρα γὰρ αἷς ἐγκεχάρακται πάντων ἡ διάνοια, ὥς φησιν, " ἐπιμελῶς " καὶ οὐ παρέργως· τουτέστιν συγκεκόλληται καὶ προσήρμοσται. Τὸ δὲ σὺν ἐπιμελείᾳ καὶ φροντίδι κατεσκεμμένον ἐστὶ καὶ διηγορευμένον[b] εἰς ἀκρίβειαν, καὶ τοῦτο οὐκ ὀψὲ καὶ μόλις ἀλλ' " ἐκ νεότητος "· μονονουχὶ λέγων, " ἐξ αὐτῶν τῶν σπαργάνων," ὥσπερ τι μέρος ἡνωμένον.[c]

Harris, pp. 24-25, from Joh. Monachus (Mangey ii. 663 = Cod. Rupef. f. 138 a, ἐκ τοῦ Περὶ μετονομαζομένων).

---

[a] οὐ om. Cod. Coislin. vid.
[b] διηρευνημένον ex Arm. conieci.
[c] ἡνωμένον ex Lat. con. Mangey : τεινόμενον Codd.

GENESIS, BOOK II

59. (Gen. ix. 4) Τί ἐστιν· "ἐν αἵματι ψυχῆς κρέας οὐ φάγεσθε";

Ἔοικεν διὰ τούτου δηλοῦν ὅτι ψυχῆς οὐσία αἷμά ἐστιν· ψυχῆς μέντοι τῆς αἰσθητικῆς[a] οὐχὶ τῆς κατ' ἐξοχὴν γενομένης ἥτις ἐστὶν λογική τε καὶ νοερά. Τρία γὰρ μέρη ψυχῆς· τὸ μὲν θρεπτικόν, τὸ δὲ αἰσθητικόν, τὸ δὲ λογικόν. Τοῦ μὲν οὖν λογικοῦ τὸ θεῖον πνεῦμα οὐσία κατὰ τὸν θεόλογον, φησὶν γὰρ ὅτι ἐνεφύσησεν εἰς τὸ πρόσωπον αὐτοῦ πνοὴν ζωῆς· τοῦ δὲ αἰσθητικοῦ καὶ ζωτικοῦ τὸ αἷμα οὐσία, λέγει γὰρ ἐν ἑτέροις ὅτι ψυχὴ πάσης σαρκὸς τὸ αἷμά ἐστιν· καὶ κυριώτατα ψυχῆς σαρκὸς αἷμα εἴρηκεν, περὶ δὲ σάρκα ἡ αἴσθησις καὶ τὸ πάθος οὐχ ὁ νοῦς καὶ ὁ λογισμός. Οὐ μὴν ἀλλὰ καὶ τὸ ἐν αἵματι ψυχῆς μηνύει ὅτι ἕτερόν ἐστιν ψυχὴ καὶ ἕτερον αἷμα, ὡς εἶναι ψυχῆς μὲν ἀψευδῶς οὐσίαν πνεῦμα, μὴ καθ' αὑτὸ δὲ χωρὶς αἵματος τόπον ἐπέχειν ἀλλ' ἐμφέρεσθαι καὶ συγκεκρᾶσθαι αἵματι.

Harris, pp. 25-26, from Cod. Reg. 923, f. 376 b and Cod. Rupef. f. 279 b.

62. (Gen. ix. 6) Διατί, ὡς περὶ ἑτέρου θεοῦ, φησι τὸ "ἐν εἰκόνι θεοῦ ἐποίησα τὸν ἄνθρωπον" ἀλλ' οὐχὶ τῇ ἑαυτοῦ;

Παγκάλως καὶ σοφῶς τουτὶ κεχρησμῴδηται. Θνητὸν γὰρ οὐδὲν ἀπεικονισθῆναι πρὸς τὸν ἀνωτάτω καὶ πατέρα τῶν ὅλων ἐδύνατο, ἀλλὰ πρὸς τὸν δεύτερον θεόν, ὅς ἐστιν ἐκείνου λόγος. Ἔδει γὰρ τὸν λογικὸν ἐν ἀνθρώπου ψυχῇ τύπον ὑπὸ θείου λόγου χαραχθῆναι, ἐπειδὴ ὁ πρὸ τοῦ λόγου θεὸς κρείσσων ἐστὶν ἢ πᾶσα λογικὴ φύσις· τῷ δὲ ὑπὲρ τὸν λόγον ἐν τῇ βελτίστῃ καί τινι ἐξαιρέτῳ καθεστῶτι ἰδέᾳ οὐδὲν θέμις ἦν γεννητὸν ἐξομοιοῦσθαι.

Harris, p. 26, from Eusebius, Praep. Evang. vii. 13, ἐκ τοῦ πρώτου μοι κείσθω τῶν Φίλωνος ζητημάτων καὶ λύσεων.

64. (Gen. ix. 13-17)
(a) Τινὲς δέ φασι· μήποτε παρὰ τὴν ἶριν ἕτερα ἄττα μηνύει, τουτέστιν ἄνεσιν καὶ ἐπίτασιν τῶν ἐπιγείων μήτε τῆς ἀνέσεως εἰς ἔκλυσιν ὑφιεμένης παντελῆ καὶ ἀναρμοστίαν μήτε τῆς ἐπιτάσεως ἄχρι ῥήξεως ἐπιτεινομένης ἀλλὰ μέτροις ὡρισμένοις ἑκατέρας δυνάμεως σταθμηθείσης. Ὁ γὰρ μέγας κατακλυσμὸς ῥήξει γέγονεν, ὡς καὶ αὐτός φησιν· "ἐρράγησαν αἱ πηγαὶ τῆς ἀβύσσου" ἀλλ' οὐκ

---

[a] αἰσθητικῆς καὶ τῆς ζωτικῆς ex Lat. con. Harris.

ἐπιτάσει ποσῇ τινι.[a] Ἄλλως τέ φασιν· οὐκ ἔστιν ὅπλον τὸ τόξον ἀλλ' ὄργανον ὅπλου, βέλους τιτρώσκοντος, ὅπερ καθικνεῖται τοῦ πόρρω, τοῦ πλησίον ἀπαθοῦς διαμένοντος. Οὕτως οὖν, φησίν, οὐ πάντες καταλυθήσονται, κἂν τοῦτό τινας ὑπομένειν συμβῇ. Τὸ οὖν τόξον συμβολικῶς θεοῦ δύναμίς ἐστιν ἀόρατος ἑκάτερον κυβερνῶσα, καὶ τὴν ἐπίτασιν καὶ τὴν ἄνεσιν, τῷ ἀέρι ἐκ θεοῦ ἐνυπάρχουσα.

Wendland, pp. 59-60, from Procopius 300 c-d.

(b) Ἔστιν οὖν θεοῦ δύναμις ἀόρατος συμβολικῶς τὸ τόξον, ἥτις ἐνυπάρχουσα τῷ ἀέρι ἀνειμένῳ κατὰ τὰς αἰθρίας καὶ ἐπιτεινομένη κατὰ τὰς νεφώσεις οὐκ ἐᾷ τὰ νέφη δι' ὅλου εἰς ὕδωρ ἀναλύεσθαι τῷ μὴ γενέσθαι καθόλου κατακλυσμόν. Κυβερνᾷ γὰρ καὶ ἡνιοχεῖ τὴν πύκνωσιν τοῦ ἀέρος, πεφυκότος μάλιστα τότε ἀπαυχενίζειν καὶ ἐνυβρίζειν διὰ πλησμονῆς κόρου.

Harris, pp. 26-27, from Cat. Lips. 1, col. 160, Φίλωνος ἐπισκόπου, "also in Cod. Burney, fol. 37 b, with frequent inaccuracy of transcription."

65. (Gen. ix. 18-19)
Εἰ δὲ μνησθεὶς τετάρτου τοῦ Χανααν ἐπήνεγκε· "τρεῖς οὗτοι υἱοὶ τοῦ Νῶε," δέον, φασίν, εἰπεῖν τέσσαρες, οὐκ ἀλόγως. Διὰ γὰρ τὴν ὁμοιοτροπίαν εἰς ἓν συλλαμβάνει τῷ πατρὶ τὸν υἱόν. Οἳ καί φασιν ὡς εἰκότως νῦν τοῦ Χὰμ ὑπογράφει τὴν γενεὰν εἰς ἔμφασιν τοῦ ὅτι πατὴρ ἤδη γεγονὼς τὸν ἑαυτοῦ πατέρα οὐκ ἐτίμησεν οὐδὲ μετέδωκε τῷ γεννήσαντι ὧν ἂν παρὰ τοῦ παιδὸς ἠξίου τυχεῖν, καὶ ὡς νεωτεροποιὸν πρὸς ἁμαρτίαν ἐκάλεσεν εἰκότως νεώτερον. Ἐπίτηδες δὲ ἴσως ἐμνήσθη καὶ τοῦ Χανααν τοῦ τῶν Χαναναίων οἰκιστοῦ πόρρωθεν ἐλέγχων τὸ δυσγενές, ὧν τὴν γῆν ἀφελὼν τῷ θεοφιλεῖ παρέσχε λαῷ.

Wendland, p. 61, from Procopius 301 d, 304 a.

66. (Gen. ix. 20)
Ἐξομοιοῖ δὲ τὸν Νῶε τῷ πρώτῳ διαπλασθέντι ἀνθρώπῳ. Ἐξῆλθε γὰρ ἑκάτερος, ὁ μὲν τοῦ παραδείσου, ὁ δὲ τῆς κιβωτοῦ. Ἄρχει γεωργίας ἑκάτερος μετὰ κατακλυσμόν· καὶ γὰρ ἐν τῇ τοῦ κόσμου γενέσει τρόπον τινὰ κατεκέκλυστο ἡ γῆ. Οὐ γὰρ ἂν ἔλεγε "συναχθήτω τὸ ὕδωρ εἰς τὴν συναγωγὴν μίαν καὶ ὀφθήτω ἡ ξηρά."

Wendland, p. 63, from Procopius 305 a.

[a] ποσῇ τινι] περιττῇ con. Wendland.

δ8. (Gen. ix. 20)

Εἴποι δ' ἄν τις ἐκ τῶν ῥητῶν ὡς οὐδὲ τὸν οἶνον ὅλον ἀλλ' ἐκ
τοῦ οἴνου πίνει δι' ἐγκράτειαν, δι' ἣν ἐμέτρει τὴν χρῆσιν, τοῦ
ἀκράτους οὐκ ἀπαλλαττομένου τῶν συμποσίων πρὶν ⟨ἄν⟩ ὅλον
ἐκπίῃ τὸν ἄκρατον· εἶτα καὶ τῷ μεθύειν ἡ γραφὴ νῦν ἀντὶ τῆς
οἰνώσεως κέχρηται. Διττὸν γὰρ τὸ μεθύειν, ἢ τὸ παρ' οἶνον ληρεῖν,
ὅπερ ἁμάρτημα καὶ φαύλου ἴδιον, ἢ τὸ οἰνοῦσθαι, ὅπερ καὶ εἰς
σοφὸν πίπτει.[a]

Wendland, p. 63, from Procopius 305 ᴀ. The variant to
the last sentence, given in the footnote, is printed by Harris,
p. 27, from Mai, *Script. Vet.* vii. 104, from Cod. Vat. 1553,
ἐκ τοῦ α' τῶν ἐν Γενέσει ζητημάτων.

71. (Gen. ix. 22)

Τοῦ δὲ Χὰμ αὔξει τὸ ἔγκλημα, πρῶτον μὲν ἐκ τοῦ ὑπεριδεῖν,
δεύτερον δ' ἐκ τοῦ εἰπεῖν καὶ οὐχ ἑνὶ μόνῳ τῶν ἀδελφῶν[b] ἀλλ'
ἀμφοτέροις· εἰ δὲ καὶ πλείους ἦσαν, ἅπασιν ἐξελάλησεν αὐτῶ διαχλευά-
ζων πρᾶγμα οὐ χλεύης ἀλλ' αἰδοῦς καὶ εὐλαβείας ἄξιον ὄν. Εἶτα
οὐκ ἔνδον ἀλλ' ἔξω διήγγειλεν· ὅπερ ἐμφαίνει τὸ μὴ ἀκηκοέναι
μόνον τοὺς ἀδελφοὺς ἀλλὰ καὶ τοὺς ἔξω περιεστῶτας ἄνδρας τε
καὶ γυναῖκας.[c]

Wendland, p. 62, from Procopius 304 c. The variant to
the last sentence, given in the footnote, is printed by Harris,
p. 27, from Cat. Lips. 1, col. 163, also from Cat. Burney,
f. 37 b, Φίλωνος ἐπισκόπου.

72. (Gen. ix. 23)

Ὁ εὐχερὴς καὶ ἀπερίσκεπτος τὰ ἐπ' εὐθείας καὶ πρὸς ὀφθαλμῶν
μόνον ὁρᾷ· ὁ δὲ φρόνιμος καὶ τὰ κατόπιν, τουτέστι τὰ μέλλοντα·
ὥσπερ γὰρ τὰ ὀπίσω τῶν ἔμπροσθεν ὑστερίζει, οὕτω καὶ τὰ
μέλλοντα τῶν ἐνεστώτων. Ὧν τὴν θεωρίαν ὁ ἀστεῖος μέτεισιν,
αὐγαίως[d] πάντοθεν ὀμματωθείς· πᾶς οὖν σοφὸς οὐκ ἄνθρωπος

[a] Διττὸν . . . πίπτει] Διττὸν τὸ μεθύειν· ἐν μὲν τὸ ληρεῖν παρ'
οἶνον, ὅπερ ἐστὶ φαύλου ἴδιον ἁμάρτημα· ἕτερον δὲ τὸ οἰνοῦσθαι,
ὅπερ εἰς σοφὸν πίπτει Cod. Vat.
[b] Post ἀδελφῶν verba τὸ τοῦ πατρὸς ἀκούσιον ἁμάρτημα ex
Arm. suppl. Wendland.
[c] τὸ μὴ ἀκηκοέναι . . . γυναῖκας] οὐ μόνον τοὺς ἀδελφοὺς
ἀκηκοέναι ἀλλὰ καὶ τοὺς περιεστῶτας ἄνδρας ἔξω ὁμοῦ καὶ γυναῖκας
Cat. Lips.
[d] Λυγκέως ⟨δίκην⟩ ex Arm. con. Harris : Ἄργος ὡς con. Post.

ἀλλὰ νοῦς καταθεώμενος καὶ περιαθρῶν περιπέφρακται πρὸς τὰ
ἐνεστῶτα καὶ τὰ ἀδοκήτως κατασπιλάζοντα.

Harris, p. 28, from Cod. Rupef. f. 142, Φίλωνος· ἐκ τῶν ἐν
Γενέσει ζητημάτων.

77. (Gen. ix. 27) Καὶ πῶς Χὰμ καὶ αὐτὸς ὢν ἀσεβὴς οὐ τῆς
αὐτῆς μετέσχε κατάρας;

Ἄλλοι δέ φασιν ὡς ὁ μὲν Χαναὰν ἔλαβε τὴν κατάραν οὐκ ὢν
ἀλλότριος τῆς πατρικῆς προαιρέσεως, ὁ δὲ Χὰμ εἰς πατέρα ἁμαρ-
τήσας εἰς υἱὸν κατηράθη ἄξιον ὄντα καὶ τῶν ἰδίων κακῶν τῆς
κατάρας. Ἀλλὰ καὶ μειζόνως ἤλγει διὰ τοῦ παιδὸς τιμωρούμενος·
μεῖζω γὰρ ὢν ⟨αὐτοὶ⟩ πάσχομεν τὰ τῶν παίδων ἐστὶν εἰς συμφοράν,
καὶ[a] μάλιστα ἡνίκα γινώσκομεν ὡς ἀρχηγοὶ καὶ διδάσκαλοι τῶν
κακῶν αὐτοῖς βουλευμάτων γεγόναμεν.

Wendland, pp. 60-61, from Procopius 301 c-d and Theodoret, Quaest. lviii. (cf. Cat. Lips. 165-166).

[a] Post καὶ lacuna est quam per verbum ἀνιώμεθα suppl.
Wendland.

3. (Gen. xv. 9)

Ἀτόπως δρῶσιν ὅσοι ἐκ μέρους τινὸς κρίνουσι τὸ ὅλον ἀλλὰ τὸ ἐναντίον[a] ἐκ τοῦ ὅλου τὸ μέρος. Οὕτω γὰρ ἄμεινον καὶ σῶμα[b] καὶ πρᾶγμα δογματίζοιτο ἄν. Ἔστιν οὖν ἡ θεία νομοθεσία τρόπον τινὰ ζῷον ἡνωμένον, ἣν ὅλον δι' ὅλου χρὴ μεγάλοις ὄμμασι περισκοπεῖν, καὶ τὴν βουλὴν τῆς συμπάσης γραφῆς ἀκριβῶς καὶ τηλαυγῶς περιαθρεῖν, μὴ κατακόπτοντας τὴν ἁρμονίαν, μηδὲ τὴν ἕνωσιν διαρτῶντας. Ἑτερόμορφα γὰρ καὶ ἑτεροειδῆ φανεῖται τῆς κοινωνίας στερούμενα.

Harris, p. 29, from Dam. Par. 774, from Cod. Rupef.

7. (Gen. xv. 11a)

Πᾶσα ἡ ὑπὸ τὴν σελήνην φύσις μεστὴ πολέμων καὶ κακῶν ἐμφυλίων ἐστὶ καὶ ξένων.

Harris, p. 29, from Mai, *Script. Vet.* vii. 98, from Cod. Vat. 1553, ἐκ τοῦ γ' τῶν ἐν Γενέσει ζητημάτων.

8. (Gen. xv. 11b)

Ἕνεκα μὲν τῶν φαύλων οὐδεμία πόλις ἠρέμησεν ἄν. Διαμένουσι δὲ ἀστασίαστοι δι' ἑνὸς ἢ δευτέρου δικαιοσύνη ἀσκοῦντος[c] οὗ ἡ ἀρετὴ τὰς πολιτικὰς[d] νόσους ἰᾶται, γέρας ἀπονέμοντος τοῦ φιλαρέτου[e] θεοῦ καλοκἀγαθίας[f] τοῦ μὴ μόνον αὐτὸν ἀλλὰ καὶ τοὺς πλησιάζοντας ὠφελεῖσθαι.[g]

Harris, pp. 29-30, from Mangey ii. 661, from Joh.

[a] οὐ τὸ ἐναντίον con. Harris.   [b] ὄνομα con. Harris.
[c] οἰκοῦντος Cod. Rupef. : συνοικοῦντος Anton Melissa.
[d] πολεμικὰς Joh. Monachus.
[e] φιλανθρώπου Joh. Monachus.
[f] καλοκἀγαθῶν Cod. Rupef.
[g] ὠφελεῖν Anton Melissa.

APPENDIX A, GREEK FRAGMENTS

Monachus (=Cod. Rupef. f. 33 b), and from Anton Melissa, col. 1105.

11. (Gen. xv. 15)

Ἐναργῶς ἀφθαρσίαν ψυχῆς αἰνίττεται μετοικιζομένης ἀπὸ τοῦ θνητοῦ σώματος. Τὸ[a] γὰρ τῷ τελευτῶντι φάσκειν " ἀπελεύσῃ ⟨πρὸς τοὺς⟩ πατέρας σου " τί ἕτερον ἢ ζωὴν ἑτέραν παρίστησι τὴν ἄνευ σώματος, καθ' ἣν ψυχὴν μόνην συμβαίνει ζῆν. Πατέρας δὲ Ἀβραὰμ οὐ δήπου τοὺς γεννήσαντας αὐτὸν πάππους καὶ προγόνους παρείληφεν· οὐ γὰρ πάντες ἐπαινετοὶ γεγόνασιν· ἀλλ' ἔοικεν αἰνίττεσθαι πατέρας οὓς ἑτέρωθι καλεῖν ἀγγέλους εἴωθεν. Εἰ δὲ καὶ τοὺς περὶ τὸν Ἄβελ καὶ Ἐνὼς καὶ Σὴθ καὶ Ἐνὼχ καὶ Νῶε φήσεις, οὐχ ἁμαρτήσει[b] τοῦ πρέποντος . . . μακρὸν γὰρ αἰῶνα τείνουσι[c] μυρίοι τῶν ἀφρόνων, καλὸν δὲ καὶ σπουδαῖον μόνος ὁ φρονήσεως ἐραστής.

Wendland, pp. 67-68, from Cat. Barb. vi. 8, f. 128, Φίλωνος Ἑβραίου . . . φίλωνος ἐπισκόπου (cf. Cat. Lips. 209, Ἀδήλου).

12. (Gen. xv. 16)

Καὶ οὕτω μὲν ἐπὶ τοῦ νοητοῦ, οὐδὲν δὲ ἧττον κἀπὶ τοῦ αἰσθητοῦ ἐστι συνιδεῖν ἐν ταῖς τῶν ζῴων γενέσεσι· πρῶτον μὲν γάρ ἐστι σπέρματος καταβολή, δεύτερον δὲ ἡ εἰς τὰ γένη διανομή, τρίτον αὔξησις, καὶ τέταρτον τελείωσις.

Staehle, p. 30, from Joh. Lydus, p. 29, 7-11.

18. (Gen. xvi. 1)

Στεῖρα ἡ τοῦ ἔθνους μήτηρ εἰσάγεται, πρῶτον μὲν[d] ἵνα παράδοξος ἡ τῶν ἐγγόνων σπορὰ φαίνηται θαυματουργηθεῖσα, δεύτερον δὲ ὑπὲρ τοῦ μὴ[e] συνουσίᾳ μᾶλλον ἀνδρὸς ἀλλ' ἐπιφροσύνῃ[f] θείᾳ συλλαμβάνειν τε καὶ τίκτειν.[g] Τὸ γὰρ στεῖραν οὖσαν ἀποκύειν οὐ γεννήσεως ἀλλὰ θείας δυνάμεως ἔργον ἦν.[h]

Wendland, pp. 68-69, from Cat. Barb. vi. 8, f. 129 (cf. Theodoret, Quaest. lxxv), and Procopius 349 c.

[a] τὸ Wendland : τῷ codd.
[b] Wendland : ἁμαρτήσεις codd.
[c] Wendland : τίνουσι codd.
[d] πρῶτον μὲν om. Procopius.
[e] δεύτερον . . . μὴ] καὶ ἵνα μὴ Procopius.
[f] εὐφροσύνῃ Cat. Barb.
[g] θείᾳ . . . τίκτειν] θεοῦ συλλαμβάνῃ καὶ τίκτῃ Procopius.
[h] τὸ γὰρ . . . ἦν om. Procopius vid.

20. (Gen. xvi. 2)

Ὁρᾷς ταύτης τὸ σῶφρον καὶ τὸ ἄφθονον προσέτι καὶ φίλανδρον
καὶ τοῦ Ἀβραὰμ τὴν ἀπάθειαν.

Wendland, p. 69, from Procopius 352 A (*cf.* Cat. Lips. 213,
Ἀδήλου).

21. (Gen. xvi. 3)

Οὐχ ὥσπερ οἱ ἀσελγεῖς ὀλιγωρίᾳ τῶν ἀστῶν[a] ἐπὶ τὰς θεραπαίνας
ἐκμαίνονται. Ὁ δὲ Ἀβραὰμ τότε βεβαιότερος περὶ τὴν σύνοικον,
ὅτε παλλακίδι χρῆσθαι παρήγγελλον οἱ καιροί, καὶ τότε ταύτην
εὗρε γυναῖκα παγιωτέραν, ὅτε παρεισῆλθεν ἑτέρᾳ. Πρὸς μὲν γὰρ
τὴν παλλακίδα μίξις ἦν σωμάτων ἕνεκα παίδων γενέσεως, πρὸς
δὲ τὴν γαμετὴν ἕνωσις ψυχῆς ἁρμοζομένης ἔρωτι θείῳ.

Wendland, p. 69, from Procopius 352 A (*cf.* Cat. Lips. 215,
Εὐσεβίου : " Philonische Gedanken sind durch eine ver-
mittelnde Quelle, Eusebius, übergegangen ").

22. (Gen. xvi. 4)

Κατὰ καιρὸν κυρίαν ἐκάλεσεν, ὅτε τῆς παρὰ τῆς θεραπαίνης[b]
ἠλάττωται. Τοῦτο δὲ καὶ εἰς πάντα διατείνει τοῦ βίου τὰ πράγ-
ματα· κυριώτερος[c] γὰρ ὁ φρόνιμος πένης ἄφρονος πλουσίου καὶ ὁ
ἄδοξος ἐνδόξου καὶ ὁ νοσῶν ὑγιαίνοντος. Τὰ μὲν γὰρ σὺν φρονήσει
πάντα κύρια, τὰ δὲ ἐν ἀφροσύνῃ δοῦλα καὶ ἄκυρα. Οὐκ εἶπε δὲ
" ἠτίμασε τὴν κυρίαν αὐτῆς " ἀλλ᾽ " ἠτιμάσθη ἡ κυρία." Οὐ γὰρ
ἐθέλει κατηγορεῖν, δηλῶσαι δὲ τὸ συμβεβηκός.

Wendland, pp. 69-70, from Procopius 352 B (*cf.* Cat. Lips.
215, Ἀδήλου).

23. (Gen. xvi. 5)

Τὸ " ἐκ σοῦ " οὐκ ἀντὶ τοῦ " ὑπὸ σοῦ " . . . ἀλλ᾽ ἔστι χρονικὸν
τῷ ἑξῆς συναπτόμενον· ἐξ οὗ σοι καὶ ἀφ᾽ οὗ χρόνου ἐγὼ " δέδωκα
τὴν παιδίσκην μου." Οὐ γὰρ γυναῖκα εἶπεν ἢ γαμετὴν τὴν ἐξ
αὐτοῦ κύουσαν.

Wendland, p. 70, from Procopius 352 B (the next two
sentences in Procopius do not belong here).

---

[a] ἀστείων ex Arm. con. Wendland.
[b] θεραπαίνης τιμῆς con. Wendland.
[c] κυριώτερον Mai.

APPENDIX A, GREEK FRAGMENTS

24. (Gen. xvi. 6)

Ἔπαινον ἔχει τὸ ῥητὸν τοῦ σοφοῦ μήτε γυναῖκα μήτε γαμετὴν ἀλλὰ παιδίσκην εἰπόντος τῆς γαμετῆς τὴν ἐξ αὐτοῦ κύουσαν.

Wendland, p. 70, from Cat. Barb. vi. 8, f. 130, Φίλωνος ἐπισκόπου.

26. (Gen. xvi. 6)

Οὐ γάρ[a] πᾶσα ψυχὴ δέχεται νουθεσίαν ἀλλ᾽ ἡ μὲν ἵλεως ἀγαπᾷ τοὺς ἐλέγχους καὶ τοῖς παιδεύουσι μᾶλλον οἰκειοῦται, ἡ δὲ ἐχθρὰ μισεῖ καὶ ἀποστρέφεται[b] καὶ ἀποδιδράσκει τοὺς πρὸς ἡδονὴν λόγους, τῶν ὠφελεῖν δυναμένων προκρίνουσα.

Wendland, pp. 70-71, from Procopius 352 B = Harris, p. 30, from Cat. Lips. col. 216, Προκοπίου.

29. (Gen. xvi. 8)

Καὶ τὸ εὔγνωμον δὲ αὐτῆς παρίσταται ἐκ τοῦ λέγειν Σάρραν κυρίαν καὶ μηδὲν περὶ αὐτῆς φαῦλον εἰπεῖν. Καὶ τὸ τοῦ ἤθους δὲ ἀνυπόκριτον πῶς οὐκ ἐπαινετόν; ὁμολογεῖ γὰρ ὁ πέπονθεν, ὅτι τὸ πρόσωπον, λέγω δὲ τὴν φαντασίαν τῆς ἀρετῆς καὶ σοφίας, καταπέπληκται καὶ τὸ τῆς ἐξουσίας βασιλικόν· οὐ γὰρ ὑπομένει τὸ ὕψος καὶ μέγεθος θεωρεῖν ἀλλ᾽ ἀποδιδράσκει· ἔνιοι γὰρ οὐ μίσει τῷ πρὸς ἀρετὴν φεύγουσιν αὐτήν, ἀλλ᾽ αἰδοῖ κρίνοντες ἑαυτοὺς ἀναξίους συμβιοῦν τῇ δεσποίνῃ.

Wendland, p. 71, from Procopius 354 B.

30. (Gen. xvi. 9)

Τὸ ὑποτάττεσθαι τοῖς κρείττοσιν ὠφελιμώτατον. Ὁ μαθὼν ἄρχεσθαι καὶ ἄρχειν εὐθὺς μανθάνει. Οὐδὲ γὰρ εἰ πάσης γῆς καὶ θαλάττης τὸ κράτος ἀνάψοιτό τις, ἄρχων ἂν εἴη πρὸς ἀλήθειαν, εἰ μὴ μάθοι καὶ προπαιδευθείη τὸ ἄρχεσθαι.

Harris, p. 30, " The first sentence from Mai, *Script. Vet.* vii. 103, *e* Cod. Vat. 1553, ἐκ τοῦ πρώτου τῶν ἐν τῇ Γενέσει ζητημάτων. Also Dam. Par. 359 and Cod. Reg. 923, fol. 74, in each case referred to Greg. Nazianz. The last part in Dam. Par. 359 as from Philo, and in Cod. Reg. *l.c.*, ἐκ τοῦ α´ τῶν ἐν Γενέσει ζητημάτων."

[a] γὰρ om. Cat. Lips.
[b] καὶ ἀποστρέφεται om. Procopius.

38. (Gen. xvi. 16)

(a) Ὁ γὰρ ἐξ ἀριθμὸς γεννητικώτατός ἐστιν ὡς ἀρτιοπέριττος, μετέχων καὶ τῆς δραστικῆς οὐσίας κατὰ τὸν περιττὸν καὶ τῆς ὑλικῆς κατὰ τὸν ἄρτιον. Ὅθεν καὶ ἀρχαῖοι γάμον καὶ ἁρμονίαν αὐτὸν ἐκάλεσαν.

Staehle, p. 33, from Joh. Lydus, p. 32, 4-8.

(b) Μακαρία φύσις ἡ ἐπὶ παντὶ χαίρουσα καὶ μηδενὶ δυσαρεστοῦσα τῶν ἐν τῷ κόσμῳ τὸ παράπαν,ᵃ ἀλλ᾽ εὐαρεστοῦσαᵇ τοῖς γινομένοις ὡς καλῶς καὶ συμφερόντως γινομένοις.

Harris, p. 97 (" unidentified," but located by Früchtel), from Dam. Par. 372 and 675, also Cod. Reg. 923, f. 38 b, and Georgius Monachus, col. 1116.

40. (Gen. xvii. 1-2)

Ἢ ὡς μήπω ἀμέμπτῳ ἢ ὡς τοιούτῳ μέν, δεομένῳ δὲ ἀεὶ ἐνεργεῖν τὸ ἄμεμπτον, ὡς ἂν διὰ παντὸς ἄμεμπτος ᾖ. Τὸ δὲ " θήσομαι τὴν διαθήκην μου " ὡς περὶ ἄθλου ἐπαγγελία, καὶ αὐτῆς διδομένης τῷ εὐαρεστοῦντι ἐναντίον αὐτοῦ καὶ γενομένῳ ἀμέμπτῳ. Ἐπάγει δὲ καί· " πληθυνῶ σε σφόδρα."

Wendland, p. 71, from Procopius 353 c (" die philonische Vorlage hat Pr. wohl auch hier . . . nicht selbst benutzt; denn die Uebereinstimmung ist keine wörtliche ").

41. (Gen. xvii. 3)

Τὸ δὲ μέγεθος τῶν ἐπαγγελιῶν καὶ τὸ τὸν θεὸν ἀξιοῦν αὐτοῦ θεὸν εἶναι καταπλαγεὶς ἔπεσεν ἐπὶ τὸ πρόσωπον.

Wendland, p. 72, from Procopius 356 в, " passt durchaus in philonische Gedankenkreise."

48. (Gen. xvii. 12)

Οἴησις, ὡς ὁ τῶν ἀρχαίων λόγος, ἐστὶν ἐκκοπὴ προκοπῆς· ὁ γὰρ κατοιόμενος βελτίωσιν οὐκ ἀνέχεται.

Harris, p. 99 (" unidentified," but located by Früchtel), from Dam. Par. 704 (" note that on p. 629 this is given to Cyril, and so in Cod. Reg. 923, f. 36 b ").

ᵃ τῶν . . . παράπαν om. Georg. Mon.
ᵇ εὐχαριστοῦσα Georg. Mon.: τῶν . . . εὐαρεστοῦσα om. Cod. Reg.

52. (Gen. xvii. 14)

Οὐδὲν τῶν ἀκουσίων ἔνοχον ἀποφαίνει ὁ νόμος, ὁπότε καὶ τῷ φόνον ἀκούσιον δράσαντι συγγινώσκει. . . . Τὸ δὲ ὀκτὼ ἡμερῶν μετὰ γέννησιν βρέφος εἰ μὴ περιτέμνηται, τί ἀδικεῖ ὡς καὶ θανάτου τιμωρίαν ὑπομένειν; Ἔνιοι μὲν οὖν φασιν ἀναφορικὸν εἶναι τὸν τῆς ἑρμηνείας[a] τρόπον ἐπὶ τοὺς γονεῖς, καὶ ἐκείνους κολάζεσθαι οἴονται δεινῶς, ὡς ὀλιγωρηκότας τῆς τοῦ νόμου διατάξεως. Ἔνιοι δὲ ὅτι ὑπερβολῇ χρώμενος κατὰ τοῦ βρέφους, ὅσα τῷ δοκεῖν, ἠγανάκτησεν, ἵνα τοῖς τελείοις καταλύσασι[b] τὸν νόμον ἀπαραίτητος ἐπάγηται τιμωρία[c] οὐκ ἐπειδὴ τὸ ἔργον τῆς περιτομῆς ἀναγκαῖον ἀλλ' ὅτι ἡ διαθήκη ἀθετεῖται, τοῦ σημείου, δι' οὗ γνωρίζεται, μὴ πληρουμένου.

Harris, p. 31, from Cat. Ined. Cod. Reg. 1825 (Mangey ii. 675), and Cat. Burney, f. 45, Φίλωνος Ἑβραίου, also Cat. Lips. 1, col. 225 (" the last sentence looks like an added gloss ").

Οὐδὲν τῶν ἀκουσίων ἔνοχον ἀποφαίνει ὁ νόμος, ὁπότε καὶ τῷ φόνον ἀκούσιον δράσαντι συγγινώσκει. Τί οὖν ἀδικεῖ τὸ ὀκτὼ ἡμερῶν βρέφος, εἰ μὴ περιτμηθήσεται; ἀλλ' ἢ τὴν ἀναφορὰν ἐπὶ τοὺς γονεῖς ἐκληπτέον κολαζομένους, εἰ μὴ περιτέμοιεν τὸ παιδίον, ἢ γοῦν ὑπερβολικῶς κατὰ τοῦ βρέφους, ὅσα τῷ δοκεῖν, ἠγανάκτησεν, ἵνα τοῖς τελείοις ἀπαραίτητος γίνηται.

Wendland, pp. 72-73, from Procopius, Cod. Aug. f. 98[r] (Migne, p. 357 A).

---

58. (Gen. xvii. 19) Καὶ ἰδοὺ Σάρρα ἡ γυνή σου τέξεταί σοι υἱόν.

Ἡ ὁμολογία, φησίν, ἡ ἐμὴ κατάφασίς ἐστιν ἀκραιφνής, ἀμιγὴς ἀρνήσεως καὶ ἡ σὴ πίστις οὐκ ἀμφίβολος ἀλλ' ἀνενδοίαστος, αἰδοῦς καὶ ἐντροπῆς μετέχουσα. Ὅθεν ὁ προείληφας γενησόμενον διὰ

---

[a] τιμωρίας Cat. Lips., Burney.
[b] καταλύουσι Cat. Lips.
[c] ἀπαραιτήτως ἐπάγηται τιμωρίας Cat. Burney.

τὴν πρὸς ἐμὲ πίστιν, γενήσεται πάντως· τοῦτο γὰρ μηνύει τὸ " ναί."

Wendland, p. 73, from Procopius, Cod. Aug. f. 98ᵛ (Migne, p. 358).

61. (Gen. xvii. 24-25)

Ὁ γὰρ τῶν δεκατριῶν ἀριθμὸς συνέστηκεν ἐκ τῶν πρώτων δυοῖν τετραγώνων, τοῦ τέσσαρα καὶ τοῦ ἐννέα, ἀρτίου τε καὶ περιττοῦ, πλευρὰς ἐχόντων τοῦ μὲν ἀρτίου τὸ ὑλικὸν εἶδος δυάδα, τοῦ δὲ περιττοῦ τὴν δραστήριον ἰδέαν τριάδα.   Οὗτος οὖν ὁ ἀριθμὸς ἡ μεγίστη καὶ τελειοτάτη τῶν ἑορτῶν γέγονε τοῖς ἀρχαίοις[a] ἐπιτήρησις.

Staehle, p. 59, from Joh. Lydus, 45, 12-18.

[a] ἀρχαῖος Staehle.

GENESIS, BOOK IV

8. (Gen. xviii. 6-7)

(a) Μεγίστη δὲ ἡ τῆς τριάδος καὶ κατ' αἴσθησιν δύναμις. Ὁ γὰρ κατ' αὐτὴν ἀριθμὸς τοῖς γενητοῖς ἐπιδέδωκε γένεσιν, αὔξησιν, τροφήν, καὶ οὐχ ἁπλῶς εἴρηται· "τριχθὰ δὲ πάντα δέδασται." . . . Διὰ μὲν τοῦτο οἱ Πυθαγόρειοι τριάδα μὲν ἐν ἀριθμοῖς, ἐν δὲ σχήμασι τὸ ὀρθογώνιον τρίγωνον ὑποτίθενται στοιχεῖον τῆς τῶν ὅλων γενέσεως. Ἕν μὲν οὖν μέτρον ἐστί, καθ' ὃ συνέστη ὁ ἀσώματος καὶ νοητὸς κόσμος. Δεύτερον δὲ μέτρον, καθ' ὃ ἐπάγη ὁ αἰσθητὸς οὐρανός, πέμπτην λαχὼν καὶ θειοτέραν οὐσίαν, ἄτρεπτον καὶ ἀμετάβολον. Τρίτον δὲ καθ' ὃ ἐδημιουργήθη τὰ ὑπὸ σελήνην, ἐκ τῶν τεσσάρων δυνάμεων, γένεσιν καὶ φθορὰν ἐπιδεχόμενα.

Staehle, pp. 25-26, from Joh. Lydus, pp. 25, 12-16 and 28, 8-16.

(b) Οὐ θέμις τὰ ἱερὰ μυστήρια ἐκλαλεῖν ἀμυήτοις ἄχρις ἂν καθαρθῶσιν[a] τελείᾳ καθάρσει, ὁ γὰρ ἀνοργίαστος καὶ εὐχερής, ἀσώματον καὶ νοητὴν φύσιν ἀκούειν ἢ βλέπειν ἀδυνατῶν, ὑπὸ τῆς φανερᾶς ὄψεως ἀπατηθεὶς μωμήσεται τὰ ἀμώμητα. Τοῖς ἀμυήτοις ἐκλαλεῖν μυστήρια καταλύοντός ἐστι τοὺς θεσμοὺς τῆς ἱερατικῆς τελετῆς.

Harris, p. 69 (" unidentified," but located by E. Bréhier), from Dam. Par. 533 (cf. Dam. Par. 782=Cod. Rupef. f. 189, and Cod. Reg. 923, f. 25 b, " by the last two expressly referred to II. Quaest. in Gen.").

10. (Gen. xviii. 8) Αὐτὸς δὲ παρειστήκει αὐτοῖς ὑπὸ τὸ δένδρον.

Αὐτουργῶν δὲ τὴν ὑπηρεσίαν ὁ τῃ' καὶ δέκα κεκτημένος οἰκογενεῖς καὶ πολλοὺς ἀργυρωνήτους τὴν θείαν ὑπόνοιαν περὶ αὐτῶν δείκνυσιν οὐ συγχωρῶν οἰκέταις τὴν ἱερατικὴν θεοῦ διακονίαν, αὐτὸς δὲ ταύτην, εἰ καὶ πρεσβύτης, ἀναδεχόμενος.

Wendland, p. 74, from Procopius, Cod. Aug. f. 100[v] (cf. Ἀκακίου, Cat. Lips. 234).

[a] ἄχρι καθαρσῶσι Cod. Reg.

20. (Gen. xviii. 16)

Μόλις διαζεύγνυνται δυσαποσπάστως ἔχων, ὡς βούλεσθαι καὶ ἀποδημεῖν. Ἄμεινον δὲ τοῦ πέμπειν κοινωνικώτατον ἦθος ἐμφαῖνον.
Wendland, p. 74, from Procopius 368 B.

24. (Gen. xviii. 21)

Ἡμᾶς τοίνυν διδάσκει μὴ ἐπιτρέχειν πίστει κακῶν μέχρι⟨ς ἂν⟩ πεισθῶμεν τῇ θέᾳ.
Wendland, p. 74, from Procopius, Cod. Aug. f. 101ᵛ (Migne, p. 368 c, cf. Cat. Lips. 239 Β-Γ).

30. (Gen. xix. 1)

Τῷ μὲν Ἀβραὰμ φαίνονται τρεῖς, καὶ μεσημβρίας· τῷ δὲ Λὼτ δύο, καὶ ἑσπέρας. Φυσικώτατα διάφορον εἰσηγεῖται ὁ νόμος τελείου καὶ προκόπτοντος· ὁ μὲν οὖν τέλειος τριάδα φαντασιοῦται ἐν ἀσκίῳ φωτὶ καὶ μεσημβρινῷ, μεστὴν διηνεκῆ καὶ πληρεστάτην οὐσίαν· ὁ δὲ δυάδα, διαίρεσιν καὶ τομὴν καὶ κενὸν ἔχουσαν ἐν ἑσπερινῷ σκότει.
Harris, p. 32, from Pitra, *Anal. Sacr.* ii. 23 *e* Cod. Coislin. 276 (?), f. 10 " with heading, φησὶ γὰρ τοῦτο ὁ ἐν λόγοις ἐξαίρετος Φίλων."

Πρὸς μὲν Ἀβραὰμ οἱ τρεῖς ἄνδρες καὶ μεσημβρίας, εἰς Σόδομα δὲ οἱ δύο ἄγγελοι καὶ ἑσπέρας.
Wendland, p. 74, from Procopius, Cod. Aug. f. 102ʳ (Migne, p. 370 c=Cat. Lips. 241-242, Ἀδήλου).

33. (Gen. xix. 2)

(a) Τῷ μὲν Ἀβραὰμ εὐχερῶς ἐπείσθησαν, τῷ δὲ Λὼτ μετὰ βίας.
Wendland, p. 75, from Procopius 370 D.

(b) Στενοχωρεῖται πᾶς ἄφρων, θλιβόμενος ὑπὸ φιλαργυρίας καὶ φιλοδοξίας καὶ φιληδονίας καὶ τῶν ὁμοιοτρόπων ἅπερ οὐκ ἐᾷ τὴν διάνοιαν ἐν εὐρυχωρίᾳ διάγειν.ᵃ
Harris, p. 32, from Dam. Par. 362, ἐκ τοῦ β′ τῶν ἐν Γενέσει, and Cod. Reg. 923, ἐκ τῶν δ′, " also Cod. Barocc. 143 . . . (Mangey ii. 674), and in Cod. Rupef. f. 73 b without a title."

———
ᵃ διαβαίνειν Cod. Barocc.

APPENDIX A, GREEK FRAGMENTS

40. (Gen. xix. 10)

Νόμος ἔστω κατὰ τῶν σεμνὰ καὶ θεῖα οὐ[a] σεμνῶς καὶ θεοπρεπῶς ὁρᾶν ἀξιούντων, κόλασιν ἐπιφέρειν ἀορασίας.

Harris, pp. 32-33, from Dam. Par. 341, "where it is ascribed to Clem. Alex.," and Cod. Reg. 923, f. 62 b, ἐκ τοῦ δ' τῶν ἐν Γενέσει ζητημάτων.

43. (Gen. xix. 14)

Οἱ ἐν ταῖς ἀφθόνοις χορηγίαις πλούτου καὶ δόξης καὶ τῶν ὁμοιοτρόπων ὑπάρχοντες, καὶ ἐν ὑγιείᾳ καὶ εὐαισθησίᾳ σώματος καὶ εὐεξίᾳ ζωῆς καὶ τὰς διὰ πασῶν τῶν αἰσθήσεων ἡδονὰς καρπούμενοι[b] νομίζοντες τῆς ἄκρας εὐδαιμονίας ἀφῖχθαι,[c] μεταβολὴν οὐ προσδοκῶσιν, ἀλλὰ καὶ τοὺς λέγοντας ὅτι πάντα περὶ τὸ σῶμα καὶ ἐκτὸς ἐπικαίρως ἔχει, γέλωτα καὶ χλεύην τίθενται.

Harris, p. 33, from Mai, Script. Vet. vii. 101 e Cod. Vat. 1553, Φίλωνος· ἐκ τῶν δ' τῶν ἐν Γενέσει ζητημάτων.

44. (Gen. xix. 16)

. . . τῆς χειρὸς αὐτοῦ· οὐκ ἄρα λόγοις μόνον ἡμᾶς παρακαλεῖ πρὸς ἁμαρτίας ἀποφυγήν, ἀλλὰ καὶ ἐνεργὸν τὴν ἐπικουρίαν χαρίζεται.

Wendland, p. 75, n. 1, from Procopius, Cod. Aug. f. 102[v] = Migne, p. 371 B (" wahrscheinlich geht auf Philons Einfluss zurück ").

47. (Gen. xix. 18-20)

Ὁ σοφὸς ἠρεμίαν καὶ ἀπραγμοσύνην καὶ σχολὴν μεταδιώκει[d] ἵνα τοῖς θείοις θεωρήμασιν ἐν ἡσυχίᾳ ἐντύχῃ. Ὁ φαῦλος πόλιν τε καὶ τὸν κατὰ πόλιν ὄχλον τε καὶ φυρμὸν ἀνθρώπων ὁμοῦ καὶ πραγμάτων μεταδιώκει. Φιλοπραγμοσύναι γὰρ καὶ πλεονεξίαι, δημοκοπίαι τε καὶ δημαρχίαι τῷ τοιούτῳ τιμαί, τὸ δὲ ἡσυχάζειν ἀτιμώτατον.

Harris, p. 33, " the first sentence is Dam. Par. 376, also Cod. Reg. 923, f. 85, where it is ἐκ τοῦ α' τῶν ἐν Γενέσει, and Maximus ii. 599 . . . the last part is found in Anton Melissa (Migne, Patr. Gr. 136, col. 1193 . . .)."

[a] μὴ Cod. Reg.
[b] Harris (p. 110) : κρατούμενοι codd.
[c] Harris : ἠφίχθαι codd. : ἐφικέσθαι prop. Harris.
[d] καὶ σχολὴν μεταδιώκει] διώκει Maximus.

216

GENESIS, BOOK IV

51. (Gen. xix. 23)

(a) Διὰ τί, " ἐξῆλθεν ὁ
ἥλιος ἐπὶ τὴν γῆν, καὶ Λὼτ
εἰσῆλθεν εἰς Σηγώρ";

Καί φησιν· Ὁ αὐτὸς χρόνος
γίνεται καὶ τοῖς προκόπτουσιν
εἰς σωτηρίαν, καὶ τοῖς ἀνιάτως
ἔχουσι πρὸς κόλασιν. Καὶ ἐν
ἀρχῇ δὴ ἡμέρας εὐθὺς ἀνατείλαντος τοῦ ἡλίου τὴν δίκην
ἐπάγει, βουλόμενος δεῖξαι ὅτι
ἥλιος καὶ ἡμέρα καὶ φῶς καὶ
ὅσα ἄλλα[a] ἐν κόσμῳ καλὰ καὶ
τίμια μόνοις ἀπονέμεται τοῖς
ἀστείοις, φαύλῳ δὲ οὐδενὶ τῶν
ἀθεράπευτον κακίαν ἐχόντων.

Harris, p. 34, from Cat.
Ined. Cod. Reg. 1825 (Mangey ii. 675), Cat. Burney,
f. 37 and Cat. Lips. 1, col.
251.

Οὐ μεσημβρίας γίνεται ὁ τοῦ
πυρὸς ὑετός, ἀλλ' ὄρθρου ὅτε
καταψύχει πως ὁ ἀήρ . . . ὅρα
δὲ πάλιν ἱστορικώτερον, ὡς ὁ
αὐτὸς χρόνος γίνεται καὶ τοῖς
προκόπτουσιν εἰς σωτηρίαν καὶ
τοῖς ἀνιάτοις εἰς κόλασιν.
Ἡλίου γὰρ ἀνατείλαντος ἑκάτερον γέγονεν.

Wendland, p. 75, from
Procopius 373 A and Cod.
Aug. f. 104[r] (Migne, p. 375).

(b) Ἐκ τοῦ οὐρανοῦ, ἐξ οὗ
γίνονται οἱ ἐτήσιοι χειμῶνες καὶ
ὑετοὶ πρὸς αὔξησιν τῶν φυο-
μένων, ὅσα σπαρτὰ καὶ δένδρα
πρὸς γένεσιν καρπῶν εἰς ἀνθρώπων καὶ τῶν ἄλλων ζῴων τρο-
φάς, καταρραγῆναί φησι τὸ
θεῖον καὶ τὸ πῦρ ἐπὶ φθορᾷ τῶν
κατὰ γῆν ἁπάντων ἵν' ἐπιδεί-
ξηται ὅτι καὶ τῶν καιρῶν καὶ
τῶν ἐτησίαν ὡρῶν αἴτιος οὔθ'
ὁ οὐρανὸς οὔθ' ὁ ἥλιος οὔθ' αἱ
τῶν ἄλλων ἀστέρων χορεῖαι καὶ
περιπολήσεις, ἀλλ' ἡ τοῦ πα-
τέρος δύναμις.[b] Δηλοῖ δὲ καὶ
ἡ τεθαυματουργημένη πρᾶξις οὐ

Ἐξ οὐρανοῦ δὲ τὸ πῦρ πρὸς
φθοράν, ὅθεν ὑετοὶ πρὸς ζωήν,
ὡς ἂν δειχθῇ μὴ τῶν καρπῶν
αἴτιος ὑπάρχων οὐρανὸς καὶ
ἀστέρες ὡς οὐδὲ τῶν ὄμβρων,
ἀλλ' ὁ πέμπων τούτους θεός,
ὅς γε καὶ τὸ πῦρ ἀντὶ τούτων
ἀπέστειλε παρὰ φύσιν ἐπὶ τὰ
κάτω πεμφθέν.

Wendland, p. 75, from
Procopius, Cod. Aug. f. 104[r]
(Migne, p. 375).

---

[a] ἄλλα om. Cat. Burney.
[b] ἐφεδρεύοντος μὲν ὡς ἅρματι πτηνῷ σύμπαντι τῷ κόσμῳ,
ἡνιοχοῦντος δ' αὐτὸν ὡς βέλτιστ' ἂν νομίσειεν ex Arm. add.
Lewy.

217

τὸ καθεστὸς[a] ἐπὶ τῶν στοιχείων ἔθος ἀλλά τινα δύναμιν
αὐτοκρατῆ καὶ αὐτεξούσιον
μεταστοιχειοῦσαν, ὡς ἂν προ-
έληται, τὰ σύμπαντα.
Lewy, p. 58, from Catt.
Len. f. 63ʳ, Barb. f. 141ᵛ-142ʳ,
Mosq. f. 217 ʳ⁻ᵛ, Φιλ. ἐπισκ.

(c) Φύσει μὲν γὰρ κοῦφα
θεῖον καὶ πῦρ ἐστιν καὶ διὰ
τοῦτο ἄνω φοιτᾷ· τὸ δὲ τῆς
ἀρᾶς κεκαινουργημένον ἤλλαξε
πρὸς τοὐναντίον τὴν κίνησιν
ἄνωθεν κάτω βιαζόμενον ἐνεχ-
θῆναι τὰ κουφότατα ὡς τὰ τῶν
ὄντων βαρύτατα.
Lewy, p. 58, from Catt.,
as in (b) above.

Φύσει μὲν κοῦφα θεῖον καὶ
πῦρ· τὸ δὲ τῆς ἀρᾶς κεκαινουργημένον ἤλλαξε πρὸς τοὐναντίον
τὴν κίνησιν.
Harris, p. 34, from Cat.
Burney, f. 46 b, Φίλωνος
ἐπισκόπου, and Cat. Lips.
col. 252, Ἀδήλου.

52. (Gen. xix. 26)

Οἱ δὲ ἄγγελοι παραγγέλλουσι μὴ ἀποκλίνειν ὀπίσω. Ἤιδεσαν
γὰρ ὅτι οἱ μὲν ἴσως ἐφησθήσονται ταῖς συμφοραῖς ἰδόντες—χαίρειν
δὲ ἐπὶ ταῖς τῶν ἑτέρων[b] ἀτυχίαις εἰ καὶ δίκαιον, ἀλλ' οὐκ ἀνθρώ-
πινον· τὸ γὰρ μέλλον ἄδηλον—, οἱ δὲ ἴσως μαλακισθήσονται καὶ
πλέον τοῦ μετρίου δυσανασχετήσουσι περιαλγοῦντες ἡττώμενοι
φίλων καὶ συνηθείας. Καὶ πάλιν αὕτη τρίτη αἰτία· θεοῦ γάρ,
φησίν, ὦ[c] ἄνθρωποι, κολάζοντος μὴ κατανοεῖτε. Ἀπόχρη γὰρ
ὑμῖν τοῦτο γνῶναι, ὅτι ὑπέμειναν τιμωρίαν οὓς ἔχρην[d]· τὸ δὲ πῶς
ὑπέμειναν[e] περιεργάζεσθαι προπετείας καὶ θράσους, οὐκ εὐλαβείας
ἂν εἴη.
Wendland, p. 76, from Procopius, Cod. Aug. f. 104ʳ
(Migne, p. 375). The phrase χαίρειν . . . ἀνθρώπινον is also in
Harris, p. 34, from Dam. Par. 509, ascribed to Nilus, and
Cod. Reg. 923, f. 154 b, ascribed to Philo, and Mai, *Script.*

---

[a] ex Arm. Lewy : καθ' ἕκαστον codd.
[b] ἐχθρῶν Cod. Reg.
[c] ὡς Catt. Lips., Burney.
[d] ἀπόχρη . . . ἔχρην] ὅτι μὲν γὰρ τιμωροῦνται ἔχρην γνῶναι
Catt. Lips., Burney.
[e] ὑπέμειναν om. Catt. Lips., Burney.

GENESIS, BOOK IV

Vet. vii. 102, from Cod. Vat. 1553, ἐκ τοῦ γ´ τῶν ἐν Γενέσει ζητημάτων. The last part, θεοῦ γάρ . . . εὐλαβείας (ἂν εἴη), is also in Harris, pp. 34–35, from Cat. Lips. col. 248 and Cat. Burney, f. 46 b, Φίλωνος ἐπισκόπου.

54. (Gen. xix. 29) Ἐμνήσθη δὲ ὁ θεὸς τοῦ Ἀβραὰμ καὶ ἐξαπέστειλε τὸν Λώτ.

Ὥστε διὰ τὸν Ἀβραὰμ διασέσωσται (καὶ αὐτός τι μέρος εἰσενεγκών).

Wendland, p. 76, from Procopius, Cod. Aug. f. 104ʳ.

56. (Gen. xix. 31–32) Ἐπότισαν δὲ τὸν πατέρα αὐτῶν οἶνον ἐν νυκτί.

. . . δι᾽ ὧν δέ φασι " καὶ οὐδείς ἐστιν ἐπὶ τῆς γῆς ὃς εἰσελεύσεται πρὸς ἡμᾶς," δεικνύουσιν ὡς οὐ πάθος ἀκολασίας ἤλασεν αὐτὰς ἐπὶ τοῦτο ἀλλὰ φειδὼ τοῦ γένους, ὅθεν εὐσύγγνωστοι. . . . Οὕτως οἰκονομία τις ἦν καὶ ἐπὶ τῶν θυγατέρων τοῦ Λώτ, ἐπειδὴ μὴ δι᾽ ἀκολασίαν καὶ παίδων ἐπιθυμίαν τὸ γεγονός.

Wendland, p. 77, from Procopius, Cod. Aug. f. 104ᵛ (Migne, p. 378 A, *cf.* Theodore, Cat. Lips. 255) and Procopius 474 A.

64. (Gen. xx. 4–5) Οὐχ ὡς τὸ ἑκουσίως ἁμαρτάνειν ἐστὶν ἄδικον, οὕτω τὸ ἀκουσίως καὶ κατ᾽ ἄγνοιαν εὐθὺς δίκαιον, ἀλλὰ τάχα που μεθόριον ἀμφοῖν, δικαίου καὶ ἀδίκου, τὸ ὑπό τινων καλούμενον ἀδιάφορον. Ἁμάρτημα γὰρ οὐδὲν ἔργον δικαιοσύνης.

Harris, p. 35, from Dam. Par. 520 and Cod. Reg. 923. See also Wendland, p. 78, who prints a brief paraphrase from Procopius 380 A, ὁ μὲν δίκαιος οὐκ ἐν ἀγνοίᾳ ἀλλ᾽ ἐπιστήμῃ.

67. (Gen. xx. 10–11) Οὐ πάντα ἀληθῆ λεκτέον ἅπασιν· ὅθεν καὶ νῦν ὁ ἀστεῖος ὅλον οἰκονομεῖ τὸ πρᾶγμα μεταθέσει καὶ ἀπαλλαγῇ τῶν ὀνομάτων.

Harris, p. 35, from Mai, *Script. Vet.* vii. 106 = Cod. Vat. 1553, ἐκ τῶν ἐν Γενέσει ζητημάτων.

69. (Gen. xx. 16) Τὸ δὲ " πάντα ἀλήθευσον᾽ ᾽ ἀφιλοσόφου καὶ ἰδιώτου παράγγελμα·

APPENDIX A, GREEK FRAGMENTS

εἰ μὲν γὰρ ὁ μὲν ἀνθρώπων βίος εὐώδει μηδὲν παραδεχόμενος ψεῦδος, εἰκὸς ἦν ἐπὶ παντὶ πρὸς πάντας ἀληθεύειν· ἐπειδὴ δὲ ὑπόκρισις ὡς ἐν θεάτρῳ[a] δυναστεύει καὶ τὸ ψεῦδος παραπέτασμα τῆς ἀληθείας ἐστί, τέχνης δεῖ τῷ σοφῷ πολυτρόπου, καθ᾽ ἣν ὠφελήσει μιμούμενος τοὺς ὑποκριτὰς οἳ ἄλλα λέγοντες ἕτερα δρῶσιν ὅπως διασώσωσιν οὓς δύνανται.

Harris, p. 35, from Mai, *Script. Vet.* vii. 106 = Cod. Vat. 1553.

73. (Gen. xxiii. 2-3)

Προπάθεια καὶ οὐ πάθος τοῦ Ἀβραὰμ διὰ τούτων δεδήλωται. Οὐ γὰρ εἴρηται ὅτι ἐκόψατο ἀλλ᾽ ὅτι ἦλθε κόψασθαι. Τοῦτο δηλοῖ καὶ τὸ " ἀνέστη Ἀβραὰμ ἀπὸ τοῦ νεκροῦ," μὴ προλεχθέντος τοῦ " ἐκόψατο."

Wendland, p. 78, from Procopius, Cod. Aug. f. 110ʳ (Migne, p. 394, *cf.* Cat. Lips. 285, Εὐσεβίου).

74. (Gen. xxiii. 4)

Οὕτως γὰρ ὁ σοφίας ἐραστὴς οὐδενὶ τῶν εἰκαιοτέρων, καὶ ἂν συμπεφυκὼς τυγχάνῃ, σύνεστιν ἢ συνδιατρίβει πονηροτάτῳ, διεζευγμένος τῶν πολλῶν διὰ λογισμῶν, δι᾽ οὓς οὔτε συμπλεῖν οὔτε συμπολιτεύεσθαι οὔτε συζῆν λέγεται.

Harris, p. 69 (" unidentified," but located by Früchtel), from Dam. Par. 754 (Cod. Rupef.), ἐκ τοῦ ε´ τῶν αὐτῶν.

76. (Gen. xxiii. 5-6)

Τῶν μὲν ἀφρόνων βασιλεὺς οὐδείς, καὶ ἂν τὸ πάσης γῆς καὶ θαλάσσης ἀνάψηται κράτος· μόνος δὲ ὁ ἀστεῖος καὶ θεοφιλής, καὶ ἂν τῶν παρασκευῶν καὶ τῶν χορηγιῶν ἄμοιρῇ, δι᾽ ὧν πολλοὶ κρατύνονται τὰς δυναστείας. Ὥσπερ γὰρ τῷ κυβερνητικῆς ἢ ἰατρικῆς ἢ μουσικῆς ἀπείρῳ παρέλκον πρᾶγμα οἴακες καὶ φαρμάκων σύνθεσις καὶ αὐλοὶ καὶ κιθάραι, διότι μηδενὶ τούτων χρήσθαι πρὸς ὃ πέφυκε, κυβερνήτῃ δὲ καὶ ἰατρῷ καὶ μουσικῷ λέγοιτο ἂν ἐφαρμόζειν· δεόντως οὕτως, ἐπειδὴ τέχνη τίς ἐστι βασιλικὴ καὶ τεχνῶν ἀρίστη, τὸν μὲν ἀνεπιστήμονα χρήσεως ἀνθρώπων ἰδιώτην νομιστέον, βασιλέα δὲ μόνον τὸν ἐπιστήμονα.

Harris, p. 36, the first few lines (to θεοφιλής) from Dam. Par. 396 and 776 = Cod. Rupef. f. 115 b, ἐκ τοῦ α´ τῶν ἐν

[a] ex Arm. Harris : ἑκατέρῳ codd.

GENESIS, BOOK IV

Γενέσει ζητημάτων, and Cod. Reg. 923, f. 97, ἐκ τοῦ α' τῶν ἐν Γενέσει, the rest of the passage from Dam. Par. 776.

80. (Gen. xxiii. 9, 11)
Τὸ σπήλαιον τὸ διπλοῦν δύω εἰσὶν ἀντρώδεις ὑπωρείαι· ἡ μὲν ἐκτός, ἡ δὲ εἴσω· ἢ δύω περίβολοι· ὁ μὲν περιέχων, ὁ δὲ περιεχόμενος.
Harris, p. 36, from Cat. Lips. col. 288, Προκοπίου.

81. (Gen. xxiii. 11)
Τοῦ δὲ Ἀβραὰμ μόνον τὸ σπήλαιον αἰτοῦντος ὁ Ἐφρὼν ὁρῶν αὐτοῦ τὴν σοφίαν καὶ τὸν ἀγρὸν ἐπιδίδωσιν, οἰόμενος δεῖν ἀφθόνους ἐπιδαψιλεύεσθαι χάριτας.
Wendland, p. 78, from Procopius, Cod. Aug. f. 110ʳ = Cat. Lips. 288, Ἀδήλου.

86. (Gen. xxiv. 2)
Λεχθείη δ' ἂν καὶ ὅτι ἐπὶ μνηστείαν καὶ γάμον πέμπων τὸν παῖδα ὁ Ἀβραὰμ κατὰ τῶν γαμικῶν ὀργάνων ἐξώρκισε, καθαρὰν ὁμιλίαν καὶ γάμον ἀνεπίληπτον, αἰνιττόμενος οὐχ ἡδονὴν τὸ τέλος ἀλλὰ γνησίους ἔχοντα παῖδας.ᵃ
Wendland, pp. 78-79, from Procopius, Cod. Aug. f. 110ᵛ (Migne, p. 365, cf. Theodoret, Quaest. lxxiv).

88. (Gen. xxiv. 3) Διατί δὲ μὴ τῷ υἱῷ παραγγέλλει μὴ λαβεῖν Χαναυῖτιν, ὥσπερ ὕστερον τῷ Ἰακὼβ οἱ γονεῖς, ἀλλὰ τῷ παιδί;
. . . καίτοι τελείου τυγχάνοντος Ἰσαὰκ καὶ ἡλικίαν ἔχοντος γάμου . . . καὶ εἰ μὲν ἤμελλε πείθεσθαι, εἰκὸς ἦν αὐτῷ μᾶλλον παρεγγυᾶν· εἰ δὲ ἀπειθεῖν, περιττὴ τοῦ παιδὸς ἡ διακονία. Τὸ γὰρ εἰπεῖν ὅτι, χρησμῷ τῆς γῆς ἐξελθών, πέμπειν εἰς αὐτὴν οὐκ ἠξίου τὸν υἱόν, [εἰ καὶ εὔλογον, ὅμως ἀπαρέσκει τισί] διὰ τὸ μηδ' ἂν τὸν Ἰακώβ, εἰ τοῦτο ἦν ἀληθές, ὑπὸ τῶν γονέων ἐνταῦθα πεμφθῆναι.
Harris, p. 37, from Cat. Lips. col. 292, Προκοπίου.

99. (Gen. xxiv. 16)
(α) Διαγράφει τὸ κάλλος ἵνα μᾶλλον τὴν σωφροσύνην θαυμάσωμεν. Οὐ τὸ κάλλος γὰρ πάντως ἀσελγές, ὡς οὐδὲ σῶφρον ἡ

ᵃ γνησίων παίδων γένεσιν scripsisse Philonem ex Ambr. De Abr. i. 83 con. Wendland.

ἀμορφία. Οὐ σῶμα γὰρ τούτων ἀλλ' ἡ προαίρεσις αἴτιον. Διπλασιάζει δὲ τὸ " παρθένος ἦν," τὸ κατ' ἄμφω σῶφρον ἐμφαίνουσα. Ἔστι γὰρ ἀσελγείαις διεφθάρθαι ψυχήν, ἀκεραίου τοῦ σώματος μένοντος.

Wendland, p. 79, from Procopius 398 B (" zum guten Teile philonisch erscheint mir die Stelle ").

(b) Ἀναιδὲς βλέμμα καὶ μετέωρος αὐχὴν καὶ συνεχὴς κίνησις ὀφρύων[a] καὶ βάδισμα σεσοβημένον καὶ τὸ ἐπὶ μηδενὶ τῶν φαύλων ἐρυθριᾶν σημεῖά ἐστι ψυχῆς αἰσχίστης, τοὺς ἀφανεῖς τῶν οἰκείων ὀνειδῶν τύπους[b] ἐγγραφούσης τῷ φανερῷ σώματι.

Harris, p. 37, from Dam. Par. 658 and Cod. Reg. 923, f. 292, ἐκ τοῦ εʹ τῶν ἐν Γενέσει, also Cramer, Anec. Oxon. iv. 254 e Cod. Bodl. Clark, f. 11 b, Maximus ii. 633, Anton Melissa (Patr. Gr. 136, col. 1225), referring to Greg. Nazianz., and Tischendorf, Philonea, p. 154 e Cod. Cahirino.

100. (Gen. xxiv. 16)

Φυσικώτατα ταῦτα δέδεικται· κατάβασιν μὲν ψυχῆς τὴν δι' οἰήσεως ἀνάβασιν, ἄνοδον δὲ καὶ ὕψος τὴν ἀλαζονείας ὑπονόστησιν.

Harris, p. 102 (" unidentified," but located by Früchtel), from Cod. Rupef. f. 264.

102. (Gen. xxiv. 17)

Ἄξιον ἀποδέχεσθαι τὸ μηδενὸς ὀρέγεσθαι τῶν ὑπὲρ δύναμιν· πᾶν γὰρ τὸ συμμετρίαν ἔχον, ἐπαινετόν . . . ἀναγκαῖον οὖν τῷ μὲν εὐφυεῖ πλείους εἶναι τὰς διδασκαλίας, ἐλάττους δὲ τῷ ἀφυεῖ διὰ τὴν ἐν ταῖς ἀνάγκαις[c] ἀρίστην ἰσότητα . . . καὶ τοῦτό γέ ἐστι τὸ βιωφελέστατον ἴσον.

Harris, p. 38, from Mai, Script. Vet. vii. 106, from Cod. Vat. 1553, Φίλωνος· ἐκ τῶν ἐν Γενέσει ζητημάτων.

104. (Gen. xxiv. 18)

Οὐχ ὡς δύναται διδάσκειν ὁ διδάσκαλος, οὕτω καὶ μανθάνειν ὁ γνώριμος, ἐπειδὴ ὁ μὲν τέλειος, ὁ δὲ ἀτελής ἐστιν. Ὅθεν προσήκει στοχάζεσθαι τῆς τοῦ παιδευομένου δυνάμεως.

Harris, p. 38, from Dam. Par. 435 and Cod. Reg. 923, f.

---

[a] ὀφθαλμῶν Dam. et Cod. Reg.
[b] τόποις Dam. et Cod. Reg.
[c] ἀναλογίαις ex Arm. conieci.

116 b, Φίλωνος· ἐκ τῆς η′ τῶν νόμων ἱερῶν ἀλληγορίας, also Mai, *Script. Vet.* vii. 99, Φίλωνος· ἐκ τοῦ θ′ τῶν ἐν Γενέσει ζητημάτων.

110. (Gen. xxiv. 22)

(a) 'Ακοῦσαι δεῖ πρῶτον, εἶτα ἐργάσασθαι· μανθάνομεν γὰρ οὐ τοῦ μαθεῖν χάριν ἀλλὰ τοῦ πρᾶξαι.

Harris, p. 38, from Mai, *Script. Vet.* vii. 99.

(b) Διαφέρει δὲ μονὰς ἑνὸς ᾗ διαφέρει ἀρχέτυπον εἰκόνος· παράδειγμα μὲν γὰρ ἡ μονάς, μίμημα δὲ τῆς μονάδος τὸ ἕν.

Staehle, p. 19, from Joh. Lydus ii. 6, p. 23, 6.

(c) . . . ἢ ἀπὸ τοῦ διακεκρίσθαι καὶ μεμονῶσθαι ἀπὸ τοῦ λοιποῦ πλήθους τῶν ἀριθμῶν καλεῖται μονάς.

Staehle, p. 19, from Theon of Smyrna, p. 19, 12 f. (*cf.* Joh. Lydus, p. 21, 20 and Moderatus *ap.* Stob. *Ecl.* i. i. 8).

130. (Gen. xxiv. 52-53)

Δεῖ γὰρ πάσης πράξεως καθαρᾶς ἀρχὴν [εἶναι] τὴν πρὸς θεὸν εὐχαριστίαν καὶ τιμήν· διὰ τοῦτο ὁ παῖς προσκυνεῖ πρότερον, εἶτα χαρίζεται τὰ δῶρα.

Harris, p. 38, from Cod. Vat. 746, f. 53, Φίλωνος, *cf.* Pitra, *Analecta Sacra* ii. 314.

131. (Gen. xxiv. 55-56)

Μετανενοήκασιν οἱ πρὸ μικροῦ λέγοντες· "'Ιδοὺ 'Ρεβέκκα ἐνώπιόν σου· λαβὼν ἀπότρεχε."

Lewy, p. 59, from Cat. Barb. f. 146ᵛ, Φιλ. ἐπ., and Cat. Len. f. 93ᵛ, Φίλωνος.

144. (Gen. xxiv. 66) Διὰ τί δὲ ὁ παῖς ὑφ' ἑτέρου πεμφθεὶς ἐπὶ τὴν πρεσβείαν ἑτέρῳ ἀποπρεσβεύει; "διηγήσατο γάρ," φησί, "τῷ 'Ισαάκ."

Εὐαγγελίζεται τούτῳ δι' ὃν ἐπέμφθη. Καὶ προτέρῳ δὲ ἐνέτυχε κατὰ τὴν ὁδόν. Πάντως δὲ καὶ τῷ 'Αβραὰμ εἶπεν, εἰ καὶ μὴ γέγραπται.

Wendland, p. 79, from Procopius 404 ᴀ.

145. (Gen. xxiv. 67) Διὰ τί δὲᵃ οὐκ εἰς τὸν τοῦ πατρὸς οἶκον ἀλλ' εἰς τὸν τῆς μητρὸς εἰσέρχεσθαι λέγεται 'Ισαὰκ ἐπὶ γάμῳ;

ᵃ δὲ om. Cat. Barb.

APPENDIX A, GREEK FRAGMENTS

Ὅτι ὁ μὲν πατὴρ πλείους ἀγαγόμενος γυναῖκας, δυνάμει[a] καὶ πλείους[b] ἔσχεν οἴκους. Οἶκος γὰρ οὐ μόνον λέγεται[c] τὸ οἰκοδόμημα ἀλλὰ καὶ τὸ ἐκ γαμικῆς συζυγίας[d] καὶ τέκνων σύστημα.[e] ἡ[f] δὲ μέχρι τελευτῆς ἐπέμεινε τῷ κουριδίῳ, ὡς διὰ τοῦτο καὶ ἕνα οἶκον ἐσχηκέναι δοκεῖν.[g]

Wendland, p. 80, from Procopius 404 Λ, and Cat. Barb. vi. 8, f. 166[r], Φίλωνος ἐπισκόπου; also, in part, Harris, p. 39, from Cat. Lips. col. 305, Προκοπίου.

148. (Gen. xxv. 5-6)

Διαφορὰν δέ φασιν ὑπαρχόντων καὶ δομάτων. τὸ μὲν γὰρ σημαίνει τὰ κτήματα καὶ ὅσα βέβαια τῶν κειμηλίων, δόματα δὲ τὰ χειρόδοτα καὶ ὧν ἡ χρῆσις ἐφήμερος.

Wendland, p. 80, from Procopius 405 B.

152. (Gen. xxv. 8)

Οὐδεὶς κενὸς πλήρης εἶναι μεμαρτύρηται ἡμερῶν.

Wendland, p. 80, from Procopius 405 B and Cat. Lips.

153. (Gen. xxv. 8)

Οὐδεὶς γὰρ προστίθεται τοῖς μὴ οὖσιν, ἄλλος δὲ προστίθεσθαι, φησί, λέγεται λαῷ μήπω γεγονότι. Ἀρχὴ γὰρ αὐτὸς καὶ προπάτωρ τοῦ γένους ἐστί. Τὸν οὖν μέλλοντα δι' αὐτὸν γενέσθαι ὡς ἤδη γεγονότα χαριζόμενος αὐτοῦ τῷ θεοπρεπεῖ τῶν ἀρετῶν ἱδρύεται ᾧ[h] καὶ λέγεται[i] προστίθεσθαι.

Wendland, p. 81, from Procopius 406 c.

165. (Gen. xxv. 27)

Ἰακὼβ δὲ ἄνθρωπος " ἄπλαστος οἰκῶν οἰκίαν," τουτέστι μηδὲν

[a] δυνάμει om. Cat. Lips.
[b] πλείστους Cat. Barb.
[c] λέγεται om. Procopius.
[d] ἐκ γαμικῆς συζυγίας] ἐξ ἀνδρὸς καὶ γυναικὸς Cat. Barb.
[e] οἶκος . . . σύστημα] λέγεται γὰρ οἶκος καὶ τὸ ἐκ γυναικὸς καὶ τέκνων σύστημα Cat. Lips.
[f] ἡ Cat. Barb.
[g] ὁ δὲ . . . δοκεῖν om. Cat. Lips.
[h] ὡς Nicephorus.
[i] Wendland : λέγεσθαι codd.

ἔχων ἐπίπλαστον ἢ ἐπείσακτον κακόν . . . καὶ τὴν αἰτίαν τούτου τοῦ ἀπλάστου ἤθους διδάσκει λέγων ὅτι οὐκ ἐρέμβετο ἔξω.
Ἴσως δὲ καὶ ἀντιδιαστέλλει τῷ κυνηγέτῃ Ἠσαῦ καὶ ἐν ὑπαίθρῳ
διάγοντι.

Wendland, p. 81, from Procopius 410 ᴀ, *cf.* Cyril *ap.* Cat.
Lips. 315 and Theodoret, *Quaest.* lxxvi.

166. (Gen. xxv. 28)
Τίς δ' ἂν οὐκ ἀγάσαιτο τὸ "ἠγάπησε τὸν Ἠσαῦ· ἡ δὲ
Ῥεβέκκα ἠγάπα τὸν Ἰακώβ"; Τὸ μὲν γὰρ παρελήλυθε· τὸ
δὲ πάρεστιν ἀεί· ἡ μὲν γὰρ ἀποδοχὴ τοῦ φαύλου κἂν συμβῇ
ποτε, ὀλιγοχρόνιός ἐστι καὶ ἐφήμερος· ἡ δὲ τοῦ σπουδαίου ἀθανατί-
ζεται.

Harris, p. 39, from Cat. Lips. col. 315, Προκοπίου.

167. (Gen. xxv. 28)
Καὶ τὸ μὲν σπουδαῖον οὐ δι' ἕτερόν τι ἀγαπᾶται· τὸ δὲ μὴ
τοιοῦτον, ἐκ τῶν χρειῶν· ἠγάπησε γάρ φησιν ὅτι ἡ θήρα αὐτοῦ
βρῶσις αὐτῷ.

Harris, p. 39, from Cat. Lips. col. 315, Προκοπίου.

168. (Gen. xxv. 29)
Καὶ τὸ ῥητὸν τῆς διηγήσεως ἔλεγχον ἔχει ἀκολάστου πρὸς νουθεσίαν τῶν θεραπεύεσθαι δυναμένων· ὁ ᵃ γὰρ τοῦ τυχόντος ἕνεκα
προεψήματος ᵇ ἐκστὰς τῶν πρεσβείων τῷ νεωτέρῳ καὶ δοῦλος
γαστρὸς ἡδονῆς ἀναγραφεὶς εἰς ὄνειδος προκείσθω τῶν μήποτε
ζῆλον ἐγκρατείας λαβόντων.

Harris, pp. 39-40, from Cat. Lips. 1, col. 318, Φίλωνος
(" but the editor remarks ἴσως τοῦ ἐπισκόπου· ἐν γὰρ τοῖς τοῦ
Ἑβραίου οὐχ εὑρίσκεται "), also Cat. Burney, f. 55, Φίλωνος
ἐπισκόπου, and Cod. Palat. 203, f. 110 *ap.* Pitra, *Anal. Sacr.*
ii. 311.

169. (Gen. xxv. 29)
Ἐπὶ μὲν τῶν σπουδαίων ἡ ἔκλειψις εἶναι λέγεται πρόσθεσις·
ἐκλείποντες γὰρ τὸν θνητὸν βίον ἀθανάτῳ ζωῇ προστίθενται· ὁ δὲ

ᵃ οὐ Arm.
ᵇ προεψημένων Cat. Burney : προσλήμματος Cod. Palat.

φαῦλος ἔκλειψιν ἀναδέχεται μόνον[a] λιμὸν ἀρετῆς ὑπομένων ἀδιά-
στατον μᾶλλον ἢ σίτων καὶ ποτῶν.

Wendland, p. 82, from Procopius, Cod. Aug. f. 115ʳ (Migne, p. 410).

172. (Gen. xxv. 31)

Τὸ μὲν ῥητὸν οἷα τῷ δοκεῖν ἐμφαίνει πλεονεξίαν νεωτέρου σφετερίζεσθαι[b] ἀδελφοῦ δίκαια ποθοῦντος. Ὁ δὲ σπουδαῖος οὐ πλεονέκτης ἅτε ὀλιγοδείας καὶ ἐγκρατείας ἑταῖρος. Σαφῶς οὖν ὁ ἐπιστάμενος ὅτι αἱ ἄφθονοι περιουσίαι τῶν φαύλων χορηγοὶ τῶν ἁμαρτημάτων καὶ ἀδικη-μάτων αὐτοῖς εἰσιν, ἀναγκαιότα-τον ἡγεῖται τὴν προσαναφλέγου-σαν ὕλην, ὡς πυρός, τῆς κακίας ἀφαιρεῖν εἰς βελτίωσιν ἠθῶν ὅπερ οὐ βλάβην ἀλλὰ μεγίστην ὠφελείαν περιποιεῖ τῷ ζημιοῦσ-θαι δοκοῦντι.

Harris, p. 40, from Cat. Lips. 1, col. 316, and Cat. Burney, f. 55, Φίλωνος ἐπι-σκόπου.

Δοκεῖ δὲ τὸ ῥητὸν πλεον-εξίαν ἐμφαίνειν τοῦ Ἰακώβ, ὅπερ ἀλλότριον σπουδαίου, εἴπερ ὀλι-γοδείας καὶ ἐγκρατείας ἑταῖρος καὶ ὠφελητικός ἐστιν ἐν τοῖς μάλιστα. Σαφῶς οὖν ἐπιστά-μενος ὅτι αἱ ἄφθονοι περιουσίαι παντὶ φαύλῳ χορηγοὶ τῶν ἁμαρτημάτων καὶ ἀδικημάτων εἰσίν, ἀναγκαιότατον ἡγεῖται τὴν προσαναφλέγουσαν ὕλην, ὡς πυρός, τῆς κακίας ἀφαιρεῖν εἰς βελτίωσιν ἠθῶν· ὅπερ οὐ βλά-βην ἀλλὰ μεγίστην ὠφέλειαν περιποιεῖ τῷ ζημιοῦσθαι δο-κοῦντι.

Wendland, pp. 82-83, from Procopius, Cod. Aug. f. 115ᵛ (Migne, p. 412).

173. (Gen. xxv. 32) Ἰδοὺ ἐγὼ πορεύομαι τελευτᾶν. Λόγιόν ἐστι τὸ εἰρημένον. Ὄντως γὰρ ὁ τοῦ φαύλου βίος ἐπὶ θάνατον σπεύδει. Οὐ φησὶ δὲ " ἵνα τί μοι πρωτοτόκια," μετὰ προσθήκης δὲ τοῦ " ταῦτα," ὅ ἐστι τὰ πρὸς ἀρετὴν ἄγοντα καὶ εὐδαιμονίαν. Ἔχω γάρ, φησί, ἐξαίρετα ἕτερα· τὸ ἤδεσθαι, τὸ ἐπιθυμεῖν, τὸ ἀκολασταίνειν, τὸ πλεονεκτεῖν καὶ ὅσα τούτων ἀδελφά.

Wendland, p. 83, from Procopius, Cod. Aug. f. 115ᵛ (Migne, p. 411).

174. (Gen. xxv. 34) Καὶ ἐφαύλισεν Ἡσαῦ τὰ πρωτοτόκια.

Κακίζει γὰρ ὥσπερ ὁ ἀστεῖος τὰ τοῦ φαύλου, καὶ ὁ φαῦλος τὰ

[a] μόνον om. Nicephorus.   [b] +ἀδικῶς Cat. Burney.

τοῦ ἀστείου καὶ βουλεύματα καὶ πράξεις καὶ λόγους. Ἀσύμφωνον
γὰρ ἁρμονία πρὸς ἀναρμοστίαν.

Wendland, p. 83, from Procopius, Cod. Aug. f. 115ᵛ
(Migne, p. 411).

179. (Gen. xxvi. 3)

Μεῖζον ἀνθρώπῳ κακὸν ἀφροσύνης οὐδέν ἐστι, τὸ ἴδιον τοῦ
λογιστικοῦ γένους, τὸν νοῦν, ζημιωθέντι.

Harris, p. 69 (" unidentified," but located by E. Bréhier),
from Dam. Par. 363 and Cod. Reg. 923, f. 76, " in both cases
as from the *sixth* book of the Questions on Genesis."

180. (Gen. xxvi. 36)

(*a*) Ἀδιαφοροῦσιν ὅρκων λόγοι θεοῦ· καὶ κατὰ τίνος ἂν ὤμοσεν
ὁ θεός, ὅτι μὴ ἑαυτοῦ; λέγεται δὲ ὀμνύναι διὰ τὴν ἡμετέραν
ἀσθένειαν τῶν ὑπολαμβανόντων ὡς ἐπ' ἀνθρώπου διαφέρειν λόγων
ὅρκους, οὕτως ἐπὶ θεοῦ. . . .

Harris, pp. 40-41, from Cat. Lips. col. 319, Προκοπίου.

(*b*) Ἐπαινεῖ δὲ καὶ τὸν υἱὸν ὡς πατρῴας ἄξιον εὐεργίας. Οὐ
γὰρ ἂν βεβαιότερον ἱδρύετο τὰς μεθ' ὅρκων γεγενημένας ἐπὶ τοῦ
πατρὸς εὐλογίας τῷ υἱῷ, εἰ μὴ καὶ τούτῳ τὴν αὐτὴν ἀρετὴν
προσεμαρτύρει.

Wendland, p. 84, from Procopius, Cod. Aug. 117ᵛ (Migne,
p. 414 A).

184. (Gen. xxvi. 5)

Διαφέρει δικαιώματα νομίμων· τὰ μὲν γάρ πως δύναται συν-
ίσθασθαι (*sic*) φύσει, τὰ δὲ νόμιμα θέσει· πρεσβύτερα δὲ τῶν θέσει
τὰ φύσει, ὥστε καὶ τὸ δίκαιον νόμῳ.

Lewy, p. 59, from Cod. Rupef. 148ʳ, τοῦ αὐτοῦ (*sc*. Φίλωνος).

188. (Gen. xxvi. 8)

Ἑβραῖοι δέ φασιν εὐσχημόνως εἰρῆσθαι τὸ " παίζειν " ἀντὶ τοῦ
συνουσιάζειν.

Wendland, p. 84, from Procopius 416 B.

189. (Gen. xxvi. 12)

Μαρτυρεῖ δὲ τὸ παρὸν ὅτι τῷ σπουδαίῳ καὶ τὰ κατὰ γεωργίαν

καὶ τἆλλα ⟨τὰ⟩ περὶ βίον εὐοδεῖ καὶ τὰ ἐπιγινόμενα πολλαπλάσια
τῶν ἐξ ἀρχῆς γίνεται.

Wendland, p. 84, from Procopius 416 в.

191. (Gen. xxvi. 15)

(*a*) Τοῖς γὰρ ἀβούλοις ἔθος
ἐστὶ μήτε στήλας μήτε μνη-
μεῖόν τι ἀπολιπεῖν τῶν καλῶν
εἰς εὐδοξίαν συμβαλλόμενον, ἢ
ὅτι ῥηγνύμενοι φθόνῳ καὶ βα-
σκανίᾳ τῆς τε περὶ ἐκείνους[a]
εὐπραγίας ὀλιγωροῦσι καὶ τῆς
αὐτῶν ὠφελείας ἄμεινον ἡγού-
μενοι βλάπτεσθαι μᾶλλον ἢ ὑφ'
ὧν οὐκ ἔτι[b] θέλουσιν εὐεργε-
τεῖσθαι.

Harris, p. 41, from Cat.
Burney, f. 55 b, and Cat.
Lips. 1, col. 323, Φίλωνος
ἐπισκόπου.

Οἱ δὲ ἐμπαθεῖς καὶ τὰ μνη-
μεῖα τῶν ἀγαθῶν ἐξαλείφουσι,
κἂν τύχωσιν ἐξ αὐτῶν ὠφε-
λούμενοι, προτιμῶντες βλάβην
μᾶλλον ἢ τὴν ἐξ ὧν μὴ θέλουσιν
εὐεργέσιαν. Ὠφέλουν γὰρ αἱ
πηγαὶ καὶ τῶν Φυλιστιεὶμ τοὺς
βουλομένους κεχρῆσθαι.

Wendland, p. 84, from Procopius, Cod. Aug. f. 118ʳ
(Migne, p. 415).

(*b*) Τί γὰρ ἐκώλυεν, εἴποι τις ἄν, ὦ πάντων ἠλιθιώτατοι, τὰς
πηγὰς ἐᾶσαι, ἃς ἕτερος εὗρεν πρὸς τὴν τῶν παρ' ὑμῖν αὐτοῖς δεο-
μένων χρῆσιν; Ἀλλ' ἀποκρίνεταί τις· " Μὴ ζήτει παρὰ βασκάνων
ἀπολογίαν εὐγνώμονα,[c] ζημίαν ὑπολαμβανόντων τὰς ὑπὸ τῶν
βελτίστων προτεινομένας χάριτας."

Lewy, p. 59, from Cat. Len. 124, f. 76ᵛ.

193. (Gen. xxvi. 18) Τὰ ἐμφραγέντα φρέατα πάλιν ὤρυξεν.[d]

Ὅτι φύσει φιλάνθρωπος ὁ
ἀστεῖος καὶ εὐμενὴς καὶ συγ-
γνώμων, οὐδενὶ μνησικακῶν τὸ
παράπαν, ἀλλὰ νικᾶν τοὺς
ἐχθροὺς ἀξιῶν ἐν τῷ ποιεῖν εὖ
μᾶλλον ἢ βλάπτειν.

Harris, p. 41, from Cat.
Lips. 1, col. 323, and Cat.
Burney, f. 55 b.

Ἰσαὰκ ὡς πᾶσιν ὢν εὐμενὴς
καὶ πρὸς τῷ μὴ μνησικακεῖν, ἐ
τῷ εὐεργετῆσαι σπουδάζων νικᾶν τὴν ἐκείνων κακίαν.

Wendland, p. 85, from
Procopius, Cod. Aug. f.
118ʳ (Migne, p. 415).

---

[a] ἐκείνων Harris.   [b] εὖ Cat. Burney : del. Wendland.
[c] εὐγενῆ Arm.   [d] ὀρύσσει ὁ Ἰσαάκ Catt. Lips. et Burney.

GENESIS, BOOK IV

194. (Gen. xxvi. 18)

Καὶ τὰ αὐτὰ ὀνόματα τίθεται, τιμῶν αὐτοῦ τὸν πατέρα καὶ μὴ συγχωρῶν εἰσάπαν τῷ φθόνῳ νικᾶν.

Wendland, p. 85, from Procopius, Cod. Aug. f. 118ʳ (Migne, p. 415).

[195, see Appendix B.]

198. (Gen. xxvii. 3-4)

Δυοῖν ὄντων υἱῶν, τοῦ μὲν ἀγαθοῦ, τοῦ δὲ ὑπαιτίου, τὸν μὲν ὑπαίτιον εὐλογήσειν φησίν· οὐκ ἐπειδὴ τοῦ σπουδαίου προκρίνει τοῦτον ἀλλ' ὅτι ἐκεῖνον οἶδε δι' αὐτοῦ κατορθοῦν δυνάμενον, τοῦτον δὲ τοῖς ἰδίοις τρόποις ἁλισκόμενον, μηδεμίαν δὲ ἔχοντα σωτηρίας ἐλπίδα, εἰ μὴ τὰς εὐχὰς τοῦ πατρός· ὧν εἰ μὴ τύχοι, πάντων ἂν εἴη κακοδαιμονέστατος.

Harris, p. 43, from Cat. Ined. Reg. 1825 (Mangey ii. 676), and Cat. Lips. 1, col. 330, Φίλωνος, ἴσως ἐπισκόπου, and Cat. Burney, f. 56 b, Φίλωνος ἑβραίου. (Harris also gives two Latin fragments, one from Cat. Zephyri, p. 83, the other from Cat. Lippomani, f. 288 b).

Ὁ δὲ Ἰσαὰκ οὐ προτιμῶν τοῦ Ἰακὼβ τὸν Ἡσαῦ αὐτὸν ἠθέλησεν εὐλογεῖν. Πῶς γὰρ ἂν σπουδαῖος προτιμᾶν ἀνείχετο τὸν ὑπαίτιον; ἀλλ' εἰδὼς ὡς ἐκεῖνος μὲν ἐκ τῶν οἰκείων τρόπων ἔχει τὴν εὐμένειαν οὗτος δὲ μίαν ἔχει σωτηρίας ἐλπίδα τὰς εὐχὰς τοῦ πατρός.

Wendland, p. 86, from Procopius, Cod. Aug. f. 118ᵛ.

200. (Gen. xxvii. 8-10)

(a) Ἐντεῦθέν ἐστι μαθεῖν τὸ τοῦ σώματος μέγεθος καὶ τὴν ἐκ κατασκευῆς φυσικὴν εὐεξίαν· ὁ γὰρ ἐν γήρᾳ δύο πίοσιν ἐρίφοις κεχρημένος προεψήμασι, τίς ἂν ὑπῆρχεν ἐν τῇ νεότητι; καὶ ταῦτα ὢν ἐγκρατὴς καὶ οὐκ ἄπληστος.

Harris, p. 44, from Cat. Lips. 1, col. 331, Προκοπίου.

(b) Οὐ διαμάχονται δὲ κατὰ τοὺς οὕτω νομίσαντας τῶν γονέων αἱ γνῶμαι, πρὸς ἓν δὲ τέλος ἐπείγονται, τῆς μὲν βουλομένης τὸν

229

APPENDIX A, GREEK FRAGMENTS

ἀγαθὸν τυχεῖν ὧν ἄξιος ἦν, τοῦ δὲ τοῦ σκαιοῦ, τὴν ἀπορίαν ἐπανορθώσασθαι τῷ ἐλέῳ τῷ εἰς αὐτόν.

Wendland, pp. 86-87, from Procopius, Cod. Aug. f. 118ᵛ= Cat. Lips. 331 Γ, Ἀδήλου (*cf.* Ambros. *De Jacob.* ii. 7).

202. (Gen. xxvii. 12-13)

Ἄξιον καὶ τὴν μητέρα τῆς εὐνοίας θαυμάσαι, τὰς κατάρας ὁμολογοῦσαν εἰσδέξασθαι[a] τὰς ὑπὲρ ἐκείνου. Καὶ τὸν υἱὸν τῆς εἰς ἀμφοτέρους τοὺς γονεῖς[b] τιμῆς. Ἀνθέλκεται γὰρ ὑπὸ τῆς πρὸς ἑκάτερον εὐσεβείας· τὸν μὲν γὰρ πατέρα ἐδεδίει, μὴ δόξῃ φενακίζειν καὶ ὑφαρπάζειν ἑτέρου γέρας, τὴν δὲ μητέρα, μὴ καὶ ταύτης νομισθῇ παρακούειν λιπαρῶς ἐγκειμένης· ὅθεν ἄγαν εὐλαβῶς καὶ ὁσίως φησὶν οὐχ "ὁ πατήρ με καταράσεται" ἀλλ' "ἐγὼ τὰς κατάρας ἐπ' ἐμαυτὸν ἄξω."[c]

Harris, p. 44, from Cat. Inedit. Reg. 1825, and Cat. Lips. 1, col. 331, and Cat. Burney, f. 56 b.

Θαυμαστὸς τῆς πρὸς ἄμφω τοὺς γονεῖς εὐσεβείας, τὸν μὲν ἵνα μὴ κινήσῃ, τῆς δὲ μὴ παρακούσῃ. Καλῶς δὲ τὸ "ἐπ' ἐμαυτὸν ἄξω." Κἂν γὰρ ἡσυχάζῃ φιλοστοργίᾳ τῇ πρὸς ἐμέ, τὸ συνειδὸς ἐπιμέμψεται ὡς ἄξια κατάρας ἐργασάμενον. Θαυμαστὴ δὲ καὶ τῆς εὐνοίας ἡ μήτηρ.

Wendland, p. 87, from Procopius 418 B.

204. (Gen. xxvii. 16)

Ὥσπερ τὰς ἄλλας ἀρετὰς ὁ ἀστεῖος, οὕτως καὶ τὴν ἀνδρείαν καθαρῶς ἐπιτετηδευκώς, ἐάν που ταύτην ἐπισκιάζῃ χάριν, καιρῶν οἰκονομίᾳ χρῆται, μένων μὲν ἐν ὁμοίῳ καὶ τῆς ἐξ ἀρχῆς προθέσεως οὐκ ἀναχωρῶν, διὰ δὲ τῶν ἀβουλήτων συντυχίας ἐναλλάττων ὥσπερ ἐν θεάτρῳ μορφὴν ἑτέραν ὑπὲρ ὠφελείας τῶν ὁρώντων· ἰατρὸς γὰρ τῶν κατὰ τὸν βίον πραγμάτων ὁ ἀστεῖος, ὃς ἕνεκα τῶν καιρῶν φρονίμως ἐνεργεῖ τὰ ἀφροσύνης, καὶ σωφρόνως τὰς ἀκολασίας καὶ τὰς δειλίας ἀνδρείως καὶ δικαίως τὰς ἀδικίας· καὶ γὰρ ἐρεῖ ποτε τὰ ψευδῆ οὐ ψευδόμενος καὶ ὑβρίσει μὴ ὢν ὑβριστής.

Harris, p. 45, from Mai, *Script. Vet.* vii. 106 e Cod. Vat. 1553, Φίλωνος· ἐκ τοῦ δ' τῶν ἐν Γενέσει ζητημάτων.

---

[a] Harris : ἐκδέξασθαι Cat. Reg.
[b] τοὺς γονεῖς add. Harris. [c] ἔξω Cat. Lips.

230

206. (Gen. xxvii. 18-19)

(a) Πάλιν ἀπατεὼν εἶναι δόξει τοῖς μὴ τὴν κατ' ἀρετὴν σκοποῦσιν οἰκονομίαν. Ἡ δὲ οἰκονομία πρὸς τὸ μὴ τοῖς ἀναξίοις δίδοσθαι τὰ καλά. Λεγέτω καὶ κατάσκοπος συλληφθείς· οὐκ εἰμὶ πολέμιος ἢ ὡς ηὐτομόληκα.

Wendland, pp. 87-88, from Procopius, Cod. Aug. f. 118ᵛ.

(b) Λεγέτω καὶ ὁ στρατηγὸς ἢ τὰ πολεμοποιοῦντα εἰρήνην πραγματευόμενος ἢ τὰ εἰρήνης πολεμεῖν διανοούμενος· ὑποδυέσθω καὶ βασιλεὺς ἰδιώτου σχῆμα εἰ μὴ δύναιτο ἑτέρως τὸ συμφέρον τῇ τε ἀρχῇ καὶ τοῖς ὑπηκόοις λαβεῖν· καὶ ὁ δεσπότης δούλου, εἵνεκα τοῦ μηδὲν ἀγνοῆσαι τῶν κατὰ τὴν οἰκίαν δρωμένων.

Harris, p. 45, from Mai, *Script. Vet.* vii. 106 e Cod. Vat. 1553, Φίλωνος· ἐκ τοῦ δ' τῶν ἐν Γενέσει ζητημάτων.

Λεγέτω καὶ στρατηγὸς τὰ πολεμοποιοῦντα εἰρήνην πραγματευόμενος ἢ τὰ εἰρηναῖα πολεμεῖν ἐγνωκώς. Οὐδὲν κωλύσει καὶ βασιλέα ἰδιώτου σχῆμα λαβεῖν τοῖς ὑπηκόοις τὸ συμφέρον θηρώμενον καὶ τὸν δεσπότην οἰκέτου μηδὲν ἀγνοεῖν ἐθέλοντα τῶν κατὰ τὸν οἶκον δρωμένων.

Wendland, p. 88, from Procopius, Cod. Aug. f. 118ᵛ.

207. (Gen. xxvii. 20)

Οὐ γὰρ ἔφθασε χρόνον προσήκοντα κυνηγέτῃ.

Wendland, p. 88, from Procopius, Cod. Aug. f. 119ʳ (Migne, p. 419).

208. (Gen. xxvii. 20)

Ὁ δὲ θεοφιλὴς ἐπὶ θεὸν τὴν αἰτίαν ἀνάγει διὰ τῆς ἀποκρίσεως.

Wendland, p. 88, from Procopius, Cod. Aug. f. 119ʳ (Migne, p. 419).

210. (Gen. xxvii. 22)

Τὴν εὐσεβῆ φωνὴν οὐκ ἂν λεχθεῖσαν ὑπὸ τοῦ Ἡσαῦ τὴν "ὃ παρέδωκεν ὁ θεὸς ἐναντίον μου" ἐπιγνοὺς Ἰσαὰκ εἶπε τὸ προκείμενον, ᾧ καὶ μαρτυρεῖν ἔοικεν ἡ γραφὴ φάσκουσα περὶ μόνων τῶν χειρῶν ὅτι "ἦσαν αἱ χεῖρες τοῦ Ἰακὼβ ὡς αἱ χεῖρες Ἡσαῦ τοῦ ἀδελφοῦ αὐτοῦ δασεῖαι," οὐκέτι δὲ καὶ περὶ φωνῆς τὸ ὅμοιον· οὐ γὰρ ἐν ἰδιότητι προφορᾶς ἀλλ' ἐν τοῖς λεχθεῖσιν ἦν ἡ φωνή.

Wendland, pp. 88-89, from Procopius, Cod. Aug. f. 119ʳ (Migne, p. 419).

APPENDIX A, GREEK FRAGMENTS

211. (Gen. xxvii. 23)

Τὰ αὐτὰ καθήκοντα[a] πολλάκις ἐνεργοῦσιν ὅ τε ἀστεῖος καὶ ὁ
φαῦλος, ἀλλ᾽ οὐκ ἀπὸ τῆς αὐτῆς διανοίας ἀμφότεροι[b]· ὁ μὲν γὰρ
κρίνων ὅτι καλόν, ὁ δὲ μοχθηρὸς[c] μνώμενός τι τῶν εἰς πλεονεξίαν.

Harris, p. 70 (" unidentified," but located by E. Bréhier).
from Mai, *Script. Vet.* vii. 100 e Cod. Vat. 1553, Φίλωνος·
ἐκ τῶν δ᾽ ἐν Γεν. ζητημ., and from Cod. Rupef. f. 337 b.

227. (Gen. xxvii. 34)

Οὐκ ἐπὶ τῷ μὴ τυχεῖν[d] τῶν εὐλογιῶν οὕτω δυσχεραίνει ὡς ἐπὶ
τῷ τὸν ἀδελφὸν αὐτοῦ[e] ἀξιωθῆναι. Βάσκανος γὰρ ὢν ἐπιμε-
λέστερον προκρίνει τῆς ἰδίας ὠφελείας τὴν ἐκείνου ζημίαν. Ταῦτα
γὰρ ἐμφαίνεται διὰ τοῦ μέγα καὶ πικρὸν ἀνοιμῶξαι[f] καὶ ἐπιλέγειν·
" Εὐλόγησον δὴ[g] καὶ ἐμέ, πάτερ."

Harris, p. 46, from Cat. Ined. Regia, 1825 (Mangey ii. 676),
and Cat. Lips. 1, col. 339, Προκοπίου, and Cat. Burney, f. 57 b,
Φίλωνος ἑβραίου, also in Wendland, pp. 89-90, from Procopius 421 c.

228. (Gen. xxvii. 35)

Ἀλλ᾽ εἴ γε μετὰ δόλου ἔλα-
βεν, εἴποι τις ἄν,[h] οὐκ ἐπαινετός.
Τί οὖν φησί· " Καὶ εὐλογημένος ἔσται[i] "; Ἀλλ᾽ ἔοικεν
αἰνίττεσθαι διὰ τοῦ λεχθέντος
ὅτι οὐ πᾶς δόλος ὑπαίτιός ἐστιν,
ἐπεὶ καὶ λῃστὰς νυκτοφύλακες,
καὶ πολεμίους στρατηγοί, οὓς
ἀδόλως συλλαβεῖν οὐκ ἔστιν,
ἐνεδρεύοντες κατορθοῦν δοκοῦσι.
Καὶ τὰ λεγόμενα στρατηγήματα
τοιοῦτον λόγον ἔχει καὶ τὰ τῶν
ἀθλητῶν ἀγωνίσματα· καὶ γὰρ
ἐπὶ τούτων ἡ ἀπάτη νενόμισται

Πῶς οὖν ἐπιφέρεις· " Καὶ
εὐλογημένος ἔσται "; Αἰνίττεται τοίνυν ὡς οὐ πᾶς δόλος
ὑπαίτιος. Τοιαῦτα γὰρ καὶ τὰ
λεγόμενα στρατηγήματα, καὶ
ἐπὶ τῶν ἀθλητῶν ὁμοίως οἱ μετὰ
δόλου νικῶντες θαυμάζονται
στεφανούμενοι· οἷς ἰσοδύναμεῖ
τὸ " μετὰ δόλου " τῷ " μετὰ
τέχνης." Οὐδὲν δὲ ἀτέχνως ὁ
σπουδαῖος ποιεῖ.

Wendland, p. 90, from
Procopius, Cod. Aug. f.
121ᵛ.

---

[a] καθηκόντως Cod. Rupef.   [b] ἀμφότεροι om. Cod. Rupef.
          [c] μοχθηρῶς Cod. Rupef.
[d] +φασί Procop.   [e] αὐτῶν Procop.
      [f] ἐκβοῆσαι Cat. Lips. : βοῆσαι Cat. Burney.
                [g] δὲ Procop.
[h] εἴποι τις ἄν] ἴσως εἴποι τις Catt. Lips. et Burney.
      [i] ἔστω Catt. Lips. et Burney.

τίμιον, καὶ οἱ δι' ἀπάτης περιγενόμενοι[a] τῶν ἀντιπάλων, βραβείων ἀξιοῦνται καὶ στεφάνων. Ὥστε οὐ διαβολὴ τὸ " μετὰ δόλου " ἀλλ' ἐγκώμιον ἰσοδυναμοῦν τῷ " μετὰ τέχνης." Οὐδὲν γὰρ ἀτέχνως πράττει ὁ σπουδαῖος.

Harris, p. 46, from Cat. Ined. Regia, 1825 (Mangey ii. 676), and Cat. Lips. 1, col. 340, Ἀδήλου, and Cat. Burney, f. 57 b.

[a] περιγινόμενοι Catt. Lips. et Burney.

UNIDENTIFIED FRAGMENTS FROM QUAESTIONES IN GENESIN[a]

1. Τῶν φαύλων πλούσιος οὐδεὶς καὶ ἂν τὰ πανταχοῦ μέταλλα κέκτηται· ἀλλ' εἰσὶ πάντες οἱ ἄφρονες πένητες.

Harris, p. 69, from Dam. Par. 362 and Cod. Reg. 923, f. 76, " in each case with reference to II Quaest. in Gen."

2. Μελέτη τροφὸς[b] ἐπιστήμης.

Harris, p. 69, from Dam. Par. 405, and Cod. Reg. 923, f. 105, and Mai, *Script. Vet.* vii. 99 e Cod. Vat. 1553, ἐκ τῶν ἐν Γενέσει ζητημάτων.

3. Ὥσπερ κίονες οἰκίας ὅλας ὑπερείδουσιν, οὕτω καὶ αἱ θεῖαι δυνάμεις τὸν σύμπαντα κόσμον καὶ τοῦ ἀνθρωπείου τὸ ἄριστον καὶ θεοφιλέστατον γένος.

Harris, p. 69, from Dam. Par. 749=Cod. Rupef. f. 29, ἐκ τοῦ α' τῶν ἐν Γενέσει ζητημάτων.

4. Ἐάν τις κατ' οἰκίαν ἢ κώμην ἢ πόλιν ἢ ἔθνος γένηται φρονήσεως ἐραστής, ἀνάγκη τὴν οἰκίαν καὶ τὴν πόλιν ἐκείνην ἀμείνονι βίῳ χρήσασθαι· ὁ γὰρ ἀστεῖος κοινὸν ἀγαθόν ἐστιν ἅπασιν, ἐξ ἑτοίμου τὴν ἀφ' ἑαυτοῦ προτείνων ὠφελείαν.

Harris, p. 69, from Dam. Par. 750=Cod. Rupef. f. 33 b, " from I Quaest. in Gen."

5. Ἀνθρώποις τὸ εὐμετάβλητον διὰ τὴν ἐν τοῖς ἐκτὸς ἀβε-

---

[a] Omitting the six fragments located by Früchtel and Bréhier, and printed above. The unidentified fragments, which are unnumbered in Harris, have been numbered by me.

[b] + ἐστιν Codd. Reg. et Vat.

αιότητα συμβαίνειν ἀνάγκη. Οὕτω γοῦν φίλους ἑλόμενοι πολλάκις καὶ βραχύν τινα αὐτοῖς διατρίψαντες χρόνον, οὐδὲν ἐγκαλεῖν ἔχοντες ἀπεστράφημεν ὡσεὶ ἐχθρῶν.

Harris, pp. 69-70, from Dam. Par. 776 (Cod. Rupef.), ἐκ τῶν ἐν Γενέσει ζητουμένων.

6. Τὸ ἐπαισθάνεσθαι τῶν ἐσφαλμένων καὶ ἑαυτοῦ καταμέμφεσθαι πρὸς δικαίου ἀνδρός· τὸ δὲ ἀνεπαισθήτως διακεῖσθαι—ἀργαλεώτερα ποιεῖ τῇ ψυχῇ τὰ δεινά—πρὸς κακοῦ ἀνδρός.

Harris, p. 70, from Dam. Par. 777 (Cod. Rupef.), ἐκ τῶν αὐτῶν (sc. τῶν ἐν Γενέσει ζητημάτων).

7. Ἐπειδὴ πρὸς πολλὰ τῶν κατὰ τὸν βίον τυφλὸς ὁ τῶν μὴ πεφιλοσοφηκότων νοῦς, χρηστέον[a] τοῖς βλέπουσι τὰς τῶν πραγμάτων ἰδέας πρὸς ὁδηγίαν.

Harris, p. 70, from Dam. Par. (Cod. Reg. 923, f. 315 b), "referred to Philo on Genesis," and John Monachus (Mangey ii. 667)=Cod. Rupef. f. 256 b, ἐκ τῶν ἐν Γεν. ζητ.

8. Ἐν θεῷ μόνον τὸ τέλειον καὶ ἀνενδεές, ἐν δὲ ἀνθρώπῳ[b] τὸ ἐπιδεὲς καὶ ἀτελές. Διδακτὸς γὰρ ὁ ἄνθρωπος, καὶ ἂν γὰρ σοφώτατος ἄλλος ἀπ᾿ ἄλλου,[c] ἀλλ᾿ οὐ ἀδιδάκτως οὐδὲ αὐτοφυῶς· καὶ εἰ ἐπιστημονικώτερος ἕτερος ἑτέρου, οὐκ ἐμφύτως ἀλλὰ μεμαθημένως.

Harris, p. 70, from Dam. Par.=Cod. Reg. 923, f. 335, "from Quaest. in Gen.," and John Monachus (Mangey ii. 667)=Cod. Rupef. f. 262 b.

9. Εἰώθασιν οἱ ἄνθρωποι ἐκ πλουσίων γενόμενοι πένητες ἐξαίφνης ἢ ἐξ ἐνδόξων καὶ μεγάλων ἄδοξοι καὶ ταπεινοὶ ἢ ἐξ ἀρχόντων ἰδιῶται ἢ ἐξ ἐλευθέρων δοῦλοι, ταῖς τύχαις συμμεταβάλλειν τὰ φρονήματα, φάσκοντες οὐ προνοεῖσθαι τῶν ἀνθρωπίνων πραγμάτων τὸ θεῖον, οὐ γὰρ ἂν χρήσασθαι μεγάλαις καὶ ἀπροσδοκήτοις μεταβολαῖς καὶ κακοπραγίαις· ἀγνοοῦντες πρῶτον μὲν ὅτι τούτων οὐδέν ἐστι κακὸν οὐδὲ γὰρ τἀναντία ἀγαθά, ὅτι μὴν τὸ

[a] χρητέον Cod. Reg.
[b] ἀνθρώποις Cod. Reg.
[c] σοφώτατος . . . ἄλλου] σοφώτερος ἄλλος ἀλλήλου Cod. Reg.

APPENDIX A, GREEK FRAGMENTS

δοκεῖν οὐκ ἀλήθεια· δεύτερον δὲ ὅτι πολλάκις ταῦτα συμβαίνει διὰ νουθεσίαν, ἕνεκα τῶν ἀδιαφόρων ἐξυβριζόντων· οὐ γὰρ πάντες φέρειν τὰ ἀγαθὰ δύνανται· τρίτον δέ, ὡς ἔφην, πρὸς ἀπόπειραν ἠθῶν· ἀκριβεστάτη γὰρ βάσανος οἱ πρὸς ἑκάτερα καιροί.

Harris, p. 70, from Mai, *Script. Vet.* vii. 101 *e* Cod. Vat. 1553, Φίλωνος· ἐκ τοῦ α' τῶν ἐν Γεν. ζητημ.

10. Τὸ ἐπιορκεῖν ἀνόσιον καὶ ἀλυσιτελέστατον.

Harris, p. 70, from Dam. Par. 784 (Cod. Rupef.), *ἐκ τῶν ἐν Γενέσει ζητημάτων*, "also Dam. Par. 751 (Cod. Rupef.), apparently referred to the Questions on Exodus."

11. Οἱ ἑαυτῶν μόνον ἕνεκα πάντα πράττοντες φιλαυτίαν,[a] μέγιστον κακόν, ἐπιτηδεύουσιν, ὃ ποιεῖ τὸ ἄμικτον, τὸ ἀκοινώνητον, τὸ ἄφιλον,[b] τὸ ἄδικον, τὸ ἀσεβές. Τὸν γὰρ ἄνθρωπον ἡ φύσις κατεσκεύασεν οὐχ ὡς τὰ μονωτικὰ θηρία ἀλλ' ὡς ἀγελαῖα καὶ σύννομα, κοινωνικώτατον, ἵνα μὴ μόνῳ ἑαυτῷ ζῇ ἀλλὰ καὶ πατρὶ καὶ μητρὶ[c] καὶ ἀδελφοῖς καὶ γυναικὶ καὶ τέκνοις καὶ τοῖς ἄλλοις συγγενέσι καὶ φίλοις, καὶ δημόταις καὶ φυλέταις[d] καὶ πατρίδι καὶ ὁμοφύλοις καὶ πᾶσιν ἀνθρώποις, ἔτι μέντοι καὶ τοῖς μέρεσι τοῦ παντός, καὶ τῷ ὅλῳ κόσμῳ[e] καὶ πολὺ πρότερον τῷ πατρὶ καὶ ποιητῇ· δεῖ γὰρ εἶναι, εἴγε ὄντως ἐστὶ λογικός, κοινωνικόν, φιλόκοσμον, φιλόθεον ἵνα γένηται καὶ θεοφιλής.[f]

Harris, p. 71, from John Monachus (Mangey ii. 662), and Mai, *Script. Vet.* vii. 108 *e* Cod. Vat. 1553, ἐκ τοῦ β' τῶν ἐν Γεν. ζητημάτων, and Cod. Reg. 923, f. 20 b, Φίλωνος. "Maximus (ii. 686) gives the first sentence . . . Further in Dam. Par. 721 the whole passage is ascribed to the Abbot Isaiah."

12. Τρεπτοὶ πολύτρεπτον διαπερῶντες βίον, καὶ συμφορὰς καθημέραν ἐνειλούμενοι, ἥκιστα τῆς εὐδαιμονίας ἠφῖχθαί[g] τινα πρὸ τέλους ὑπολαμβάνομεν.

Harris, p. 71, from Mai, *Script. Vet.* vii. 102 *e* Cod. Vat. 1553, Φίλωνος· ἐκ τῶν ἐν Γεν. ζητημ.

---

[a] φιλαυτίᾳ τὸ Cod. Vat. : φιλαυτίας Maximus.
[b] τὸ ἄφιλον om. Cod. Vat.   [c] καὶ μητρὶ om. Cod. Vat.
[d] καὶ φίλοις . . . φυλέταις om. Cod. Vat.
[e] ἔτι . . . κόσμῳ om. Cod. Vat.
[f] δεῖ γὰρ . . . θεοφιλής om. Cod. Vat.
[g] ἀφῖχθαί con. Harris.

236

13. Συγκρύπτεται διὰ φιλίαν νόθου πράγματος καὶ ἀδόκιμον[a] τὸ γνήσιον καὶ δοκιμώτατον.

Harris, p. 71, from Mai, *Script. Vet.* vii. 103, Φίλωνος· ἐκ τοῦ δ′ τῶν ἐν Γεν. ζητημ.

14. Τοὺς ἄρξαντας εἴτε τῶν ἀγαθῶν εἴτε καὶ πονηρῶν βουλευμάτων, καὶ μάλιστα ὅταν ἐφαρμόσῃ τοῖς βουλεύμασι τὰ ἔργα, ἴσους ἡγητέον τοῖς καὶ τελειώσασιν αὐτά· τὸ μὲν γὰρ μὴ φθάσαι πρὸς τὸ πέρας ἐλθεῖν, ἕτερα καὶ πολλὰ αἴτια· ἡ δὲ γνώμη καὶ σπουδὴ τῶν προελομένων ἔφθακεν δυνάμει καὶ πρὸς τὸ πέρας.

Harris, p. 71, from Mai, *Script. Vet.* vii. 105 *e* Cod. Vat. 1553, Φίλωνος· ἐκ τοῦ β′ τῶν ἐν Γεν. ζητημ.

15. Ὁ εὐλαβέστερος τρόπος οὐχ οὕτως ἐπὶ τοῖς ἰδίοις ἀγαθοῖς γέγηθεν ὡς ἐπὶ τοῖς τοῦ πέλας κακοῖς ἀνιᾶται ἢ φοβεῖται· ἀνιᾶται μὲν ὅτ′ ἀνάξιος ὢν ἀτυχῇ, φοβεῖται δὲ ὅτ′ ἂν ἐπιτηδέως κακοπαθῇ.

Harris, p. 71, from Mai, *Script. Vet.* vii. 107, Φίλωνος· ἐκ τοῦ δ′ τῶν ἐν Γεν. ζητημ.

16. Τί οὖν ἐνεθυμήθη; ὅτι διὰ τὸ εὐαρεστεῖν πεποίηται ὁ ἄνθρωπος, οὐ κατ′ ἀντιστροφήν, διότι ἐποίησεν, ἀλλ′ ὡς μὴ ἐμμεῖναν τὸ ποίημα τῇ εἰς εὐαρέστησιν ποιήσει. Πρὸς οὖν τὸ ποίημα ὁ λόγος, ὥσπερ σοφιστὴς διαλογεῖται, οὐ διότι πεφύτευκεν ὁ θεὸς ἀλλ′ ὅτι προελθὸν διὰ ῥαθυμίαν διαμαρτάνει τῆς ἐγχειρήσεως.

Harris, p. 71, from Pitra, *Anal. Sacr.* ii. 307 = Cod. Coislin. 276, f. 221, ἐκ τῶν εἰς Γεν. ζητημ.

17. Τὰ γὰρ τοῦ πολέμου ἀριστεῖα δίδωσι τῷ ἱερεῖ καὶ τὰς τῆς νίκης ἀπαρχάς. Ἱεροπρεπεστάτη δὲ καὶ ἁγιωτάτη πασῶν ἀπαρχῶν ἡ δεκάτη διὰ τὸ παντέλειον εἶναι τὸν ἀριθμόν, ἀφ′ οὗ καὶ τοῖς ἱερεῦσι καὶ νεωκόροις αἱ δεκάται προστάξει νόμου καρπῶν καὶ θρεμμάτων ἀποδίδονται, ἄρξαντος τῆς ἀπαρχῆς Ἀβραάμ, ὃς καὶ τοῦ γένους ἀρχηγέτης ἐστίν.

Harris, pp. 71-72, from Cramer, *Catena in Heb.* p. 580, *e* Cod. Paris 238, ". . . seems to belong to the Questions on Genesis xiv. 18, being found in a codex which quotes the Questions on Gen. iv. 4 and seems to have no other Philonea. This part of the Questions is lost in the Armenian."

---

[a] l. ἀδοκίμου (?).

EXODUS, BOOK I

1. (Ex. xii. 2)

῞Οταν οἱ τῶν σπαρτῶν καρποὶ τελειωθῶσιν, οἱ τῶν δένδρων γενέσεως ἀρχὴν λαμβάνουσιν ἵνα δολιχεύωσιν αἱ τοῦ θεοῦ χάριτες τὸν αἰῶνα, παρ᾽ ἄλλων ἄλλαι διαδεχόμεναι καὶ συνάπτουσαι τέλη μὲν ἀρχαῖς, ἀρχὰς δὲ τέλεσιν, ἀτελεύτητοι ὦσιν.

Harris, p. 47, from Dam. Par. 789 = Cod. Rupef. f. 142 b, ἐκ τοῦ α᾽ τῶν ἐν Ἐξόδῳ.

6. (Ex. xii. 4b)

Ὑπερβολαὶ καὶ ἐλλείψεις ἀνισότητα ἐγέννησαν. Ἀνισότης δέ, ἵνα αὐτὸς μυθικώτερον χρήσωμαι[a] τοῖς ὀνόμασιν, μητὴρ ἀδικίας ἐστίν, ὡς ἔμπαλιν ἰσότης δικαιοσύνης· ὑπερβολῆς δὲ καὶ ἐλλείψεως μέσον τὸ αὐταρκές· ἐν ᾧ τὸ ἱερὸν γράμμα περιέχεται τὸ " μηδὲν ἄγαν."

Harris, p. 47, from Mai, Script. Vet. vii. 106 e Cod. Vat. 1553, Φίλωνος· ἐκ τοῦ α᾽ τῶν ἐν Ἐξόδῳ ζητημάτων.

7. (Ex. xii. 5a)

(a) Λέγεται ὑπὸ φυσικῶν ἀνδρῶν, οὐδὲν ἕτερον εἶναι θῆλυ ἢ ἀτελὲς ἄρσεν.

Harris, p. 47, from Dam. Par. 777 = Cod. Rupef. f. 134, ἐκ τῶν ἐν Ἐξόδῳ ζητημάτων, and Anton Melissa, Migne, col. 1088.

(b) ῎Ενιοι προκόψαντες ἐπ᾽ ἀρετὴν ὑπενόστησαν πρὶν ἐφικέσθαι τοῦ τέλους, τὴν ἄρτι φυομένην ἀριστοκράτειαν ἐν ψυχῇ καθελούσης τῆς παλαιᾶς ὀλιγοκρατείας,[b] ἢ πρὸς ὀλίγον ἠρεμήσασα πάλιν ἐξ ὑπαρχῆς μετὰ πλείονος δυνάμεως ἀντεπέθετο.[c]

Harris, pp. 47–48, from Dam. Par. 343, and Cod. Reg. 913,

[a] edd. : χρήσομαι Cod. Vat.
[b] παλαιᾶς ὀλιγοκρατείας] ὀχλοκρατίας Anton Melissa.
[c] ἐναπέθετο Dam.

238

f. 84, ἐκ τοῦ α' τῶν ἐν Ἐξαγω [sc. Ἐξαγωγῇ = Ἐξόδῳ] ζητημάτων, and Anton Melissa (Migne, col. 1117).

19. (Ex. xii. 11)

Αἱ μὲν γὰρ ζῶναι στάσιν ἐμφαίνουσι καὶ συναγωγὴν ἡδονῶν καὶ τῶν ἄλλων παθῶν ἃ τέως ἀνεῖτο καὶ κεχάλαστο· οὐκ ἀπὸ δὲ σκοποῦ προσέθηκε τὸ δεῖν ζώννυσθαι κατὰ τὴν ὀσφύν· ὁ γὰρ τόπος ἐκεῖνος εἰς φάτνην ἀποκέκριται πολυκεφάλῳ θρέμματι τῶν ἐν ἡμῖν ἐπιθυμιῶν.

Harris, p. 48, from Pitra, Anal. Sacr. ii. 313 e Cod. Vat. 1611, f. 181.

21. (Ex. xii. 17)

Ἄνδρες ἀγαθοί, τροπικώτερον εἰπεῖν, κίονές[a] εἰσι δήμων ὅλων, ὑπερείδοντες, καθάπερ οἰκίας μεγάλας, τὰς πόλεις καὶ τὰς πολιτείας.

Harris, p. 48, from John Monachus (Mangey ii. 661) = Cod. Rupef. f. 33 b, ἐκ τοῦ Περὶ μέθης, and Cod. Rupef. f. 200 b, and Anton Melissa (Migne, col. 1105).

[a] κρείττονές Cod. Rupef.

EXODUS, BOOK II

1. (Ex. xx. 25b) Τί ἐστι· "τὸ γὰρ ἐγχειρίδιόν σου" καὶ τὰ ἑξῆς;

Οἱ τὴν φύσιν παρεγχειρεῖν τολμῶντες καὶ τὰ ἔργα τῆς φύσεως ἐγχειρήμασιν ἰδίοις μεταμορφοῦντες τὰ ἀμίαντα μιαίνουσι. Τέλεια γὰρ καὶ πλήρη τὰ τῆς φύσεως, προσθήκης οὐδεμιᾶς δεόμενα.

Harris, p. 49, from Cat. Ined. Regia, 1825 (Mangey ii. 677), and Cat. Lips. 1, col. 785, Φίλωνος ἑβραίου.

2. (Ex. xxii. 21 [Heb. 20])

Ἐμφανέστατα παρίστησιν ὅτι προσήλυτός ἐστιν, οὐχ ὁ περιτμηθεὶς τὴν ἀκροβυστίαν ἀλλ' ὁ τὰς ἡδονὰς καὶ τὰς ἐπιθυμίας καὶ τὰ ἄλλα πάθη τῆς ψυχῆς. Ἐν Αἰγύπτῳ γὰρ τὸ Ἑβραίων γένος οὐ περιτέτμητο, κακωθὲν δὲ πάσαις κακώσεσι τῆς παρὰ τῶν ἐγχωρίων περὶ τοὺς ξένους ὠμότητος, ἐγκρατείᾳ καὶ καρτερίᾳ συνεβίου οὐκ ἀνάγκῃ μᾶλλον ἢ ἐθελουσίῳ γνώμῃ διὰ τὴν ἐπὶ τὸν σωτῆρα θεὸν καταφυγήν, ὃς ἐξ ἀπόρων καὶ ἀμηχάνων ἐπιπέμψας τὴν εὐεργέτιν δύναμιν ἐρρύσατο τοὺς ἱκέτας.[a] Διὰ τοῦτο προστίθησιν· "Ὑμεῖς γὰρ οἴδατε τὴν ψυχὴν τοῦ προσηλύτου." Τίς δὲ προσηλύτου διάνοιά ἐστιν; Ἀλλοτρίωσις τῆς πολυθέου δόξης, οἰκείωσις δὲ τῆς πρὸς τὸν ἕνα καὶ πατέρα τῶν ὅλων τιμῆς. Δεύτερον ἐπήλυδας ἔνιοι καλοῦσι τοὺς ξένους. Ξένοι δὲ καὶ οἱ πρὸς τὴν ἀλήθειαν αὐτομοληκότες, τὸν αὐτὸν τρόπον τοῖς ἐν Αἰγύπτῳ ξενιτεύσασιν. Οὗτοι μὲν γὰρ ἐπήλυδες χώρας, ἐκεῖνοι δὲ νομίμων καὶ ἐθῶν εἰσι,[b] τὸ δὲ ὄνομα κοινὸν ἑκατέρων "ἐπηλύδων" ὑπογράφεται.

Harris, pp. 49-50, from Cat. Reg. 1825 (Mangey ii. 677), and Cat. Lips. 1, col. 810, Φίλωνος ἑβραίου, and Cat. Burney, f. 13 b. The variant reading is in Wendland, p. 95, from Procopius, Cod. Aug. f. 217ᵛ (Migne, p. 622).

[a] οἰκέτας Cat. Lips.

[b] οὗτοι μὲν ... εἰσι] οὐ τὸν αὐτὸν τρόπον, αὐτοὶ μὲν γὰρ χώρας, οἱ δὲ πρὸς αὐτοὺς ἰόντες νόμων καὶ πολιτείας Procopius.

EXODUS, BOOK II

3. (Ex. xxii. 22 [Heb. 21])

(a) Οὐδένα μέν, οὐδὲ[a] τῶν ἄλλων, οὔτε ἄρρενα οὔτε θήλειαν,
ἀφίησιν ἀδικεῖν ὁ νόμος.[b] Ἐξαιρέτου δὲ προνοίας μεταδίδωσιν
χήραις καὶ ὀρφανοῖς,[c] ἐπειδὴ τοὺς ἀναγκαίους βοηθοὺς καὶ κηδεμόνας ἀφήρηνται, χῆραι μὲν ἄνδρας, ὀρφανοὶ δὲ γονεῖς.[d] Βούλεται
γὰρ τῇ φυσικῇ κοινωνίᾳ χρωμένους τὰς ἐνδείας ὑπὸ τῶν ἐν περιουσίᾳ ἀναπληροῦσθαι.[e]

Harris, p. 50, from Mai, *Script. Vet.* vii. 104 e Cod. Vat.
1553, Φίλωνος· ἐκ τοῦ τελευταίου τῶν ἐν Ἐξόδῳ ζητημάτων,
and Cod. Reg. 923, f. 32 b, and Cod. Rupef. f. 220 b, and
Cat. Ined. Reg. 1825 (Mangey ii. 678), and Cat. Lips. 1, col.
805, and Cat. Burney, f. 136. The variant to the first part
of the second sentence is in Wendland, p. 95, from Procopius, Cod. Aug. f. 217[v] (Migne, p. 622).

(b) Ψυχαὶ δέ, ὅταν προσκολληθῶσι θεῷ, ἐκ γυναικῶν γίνονται
παρθένοι, τὰς μὲν γυναικώδεις ἀποβάλλουσαι φθορὰς τῶν ἐν
αἰσθήσει καὶ πάθει· τὴν δὲ ἄψευστον[f] καὶ ἀμιγῆ παρθένον, ἀρέ-
σκειαν θεοῦ, μεταδιώκουσι· κατὰ λόγον οὖν αἱ τοιαῦται ψυχαὶ
χηρεύουσιν, ἄνδρα τὸν τῆς φύσεως ὀρθὸν νόμον προσσυμβιοῦσιν
καὶ πατέρα τὸν αὐτόν, ἃ χρὴ πράττειν παραγγέλλοντα καθάπερ
ἐγγόνοις μετὰ τῆς ἀνωτάτω κηδεμονίας.

Harris, p. 51, from Pitra, *Anal. Sacr.* ii. 308 e Cod. Coislin.
276, f. 183.

4. (Ex. xxii. 23 [Heb. 22])

Καὶ κακοῦν ἀπαγορεύει οὐ τοσοῦτον τὴν σωματικὴν κάκωσιν
ὅσον τὴν ψυχικήν. Ὀρφανοῖς γὰρ γινέσθω μηδεὶς ἀφροσύνης ἢ
ἀκολασίας διδάσκαλος, ἀλλὰ τῶν ἐναντίων, ἐν ὅσῳ τὰς ψυχὰς
ἔχουσιν ἁπαλὰς πρὸς τὴν τῶν θείων χαρακτήρων ὑποδοχήν.

Wendland, p. 95, from Procopius, Cod. Aug. f. 217[v]
(Migne, p. 622).

6. (Ex. xxii. 28b [Heb. 27b])

(a) Προνοεῖται τῶν ἰδιωτῶν ὡς μὴ περιπίπτοιεν ἀνηκέστοις

[a] οὐδένα . . . οὐδὲ] οὐ δυναμένου δὲ Cod. Vat.
[b] οὐδένα . . . νόμος om. Codd. Reg., Rupef., et Catt. Ined.
Reg., Lips., Burney.
[c] ἐξαιρέτου . . . ὀρφανοῖς] ἐξαιρέτου δὲ προνοίας διὰ τὴν
ἐρημίαν μεταδίδωσιν ὀρφανοῖς τε καὶ χήραις Procopius.
[d] ἐπειδὴ . . . γονεῖς om. Catt. Lips., Burney.
[e] βούλεται . . . ἀναπληροῦσθαι om. Cod. Vat.
[f] ex Arm. Pitra : ἄψαυστον Cod. Coislin.

241

τιμωρίαις· οἱ γὰρ κακῶς ἀκούσαντες ἄρχοντες τοὺς εἰπόντας[a] οὐ μετὰ δίκης ἀμυνοῦνται· καταχρήσονται δυναστείαις εἰς πανωλεθρίαν. Ἐπεί, φησίν, οὐ περὶ παντὸς ἄρχοντος ἔοικε νομοθετεῖν ἀλλ' ὡσανεὶ τοῦ λαοῦ τοῦδε ἢ ἔθνους ἡγεμόνα σπουδαῖον ὑποτίθεται,[b] διὰ πλειόνων, καταχρηστικῶς δὲ δυνατοὺς ἢ ἱερεῖς ἢ προφήτας ἢ ἁγίους ἄνδρας ὡς Μωϋσέα. " Ἰδοὺ γάρ, ἔθηκά σε θεὸν Φαραώ," ἐλέχθη πρὸς Μωϋσῆν.

Harris, p. 51, from Cat. Lips. 1, col. 805, Φίλωνος ἑβραίου, and Cat. Burney, f. 136.

(b) Τῷ ἀγαθῷ ἀνδρὶ βλασφημία μὲν ἀλλότριον, ἔπαινος δὲ οἰκειότατον· οὐδὲν γὰρ οὕτως εὐάγωγον εἰς εὔνοιαν ὡς εὐφημία.

Lewy, pp. 59-60, from Dam. Par.=Cod. Const. Metoch. 274, Φίλωνος.

Οὐδὲν οὕτως εὐάγωγον εἰς εὔνοιαν ὡς ἡ τῶν εὐεργετημάτων εὐφημία.

Harris, p. 51, from Anton Melissa (Migne, col. 1149).

9. (Ex. xxiii. 1a)

Μάταιόν φησιν οὔτε ἀκοαῖς οὔτε ἄλλῃ τινὶ τῶν αἰσθήσεων προσιτέον· ἐπακολουθοῦσι γὰρ ταῖς ἀπάταις αἱ μέγισται ζημίαι. Διὸ καὶ παρ' ἐνίοις νομοθέταις ἀπείρηται μαρτυρεῖν ἀκοή,[c] ὡς τὸ μὲν ἀληθὲς ὄψει πιστευόμενον,[d] τὸ δὲ ψεῦδος[e] ἀκοῇ.

Harris, pp. 51-52, from Cat. Reg. Ined. 1825, and Cat. Lips. 1, col. 807, and Cat. Burney, f. 136 b. The second sentence is in Wendland, pp. 95-96, from Procopius, Cod. Aug. f. 218[r] (Migne, p. 623).

10. (Ex. xxiii. 3)

Πενία καθ' ἑαυτὴν μὲν ἐλέου χρῄζει εἰς ἐπανόρθωσιν ἐνδείας, εἰς δὲ κρίσιν ἰοῦσα βραβευτῇ χρῆται τῷ τῆς ἰσότητος νόμῳ. Θεῖον γὰρ ἡ δικαιοσύνη καὶ ἀδέκαστον· ὅθεν καὶ ἐν ἑτέροις εὖ εἴρηται ὅτι[f] ' ἡ κρίσις τοῦ θεοῦ δικαία[g] ἐστίν."

Harris, p. 52, from Cat. Reg. Ined. 1825, and Cat. Lips. 1,

---

[a] ἀπόντας Cat. Burney.   [b] ὑπερτίθεται Cat. Burney.

[c] διὸ . . . ἀκοῇ] διὸ παρ' ἐνίοις ἀπείρηται νομοθέταις ἀκοὴν μαρτυρεῖν Procopius.

[d] πιστούμενον Procopius.   [e] ψευδὲς Procopius.

[f] ὅθεν . . . ὅτι] διὸ καὶ εἴρηται Procopius.

[g] δικαία om. Procopius, cf. Wendland ad loc., " fehlt in fast allen mss. der Cat. Lips."

col. 807, and Cat. Burney, f. 136 b. The second sentence is in Wendland, p. 96, from Procopius, Cod. Aug. f. 218ʳ (Migne, p. 623).

11. (Ex. xxiii. 4)

Ἡμερότητος ὑπερβολὴ πρὸς τὸ μὴ βλάπτειν τὸν ἐχθρὸν ἔτι καὶ συνωφελεῖν πειρᾶσθαι· δεύτερον δὲ παραίτησις πλεονεξίας ᵃ· ὁ γὰρ μηδ' ἐχθρὸν ζημιοῦν ὑπομένων τίνα τῶν ἄλλων ἐθελήσειεν ἂν βλάπτειν ἐπ' ὠφελείᾳ ἰδίᾳ; Lewy, p. 60, from Dam. Par. = Cod. Const. Metoch. 274, Φίλωνος.

Ἡμερότητος ὑπερβολὴ πρὸς τῷ μὴ βλάπτειν τὸν ἐχθρὸν ἔτι καὶ ὠφελεῖν πειρᾶσθαι. Τίνα δὲ καὶ ἀδικήσειεν ⟨ἂν⟩ ὁ μηδὲ τὸν ἐχθρὸν ζημιῶν; Ἔτι δὲ καὶ στάσιν καθαιρεῖ καὶ δυσμένειαν προκατάρχων εἰρήνης. Φιλικὸν γὰρ τὸ ἔργον καὶ πρὸς ἀμοιβὴν ἐφέλκει τὸν μὴ λίαν ἀγνώμονα. Διδαχθεὶς δέ τις μηδὲ βοσκημάτων ὑπερορᾶν πρὸς τίνα τῶν ἀνθρώπων οὐκ ἂν εἴη φιλάνθρωπος; Wendland, p. 96, from Procopius, Cod. Aug. f. 218ʳ (Migne, p. 623).

13. (Ex. xxiii. 20-21)

(a) Οἱ ἀφυλάκτως ὁδοιποροῦντες διαμαρτάνουσιν τῆς ὀρθῆς καὶ λεωφόρου ὡς πολλάκις εἰς ἀνοδίας καὶ δυσβάτους καὶ τραχείας ἀτραποὺς ἐκτρέπεσθαι. Τὸ παραπλήσιόν ἐστι ὅτε καὶ αἱ ψυχαὶ τῶν νέων ᵇ παιδείας ἀμοιροῦσιν,ᶜ καθάπερ ῥεῦμα ἀνεπίσχετον ᵈ ὅπη μὴ λυσιτελὲς ῥεμβεύονται. Harris, p. 52, from Cod. Reg. 923, f. 302 b, " from the Quaest. in Exod."

(b) Ὁ πεινῶν καὶ διψῶν ἐπιστήμης καὶ τοῦ μαθεῖν ἃ μὴ οἶδεν, τὰς ἄλλας μεθιέμενος φροντίδας, ἐπείγεται πρὸς ἀκρόασιν, καὶ νύκτωρ καὶ μεθ' ἡμέραν θυρωρεῖ τὰς τῶν σοφῶν οἰκίας. Harris, p. 52, from Dam. Par. 613 = Cod. Reg. f. 230.

ᵃ δεύτερον . . . πλεονεξίας ex Arm. con. Lewy.
ᵇ νεῶν Harris.
ᶜ Harris : ἀμοιρῶσιν Cod. Reg.
ᵈ Harris : ἀνεπίσχετο Cod. Reg.

14. (Ex. xxiii. 18a)

'Αντὶ τοῦ οὐ δεῖ ζυμωτὸν
παρεῖναι ἐπὶ τῶν θυσιαζομένων
ἀλλὰ πάντα τὰ προσαγόμενα εἰς
θυσίαν ἤτοι προσφορὰν ἄζυμα
δεῖ εἶναι, αἰνίττεται διὰ συμβόλου δύο τὰ ἀναγκαιότατα· ἐν
μὲν τὸ καταφρονεῖν ἡδονῆς,
ζύμη γὰρ ἥδυσμα τροφῆς, οὐ
τροφή· ἕτερον δὲ τὸ μὴ δεῖν
ἐπαίρεσθαι φυσωμένους διὰ κενῆς[a] οἰήσεως. 'Ανίερον γὰρ
ἑκάτερον, ἡδονῇ τε καὶ οἴησις,
μητρὸς μιᾶς ἀπάτης ἔγγονα.
Τὸ αἷμα τῶν θυσιῶν δεῖγμα
ψυχῆς ἐστι σπενδομένης θεῷ,
μιγνύναι δὲ τὰ ἄμικτα οὐχ
ὅσιον.

Harris, p. 53, from Cat.
Reg. Ined. 1825 (Mangey ii.
678), and Cat. Lips. 1, col.
816, and Cat. Burney, f. 138.

Αἰνίττεται δὲ διὰ συμβόλου
καταφρονεῖν ἡδονῆς—ζύμη γὰρ
ἥδυσμα τροφῆς, οὐ τροφή—, καὶ
τὸ μὴ δεῖν ὑπὸ κενῆς φυσωμένους οἰήσεως αἴρεσθαι. Τὸ δὲ
αἷμα τῶν θυσιῶν δεῖγμα ψυχῆς
ἐστι σπενδομένης θεῷ. Μιγνύναι δὲ τὰ ἄμικτα οὐχ ὅσιον.

Wendland, pp. 96-97, from
Procopius, Cod. Aug. f. 220ʳ
(Migne, p. 627).

15. (Ex. xxiii. 18b)

(a) Κελεύει τὰ στέατα αὐθήμερον ἀναλίσκεσθαι γινόμενα
ὕλην ἱερᾶς φλογός.

Harris, p. 53, from Cat.
Burney, f. 138, and Cat. Lips.
1, col. 816, 'Αδήλου.

Ὕλη δὲ τῆς ἱερᾶς γινέσθω
φλογός.

Wendland, p. 97, from
Procopius, Cod. Aug. f. 220ʳ
(Migne, p. 627).

(b) Ψυχὴ πᾶσα ἣν εὐσέβεια λιπαίνει τοῖς ἰδίοις ὀργίοις, ἀκοιμήτως ἔχει πρὸς τὰ θεῖα καὶ διανίσταται πρὸς τὴν θέαν τῶν θέας
ἀξίων. Τοῦτο γὰρ τὸ πάθος τῆς ψυχῆς ἐν ἑορτῇ μεγίστῃ καὶ
καιρὸς ἀψευδὴς εὐφροσύνης.

Harris, p. 101 (" unidentified," but located by Früchtel),
from Cod. Rupef. f. 153 b.

16. (Ex. xxiii. 22)

Φωνὴν θεοῦ τὸν πρὸ μικροῦ
λεχθέντα ἄγγελον ὑπονοητέον

Τὸν προφήτην φασί τινες καὶ
τὴν ἐν αὐτῷ τοῦ λαλοῦντος

[a] καινῆς Cat. Lips.

μηνύεσθαι. Τοῦ γὰρ λέγοντος ὁ προφήτης ἄγγελος κυρίου ἐστιν. Ἀνάγκη[a] γὰρ τὸν ἀκοῇ ἀκούοντα, τουτέστι τὸν τὰ λεγόμενα βεβαίως παραδεχόμενον, ἔργοις ἐπιτελεῖν τὰ λεχθέντα. Λόγου γὰρ πίστις ἔργον· ὁ δὲ καὶ τοῖς εἰρημένοις καταπειθὴς καὶ ἐνεργῶν τὰ ἀκόλουθα, σύμμαχον καὶ ὑπερασπιστὴν ἐξ ἀνάγκης ἔχει τὸν διδάσκαλον, ὅσα μὲν τῷ δοκεῖν, βοηθοῦντα τῷ γνωρίμῳ, τὸ δὲ ἀληθὲς τοῖς αὐτοῦ δόγμασι καὶ παραγγέλμασιν, ἅπερ οἱ ἐναντίοι καὶ ἐχθροὶ βούλονται καθαιρεῖν.

Harris, p. 54, from Cat. Reg. Ined. 1825 (Mangey ii. 678), and Cat. Lips. 1, col. 818, and Cat. Burney, f. 139, " glossed by a Christian commentator."

φωνήν, οὗ παρακελεύεται εἰσακούειν. Λόγου δὲ πίστις ἔργον. Ὁ δὲ καὶ πεισθεὶς καὶ πράξας ἕξει πάντως ὑπερασπιστὴν τὸν διδάσκαλον συμμαχοῦντα δι᾽ αὐτοῦ τοῖς δόγμασιν, ἅπερ οἱ ἐναντίοι βούλονται καθαιρεῖν.

Wendland, p. 97, from Procopius, Cod. Aug. f. 221[r] (Migne, p. 630).

17. (Ex. xxiii. 24c)

Στῆλαί εἰσι τὰ δόγματα συμβολικῶς, ἅπερ ἑστάναι καὶ ἐρηρεῖσθαι δοκεῖ. Τῶν δὲ κατεστηλιτευμένων δογμάτων ἀστεῖά ἐστιν, ἃ καὶ θέμις ἀνακεῖσθαι καὶ βεβαίαν ἔχειν τὴν ἵδρυσιν· τὰ δὲ ἐπίληπτα, ὧν τὴν καθαίρεσιν ποιεῖσθαι λυσιτελές. Τὸ δὲ " καθαιρῶν καθελεῖς " καὶ " συντρίβων συντρίψεις " τοιοῦτον ὑποβάλλει νοῦν. Ἔνιά τινες καθαιροῦσιν ὡς ἀναστήσοντες, καὶ συντρίβουσιν ὡς αὖθις ἁρμοσόμενοι· βούλεται δὲ τὰ καθαιρεθέντα

Τὰ δόγματα συμβολικῶς, ἅπερ ἑστάναι καὶ ἐρηρεῖσθαι δοκεῖ. Τῶν δὲ κατεστηλιτευμένων[b] δογμάτων τὰ μὲν ἀστεῖα θέμις ἀνακεῖσθαι καὶ βεβαίαν ἔχειν τὴν ἵδρυσιν, τὰ δὲ ἐπίληπτα καθαιρεῖσθαι ὡς μὴ πάλιν ἀναστησόμενα μηδὲ ἁρμοσόμενα. Τοιαύτη γὰρ ἔμφασις ἡ τοῦ " καθαιρῶν καθελεῖς " καὶ " συντρίβων συντρίψεις."

Wendland, pp. 97-98, from Procopius, Cod. Aug. f. 221[r] (Migne, p. 630).

[a] l. ἀνάγκη.
[b] Wendland : κατεστηλευμένων Cod. Aug.

ἅπαξ καὶ συντριβέντα μηκέτι
τυχεῖν ἀνορθώσεως ἀλλ' εἰς
ἅπαν ἠφανίσθαι τὰ ἐναντία τοῖς
ἀγαθοῖς καὶ καλοῖς.

Harris, pp. 54-55, from
Cat. Reg. Ined. 1825 (Mangey ii. 678), and Cat. Lips.
1, col. 820, and Cat. Burney,
f. 139.

18. (Ex. xxiii. 25b)

Τροφὴν καὶ ὑγίειαν αἰνίτ-
τεται· τροφὴν μὲν δι' ἄρτου καὶ
ὕδατος· ὑγίειαν διὰ τοῦ μαλακίαν ἀποστρέφειν. Δεύτερον,
ἐγκράτειαν εἰσηγεῖται, τὴν τῶν
ἀναγκαίων μετουσίαν, μόνον
ἐπειπών . . . πρὸς δὲ τούτοις,
μάθημα ἡμᾶς αἰσιώτατον ἀνα-
διδάσκει, δηλῶν ὅτι οὔτε ἄρτος
οὔτε ὕδωρ καθ' ἑαυτὰ τρέφου-
σιν· ἀλλ' ἔστιν ὅτε καὶ βλά-
πτουσι μᾶλλον ἢ ὠφελοῦσιν, ἐὰν
μὴ θεῖος λόγος καὶ τούτοις
χαρίσηται τὰς ὠφελητικὰς[a] δυ-
νάμεις· ἧς χάριν αἰτίας φησὶν
" εὐλογήσω τὸν ἄρτον σου καὶ
τὸ ὕδωρ," ὡς οὐχ ἱκανὰ καθ'
ἑαυτὰ τρέφειν ἄνευ θείας[b] καὶ
ἐπιφροσύνης.

Harris, p. 55, from Cat.
Lips. 1, col. 820, Ἀδήλου.

Τροφὴν καὶ ὑγίειαν ἐπαγγέλλεται, καὶ τῶν ἀναγκαιοτάτων
μόνων μνησθεὶς ἐδίδαξε τὴν
ἐγκράτειαν. Καὶ μάθημα δὲ
παρέδωκεν αἰσιώτατον, ὡς οὐδὲν τούτων τρέφει καθ' ἑαυτό,
βλάπτει δὲ μᾶλλον ἢ ὠφελεῖ,
μὴ τοῦ θεοῦ δύναμιν ὠφελητικὴν
διὰ τῆς εὐλογίας παρέχοιτος.

Wendland, p. 98, from
Procopius, Cod. Aug. f. 221ʳ
(Migne, p. 630).

19. (Ex. xxiii. 26a)

Ἀγονίαν[c] καὶ στείρωσιν ἐν κατάραις τάττων Μωϋσῆς οὗ φησιν
ἔσεσθαι παρὰ τοῖς τὰ δίκαια καὶ νόμιμα δρῶσιν· ἆθλον γὰρ τοῖς τὸ
ἱερὸν γράμμα τοῦ νόμου φυλάττουσι παρέχει τὸν ἀρχαιότερον

---

[a] Wendland : ἀφελητικὰς Cat. Lips.
[b] post θείας lacunam esse stat. Harris.
[c] Harris : ἀγωνίαν Cod. Vat.

νόμον τῆς ἀθανάτου φύσεως, ὃς ἐπὶ σπορᾷ καὶ γενέσει τέκνων ἐτέθη πρὸς τὴν τοῦ γένους διαμονήν.

Harris, p. 55, from Mai, *Script. Vet.* vii. 105 *e* Cod. Vat. 1553, Φίλωνος· ἐκ τοῦ β' τῶν ἐν Γενέσει [*sic*] ζητημάτων.

20. (Ex. xxiii. 26b)

Πάγκαλον δέ φασι τὸ μήτε μησὶ μήτε ἐνιαυτοῖς καταριθμεῖσθαι τὸν βίον τῶν ἱκετῶν. Τῷ γὰρ ὄντι ἑκάστου σοφοῦ ἡμέρα ἰσότιμός ἐστιν αἰῶνι. Εὖ δὲ καὶ τὸ '' ἀναπληρώσω '' διὰ τὰ κενὰ φρονήσεως καὶ ἀρετῆς ἐν ψυχῇ διαστήματα τοῦ προκόπτοντος, ὃν βούλεται καθάπερ μουσικὸν ὄργανον διὰ πάντων ἡρμόσθαι πρὸς μίαν συμφωνίαν βουλημάτων καὶ λόγων καὶ πράξεων.

Wendland, pp. 98-99, from Procopius, Cod. Aug. f. 221ᵛ (Migne, p. 629).

21. (Ex. xxiii. 27a)

Καὶ τὸν φόβον ἀποστελῶ ἡγούμενόν σου.

Τὸ μὲν ῥητὸν ἐμφανές· εἰς κατάπληξιν ἐχθρῶν ἰσχυρὰ δύναμις ὁ φόβος, ὑφ' οὗ μᾶλλον ἢ τῆς τῶν ἀντιπάλων ἐφόδου ῥώμη ἁλίσκεται. Τὸ δὲ πρὸς διάνοιαν οὕτως· δυοῖν οὐσῶν αἰτιῶν, ὧν ἕνεκα τὸ θεῖον ἄνθρωποι τιμῶσιν, ἀγάπης καὶ φόβου, τὸ μὲν ἀγαπᾶν ἐστιν ὀψίγονον· τὸ δὲ φοβεῖσθαι συνίσταται πρότερον, ὥστε οὐκ ἀπὸ σκοποῦ λελέχθαι τὸ ἡγεῖσθαι τὸν φόβον, τῆς ἀγάπης ὕστερον καὶ ὀψὲ προσγενομένης.

Harris, p. 56, from Pitra, *Anal. Sacr.* ii. 313 *e* Cod. Palat. Vat. 203, f. 261, and Cat. Lips. 1, col. 822, and Cat. Burney, f. 139 b.

Καὶ τὸν φόβον μου ἀποστελῶ ἡγούμενόν σου, ὑφ' οὗ μᾶλλον ἢ τῆς τῶν ἀντιπάλων ῥώμης οἱ πολέμιοι ἁλίσκονται. Προηγεῖται δὲ τῆς ἀγάπης ὁ φόβος, ἢ τοῖς τελείοις ἐγγίνεται. Δι' ἀμφοῖν γὰρ τιμᾶται θεός.

Wendland, p. 99, from Procopius, Cod. Aug. f. 222ʳ (Migne, p. 629).

24. (Ex. xxiii. 28)

Σύμβολον δὲ ὑποληπτέον εἶναι τοὺς σφῆκας ἀνελπίστου δυνάμεως θείᾳ πομπῇ σταλησο-

Οἱ σφῆκες ἐξ ἀφανοῦς οὐ προειδομένους τιτρώσκουσι τὰ καιριώτατα, κεφαλήν τε καὶ τὰ

247

μένης, ἥτις ἀφ' ὑψηλοτέρων
κατὰ κράτος ἐπιφέρουσα[a] τὰς
πληγάς, εὐστοχήσει πᾶσι τοῖς
βλήμασι, καὶ διαθεῖσα οὐδὲν
ἀντιπείσεται[b] τὸ παράπαν.

Harris, p. 56, from Cat.
Reg. Ined. 1825 (Mangey ii.
679), and Cat. Lips. 1, col.
823, and Cat. Burney, f. 139 b.

ἐν αὐτῇ . . . σημαίνοι δ' ἂν καὶ
θείαν πομπὴν ἀνελπίστου δυνάμεως στελλομένης ἐξ οὐρανοῦ.

Wendland, p. 99, from
Procopius, Cod. Aug. f. 222ʳ
(Migne, p. 629).

25. (Ex. xxiii. 29)

(a) 'Εὰν τοῦ ἄρτι πρῶτον
εἰσαγομένου καὶ μανθάνοντος
σπουδάσῃς, πᾶσαν τὴν ἀμάθειαν
ἐκτεμών, ἀθρόαν ἐπιστήμην
εἰσοικίσαι τοὐναντίον οὗ διανοῇ
πράξεις· οὔτε γὰρ τὴν ἀφαίρεσιν
ἑνὶ καιρῷ γινομένην ὑπομενεῖ,
οὔτε τὴν ἄφθονον ῥύμην καὶ
φορὰν τῆς διδασκαλίας χωρήσει,
ἀλλὰ καθ' ἑκάτερον τό τε ἐκτεμνόμενον καὶ προστιθέμενον
ὀδυνηθεὶς καὶ περιαλγήσας ἀφη-
νιάσει.[c] Τὸ δὲ ἡσυχῇ καὶ με-
τρίως ἀφαιρεῖν μέν τι[d] τῆς
ἀπαιδευσίας, προστιθέναι δὲ τῆς
παιδείας τὸ ἀνάλογον ὠφελείας
γένοιτ' ἂν ὁμολογουμένης αἴτιον.

Harris, pp. 56-57, from
John Monachus (Mangey ii.
663)=Cod. Rupef. f. 137,
and Pitra, Anal. Sacr. ii. 312
e Cod. Palat. 203, f. 261, and
Cod. Vat. 1553, f. 129. "The
latter ᴍs. seems to be the one
used by Mai, Script. Vet.
vii. 100. . . ."

Τὰ γὰρ θηρία φεύγει τὰς τῶν
πλειόνων ἀνθρώπων οἰκήσεις
ὡς ἡγεμόνων τῇ φύσει καὶ τὰς
ἐρήμους πληροῖ. 'Αλλ' οὐδὲ τὰς
τῶν εἰσαγομένων ψυχὰς ἔστιν
ὑφ' ἓν ἀπαλλάττειν ἀγνοίας καὶ
πληροῦν ἐπιστήμης. Οὐ φέρουσι
γὰρ οὔτε τὴν ἐκείνης ἀφαίρεσιν
οὔτε τὴν ἄφθονον τῆς διδασκαλίας φοράν.

Wendland, p. 100, from
Procopius, Cod. Aug. f. 222ʳ
(Migne, p. 629).

---

[a] κατὰ κράτος ἐπιφέρουσα ex Arm. conieci : κατ' ἄκρον τὸ
οὖς ὑποφέρουσα codd.   [b] Mangey : ἀντιπεσεῖται codd.

[c] ἀπεράσει Cod. Vat. (vid.) ap. Mai.

[d] τι] κατ' ὀλίγον Mai.

(*b*) Ὁ δὲ ἀγαθὸς ἰατρὸς οὐ μιᾷ ἡμέρᾳ τῷ νοσοῦντι πάντα ἀθρόα τὰ ὑγιεινὰ προσφέρειν[a] ἂν ἐθελήσειεν, εἰδὼς βλάβην ἐργαζόμενος μᾶλλον ἤπερ ὠφέλειαν,[b] ἀλλὰ διαμετρησάμενος τοὺς καιροὺς ἐπιδιανέμει τὰ σωτήρια καὶ ἄλλοτε ἄλλα προστιθεὶς πρᾴως ὑγίειαν ἐμποιεῖ.

Harris, pp. 57-58, from Cod. Rupef. f. 137, and Mai, *Script. Vet.* vii. 100 *e* Cod. Vat. 1553, f. 129 (*vid.*), and Dam. Par. 567, and Cod. Reg. f. 210 b.

26. (Ex. xxiii. 33b)

Ὥσπερ οἱ προσπταίσαντες, ἀρτίοις βαίνειν ποσὶν ἀδυνατοῦντες, μακρὰν τοῦ κατὰ τὴν ὁδὸν τέλους ὑστερίζουσι προκάμνοντες[c]· οὕτω καὶ ἡ ψυχὴ τὴν πρὸς εὐσέβειαν ἄγουσα ὁδὸν ἀνύειν κωλύεται, προεντυγχάνουσα ταῖς ἀσεβέσιν ἀνοδίαις. Αὗται γὰρ εἰσιν ἐμπόδιοι καὶ προσπταισμάτων αἰτίαι, δι' ὧν κυλλαίνων ὁ νοῦς ὑστερίζει τῆς κατὰ φύσιν ὁδοῦ. Ἡ δὲ ὁδός ἐστιν ἡ ἐπὶ τὸν πατέρα τῶν ὅλων τελευτῶσα.

Harris, p. 58, from Dam. Par. 774=Cod. Rupef., ἐκ τοῦ α' τῶν ἐν Ἐξόδῳ ζητημάτων.

Τοῦτο γὰρ παθὼν ὁδοιπόρος προκάμνει, πρὶν εἰς τὸ τέλος ἐλθεῖν τῆς ὁδοῦ, καὶ ψυχὴ πρὸς θεὸν ὁδεύειν ἐθέλουσα δυσσεβέσιν ἀνοδίαις τῆς εὐθείας ἀπείργεται.

Wendland, p. 101, from Procopius, Cod. Aug. f. 222[v] (Migne, p. 631).

28. (Ex. xxiv. 1b)

Οὐχ ὁρᾷς ὅτι τοῦ πυρὸς ἡ δύναμις τοῖς μὲν ἀφεστηκόσι μεμετρημένον διάστημα παρέχει φῶς, κατακαίει δὲ τοὺς ἐγγίζοντας; Ὅρα μὴ τοιοῦτόν τι πάθῃς τῇ διανοίᾳ, μή σε ὁ πολὺς πόθος ἀδυνάτου πράγματος ἀναλώσῃ.

Harris, p. 58, from Dam. Par. 748=Cod. Rupef. f. 22 b.

[a] ἐπιφέρειν Dam. et Cod. Reg.
[b] ὑγίειαν Mai.
[c] προκάμνοντες ex Arm. et Procop. conieci : προσκάμνοντες Cod. Rupef.

APPENDIX A, GREEK FRAGMENTS

37. (Ex. xxiv. 10)

Οὐδεὶς αὐχήσει τὸν ἀόρατον θεὸν ἰδεῖν, εἴξας ἀλαζονείᾳ.[a]

Harris, p. 59, from John Monachus (Mangey ii. 662)=
Cod. Rupef. f. 55.

38. (Ex. xxiv. 11a)

Τὸ μὲν ῥητὸν διήγημα φανερὰν ἔχει τὴν ἀπόδοσιν ὡς ἁπάντων
σώων διατηρηθέντων, τὸ δὲ πρὸς διάνοιαν τὸ πάντας περὶ τὴν
εὐσέβειαν συμφώνους[b] εἶναι καὶ ἐν μηδενὶ τῶν ἀγαθῶν διαφωνεῖν.

Harris, p. 59, from Cat. Reg. Ined. 1825 (Mangey ii. 679),
and Cat. Lips. 1, col. 829, and Cat. Burney, f. 141.

40. (Ex. xxiv. 12a)

Ἐνίοις ἀψίκορος ἐγγίνεται λογισμός, οἳ πρὸς ὀλίγον ἀναπτεροφορηθέντες αὐτίκα ὑπενόστησαν, οὐκ ἀναπτάντες μᾶλλον ἢ ὑποσυρέντες εἰς ταρτάρου, φησίν, ἐσχατίας. Εὐδαίμονες δὲ οἱ μὴ
παλινδρομοῦντες.

Harris, p. 59, from Dam. Par. 784=Cod. Rupef., Φίλωνος
ἐκ τῶν ἐν Ἐξόδῳ ζητημάτων.

45. (Ex. xxiv. 16a)

(a) Ἐναργέστατα δυσωπεῖ
τοὺς ἐγγὺς ὑπὸ ἀσεβείας εἴτε
ἠλιθιότητος οἰομένους τοπικὰς
καὶ μεταβατικὰς κινήσεις εἶναι
περὶ τὸ θεῖον. Ἰδοὺ γὰρ ἐμφανῶς οὐ τὸν οὐσιώδη θεὸν τὸν
κατὰ τὸ εἶναι μόνον ἐπινοούμενον κατεληλυθέναι φησίν,
ἀλλὰ τὴν δόξαν αὐτοῦ. Διττὴ
δὲ ἡ περὶ τὴν δόξαν ἐκδοχή· ἡ
μὲν παρουσίαν ἐμφαίνουσα τῶν
δυνάμεων, ἐπεὶ καὶ βασιλέως
λέγεται δόξα ἡ στρατιωτικὴ
δύναμις· ἡ δὲ τῇ δοκήσει αὐτοῦ
μόνου καὶ ὑπολήψει δόξης θείας,
ὡς ἐνειργάσθαι ταῖς τῶν παρόν-

Ἐλέγχει τοὺς οἰομένους μεταβατικὰς δυνάμεις εἶναι περὶ
θεόν. Οὐ γὰρ τὸν οὐσιώδη θεὸν
τὸν κατὰ τὸ εἶναι μόνον ἐπινοούμενον κατεληλυθέναι φησίν,
ἀλλὰ τὴν δόξαν αὐτοῦ, ἢ δυνάμεων παρουσίαν ἐμφαίνων—
ἐπεὶ καὶ βασιλέως λέγεται δόξα
δύναμις στρατιωτική—, ἢ δόκησιν αὐτὸ μόνον καὶ δόξης θείας
ὑπόληψιν, ἢ τῶν παρόντων ὡς
ἐπὶ τοιούτῳ τὴν φαντασίαν
ἐτύπωσεν ὡς ἥκοντος θεοῦ πρὸς
βεβαιοτάτην πίστιν τῶν μελλόντων νομοθετεῖσθαι.

Wendland, p. 101, from

---

[a] ἀλογιστίᾳ Mangey.

[b] σύμφρονας Cat. Reg.

των διανοίαις φαντασίαν ἀφίξεως
θεοῦ, ὡς ἥκοντος εἰς βεβαιοτάτην πίστιν τῶν μελλόντων
νομοθετεῖσθαι.

Harris, p. 60, from Cat.
Reg. Ined. 1825 (Mangey
ii. 679), and Cat. Lips. 1, col.
382.

Procopius, Cod. Aug. f. 224ʳ
(Migne, p. 633 ?).

(b) Ἄβατος καὶ ἀπροσπέλαστος ὄντως ἐστὶν ὁ θεῖος χῶρος,
οὐδὲ τῆς καθαρωτάτης διανοίας τοσοῦτον ὕψος προσαναβῆναι
δυναμένης ὡς θίξει μόνον ἐπιψαῦσαι.

Harris, p. 60, from Dam. Par. 748 = Cod. Rupef. 22 b,
ἐκ τοῦ αὐτοῦ ἤτοι τοῦ τελευταίου τῶν ἐν Ἐξόδῳ ζητουμένων.

46. (Ex. xxiv. 16b)

Τὸν ἴσον ἀριθμὸν ἀπένειμε καὶ τῇ τοῦ κόσμου γενέσει καὶ τῇ
τοῦ ὁρατικοῦ γένους ἐκλογῇ, τὴν ἑξάδα· βουλόμενος ἐπιδεῖξαι ὅτι
αὐτὸς καὶ τὸν κόσμον ἐδημιούργησε καὶ τὸ γένος εἵλετο. Ἡ δὲ
ἀνάκλησις τοῦ προφήτου δευτέρα γένεσίς ἐστι τῆς προτέρας
ἀμείνων. Ἑβδόμῃ δὲ ἀνακαλεῖται ἡμέρᾳ, ταύτῃ διαφέρων τοῦ
πρωτοπλάστου· ὅτι ἐκεῖνος μὲν ἐκ γῆς καὶ μετὰ σώματος συνί-
στατο· οὗτος δὲ ἄνευ σώματος· διὸ τῷ μὲν γηγενεῖ ἀριθμὸς οἰκεῖος
ἀπενεμήθη ἑξάς· τούτῳ δὲ ἡ ἱερωτάτη φύσις τῆς ἑβδομάδος.

Harris, pp. 60-61, from Cat. Lips 1, col. 832, Προκοπίου.

47. (Ex. xxiv. 17)

Τὸ δὲ εἶδος τῆς δόξης κυρίου
φησὶν ἐμφερέστατον εἶναι φλογί,
μᾶλλον δὲ οὐκ εἶναι ἀλλὰ φαίνεσθαι τοῖς ὁρῶσι· τοῦ θεοῦ
δεικνύντος ὅπερ ἐβούλετο δοκεῖν
εἶναι πρὸς τὴν τῶν θεωμένων
κατάπληξιν, μὴ ὢν τοῦτο ὅπερ
ἐφαίνετο. Ἐπιφέρει γοῦν τὸ
" ἐνώπιον τῶν υἱῶν Ἰσραήλ,"
ἐναργέστατα μηνύων ὅτι φαντασία φλογὸς ἦν ἀλλ' οὐ
φλὸξ ἀληθής. Ὥσπερ δὲ ἡ φλὸξ

Ἐδείκνυε δὲ πῦρ θεός, οὐχ
ὅπερ ἦν ἀλλ' ὅπερ ἠβούλετο
δοκεῖν· ὁ δηλῶν ἐπήνεγκεν
" ἐνώπιον τῶν υἱῶν Ἰσραήλ."
Τὸ δὲ σύμβολον ὅτι δαπανητικὸν τὸ θεῖον λογισμῶν ἀσεβῶν,
ὡς καὶ τῆς ὕλης τὸ πῦρ.

Wendland, p. 102, from
Procopius, Cod. Aug. f. 224ʳ
vid.

251

APPENDIX A, GREEK FRAGMENTS

πᾶσαν τὴν παραβληθεῖσαν ὕλην
ἀναλίσκει, οὕτως, ὅταν ἐπιφοι
τήσῃ εἰλικρινὴς τοῦ θεοῦ ἔννοια
τῇ ψυχῇ, πάντας τοὺς ἑτερο
δόξους ἀσεβείας λογισμοὺς δια
φθείρει, καθοσιοῦσα τὴν ὅλην
διάνοιαν.

Harris, p. 61, from Cat.
Ined. Reg. 1825, and Cat.
Lips. 1, col. 832 (Mangey
ii. 679).

49. (Ex. xxiv. 18b)

(a) Ὅτι ἔμελλε κατάκριτος
ἔσεσθαι ἡ ἀποικισθεῖσα γενεὰ
καὶ ἐπὶ τεσσαράκοντα ἔτεα
φθείρεσθαι· μυρία μὲν εὐεργετη
θεῖσα, διὰ μυρίων δὲ ἐπιδειξα
μένη τὸ ἀχάριστον.

Harris, p. 61, from Cat.
Ined. Reg. 1825 (Mangey
ii. 680), and Cat. Lips. 1, col.
833.

Τεσσαράκοντα δὲ μένει τὰς
πάσας ἡμέρας ἐν ὄρει Μωϋσῆς,
ὅσα ἔμελλεν ἔτη τῶν εὖ παθόν
των ἡ ἀγνώμων φθείρεσθαι
γενεά.

Wendland, p. 102, from
Procopius (Migne, p. 635 a).

(b) Ὑπὲρ ὧν ἐν ἰσαρίθμοις ἡμέραις ἱκέτευε τὸν πατέρα καὶ
μάλιστα παρὰ τοιοῦτον καιρόν, ἐν ᾧ δίδονται νόμοι καὶ φορητὸν
ἱερόν, ἡ σκηνή. Τίσι γὰρ οἱ νόμοι; ἆρά γε τοῖς ἀπολλυμένοις;
Ὑπὲρ τίνων δὲ αἱ θυσίαι; [ἆρα] τῶν μικρὸν ὕστερον φθαρησο
μένων· προῄδει γὰρ ὡς προφήτης τὰ ἐσόμενα.

Harris, p. 62, from Cat. Lips. 1, col. 834, Προκοπίου. (Cf.
Wendland, p. 102, " Von hier an folgt Pr. dem Philo nicht
mehr als Quelle ").

50. (Ex. xxv. 2)

(a) Τὴν καρδίαν ἀντὶ τοῦ ἡγεμονικοῦ παρείληφεν ἡ γραφή.

Harris, p. 62, from Mai, *Script. Vet.* vii. 103 *e* Cod. Vat.
1553, Φίλωνος· ἐκ τοῦ τελευταίου τῶν ἐν Ἐξόδῳ ζητημάτων.

(b) Οὐ γὰρ ἐν ὕλαις ἀλλ᾽ ἐν εὐσεβεῖ[a] διαθέσει τοῦ κομίζοντος ἡ
ἀληθὴς ἀπαρχή. Ὁ μὴ ἐκ προαιρέσεως ἀπάρχων θεῷ, καὶ ἂν τὰ

----

[a] Mangey : εὐσεβείᾳ codd.

μεγάλα[a] πάντα κομίζῃ μετὰ τῶν βασιλικῶν θησαυρῶν, ἀπαρχὰς
οὐ φέρει.

Harris, p. 62, from John Monachus (Mangey ii. 670), ἐκ
τοῦ τελευταίου τῶν ἐν Ἐξόδῳ ζητημάτων. (I have transposed
the order of the two sentences to agree with the Armenian.
This makes it unnecessary to accept Harris' suggestion that
the last sentence [οὐ γὰρ . . . ἀπαρχή] is a gloss.)

55. (Ex. xxv. 10b [Heb. 11b]).

(a) Οἱ ἀστέρες στρέφονται καὶ εἰλοῦνται κύκλον· οἱ μὲν κατὰ
τὰ αὐτὰ τῷ σύμπαντι οὐρανῷ, οἱ δὲ καὶ κινήσεσιν ἰδίαις ⟨ἃς⟩
ἔλαχον ἐξαιρέτοις.

Harris, p. 63, from John Monachus (Mangey ii. 670), ἐκ
τοῦ β′ ἐν Ἐξόδῳ ζητημάτων.

(b) Ὁ τῶν ἀνθρώπων βίος, ὁμοιούμενος πελάγει, κυματώσεις
καὶ στροφὰς παντοίας προσεπιδέχεται[b] κατά τε εὐπραγίας καὶ
κακοπραγίας.[c] Ἵδρυται γὰρ οὐδὲν τῶν γηγενῶν ἀλλ' ὧδε καὶ
ἐκεῖσε διαφέρεται, οἷα σκάφος θαλαττεῦον ὑπ' ἐναντίων πνευμάτων.[d]

Harris, p. 63, from Anon. Coll. Florilega Cod. Barocc. 143
(Mangey ii. 674), and Dam. Par. 506, " ascribed to Nilus,"
and Cod. Reg. 923, f. 156 b, " ascribed to the ii. Quaest. in
Genesim [sic]."

62. (Ex. xxv. 17a [Heb. 18a]) Τίνα τὰ χερουβίμ;

Τὰ χερουβὶμ ἑρμηνεύεται μὲν ἐπίγνωσις πολλή, ᾗ[e] ἐν ἑτέροις
ὄνομα ἐπιστήμη πλουσία καὶ κεχυμένη. Σύμβολα δέ ἐστι δυεῖν
τοῦ Ὄντος δυνάμεων ποιητικῆς τε καὶ βασιλικῆς. Πρεσβυτέρα
δὲ ἡ ποιητικὴ τῆς βασιλικῆς κατ' ἐπίνοιαν. Ἰσήλικες γὰρ αἴγε[f]
περὶ τὸν θεὸν ἅπασαι δυνάμεις, ἀλλὰ προεπινοεῖταί πως ἡ ποιητικὴ
τῆς βασιλικῆς· βασιλεὺς γάρ τις οὐχὶ τοῦ μὴ ὄντος ἀλλὰ τοῦ γε-
γονότος· ὄνομα δὲ ἔλαχεν ἐν τοῖς ἱεροῖς γράμμασιν ἡ μὲν ποιητικὴ

---

[a] μέταλλα con. Harris.
[b] προσδέχεται Dam. : προσενδέχεται Cod. Reg.
[c] καὶ κακοπραγίας om. Cod. Barocc.
[d] πραγμάτων Dam.
[e] ᾗ ins. Harris.
[f] Harris : αἴτε codd.

253

APPENDIX A, GREEK FRAGMENTS

θεός, τὸ γὰρ ποιῆσαι θεῖναι ἔλεγον οἱ παλαιοί· ἡ δὲ βασιλικὴ κύριος, ἐπειδὴ τὸ κῦρος ἁπάντων ἀνακεῖται τῷ βασιλεῖ.

Harris, pp. 63-64, from Tischendorf, *Philonea*, p. 144 *e* Cod. Vat. 379, f. 385 (" This and the following passages [to § 99] were first edited by Grossmann in an inaugural dissertation, Leipsic, 1856 ").

63. (Ex. xxv. 17b [Heb. 18b]) Διατί χρυσοῦ τορευτά;

Ὁ μὲν χρυσὸς σύμβολον τῆς τιμιωτάτης οὐσίας, ἡ δὲ τορεία τῆς ἐντέχνου καὶ ἐπιστημονικῆς φύσεως· ἔδει γὰρ τὰς πρώτας τοῦ Ὄντος δυνάμεις ἰδέας ἰδεῶν ὑπαρχούσας καὶ τῆς καθαρωτάτης καὶ ἀμιγοῦς καὶ τιμαλφεστάτης καὶ προσέτι τῆς ἐπιστημονικωτάτης φύσεως μεταλαχεῖν.

Harris, p. 64, from Tischendorf, *Philonea*, p. 144.

64. (Ex. xxv. 17c-18 [Heb. 18c-19]) Διατί ἐπ᾽ ἀμφοτέρων τῶν κλιτῶν τοῦ ἱλαστηρίου τὰ χερουβὶμ ἥρμοττε;

Τοὺς ὅρους τοῦ παντὸς οὐρανοῦ καὶ κόσμου δυσὶ ταῖς ἀνωτάτω φρουραῖς ὠχυρῶσθαι, τῇ τε καθ᾽ ἣν ἐποίει τὰ ὅλα θεός, καὶ τῇ καθ᾽ ἣν ἄρχει τῶν γεγονότων. Ἔμελλε γὰρ ὡς οἰκειοτάτου καὶ συγγενεστάτου κτήματος προκήδεσθαι, ἡ μὲν ποιητικὴ ἵνα μὴ λυθείη τὰ πρὸς αὐτῆς γενόμενα, ἡ δὲ βασιλικὴ ὅπως μηδὲν μήτε πλεονεκτῇ μήτε πλεονεκτῆται, νόμῳ βραβευόμενα τῷ τῆς ἰσότητος, ὑφ᾽ ἧς τὰ πράγματα διαμωνίζεται[a]. Πλεονεξία μὲν γὰρ καὶ ἀνισότης ὁρμητήρια πολέμου, λυτικὰ τῶν ὄντων· τὸ δὲ εὔνομον καὶ τὸ ἴσον εἰρήνης σπέρματα,[b] σωτηρίας αἴτια καὶ τῆς εἰσάπαν διαμονῆς.

Harris, p. 64, from Tischendorf, *Philonea*, " *ut supra.*"

65. (Ex. xxv. 19a [Heb. 20a]) Διατί φησιν· " ἐκτείνει τὰς πτέρυγας τὰ χερουβὶμ ἵνα συσκιάζῃ ";

Αἱ μὲν τοῦ θεοῦ πᾶσαι δυνάμεις πτεροφυοῦσι, τῆς ἄνω πρὸς τὸν πατέρα ὁδοῦ γλιχόμεναί τε καὶ ἐφιέμεναι· συσκιάζουσι δὲ οἷα πτέρυξι τὰ τοῦ παντὸς μέρη· αἰνίττεται δὲ ὡς ὁ κόσμος σκέπαις καὶ φυλακτηρίοις φρουρεῖται, δυσὶ ταῖς εἰρημέναις δυνάμεσι τῇ τε ποιητικῇ καὶ βασιλικῇ.

Harris, p. 65, from Tischendorf, *Philonea*, p. 146. " John Monach. (Mangey ii. 656), referring to ii. Quaest. in *Gen.*, gives the first sentence, as also Pitra, *Anal. Sac.* ii. p. xxiii *e* Cod. Coislin. (?), f. 60, with the same reference."

---

[a] διαμονίζεται Grossmann.   [b] τέρματα Grossmann.

EXODUS, BOOK II

66. (Ex. xxv. 19b [Heb. 20b]) Διατί τὰ πρόσωπα εἰς ἄλληλα
ἐκνεύει καὶ ἄμφω πρὸς τὸ ἱλαστήριον;

Παγκάλη τίς ἐστι καὶ θεοπρεπὴς ἡ τῶν λεχθέντων εἰκών· ἔδει
γὰρ τὰς δυνάμεις, τήν τε ποιητικὴν καὶ βασιλικήν, εἰς ἀλλήλας[a]
ἀφορᾶν, τὰ σφῶν κάλλη κατανοούσας καὶ ἅμα πρὸς τὴν ὠφέλειαν
τῶν γεγονότων συμπνεούσας· δεύτερον ἐπειδὴ ὁ θεός, εἶς ὤν, καὶ
ποιητής ἐστι καὶ βασιλεύς, εἰκότως αἱ διαστᾶσαι δυνάμεις πάλιν
ἕνωσιν ἔλαβον· καὶ γὰρ διέστησαν ὠφελίμως ἵνα ἡ μὲν ποιῇ, ἡ δὲ
ἄρχῃ. Διαφέρει γὰρ ἑκάτερον· καὶ ἡρμόσθησαν ἑτέρῳ τρόπῳ κατὰ
τὴν τῶν ὀνομάτων ἀΐδιον προσβολὴν ὅπως καὶ ἡ ποιητικὴ τῆς
βασιλικῆς καὶ ἡ βασιλικὴ τῆς ποιητικῆς ἔχηται. Ἀμφότεραι γὰρ
συννεύουσιν εἰς τὸ ἱλαστήριον εἰκότως· εἰ μὴ γὰρ ἦν τοῖς νῦν οὖσιν
ἵλεως ὁ θεός, οὔτ' ἂν εἰργάσθη τι διὰ τῆς ποιητικῆς οὔτ' ἂν
εὐνομήθη διὰ τῆς βασιλικῆς.

Harris, p. 65, from Tischendorf, *Philonea*, p. 147.

67. (Ex. xxv. 21a [Heb. 22a]) Τί ἐστι· "γνωσθήσομαί σοι
ἐκεῖθεν";

Γνῶσιν καὶ ἐπιστήμην ὁ εἰλικρινέστατος καὶ προφητικώτατος
νοῦς λαμβάνει τοῦ ὄντος οὐκ ἀπ' αὐτοῦ τοῦ ὄντος, οὐ γὰρ χωρήσει
τὸ μέγεθος, ἀλλ' ἀπὸ τῶν πρώτων αὐτοῦ καὶ δορυφόρων δυνάμεων.
Καὶ ἀγαπητὸν ἐκεῖθεν εἰς τὴν ψυχὴν φέρεσθαι τὰς αὐγὰς ἵνα
δύνηται διὰ τοῦ δευτέρου φέγγους τὸ πρεσβύτερον καὶ αὐγοειδέστερον θεάσασθαι.

Harris, p. 66, from Tischendorf, *Philonea*, p. 148.

68. (Ex. xxv. 21b [Heb. 22b]) Τί ἐστι· "λαλήσω ἄνωθεν τοῦ
ἱλαστηρίου ἀνὰ μέσον τῶν χερουβίμ";

Ἐμφαίνει διὰ τοῦτο πρῶτον μὲν ὅτι καὶ τῆς ἵλεω καὶ τῆς ποιητικῆς καὶ πάσης δυνάμεως ὑπεράνω τὸ θεῖόν ἐστιν· ἔπειτα δὲ ὅτι
λαλεῖ κατὰ τὸ μεσαίτατον τῆς τε ποιητικῆς καὶ βασιλικῆς· τοῦτο
δὲ τοιοῦτον ὑπολαμβάνει νοῦς[b]· ὁ τοῦ θεοῦ λόγος μέσος ὢν οὐδὲν
ἐν τῇ φύσει καταλείπει κενόν, τὰ ὅλα πληρῶν καὶ μεσιτεύει καὶ
διαιτᾷ τοῖς παρ' ἑκάτερα διεστάναι δοκοῦσι, φιλίαν καὶ ὁμόνοιαν
ἐργαζόμενος· ἀεὶ γὰρ κοινωνίας αἴτιος καὶ δημιουργὸς εἰρήνης.
Τὰ μὲν οὖν περὶ τὴν κιβωτὸν κατὰ μέρος εἴρηται· δεῖ δὲ συλλήβδην
ἄνωθεν ἀναλαβόντα τοῦ γνωρίσαι χάριν τίνων ταῦτά ἐστι σύμβολα
διεξελθεῖν· ἦν δὲ ταῦτα συμβολικά. Κιβωτὸς καὶ τὰ ἐν αὐτῇ
θησαυριζόμενα νόμιμα καὶ ἐπὶ ταύτης τὸ ἱλαστήριον καὶ τὰ ἐπὶ

[a] edd. : ἀλληγορίαν codd.   [b] νοῦν Grossmann.

τοῦ ἱλαστηρίου Χαλδαίων γλώττῃ λεγόμενα χερουβίμ, ὑπὲρ δὲ τούτων κατὰ τὸ μέσον φωνὴ καὶ λόγος καὶ ὑπεράνω ὁ λέγων. Εἰ δέ τις ἀκριβῶς δυνηθείη κατανοῆσαι τὰς τούτων φύσεις, δοκεῖ μοι πᾶσι τοῖς ἄλλοις ἀποτάξασθαι ὅσα ζηλωτά, κάλλεσι θεοειδεστάτοις περιληφθείς. Σκοπῶμεν δὲ ἕκαστον οἶόν ἐστι. Τὸ πρῶτον ὁ καὶ ἑνὸς καὶ μονάδος καὶ ἀρχῆς πρεσβύτερος. Ἔπειτα ὁ τοῦ Ὄντος λόγος,[a] ἡ σπερματικὴ τῶν ὄντων οὐσία· ἀπὸ δὲ τοῦ θείου λόγου, καθάπερ ἀπὸ πηγῆς, σχίζονται αἱ[b] δύο δυνάμεις. Ἡ μὲν ποιητική, καθ᾽ ἣν ἔθηκε τὰ πάντα καὶ διεκόσμησεν ὁ τεχνίτης, αὕτη θεὸς ὀνομάζεται· ἡ δὲ βασιλική, καθ᾽ ἣν ἄρχει τῶν γεγονότων ὁ δημιουργός, αὕτη καλεῖται κύριος. Ἀπὸ δὲ τούτων τῶν δυεῖν δυνάμεων ἐκπεφύκασιν ἕτεραι· παραβλαστάνει γὰρ τῇ μὲν ποιητικῇ ἡ ἵλεως, ἧς ὄνομα εὐεργέτις, τῇ δὲ βασιλικῇ ἡ νομοθετική, ὄνομα δὲ εὐθύβολον ἡ κολαστήριος· ὑπὸ δὲ ταύτας καὶ περὶ ταύτας ἡ κιβωτός· ἔστι δὲ κιβωτὸς κόσμου νοητοῦ σύμβολον. Ἔχει δὲ τὰ πάντα ἱδρυμένα ἐν τοῖς ἐσωτάτοις ἁγίοις συμβολικῶς ἡ κιβωτός, τὸν ἀσώματον κόσμον, τὰ νόμιμα ἃ κέκληκε μαρτύρια, τὴν νομοθετικὴν καὶ κολαστήριον δύναμιν, τὸ ἱλαστήριον, τὴν ἵλεω καὶ εὐεργέτιν, τὰς ὑπεράνω τήν τε ποιητικήν, ἥτις ἐστὶ πίστις[c] τῆς ἵλεω καὶ εὐεργέτιδος, καὶ τὴν βασιλικήν, ἥτις ἐστὶ ῥίζα τῆς κολαστηρίου καὶ νομοθετικῆς. Ὑπεμφαίνεται δὲ μέσος ὧν ὁ θεῖος λόγος, ἀνωτέρω δὲ τοῦ λόγου ὁ λέγων· ἔστι δὲ καὶ ὁ τῶν κατειλεγμένων ἀριθμὸς ἑβδομάδι συμπληρούμενος νοητὸς κόσμος, καὶ δυνάμεις δύο συγγενεῖς ἥ τε κολαστήριος καὶ εὐεργέτις, καὶ ἕτεραι πρὸ τούτων δύο ἥ τε ποιητικὴ καὶ ἡ βασιλική, συγγένειαν ἔχουσαι μᾶλλον πρὸς τὸν δημιουργὸν ἢ τὸ γεγονός· καὶ ἕκτος ὁ λόγος καὶ ἕβδομος ὁ λέγων· ἐὰν δὲ ἄνωθεν τὴν καταρίθμησιν ποιῇ, εὑρήσεις τὸν μὲν λέγοντα πρῶτον, τὸν δὲ λόγον δεύτερον, τρίτην[d] δὲ τὴν ποιητικὴν δύναμιν, τετάρτην δὲ τὴν ἀρχήν, εἶτα δὲ ὑπὸ μὲν τῇ ποιητικῇ πέμπτην τὴν εὐεργέτιν, ὑπὸ δὲ τῇ βασιλικῇ ἕκτην τὴν κολαστήριον, ἕβδομον δὲ τὸν ἐκ τῶν ἰδεῶν κόσμον.

Harris, pp. 66-68, from Tischendorf, *Philonea*, pp. 148-152.

85. (Ex. xxvi. 1c)

Τὸ μὲν γὰρ ἦν ἁλουργικόν, τὸ δὲ ῥοδοειδὲς ἢ κοκκοβαφές, τὸ δὲ ὑακίνθῳ προσεοικός, ἡ δὲ βύσσος τὴν λευκὴν εἶχε χροιάν. Καὶ ταῦτα δὲ τῶν τεσσάρων στοιχείων ἦν αἰνίγματα. Ὁ μὲν γὰρ ὑάκινθος τῷ ἀέρι προσέοικε, τὸ δὲ ῥοδοειδὲς ἢ κοκκοβαφὲς τῷ πυρί, τὸ δὲ ἁλουργικὸν μηνύει τὴν θάλατταν—ἐκείνη γὰρ τρέφει

---

[a] λόγου Grossmann. [b] αἱ add. Tischendorf.
[c] πηγὴ ex Arm. conieci. [d] τρίτον Harris.

τὸν κόχλον, ἐξ οὗ τὸ τοιοῦτον γίνεται χρῶμα—, ἡ δὲ βύσσος τὴν γῆν· ἐκ ταύτης γὰρ φύεσθαι λέγεται.

Wendland, pp. 107-108, from Theodoret, *Quaest. in Exodum*, Migne, p. 284 D.

99. (Ex. xxvii. 1b)

Οὔτε πλοῦτον ἀσπάζεται τὸ θεῖον οὔτε πενίαν ἀποστρέφεται.

Harris, p. 68, from Pitra, *Anal. Sacr.* ii. 308 e Cod. Coislin. 276, f. 208.

105. (Ex. xxvii. 21b)

Οὐδὲν οὔτε ἥδιον οὔτε σεμνότερον ἢ θεῷ δουλεύειν, ὃ καὶ τὴν μεγίστην βασιλείαν ὑπερβάλλει. Καί μοι δοκοῦσιν οἱ πρῶτοι βασιλεῖς ἅμα καὶ ἀρχιερεῖς γενέσθαι, δηλοῦντες ἔργοις ὅτι χρὴ τοὺς τῶν ἄλλων δεσπόζοντας δουλεύειν τοῖς λατρεύουσι θεῷ.

Harris, p. 68, from Dam. Par. 775=Cod. Rupef. f. 113, ἐκ τοῦ β′ τῶν ἐν Ἐξόδῳ ζητημάτων.

107. (Ex. xxviii. 2)

Δόξα, ὡς ὁ παλαιὸς λόγος, ψευδής ἐστι ὑπόληψις καὶ δόκησις ἀβέβαιος.

Harris, p. 68, from Mai, *Script. Vet.* vii. 102 e Cod. Vat. 1553, ἐκ τῶν ἐν Ἐξόδῳ ζητημάτων.

117. (Ex. xxviii. 27 [Heb. 31]).

Διά τοι τοῦτο γὰρ τοῦ ἀέρος ὁ ποδήρης εἶχε τὸ χρῶμα. Ὑάκινθος δὲ ἦν, ὡς ἂν καὶ εἰς τοῦτο ἀφορῶν μετάρσιος γένηται.

Wendland, p. 108, from Theodoret, *Quaest. in Exodum*, Migne, p. 285 B.

118. (Ex. xxviii. 28 [Heb. 32])

Οἱ λάλοι, τὰ ὀφείλοντα ἡσυχάζεσθαι ῥηγνύντες, τρόπον τινὰ ὑπὸ γλωσσαλγίας προχέουσιν εἰς ὦτα ἀκοῆς οὐκ ἄξια.

Harris, p. 68, from Dam. Par. 576, and Cod. Reg. 923, f. 231, " in each case headed Φίλωνος."

UNIDENTIFIED FRAGMENTS FROM
QUAESTIONES IN EXODUM[a]

1. Ἀμήχανον ἀνθρωπίνῃ φύσει τὸ τοῦ Ὄντος πρόσωπον θεάσασθαι. Τὸ δὲ πρόσωπον οὐ κυριολογεῖται, παραβολὴ δέ ἐστιν εἰς δήλωσιν τῆς καθαρωτάτης καὶ εἰλικρινεστάτης τοῦ Ὄντος ἰδέας, ἐπειδὴ καὶ ἄνθρωπος οὐδενὶ γνωρίζεται μᾶλλον ἢ προσώπῳ κατὰ τὴν ἰδίαν ποιότητα καὶ μορφήν. Οὐ γάρ φησιν ὁ θεὸς ὅτι " οὐκ εἰμὶ ὁρατὸς τὴν φύσιν "—τίς δὲ μᾶλλον ὁρατὸς ἢ ὁ τὰ ἄλλα πάντα γεννήσας ὁρατά;—" πεφυκὼς δὲ τοιοῦτος εἰς τὸ ὁρᾶσθαι ὑπ᾽ οὐδενὸς ἀνθρώπων ὁρῶμαι " φησι. Τὸ δὲ αἴ.ιον ἡ ἀδυναμία τοῦ γενητοῦ. Καὶ ἵνα μὴ περιπλέκων μηκύνω· θεὸν γενέσθαι δεῖ πρότερον—ὅπερ οὐδὲ οἷόν τε—ἵνα θεὸν ἰσχύσῃ τις καταλαβεῖν. Ἐὰν δὲ ἀποθάνῃ μέν τις τὸν θνητὸν βίον, ζήσῃ δὲ ἀντιλαβὼν τὸν ἀθάνατον, ἴσως ὃ μηδέποτε εἶδεν ὄψεται. Αἱ φιλοσοφίαι πᾶσαι κατά τε τὴν Ἑλλάδα καὶ βάρβαρον ἀκμάσασαι, ζητοῦσαι τὰ φύσεως, οὐδὲ τὸ βραχύτατον ἠδυνήθησαν τηλαυγῶς ἰδεῖν. Σαφὴς δὲ πίστις αἱ διαφωνίαι, αἱ διαμάχαι καὶ ἑτεροδοξίαι τῶν ἑκάστης αἱρέσεως ἀνασκευαζόντων καὶ ἀνασκευαζομένων μέρη· καὶ πᾶσιν ὁρμητήρια πολέμων γεγόνασιν αἱ τῶν αἱρεσιομάχων σκιαί,[b] τυφλοῦσαι τὸν δυνάμενον βλέπειν ἀνθρώπινον νοῦν ταῖς ἀντιλογικαῖς ἔρισιν, ἀμηχανοῦντα τίνα δεῖ προσέσθαι[c] καὶ τίνα διώσασθαι. Δεῖ τὸν βουλόμενον φαντασιωθῆναι τὸν τῶν ὅλων ἄριστον, στῆναι τὸ πρῶτον κατὰ ψυχήν, ἱδρυνθέντα παγίως γνώμῃ μιᾷ, καὶ μηκέτι πρὸς πολλὰ πλάζεσθαι, ἔπειτα δὲ στῆναι ἐπὶ φύσεως καὶ γνώμης ξηρᾶς καὶ ἀγόνου πάντων,[d] ὅσα φθαρτά· ἐὰν γὰρ προσήσεταί τι τῶν μαλακωτέρων, σφαλήσεται τῆς προθέσεως. Ἀδυνατήσει καὶ τὸ ὀξυωπέστατον βλέπον ἰδεῖν τὸ ἀγένητον, ὡς τυφλωθῆναι πρότερον ἢ θεάσασθαι διὰ τὴν ὀξυαύγειαν καὶ τὸν ἐπεισρέοντα[e] χείμαρρον τῶν μαρμαρυγῶν.

Harris, pp. 72-73, from Dam. Par. 748=Cod. Rupef. f. 22 b, ἐκ τοῦ τελευταίου τῶν ἐν Ἐξόδῳ ζητουμένων.

[a] The sections have been numbered by me.
[b] Harris : οἰκίαι codd.   [c] Mangey : προέσθαι codd.
[d] Harris : παντός codd.   [e] Mangey : ἀπεισρέοντα codd.
258

EXODUS, UNIDENTIFIED

2. Ἡ φορὰ τῶν κακιῶν ἀνακυκᾷ καὶ στροβεῖ τὴν ψυχήν, ἴλιγγον αὐτῇ περιτιθεῖσα τὸν καλύπτοντα καὶ καμμύειν ἐκβιαζόμενον τὴν φύσει μὲν πρέπουσαν ὄψιν, ἐπιτηδεύσει δὲ τυφλουμένην.

Harris, p. 73, from Dam. Par. 751 (Cod. Rupef.), ἐκ τῶν ἐν Ἐξόδῳ ζητημάτων.

3. Αἱ περὶ τῶν τοῦ θεοῦ ἀρετῶν ἐναγώνιοι ζητήσεις βελτιοῦσι τὴν διάνοιαν καὶ ἀθλοῦσιν ἄθλους ἡδίστους ἅμα καὶ ὠφελιμωτάτους, καὶ μάλιστα ὅταν μή, ὡς οἱ νῦν, τὴν ψευδώνυμον κλῆσιν ὑποδυόμενοι μέχρι τοῦ δοκεῖν ὑπερμαχοῦσι τῶν δογμάτων, ἀλλὰ πάθει γνησίῳ μετ' ἐπιστήμης ἰχνηλατοῦσιν ἀλήθειαν.

Harris, p. 73, from Dam. Par. 774 (Cod. Rupef.), " referred . . . to the first . . . book of the Questions on Exodus."

4. Τὸ ἐμμελὲς καὶ εὔρυθμον οὐκ ἐν φωνῇ μᾶλλον ἢ διανοίᾳ ἐπιδείκνυσθαι πειρωμένος. Ὁ τοῦ σοφοῦ λόγος οὐκ ἐν ῥήμασι ἀλλ' ἐν τοῖς δηλουμένοις πράγμασιν ἐπιδείκνυσιν τὸ κάλλος.

Harris, p. 73, from Dam. Par. (Cod. Rupef.), " referred . . . to the second . . . book of the Questions on Exodus."

5. Τοὺς ἐντυγχάνοντας τοῖς ἱεροῖς γράμμασιν οὐ δεῖ συλλαβομαχεῖν ἀλλὰ πρὸ τῶν ὀνομάτων καὶ ῥημάτων τὴν διάνοιαν σκοπεῖν, καὶ τοὺς καιροὺς καὶ τρόπους, καθ' οὓς ἕκαστα λέγεται. Πολλάκις γὰρ αἱ αὐταὶ λέξεις ἑτέροις καὶ ἑτέροις πράγμασιν ἐφαρμόζουσιν, καὶ κατὰ τὸ ἐναντίον διαφέρουσαι λέξεις ἐπὶ τοῦ αὐτοῦ τιθέμεναι πράγματος συνάδουσιν.

Harris, p. 73, from Dam. Par. 774 (Cod. Rupef.), " referred . . . to the last book of the Questions on Exodus."

6. Περιέχει τὰ πάντα, ὑπ' οὐδενὸς περιεχόμενος. Ὡς γὰρ ὁ τόπος περιεκτικὸς σωμάτων ἐστὶ καὶ καταφυγή, οὕτω καὶ ὁ θεῖος λόγος περιέχει τὰ ὅλα καὶ πεπλήρωκεν.

Harris, p. 73, from Dam. Par. 752 (Cod. Rupef.), ἐκ τοῦ τελευταίου τῶν ἐν Ἐξόδῳ ζητημάτων.

7. Ἐντὸς φέρει τὸν ὄλεθρον ὁ τῇ κακίᾳ συζῶν ἐπεὶ σύνοικον ἔχει τὴν ἐπίβουλον καὶ πολέμιον. Ἱκανὸς γὰρ πρὸς τιμωρίαν ἡ

259

τοῦ φαύλου συνείδησις, οἴκοθεν ὡς ἐκ πληγῆς δειλίαν προτείνουσα τῇ ψυχῇ.

Harris, p. 73, from Dam. Par. 782 (Cod. Rupef.), ἐκ τῶν ἐν Ἐξόδῳ ζητουμένων.

8. Τοῦ φαύλου ὁ βίος ἐπίλυπος καὶ περιδεής, καὶ ὅσα κατὰ τὰς αἰσθήσεις ἐνεργεῖ φόβοις καὶ ὀδύναις ἀνακέκραται.

Harris, p. 73, from Dam. Par. 782 (Cod. Rupef.), " referred to Quaest. in Exod."

9. Αἱ τοῦ θεοῦ χάριτες οὐ μόνον ἀναγκαῖα παρέχονται ἀλλὰ καὶ πρὸς περιττὴν καὶ δαψιλεστέραν ἀπόλαυσιν.

Harris, p. 73, from Dam. Par. 789=Cod. Rupef. f. 277, " from ii. Quaest. in Exod."

10. Μυρία γε, οὐ λέγω τῶν ἀναγκαίων ἀλλὰ καὶ τῶν βραχυτάτων εἶναι δοκούντων, ἐκφεύγει τὸν ἀνθρώπινον νοῦν.

Harris, p. 73, from John Monachus (Mangey ii. 662), ἐκ τοῦ αʹ τῶν ἐν Ἐξόδῳ ζητ.

11. Μία ἀνάπαυσις ψυχῆς ἐστιν ἡ κρατίστη εἰς τὸ ἱερὸν τοῦ ὄντος πόθον, ἡγεμόνι χρῆσθαι θεῷ καὶ βουλευμάτων καὶ λόγων καὶ πράξεων. . . . Πέρας εὐδαιμονίας τὸ ἀκλινῶς καὶ ἀρρεπῶς ἐν μόνῳ θεῷ στῆναι.

Harris, pp. 73-74, from John Monachus (Mangey ii. 669) =Cod. Rupef. f. 178 b, ἐκ τοῦ τελευταίου τῶν ἐν Ἐξόδῳ ζητημ.

12. Πολλὰ ἀσωμένοις καὶ ἀδημονοῦσιν ἔθος ἐστὶ ψεύδεσθαι, τῶν παθῶν οὐκ ἐπιτροπευόντων ἀληθεύειν εἰ τὸ ψεῦδος οἰκεῖόν ἐστιν.

Harris, p. 74, from Mai, *Script. Vet.* vii. 96 e Cod. Vat. 1553, ἐκ τοῦ αʹ τῶν ἐν Ἐξόδῳ ζητημάτων.

13. Τὸ τῶν φαύλων ἄκριτον καὶ ἀνίδρυτον ἐν γνώμαις διασυνίστησιν μαχομένους μὲν λόγους ἀλλήλοις, μαχομένας δὲ πράξεις καὶ μηδέποτε συμφωνούσας ἑαυταῖς.

Harris, p. 74, from Mai, *Script. Vet.* vii. 100 e Cod. **Vat.** 1553, ἐκ τοῦ αʹ τῶν ἐν Ἐξόδῳ ζητημ.

EXODUS, UNIDENTIFIED

14. Τὰ βουλήματα τῶν ἀγαθῶν δεῖ βεβαιοῦσθαι τελευτησάντων οὐδὲν ἧττον ἢ ζώντων.

Harris, p. 74, from Mai, *Script. Vet.* vii. 101 *e* Cod. Vat. 1553, ἐκ τοῦ α′ τῶν ἐν Ἐξόδῳ ζητημ.

15. Τὸ μὲν " πρωτότοκον " πρὸς τὸ μητρῷον γένος, τίκτει γὰρ γύνη· τό τε " πρωτογενές " πρὸς τὸ πατρῷον, γεννᾷ γὰρ ἄρρεν· τὸ δὲ " διανοῖγον πᾶσαν μήτραν " ἵνα μὴ γενομένης πρωτοτόκου θυγατρός, εἶθ' ὕστερον ἐπιγενομένου υἱοῦ, τὸν υἱὸν ἐν πρωτοτόκοις καταριθμήσει τις, ὡς τῆς ἄρρενος ἄρχοντα γενεᾶς· ὁ γὰρ νόμος φησίν, οὐ διοίγνυσι τὴν μήτραν ὁ τοιοῦτος τὴν εὐθὺς ἐκ παρθενίας.

Harris, p. 74, from Mai, *Script. Vet.* vii. 105 *e* Cod. Vat. 1553, ἐκ τοῦ δ′ τῶν ἐν Ἐξόδῳ ζητημ. " The passage evidently belongs to Exod. xiii. 2."

16. Τὰ μέτρα πλεονάζοντα τὸν ὅρον ὑπερβαίνει ὡς γίνεσθαι τὴν μὲν ἄμετρον φρόνησιν, πανουργίαν· τὴν δὲ σωφροσύνην, φειδωλίαν· τὴν δὲ ἀνδρίαν, θρασύτητα.

Harris, p. 74, from Mai, *Script. Vet.* vii. 106 *e* Cod. Vat. 1553, ἐκ τῶν ἐν Ἐξόδῳ ζητημ.

17. Ἡ εὐφυΐα πλεονάζουσα τῇ ῥύμῃ τῆς φορᾶς πρὸς πολλὰ δὴ τῶν ἀλυσιτελῶν εἴωθε χωρεῖν· ἐν δὲ ταῖς διδασκαλίαις οὐκ ἐλάττω τὰ οὐκ ἀναγκαῖα τῶν ἀναγκαίων ἐστί· διὸ προσήκει τὸν ἔφορον καὶ ψυχῆς ὑφηγητήν, ὥσπερ γεωργὸν ἀγαθόν, τὰ ὑπερβάλλοντα περικόπτειν.

Harris, p. 74, from Mai, *Script. Vet.* vii. 108 *e* Cod. Vat. 1553, ἐκ τοῦ α′ τῶν ἐν Ἐξόδῳ ζητημάτων.

18. Ὁ σοφιστικός, γνώμης ὢν ἑτέρας, λόγοις οὐ συνᾴδουσι χρῆται· διέξεισι μὲν γὰρ ἀπνευστὶ τοὺς ἀρετῆς ἑκάστης ἐπαίνους, οἷα λόγῳ πολὺς ἐπὶ θήρᾳ τῶν ἀκουόντων· ὁ δὲ βίος ἐστὶν αὐτῶν πάντων ἀνάπλεος ἁμαρτημάτων· καὶ μοι δοκεῖ τῶν ἐπὶ σκηναῖς ὑποκριτῶν διαφέρειν οὐδέν, οἳ πολλάκις ἠμελημένοι καὶ ἄφρονες ἄνθρωποι διεφθαρμένοι τινὲς δὲ καὶ θεραπεύοντες, εἰς ἥρωας ἀσκοῦνται· μικρὸν δὲ ὕστερον ἀποθέμενοι τὴν σκευήν, τὰ τῆς ἰδίας ἀδοξίας ἀναφαίνουσι σημεῖα.

Harris, p. 74, from Mai, *Script. Vet.* vii. 106 *e* Cod. Vat. 1553, ἐκ τοῦ α′ τῶν ἐν Ἐξόδῳ ζητημάτων.

APPENDIX A, GREEK FRAGMENTS

19. Ὅρασις παρὰ τὰς ἄλλας αἰσθήσεις καὶ ταύτῃ διαφέρει ὅτ.
αἱ μὲν ἄλλαι τοῖς αἰσθητοῖς ἐγκαταμίγνυνται, οἷον ἡ γεῦσις ἀνα-
κιρνᾶται τοῖς χυμοῖς καὶ ἡ ὄσφρησις τοῖς ἐπαναδιδομένοις ἀτμοῖς
καὶ αἱ ἀκοαὶ ταῖς φωναῖς ἐκδυομέναις εἰς τὰ ὦτα· οὔτε γὰρ αὐτὴ
διὰ τοῦ βάθους τῶν σωμάτων χωρεῖ, ψαύει δὲ τῶν ἐπιφανειῶν
μόνον κατὰ τὴν προσβολήν, οὔτε τὰ σώματα εἰς τὴν ὄψιν εἰσδύεται.

Harris, p. 74, from Mai, *Script. Vet.* vii. 109 *e* Cod. Vat.
1553, ἐκ τοῦ α΄ τῶν ἐν Ἐξόδῳ ζητημάτων.

20. Οὐ πάντων κοινωνητέον πᾶσιν οὔτε λόγων οὔτε πραγμάτων
καὶ μάλιστα ἱερῶν· πολλὰ γὰρ προϋπάρξαι δεῖ τοῖς ἐφιεμένοις τῆς
μετουσίας τούτων· πρῶτον μέν, τὸ[a] μέγιστον καὶ ἀναγκαιότατον,
πρὸς τὸν ἕνα καὶ ὄντως[b] ὄντα θεὸν εὐσέβειαν καὶ ὁσιότητα, τὴν
ἐπὶ τοῖς ἀγάλμασι καὶ ξοάνοις καὶ συνόλως ἀφιδρύμασι, τελεταῖς
τε ἀτελέστοις καὶ μυστηρίοις ἀνοργιάστοις, ἀνήνυτον πλάνην
ἀπωσαμένοις· δεύτερον δὲ καθαρθῆναι τὰς ἁγνευτικὰς[c] καθάρσεις
κατά τε σῶμα καὶ ψυχὴν διὰ νόμων πατρίων καὶ ἠθῶν· τρίτον
ἀξιόπιστον τοῦ συνασμενισμοῦ παρασχεῖν ἐνέχυρον ἵνα μὴ τραπέζης[d]
μεταλαβόντες ἱερᾶς, ἀσώτων μειρακίων τρόπον, ὑπὸ κόρου καὶ
πλησμονῆς ἐναλλοιωθῶσιν ἐμπαροινοῦντες, οἷς οὐ θέμις.

Harris, p. 75, from Pitra, *Anal. Sacr.* ii. 308 *e* Cod. Coislin.
276, f. 205, ἐκ τοῦ πρώτου τῶν ἐν Ἐξόδῳ ζητημάτων, and Dam.
Par. 782 (Cod. Rupef.).

21. Φθαρτὸν καλῶ τὸν μὴ ἐφιέμενον ἀφθαρσίας ἀλλ᾽ ὀστρέου
τρόπον ἐνειλούμενον ὀστρακοδέρμῳ, ὅπερ ἐστὶν ὁ σωματικὸς ὄγκος
καὶ ὁ τῶν θνητῶν βίος.

Harris, p. 75, from Pitra, *Anal. Sacr.* ii. 308 *e* Cod. Coislin.
276, f. 245, ἐκ τοῦ τελευταίου τῶν ἐν Ἐξόδῳ ζητημάτων, and
Cod. Rupef. f. 240.

22. Μάταιον οὐδὲν οὔτε ἀκοαῖς οὔτε ἄλλῃ τινὶ τῶν αἰσθήσεων
προσιτέον· ἐπακολουθοῦσι γὰρ ταῖς ἀπάταις μάλιστα τῶν ψυχῶν
αἱ ζημίαι.

Harris, p. 75, from Cod. Rupef. f. 45, ἐκ τῶν ἐν Ἐξόδῳ
ζητουμένων.

23. Πρὸς τούτοις, εἴποι τις   Ἐθέλει δὲ μηδὲ χωρὶς ἀγώ-
ἄν, οὐκ ἐβούλετο αὐτοὺς κατα-   νων τὴν κτῆσιν αὐτοῖς ἐγγενέ-

---

[a] καὶ Dam.   [b] ὄντως om. Dam.
[c] ἀγνευούσας Dam.   [d] τροφῆς Dam.

πεσεῖν εἰς τὸ ῥάθυμον καὶ τῆς
ἐπαγγελίας κατακληρονομῆσαι
τὴν γῆν ἀγώνων χωρίς[a]· τὰ γὰρ
πόνῳ κτηθέντα παρὰ τοῖς ἔχουσι
τίμια· τὰ ἀπόνως κτηθέντα
καταφρονεῖται ῥᾳδίως· ὅθεν βουλόμενος αὐτοὺς νήφειν καὶ ἐγρη-
γορέναι καὶ ὡς ἔχοντας ἐχθροὺς
πρός τε τὸν θεὸν ἐπιστρέφειν
καὶ τῆς παρ' αὐτοῦ ἐπικουρίας
δεῖσθαι,[b] τοῦτο ποιεῖν ἐπαγγέλλεται,[b] ὁμοῦ καὶ γυμνίζων[c]
αὐτοὺς πρὸς ἀντίστασιν ἐχθρῶν.
Τοῦτο δὲ καὶ νοητῶς ὁρῶμεν
γινόμενον· ψυχὴ γὰρ διὰ τῆς
θείας συνεργείας ἀπαλλαγεῖσα
παθῶν, εἰ πρὸς τὸ ῥάθυμον
ὀλισθήσει, ὡς μηκέτι παθεῖν
ὑποπτεύουσα, ὑπὸ τῶν ἀοράτων
καὶ πονηρῶν πνευμάτων περιστοιχίζεται δίκην κυνῶν[d] αὐτῇ
ἐπιθρωσκόντων καὶ σφοδρότερον
πολεμούντων· ὅθεν καὶ λόγιον
ἡμᾶς διδάσκει μὴ πιστεύειν
ἐχθρῷ.[e]

Harris, pp. 103-104, from
Pitra, *Anal. Sacr.* ii. 312 (*vid.*)
e Cod. Pal. 203, f. 261, Cod.
Vat. 1553, f. 129, Cat. Lips.
1, col. 823, Cat. Burney, f.
140. "The previous passage
is found attached to an extract from ii. Quaest. in
Exod. xxv."

σθαι τῆς γῆς. Τὰ γὰρ πόνῳ
κτηθέντα παρὰ τοῖς ἔχουσι
τίμια, καὶ πρὸς θεὸν ἐπιστρέφει
πᾶς ἐναγώνιος ἐκ τῶν ἐχθρῶν
σωθῆναι δεόμενος. Καὶ ψυχὴ
δὲ ἀκονιτὶ γινομένη παθῶν
ἐλευθέρα πρὸς ῥαθυμίαν ὁρμᾷ[f]
καὶ τοῖς ἀοράτως πολεμοῦσι
περιστοιχίζεται.[g]

Wendland, p. 100, from
Procopius, Cod. Aug. f. 222[r]
(Migne, p. 629) *vid.*

---

[a] χωρίς τινων Cat. Burney.
[b] πορειῖν ἐπαγγείλεται Cat. Burney.
[c] γυμνάζων Cat. Burney.
[d] κυνῶν e Cat. Barb. iv. 56 add. Wendland.
[e] cf. Ecclesiasticum xii. 10.   post ἐχθρῷ add. Cat. Burney:
ἑπτὰ γὰρ πονηρίαι εἰσὶν ἐν αὐτῷ (cf. Prov. xxvi. 25, Luc. xi. 26).
[f] ὁρᾷ August. (vid.).
[g] cf. Wendland, "Es folgt eine Beziehung auf Luc. 11, 26."

APPENDIX B

APPENDIX B

ADDITIONS IN THE OLD LATIN VERSION

Selected Bibliography :
Cohn, Leopold in L. Cohn and P. Wendland, *Philonis Alexandrini Opera*, etc. (Berlin, 1896), pp. l-lii, " De antiqua versione latina."

Conybeare, Fred. C., *Philo About the Contemplative Life* (Oxford, 1895), pp. 139-145, " The Old Latin Version."

Pitra, J. B., *Analecta Sacra Spicilegio Solesmensi Parata* (Florence, 1884), Tom. ii, pp. 319-320, " De vetere Philonis interprete Latino."

Wendland, Paul, *Neu entdeckte Fragmente Philos* (Berlin, 1891), p. 85, n. 2.

In the year 1520 there appeared in Paris a volume entitled *Philonis Iudaei centum et duae quaestiones et totidem responsiones morales super Genesin.* Beside the Old Latin version of the *Quaestiones in Genesin* iv. 154-245, the volume contained the Old Latin version of the *De Vita Contemplativa* (by the same translator, according to Conybeare), Jerome's Latin translation of the *De Nominibus Hebraicis*, Budaeus' translation of the *De Mundo*, and the *Liber Antiquitatum* of Pseudo-Philo. A second and improved edition of this work was published in Basel in 1527 and was reprinted there in 1538, 1550 and 1599. It is from the edition of 1538 that Aucher took the text of the version of *QG* iv. 154-245, which is printed at the bottom of pp. 362-443 of his edition of the Armenian version of the *Quaestiones*.

The date and character of this Old Latin version have been carefully studied by the scholars mentioned above. They agree that it was made in the fourth century A.D. and that in spite of its uncouthness and freedom it is a useful check

APPENDIX B

on the ancient Armenian version, which is more faithful and more intelligible throughout.

This Old Latin version is of further interest because it contains several *Quaestiones* missing in the Armenian, namely eleven sections on Gen. xxvi. 19-35, which appear at the end of *QG* iv. 195, and three fragments added to the translation of *QG* iv. 203, 210 and 232 (beside a few glosses to other sections, which are not included here). That this group of eleven sections contains genuine material from Philo's *Quaestiones* is clear from their contents and from the fact that three of these sections (vii, viii and ix) have parallels in the Greek fragments from Procopius and the Catenae, where they are ascribed to Philo. Wendland, in particular, calls attention to the " echt philonisch " character of sections iv, vi, vii and xi ; he identifies the discussion of the number four in section ii as an interpolation from Philo's lost work Περὶ ἀριθμῶν.

The additional sections are reproduced below from Aucher's reprinting of the 1538 edition. Considerably more work should be done on the text of the Old Latin version throughout, but here, as in the footnotes to the translation, I have corrected only a few of the more obvious misprints or scribal errors.

ADDITIONS TO *QG* IV. 195 (AUCHER, PP. 395-398)

i. (Gen. xxvi. 19-22) Quare in primo dimicantur, secundo judicantur, in tertio cessant. Et primum vocatur injuria, secundum inimicitia, tertium spaciositas ? [a]

Haec pignora sunt industriae utpote aliquo in studiosam inducto disciplinam. Est enim dimicatio, dum amatores doctrinae ad institutores conferunt opponentes magistros torpori animae. Cum autem fuerit obstinatissima perseverantia, et studiosa exercitatio, jam non litigium, sed judicium est, cessante laesura congrue rationis est altius examen requirere. Provecto nanque amatore disciplinarum, infirmantur alienigenae moris eruditionis abdicato litigio atque judicio, ac per hoc merito prima momenta pro injuriis accepta sunt. Patimur enim injuriam desiderantes, amor obtinet firmitatem. In secundo autem inimicos sentimus eos, non

l. speciositas.

praevalentibus nocere alienigenarum moribus, inanem exaggerantibus inimicitiam. Tertia igitur speciositas et quia perfecta melioratio confusionem affert inimicis, inanis enim revelata est et pravitas injuriarum, et inimicitiarum insolentia.

ii. (Gen. xxvi. 23) Quid est: Ascendit inde ad puteum, sed suspensum ?

Qui enim adhuc docetur, licet promoverit et creverit, nihilominus religionis moras*a* sortitur. Cur autem perfectis approximaverit, altiores facit commemorationes. Ait enim. Puteus quaterni numeri, et in ipso numero fallit.*b* Puteus enim juramenti filia septima est, quod Hebraice legitur Bersabace*c* Berfilia Sabeae septima. Jam pervide quanta est unitas in Mathematico tractatu, et hic in prioribus translatis libris ex aperto dicente Philone quarta in omnibus corporibus et incorporalibus preciosa est pro numero quidem qui accensus est decem : in figuris autem quod secundum eam soliditatis natura constat, post signum et elogium, secundum Musicos vero omnes armonias continet, quadralitatem pertinacitate, in dimidialitatem et per omnes in duplicitate et bis per omnes in quadruplicatione haec inquit in incorporalibus. Corporalibus vero elementa mundi quatuor totidem anni momenta, debuit prius corporalia pandere, postmodum incorporalia. Hic enim ipse pro incorporalibus prosequendo coitum viri et mulieris quatuor habere vices, quod turpissimum est interpretare, ne forte quidam servi dei amatores esse eorum existiment.*d* Videtur mihi Philo ritum Judeorum sectavisse, linguam imprauisse. Si enim septimum composuisset, viginti et octo metas pacis invenisset. Denique post momenta lamentationis titulum pacis enixa est Bersabee. Quapropter inquit Moses, laudando quartum numerum sanctum et gloriosum protestatur. Ut quid autem juramentum dicitur, in opere ipso declarabo post modicum in familiari capitulo, totus liber translatus nihil tale continuit, sed coetus*e* effugere conatur.

iii. (Gen. xxvi. 24) Ut quid in nocte dominus visitatur, et ait : Ego sum deus patris tui, ne timeas, tecum enim sum ?

---

a l. mores (?).
b marg. verba sunt interpretis, quisquis hic tandem fuerit.
c l. Bersabaee *vel sim.*
d l. existimentur (?).   *e marg.* coactus.

APPENDIX B

Familiarissimum tempus animae speculatoriae, nox vagis
erroribus meridianis, et vanis aspectibus liberata, ac per hoc
nec metus pulsat, nec vacillat cogitatus absente timore, caret
autem timore pacatissima mens, cum divinitati pervigilat
perseveranter. Habet tamen lectio necessarium modum, ne
quis procerum praesumat facile occasionibus, sed prioris
acquirit meritis, digne enim dicendo : Ego sum deus patris
tui, generis censuram declaravit. Tecum autem sum pro
tua et ipsi vigilantia, cujus causa non indignatur universorum pater indignum visitare eum invisibilis animarum
medicus.

iv. (Gen. xxvi. 24) Quare Dominus*a* visitatus ostendit
semetipsum deum ?
Dominus quidem regni et dominatoris nomen est. Deus
autem appellatur pro beneficiis, quibus certius manifestatur,
quoniam sapientiam non inter subjectos ut rex, sed inter
amicos benefaciendo dinumerat. Poterat Philo pluribus
invehere, nisi computo uteretur Mathematico.

v. (Gen. xxvi. 24) Quare dicendo benedixi te, adjecit, et
multiplicabo semen tuum propter patrem tuum ?
Spontaneae disciplinae titulus perfectus, ob nullam aliam
causam divinam promeretur gratiam, nisi pro se ac pro sua
suavitate. Juvenior autem moribus et adhuc erudiens non
propter se, sed pro meritis provecta doctrinae, cujus sapientia
pro principali exemplo discentibus praeponitur, ad nanci-
scendam spem meliorem. Possunt enim hac aemulatione
parentibus similare.

vi. (Gen. xxvi. 25) Quare aedificando illic altarium, non
obtulit sacrificium, sed invocato nomine domini fixit tabernaculum suum ?
Sacrificia prae omnibus bonis sine sanguine, et victima
animalium pronorum participatio sapientiae alienarum esse
credunt, qui puro pectore placere deo desiderant, cujus gratia
sufficere credit invocationis autoris virtutem, qua princeps
atque dominator est universitatis, nullius egens. Ita illic
figere dicitur tabernaculum suum, suam nempe virtutem, in

a marg. Dominus Deus.

qua puritas illa animae inhabita commoratur,[a] firmiter sciens, dominum universorum principem sine ulla esse penuria. O pura credulitas, quae factas pridem frugum centesimas excellit.

vii. (Gen. xxvi. 26)

Quare post quartam putei fossuram a pueris factam, exiit Abimelech ad eum, et Acho[b] thalami praepositus, et Phicho princeps militiae?

Videntur mihi exploratores potius, quam pro foedere amicitiarum advenisse, in utroque parati ad praelium, si infirmum viderint: ad pacem, si potentiorem. Sensu tamen subtiliori intelligitur quartus, ut tamen in numeris insignis est, in quo constitutus studiosus per omnem felicitatem provehitur. Sequitur tamen etiam valde perfecto contraria virtus praestolanti et observanti ad incurrendum. Et est hujus fortitudo tres animae partes: mentis acumen rationabile, et animositas, et desiderium. Pro acumine quidem[c] rex, animositate princeps militiae, concupiscentia Phichol, qui libidinis videtur esse provisor. Ocholach quidem regna parcentur[d] ex utraque manu stipatus, hinc atque hinc suo protectu prohibundus, obtinente enim iracundia ut princeps militiae operatur, eo amplius pandimus dictum ex nominum translatione, est Abimelech Alido,[e] Phichol iracundia.

Ἐκπορεύεται δὲ πρὸς αὐτὸν ᾿Αβιμέλεχ καὶ οἱ μετ᾿ αὐτοῦ, κατάσκοποι μᾶλλον ἢ ἔνσπονδοι γενησόμενοι καὶ πρὸς ἑκάτερον παρεσκευασμένοι, πόλεμον μέν, εἰ ἀσθενοῦντα κατίδοιεν, εἰρήνην δέ, εἰ δυνατώτερον ἑαυτῶν.

Wendland, pp. 85-86, from Procopius, f. 118[r] (Migne, p. 415); also, except for beg. (ἐκπορεύεται . . . αὐτοῦ), in Harris, p. 42, from Cat. Ined. Reg. 1825 (Mangey ii. 675), and Cat. Burney, f. 56, Φίλωνος ἑβραίου, and Cat. Lips. 1, col. 325 " with the remark that this and the three following passages are not among the edita of Philo and do not seem to belong to him."

viii. (Gen. xxvi. 29-30) Quare dicentibus et nunc benedictus a domino facit coenam; et manducaverunt et biberunt?

[a] *marg.* inhabitare commemoratur.
[b] *marg.* Acoza.   [c] *marg.* ergo.
[d] *marg.* parenter.   [e] *marg.* Ocholach.

APPENDIX B

Non pro laude sua hospitio rogat, nec novit blandire strenuus, aut procacem medelam sapiens affectatur, sed propositis iracundiis quibus exagitati praesidere terrens sortiti sunt, nunc confitetur unum universitatis deum, benedictum eum confitetur, sed continuatione sermonis etiam praeteritum aevum declarant, quoniam et nunc et a principio ipse est sine immutatione, vel diminutione benedictionis, quem nos ipsi suspectum habuimus, nunc vero absit omnis invidia. Suscepta igitur eorum poenitentia, mensura participantur dulcedines pro existimatione, pro veritatis autem allegoriae, pro hospitio quid ipse facit convocando esse trans vos,[a] qui non perdurant in delictis, ut pote

Φιλοφρονεῖται δὲ ταῖς εὐωχίαις αὐτοὺς[b] οὐ διὰ τὸν ἔπαινον· οὐ γὰρ κολακείαν ἢ τὴν ἄμουσον θεραπείαν ὁ σοφὸς ἀσπάζεται ἀποδεξάμενος δὲ αὐτῶν τὴν μετάνοιαν ἁλῶν καὶ τραπέζης μεταδίδωσι.[c]

Wendland, p. 86, from Procopius, f. 118ʳ (Migne, p. 415); also in Harris, p. 42 (with omissions and variants indicated in footnotes), from Cat. Reg. 1825 (Mangey ii. 675), and Cat. Lips. coll. 326-327, and Cat. Burney, f. 56.

Harris adds a Latin frag. from Cat. Zephyri, p. 82 (= beg. of section):

Non quod laudaretur ab illis; nullo enim obsequio vel adulatione sapiens commovetur, sed illorum poenitentiam amplexatus.

propitialis et clementissimae naturae, hoc modo eos suscipiendo pro cibis et potis disciplinae, atque sapientiae spectaculis saginant, quarum esuriem et sitim confessi, jam nunc fruniscuntur, ut qui destinati perrexerunt, cum salute venerunt. Quidam adversarii mores ad animam nocendam, sed ex contagio virtutis sine dispendio etiam profecerunt, unde cum salute liberatos, a plurimis vitiorum nexibus insinuat curatos, praecipue et uno medicamentorum remedio pietatis.

ix. (Gen. xxvi. 32) Quare pergentibus pueris Isaac, venientes qui quartum puteum foderunt, dixerunt non invenisse aquam ?

[a] *marg.* strenuos.

[b] φιλοφρονεῖται . . . αὐτοὺς om. Catt.

[c] ἁλῶν . . . μεταδίδωσι om. Catt. : v rba σωτηρίαν τὴν ἀπὸ τῶν ὅρκων (ἀνθρώπων Bur.) ἔχοντες add. Catt. Lips. et Burney.

OLD LATIN ADDITIONS

Quod et juramentum vocat, et civitatem, puteum juramenti, fallit. Post juramenta autoris, quicquid agit justus, hoc foedere firmari sperat secundum quadrinitatis virtutem. Unde etiam valde ait severissimam vocamus virtutem, spectatissimam ad capessendum intellectum : obscure autem sensualia occupantem pro incertis eorum momentis, cunctantur enim, et immutationem capiunt variis conditionum nutibus. Nuntiat itaque divinus sermo post nativitatem quarti filii, stabilitatem non sterilitatem in creatione maxime incorporalis et intelligibilis substantiae : haec etenim ad quartum usque tenditur. Sensualis vero quinione incipit, quam non sine mercede nominavit. Naturaliter itaque quoniam finis incorporalium usque in quarto est, totius autem rei, et totius disciplinae terminus hominum incertus est, deo autem manifestus, ideo in quarto puteo non inveniunt aquam. Sicut enim puteum fodientes aquam requirunt, ita enim disciplinam sectantes finem explorant, quod est impossibile hominibus revelari. Et quidem superbi metientes, solent affirmare se summos esse Musicos, summos grammaticos, transisse vero et Philosophiae grumos, et sapientiae et totius disciplinae et virtutis metas. Astutus vero, et non sui cultor vel sui laudator, confitetur ex aperto

'Αμήχανον ὑπὸ φύσεως ἀνθρωπίνης τῆς οἱασοῦν ἐπιστήμης τὸ τέλος· οὐδὲν γὰρ ἄνθρωπος ἄκρως οἶδεν ἀλλ' οἴεται μόνον εἰδέναι· τὸ δὲ τέλος τῆς γνώσεως ἀνάκειται μόνῳ θεῷ.

Harris, p. 43, from Mai, *Script. Vet.* vii. 107 *e* Cod. Vat. 1553, Φίλωνος· ἐκ τῶν ἐν Γενέσει ζητημάτων.

quantum deest a fine, et juratus tali foedere conscientiam commendat, quod nihil perfecte homo nosse potest. Hic aliena loquitur qui tot capitulis se existimat tantum scire, finis enim scientiae deo tantum recondita est. Quem etiam testem animae vocat, quoniam pura conscientia confitetur suam ignorantiam. Sola enim novit anima, quoniam nihil novit firmiter. Juramentum igitur nihil est aliud : testimonium dei fidele, atque solidissimum. Si fidele est, certum est, nec placet illi incerta credulitas.

x. (Gen. xxvi. 34) Quare Esau quadragenarius accepit uxorem Judith filiam Beher Cetthei, et Barhatnath filiam Elom Heuaei ?

Nulla quaestio requiritur ex dicto, relatio autem intelligibilis[a] naturaliter continet. Primo quod aequiparatus annorum numerus nuptiis aptus est, et in hoc festinat pervenire. Quis enim non optabit usque ad verbum vel ad quantum videtur imitare potiora. Ut ita similitudinem rerum attingat, ita in hoc pravus et commentis eruditus subornatur insignium rerum titulis, cum sit denotationis non extraneus. Primus gradus ambitur per fallaciam deferendo, et utpote ignorando insipiens lucem et tenebras, nigrum et splendidum, bonum et malum, et alia hujuscemodi aequa ipse per numerum, possibilitate vero non solum disparia, verum etiam contraria. Et haec quidem digna zelo[b] tartareo. Inde putans prima sua commenta dirigi, et altera superducit consilia, quorum reatum verborum suffragio caelat. Accepit ergo duas uxores, quas Chaldaei vocant Judith et Basemath. Quarum una interpretatur laudatrix, secunda nominata. Vides qua festinat viri similitudo ? Se laudari atque nominari. Ego non negabo Hebraica lingua, et Syrorum loquela Basemath, suavitatem interpretari. Nominata autem Sema dicitur, non Basemath. Hoc ergo pravus ambitur, non veritate, sed fictis alatus argumentis. Nigrae enim generationis est Cetheus qui excessus interpretatur, cujus merita sectando, nomine scilicet tantum et vanae gloriae, digno domicilio habetur bestiarum. Hevet enim serpens interpretantur, excelsus atque mentis Cetheus et bestiarum merita figurae sunt ferarum, quibus cari sunt famuli iracundiae et concupiscentiae, adeo aptissimae interpretantur imas atque inferiores sortitus concupiscentiae regiones. Alterius autem uxoris nominatae pater Elom arietis est impetus, pro auspitio furiae.

xi. (Gen. xxvi. 35) Quare has ipsas dixit contendere Isaac et Rebeccae ?

Non utique ex consensu, nec enim consonat pondus figurae et concupiscentiae autori mentis. Veruntamen consistere conantur litigia adversus bonorum perseverantiam, quae est Rebecca, et turbelas et contentiones opponant, scientes illorum regimen suam esse dissipationem.

Addition to *QG* iv. 203 on Gen. xxvii. 15 (Aucher, pp. 406-407).

Quos solet philosophia summos vocare secundum malitiam et virtutem. Videtur ergo de industria dixisse, et ex aperto :

---

[a] *l.* intelligibilia.   [b] *marg.* caelo illo.

OLD LATIN ADDITIONS

rurali vero stolam aptam non esse, ideo apud matrem fuit, necdum illi donata, sed justo reservata. Tu si unam habere speciem laudabilem quasi spectabilem aut pretextam, vel urbanam censuram caeteris omnibus aut pretextam, vel Fautrix vero mater animae perseverantia, decernens ne-quando imbrui depereat, simul et unifaria contingat ruina, apud se reservando et custodiendo stolam asseverantur, qua accepta ornat palaestricum quem sollicite applicat ut patri. Et sicut est familiarissima res musicae cithara, gubernatori temonum retinaculum et medico collyrium non tempeloxii plenum,[a] qui cupiunt etiam naves aureas habere, et medica-mentorum horrea plena, ita certa censura est, et elegans pulchritudo, quasi non quidem proprium praedium alterius, sed proprium artificis digne et prospere utentes.[b]

Addition to *QG* iv. 210 on Gen. xxvii. 22 (Aucher, pp. 412-413).

Manus autem possunt esse indocti ad effecturam, multa enim inofficiose tentant agere, non ex integritate cordis, aliquoties enim et religata sibi pravi resistunt, et senectuti deferunt, et amicitiae jura conservant. Sed haec pro sua avaritia gerunt, ut captata opportunitate quosdam amplius decipiant. Ita falluntur minus sobrii modico testimonio seducti, et frivola mirantes. Cautus autem et gerendorum causas, et consilia rerum requirit, vituperabilia reprehendo, doctus et responsis divinae scripturae quae permittit justi-tiarum titulos juste sectari quam injuste.

Addition to *QG* iv. 232 on Gen. xxvii. 38 (Aucher, p. 430).[c]

Ego me confiteor legisse in Hebraeo compunctionem et taciturnitatem eiisdem literis declaratam: et aliud incredibile in psalmoza lxiiii. Non habet tibi dicit hymnus, sed tibi silet hymnus deus in Sion. Et aliud mirum non est dictum soli stare, sed tacere ejisdem aspicibus quibus etiam hymnus iacet. Vide quantam allegoriam compunctio requirit.

[a] *marg. in utroque exemplari ita legebatur ; forte* non tantopere locupletum *erat legendum.*

[b] *l.* utentis.

[c] *Aucher :* " *Addit Interp. ex se.*"

INDEX

References are to Book and Section

$E =$ *Quaestiones in Exodum*
fig. = figurative
$G =$ *Quaestiones in Genesin*
gen. = general
lit. = literal
misc. = miscellaneous
n. = note
sym. = symbolizes, is symbolized

Aaron, sym. joy, *G* iv. 16 ; sym. word, *E* ii. 27, 44 ; is possessed by prophetic spirit, *E* ii. 105

Abel, name = " brought and offered up," *G* i. 78 ; sym. good man, *G* i. 59-68

Abihu, name = " truth from God," *E* ii. 27 ; sym. help from God, *E* ii. 27

Abimelech, name = " father-king," *G* iv. 176 ; sym. foolish man, *G* iv. 61-70 ; sym. progressive man, *G* iv. 188

Abraham, name = " elect father of sound," *G* iii. 43 ; sym. wise and virtuous man, *G* iii-iv *pas-*

sim ; sym. knowledge acquired through teaching, *G* iv. 144 ; founder of race of Israel, *G* iii. 3, iv. 2, 60 ; friend of God, *G* iv. 33

Abram, name = " uplifted father," *G* iii. 43

Academics, *G* iii. 3

Active and Passive, *G* iii. 3, 18, iv. 160, 177, *E* i. 8, ii. 33 (see also Number-symbolism, Woman)

Ada, *G* i. 77

Adam, see Man

Aelian, *E* ii. 28 n.

Aetiology, *G* iv. 22

Age, see Life

Agriculture. *G* ii. 66, 67, iv. 90, 189, *E* i. 6

277

INDEX

INDEX

279

INDEX

Bracelet, sym. decad, *G* iv. 118 ; sym. memory, *G* iv. 109

Brain, as seat of mind, *G* ii. 3, *E* ii. 124

Branches of lampstand in Tabernacle, see Lampstand

Bread, sym. frugality, *G* iv. 205 ; sym. health, *E* ii. 18 ; sym. necessary food, *E* ii. 72

Breast, as seat of heart, *E* ii. 115

Breastplate of judgment (Logeion), see High Priest

Bréhier, E., *G* iv. 211 n., Appendix A *passim*

Bronze vessels of altar, see Altar

Buffalo, permitted for food, *E* ii. 101

Building, *G* i. 26

Bulls, for sacrifice, *E* ii. 99

Bury, R. G., *G* iv. 164 n.

Cain, sym. wickedness, *G* i. 58-81, iv. 4

Calf, as sacrifice, *E* ii. 32

Camel, sym. memory, *G* iv. 92, 94, 106, 109, 136, 141

Canaan, name = " being out of their minds," *G* iv. 88; name = " merchant " or " mediator," *G* ii. 65, 77 ; name = " their appearance," *G* iv. 72

Cancer (constellation), *E* ii. 76

Capricorn, *E* ii. 76

Caution, *E* ii. 13

Cave, sym. mind, *G* iv. 80

Censers of table in Tabernacle, see Table

Centre of universe, *G* i. 10

Chaldaea, sym. astrology, *G* iii. 1, iv. 88

Chaldaean Language (*i.e.* Hebrew), *G* iii. 38, 43, 49, iv. 1, 17, 97, 147, 239, *E* ii. 68

Chaldaeans, inhabit Mesopotamia, *G* iv. 243

Chance, *G* i. 78, iii. 3, iv. 43, 76, *E* ii. 55

Change, see Rest and Movement

Chariot-driving, *G* iv. 218

Cherubim in Paradise, *G* i. 57

Cherubim on ark of Tabernacle, name = " great recognition " or " knowledge poured out in abundance," *E* ii. 62 ; sym. two chief powers of God, *E* ii. 62-68

Chosen Race, see Israel

Cicero, *G* ii. 7 n.

Circumcision, lit. and fig., *G* iii. 46-52, *E* ii. 2

City, sym. soul, *G* iv. 192

City-life and Civilization, *G* iv. 47, *E* i. 1, ii. 25

Clans, *E* i. 3

Clean and Unclean, *G* ii. 12, 52, iii. 48, *E* i. 18

Clothing, lit. and fig., *G* iv. 203, 213

Cloud at Sinai, see Sinai

Colson, F. H., *G* iii. 48 n., 56 n., iv. 8 n., 159 n., *E* ii. 4 n., 13 n., 20 n., 93 n.

INDEX

Column, see Pillar

Commandments, gen., *G*, *E passim*; contrasted with precepts, rights, laws, *G* iv. 184; written on tablets of stone, *E* ii. 41

Communion, *E* ii. 39, 69, 118

Community, *E* ii. 35, 36, 78

Conception of children, *G* i. 25, ii. 7, 14, iii. 47, 56, iv. 27, 154 (see also Procreation)

Concord, see Community

Congregation, *E* i. 10

Conscience, *G* iv. 202, *E* ii. 13

Consecration, *E* ii. 51, 71

Consent, sym. by Lot's daughter, *G* iv. 55-58

Consolation, *G* iv. 146

Consonants, *G* iii. 43, iv. 117 (see also Vowels)

Constancy, sym. by Rebekah, *G* iv. 92-205, 239-241

Contemplative Life, *G* iv. 31, 47, 138-140, 146, 187, 193, *E* ii. 40

Contemplative Race, see Israel

Continence, sym. by Jacob's wife, *G* iv. 243 (see also Virtue)

Convention, contrasted with nature, *G* iv. 184

Conviction, see Conscience

Cosmopolitanism, *G* iii. 39

Counsel, sym. by Lot's daughter, *G* iv. 55-58, 121; sym. by Rebekah, *G* iv. 239

Courage, see Virtue

Covenant between God and man, *G* ii. 10, iii. 40, 42, 60, *E* ii. 34, 106

Covering, see Veils

Creation of world, *G* i. 1-3, 19, ii. 13, 16, 31, iii. 39, 49, iv. 51, 110, 164, *E* i. 1, 23, ii. 42, 46, 52, 70, 73; took place in spring, *E* i. 1 (see also God)

Cube, see Number-symbolism

Cubit, *E* ii. 111 and n.

Cups of table in Tabernacle, see Table

Curse, *G* iv. 219, *E* ii. 5, 6

Curtains of Tabernacle, sym. four elements, *E* ii. 84-88, 92

Cush, name = " sparse earth," *G* ii. 81; son of Ham and father of Nimrod, *G* ii. 81, 82

Death, lit. and fig., *G* i. 16, 45, 51, 56, 70, 74-76, ii. 7, 9, 12, 23, 45, 57, iii. 52, iv. 45, 46, 73, 77, 78, 95, 152, 173, 235, 238, 240, *E* i. 3, 38

Deception, *E* ii. 54; is sometimes justified, *G* iv. 206, 228

Dedication, see Consecration

Deer, permitted for food, *E* ii. 101

Desert, see Wilderness

Desire, see Sensual Pleasure

Dew, sym. Logos, *G* iv. 215

Didrachm (Heb. shekel), *G* iv. 110

Dio Chrysostom, *E* ii. 81 n.

Dipper, used for " north," *E* ii. 101

281

INDEX

Discipline, see Education, Training

Disease, see Health, Medicine

Divination, *G* iv. 90

Divinization, of soul, *E* ii. 40

Division, in nature, *G* i. 64, iii. 5, 6, 15, 23

Door, sym. mind's escape from sense, *E* i. 22

Door-posts, sym. reason, *E* i. 12

Doubt, see Faith

Dove, sym. reason and virtue, *G* ii. 38-44, iii. 3, 7

Drink, see Food

Drinking-trough, sym. learning, *G* iv. 234

Drunkenness, lit. and fig., *G* ii. 68, 69, 73, iv. 218, 225, *E* ii. 15, 118

Dryness and Moisture, *E* i. 8

Duality, see Number-symbolism

Dyad, see Number-symbolism

Ear, *G* i. 77, ii. 3, 13, iii. 32, iv. 110, 118, 239, *E* ii. 34 (see also Hearing)

Ear-ring, sym. learning, *G* iv. 109 ; sym. monad, *G* iv. 118

Earth, gen., *G* i. 64, ii. 18, iii. 3-6, 49, iv. 87, 215, *E* ii. 56, 85, 88, 90, 117-120 ; divided into sixty parts by astrologers, *E* ii. 81 ; sym. body, *G* ii. 66, iv. 193 ; sym. desire, *G* iv. 191 ; sym. good and evil, *G* ii. 81 ;

sym. soul, *G* iv. 28 (see also Elements)

East, *G* i. 7, iv. 149, *E* ii. 101

Ecstasy, see Inspiration, Sleep

Eden, name = " delicacies," *G* i. 7, 56

Edom, name = " flame-coloured " or " earthy," *G* iv. 171 ; sym. wickedness, *G* iv. 171

Education, gen., *G* iii. 26, 27, 30, 35, 50, iv. 16, 39, 45, 95, 98, 100-110, 114, 118, 123, 137, 144, 154, 156, 175, 191, 195, 208, 210, 217, 242-245, *E* i. 4, ii. 3, 4, 13, 16, 19, 25, 34, 36 ; encyclical or school studies, *G* iii. 19-24, 31, 35, 59, 60, iv. 203, *E* i. 5, ii. 103 ; threefold method of education through instruction (sym. by Abraham), self-teaching (sym. by Isaac) and practice (sym. by Jacob), *G* iii. 50, 51, 59, 88, iv. 91, 93, 122, 123, 127-129, 144, 175, 238, *E* i. 5

Egypt, name = " oppressing," *G* iv. 177 ; sym. external goods and senses, *G* iii. 16, 19, iv. 177 ; Israel's exodus from Egypt, *E* i. *passim*

Egyptians, *G* iii. 47, 48, *E* i. 1, 8, 10, 18, ii. 2

Einarson, B., *G* iv. 159 n.

Elders, seventy, *E* ii. 27, 31, 44

INDEX

Election of Israel, see Israel

Elements, four elements (fire, air, water, earth) gen., *G* i. 64, 71, iii. 3, 6, 15, 49, iv. 8, 51, *E* i. 4, ii. 56, 73, 81, 86, 117-120; sym. by curtains of Tabernacle, *E* ii. 84-88; sym. by garment of high priest, *E* ii. 107-124; sym. by veil of Holy of Holies, *E* ii. 92-94; fifth element (quintessence), *G* iii. 6, iv. 8, *E* ii. 73, 85; sublunary elements (air, water, earth), *G* iii. 3, 15, iv. 8, *E* ii. 33, 78, 81, 90, 91, 109

Elijah, ascends to heaven, *G* i. 86

Emerald Stones, see High Priest

Encyclical Studies, see Education

Enemies, see Foreigners

Ennead, see Number-symbolism

Enoch, *G* i. 82-86

Enosh, name = " man," *G* i. 79

Envy, *G* iv. 101, 103, 107, 142, 191-194, 226, 227, 239

Ephod, see High Priest

Ephron, name = " dust," *G* iv. 79; sym. corporeal natures, *G* iv. 79

Epicharmus, quoted on sin, *G* iv. 203

Equality and Inequality, *G* ii. 5, 12, iii. 49, iv. 35, 157, 216, *E* i. 10, 15, ii.

10, 33, 64, 81; as mother of justice, *E* i. 6; proportioned equality, *G* iv. 102, 125, *E* i. 6 n. (see also Justice, Number-symbolism)

Equinox and Solstice, *G* ii. 17, 31, 33, 45, 47, iii. 3, *E* ii. 56, 75, 113 n.; vernal and autumnal equinoxes contrasted, *E* i. 1

Esau, name = " thing made," *G* iv. 161; name = " oak," *G* iv. 161, 206, 207; sym. ignorance and evil, *G* iv. 161-238 *passim*

Eternity, *E* ii. 20, 114 (see also Immortality)

Ether, see Heaven

Ethiopians, practise circumcision, *G* iii. 48

Euphrates, sym. growth, justice, spirituality, *G* i. 12, 13; sym. pleasantness, *G* iv. 243

Euripides, quoted on good and evil, *G* iv. 203; referred to (?) as " tragic poet," *G* iv. 211

Evening, as time for sacrifice, *E* i. 11

Evil, see Good

Exodus from Egypt, *E* i. *passim*; speed of, *E* i. 14

External Goods, *G* ii. 55, 71, 76, 80, iii. 43, iv. 33, 43, 77, 80, 82, 108, 121, 134, 147-149, 186, 192, 215, 217, *E* ii. 4, 106

283

INDEX

INDEX

overseer, *G* ii. 27, 60, iv. 42, 65

philanthropic, see lover of mankind

physician, *G* ii. 29

pilot, *G* ii. 34

preserver and sustainer, *G* ii. 34, iv. 23

protector, *G* ii. 67, iv. 42, 51, 76, *E* i. 8, ii. 24, 69, 71, 72

providence, *G* iii. 3, 18, 43, iv. 25, 29, 42, 65, 87, 88

quiet, *G* iv. 140

reformer, *G* iv. 12, 65

saviour, *G* ii. 13, 25, 60, iii. 10, 15, iv. 54, 90, 131, 233, *E* i. 10, 23, ii. 2, 51

sower of spiritual seed, *G* iv. 17, 68, 99, 189, *E* ii. 3

speaker, *G* iv. 140, *E* ii. 68

splendid, *E* ii. 67

standing, *E* ii. 37

teacher, *G* ii. 16, 49, iii. 43, iv. 21, 24, 45, 101, 118, 121, 140, 184, 208, 209, *E* ii. 13, 52

triune in appearance, *G* iv. 2, 4, 8, 30

truth, God of, *G* iv. 130

unbegotten and uncreated, *G* i. 54, ii. 12, 16, iv. 1, *E* ii. 32

unbribable, *G* iv. 23, 76, *E* ii. 32

unknown, see incomprehensible

unmixed, *E* ii. 33

visible to virtuous souls, *G* iv. 1, 2, 4, *E* i. 20, ii. 32, 39, 45, 47, 51, 61, 67

without envy, *G* i. 55, iv. 101

without malice, *G* ii. 13

without need, *G* iv. 188, *E* i. 22

without passion, *G* i. 95

(*b*) glory of God, *E* ii. 45, 47

(*c*) Logos of God, see Logos

(*d*) names of God (*i.e.* God and Lord), *G* i. 57, ii. 16, 51, 53, 75, iii. 1, iv. 21, 53, 87, *E* ii. 62, 68 (see also (*f*))

(*e*) nature and God, see Nature

(*f*) power of God, esp. two chief powers or attributes, creative and royal (expressed by names " God " and " Lord," and sym. by cherubim on ark), *G* i. 54, 57, 89, ii. 16, 51, 53, 75, iii. 39, 42, 48, iv. 2, 4, 8, 9, 10, 12, 20, 25, 26, 30, 33, 53, 87, *E* i. 23 n., ii. 37, 47, 51, 61-68, 83 ; creative power older than royal power, *E* ii. 62 ; two chief powers subdivided into four powers, *E* ii. 68

(*g*) voice of God, *E* ii. 16, 48

(*h*) Word of God, see Logos

Gods of Gentiles, *G* i. 36, iv. 2, *E* i. 8, 20, ii. 5, 26 n. (see also Polytheism)

Gold, lit. and fig., *E* ii. 54, 63, 69, 73 : sym. incor-

287

INDEX

Holiness and Pollution, *G* iv. 2, 51, 63-66, 80, 95, 111, 118, 158, 186, 221, 242, *E* i. 7, 10, 12, ii. 31, 33, 45, 47, 51, 76, 83, 91, 98, 115

Holy of Holies in Tabernacle, *E* ii. 68, 91, 95 ; sym. intelligible world, *E* ii. 94, 96, 104, 106, 107, 115

Holy Place in Tabernacle, sym. sense-perceptible world, *E* ii. 91, 95, 103

Homer, quoted by name or as "the poet," *G* i. 76 (*Od.* xii. 118), iii. 3 (*Od.* xii. 39-45), 16 (*Od.* xiv. 258), iv. 2 (*Od.* xvii. 485-488), 8 (*Il.* xv. 189), 20 (*Od.* xv. 74), 183 (*Il.* iii. 179), 238 (*passim*), *E* ii. 102 (*Il. passim*)

Homonyms, *G* iv. 243

Honour, distinguished from glory, *E* ii. 67

Hope, *G* i. 79, 80, iii. 55

Horns, (*a*) on sacrificial animals, sym. battle for truth, *E* ii. 101
(*b*) of altar, see Altar

Hospitality, see Foreigners

House, sym. desire, *E* i. 12

Household Management, *G* iv. 218, 236

Humaneness, see Love of Mankind

Humility, see Pride

Hunger, lit. and fig., *G* iv. 169, 170

Hunter, sym. uncleanness, *G* iv. 165

Hur, name = "light," *E* ii. 44

Husbandman, see Agriculture

Hyacinth (colour), sym. air, *E* ii. 85, 117

Hypocrisy, *G* iv. 165

Ideas, see Incorporeality

Identity and Difference, *E* ii. 33

Idols, *E* i. 20

Ignorance, see Knowledge

Imitation of God or heaven by man, soul, etc., *G* iv. 29, 53, 115, 147, 151, 164, 181, 188, 196, 200(?), 215, *E* i. 23, ii. 42, 46, 51, 85, 104, 124

Immoderateness, see Sensual Pleasure

Immortality, *G* i. 45, 51, 55, 70, 76, 85, 86, iii. 27, 53, 57, iv. 46, 66, 103, 152, 153, 164, 169, 244, *E* i. 15, 23, ii. 38, 39, 56, 114, 118

Impiety, see Piety

Impressions, *G* iv. 1, 20, 24, 30, 94, 117, *E* ii. 13, 82, 109, 122, 124 (see also Seals)

Impulse, *G* iii. 3, 28, 52, iv. 66, 73, 78, 129, 206, 241, *E* i. 16

Incense in Tabernacle, *E* ii. 71

Incorporeality, of angels, *G* i. 92, iii. 11, *E* ii. 13 ; of forms, principles, etc., *G* ii. 4, 56, iii. 3, 22, 40, 42, 43, 49, 53, iv. 1, 8, 22, 32, 35, 73, 80, 88, 99, 110, 115, 138, 146, 160,

INDEX

Justice and Injustice, *G* i. 12, 49, 97, 98, 100, ii. 11, 36, 45, 48, 60, 67, 71, iii. 49, iv. 23, 26, 27, 64, 66, 68, 114, 115, 194, 235, *E* i. 3, 6, 12, ii. 4, 10, 19, 51, 112 (see also Equality); justice of God, see God

Kadesh, name = " holy " or " sacred," *G* iii. 36, iv. 59

Keturah, name = " incense-burning," *G* iv. 147; sym. smell, *G* iv. 147

Kid, as sacrifice, *E* ii. 32; sym. character-traits, *G* iv. 200, *E* i. 8

Kingship, *G* iv. 76, 140, 182, 206, *E* ii. 6, 72, 105

Kinship, among men, *E* i. 2, ii. 35, 36; with God, *E* ii. 29

Knops, see Lampstand

Knowledge and Ignorance, *G* ii. 49, 69, iii. 2, 3, 27, 31-33, iv. 5, 14, 19, 22, 24, 46, 64, 68, 103, 138, 161, 168, 175, 226, 227, 232, 243, 244, *E* i. 16, ii. 7, 19, 25, 36, 51, 96; knowledge contrasted with thing known and act of knowing, *E* ii. 112 (see also Education, Wisdom)

Kor (measure), *G* iii. 39

Laban, name = " whiteness," *G* iv. 117, 239, 243; sym. sense-perception, *G* iv. 117, 239

Labour, two forms of (piety and humaneness), *E* ii. 108 (see also Training)

Ladder, Jacob's, sym. ascent of soul, *G* iv. 29

Ladles, see Table

Lamb, sym. purity, *E* ii. 121; paschal, *E* ii. 32 (see also Paschal Sheep)

Lamech, *G* i. 77

Lamps, see Lampstand

Lampstand in Tabernacle, sym. sense-perceptible heaven, *E* ii. 73-81, 83, 95, 103-106; its bases, *E* ii. 80; its branches, *E* ii. 74-77; its knops, *E* ii. 74; its lamps sym. planets or stars, *E* ii. 78, 104; its lilies sym. stars, *E* ii. 74, 76; its oil sym. wisdom, *E* ii. 103; its uplifters sym. stars, *E* ii. 80: weight of, *E* ii. 81

Laughter, see Isaac, Joy

Laws of Gentiles, *E* ii. 22

Laws of Moses, gen., *G*, *E passim*; extend throughout nature, *E* ii. 59; incorruptible, *E* ii. 53: preservation and dissolution of, *E* ii. 41: world-wide purpose of, *E* ii. 42; written at God's command, *E* ii. 42, 43

Laws of Nature, see Nature

Leaf, see High Priest

Learning, see Education

Leaven, sym. pride, *E* i. 15, ii. 14

INDEX

293

INDEX

seminal substance, *E* ii. 68

source of two chief powers of God, *E* ii. 68

steward of God, *E* ii. 39

teacher, *G* iv. 91

tetrad, *E* ii. 94

unity of, *G* iv. 60

wise, *E* ii. 13

word of God, *G* iii. 15, iv. 49, 51, 59, 108, 196, 223, *E* i. 14, 15, ii. 13, 68 (?), 111

Lord, see God

Lot, sym. progressive man, *G* iv. 31-55 *passim*

Lot's Daughters, sym. consent or counsel, *G* iv. 55

Lot's Wife, sym. sense-perception, *G* iv. 52

Love, erotic, *E* ii. 13 ; of fellow-man, *G* i. 17, iv. 2, 29, 52, 142, 193, 200, 219, *E* i. 5, ii. 11, 12, 69, 108 ; of God, *G* iii. 21, iv. 20, 139, *E* ii. 12 (as implied in adjective "God-loving" *passim*) ; maternal, *E* ii. 8 ; of self, *G* i. 62, iv. 194, *E* ii. 3 ; of virtue, see Virtue ; of wisdom, see Wisdom

Lynceus, *G* ii. 72

Macedonian Empire, *G* iv. 43

Mahalath, name="from the beginning," *G* iv. 245 ; sym. sensual pleasure, *G* iv. 245

Male and Female, see Active, Number-symbolism, Woman

Mambre (Bibl. Mamre),

name="from sight," *G* iv. 1 ; sym. mind, *G* iv. 1

Man, contrasted with animals, see Animals ; contrasted with God, *G* ii. 54, 62, *E* ii. 33, 76 ; contrasted with woman, see Woman ; earthly man, moulded by God, *G* i. 4, 8, 28, 51, 87, ii. 17, 56, 66, iv, 164, *E* ii. 46 ; heavenly man, made in God's image, *G* i. 4, 8, 93, ii. 56, iv. 164, *E* ii. 47 ; mixture of opposites, *G* iv. 203, 206, 220 ; sym. mind, see Mind ; "rational, mortal animal," *G* iii. 43 ; "tame animal by nature," *E* i. 16

Manna, sym. spiritual food, *G* iv. 102

Marriage, see Family, Number-symbolism

Mars (planet), *E* ii. 75

Matter, gen., *G, E passim* ; "mother of created things," *G* iv. 160 ; of sublunary elements is one, *E* ii. 88

Measure and Measuring, *G* iv. 8, 102, *E* ii. 33, 52, 82 ; sym. by Logos, see Logos

Medicine and Medical Care, *G* ii. 41, 79, iii. 25, 48, iv. 35, 45, 47, 76, 147, 200, 201, 204, 218, *E* ii. 25

Megalopolis, *i.e.* the world, *E* i. 1, ii. 42

294

INDEX

Mountains, sym. senses, *G* ii. 21; sym. wisdom, *G* iv. 46, 49

Mourning, *G* iv. 73, *E* i. 3

Mouth, organ of food and speech (*q.v.*), *E* ii. 118

Muses, *G* i. 6

Music and Musical Harmony, *G* iii. 3, 38, 48, iv. 27, 29, 76, 95, *E* ii. 37, 38, 93 (?), 103, 120

Mysteries, *G* iv. 8, 35 (?), 110, *E* i. 13 n., ii. 52

Nadab, name = "voluntary," *E* ii. 27; sym. voluntary vision, *E* ii. 27

Nahor, name = "rest of light," *G* iv. 93; sym. wisdom, *G* iv. 93

Nakedness, lit. and fig., *G* i. 30, 40, ii. 69, 70, 72, iv. 22

Names, gen., *G* i. 20-22, iii. 43, 67, iv. 194, 243, *E* ii. 66

Nature, beauty of, *G* iv. 245; conceals itself, *G* iv. 1, 21, 22; contemplation of, *E* ii. 31; convention and nature, *G* iv. 184; female and passive, *G* iii. 3; God and nature, *G* iii. 41, iv. 21, 42, 51, 87, 88, *E* ii. 51, 68; harmony and order in nature, *G* ii. 55, iii. 5, 15, 38, iv. 23, 29, 46, 110, 114, *E* ii. 58, 59, 68, 74, 76, 78, 118, 120; healer, *G* ii. 41; law of nature, *G* iv. 90, 152, 184, 205,

E ii. 19, 59 (?); mother and provider, *G* ii. 60, 80, *E* ii. 12; perfection of, *E* ii. 1; self-producing, *G* iii. 39; teacher, *G* iii. 27, 54, 59; two species of (corporeal and incorporeal), *E* ii. 54

Navigation, *G* iv. 76, 90, 218, 236, *E* ii. 44, 55

Necessity, *G* i. 21, 68, ii. 45, 50, iv. 29, 34, 74, 133, 162, 222, *E* ii. 58, 89 (?)

Night, as time for sacrifice, *E* i. 11, 13, 18

Nilsson, M. P., *E* ii. 76 n.

Nimrod, name = "Ethiopian," *G* ii. 82; sym. evil, *G* ii. 82

Noah, name = "rest," *G* i. 87; name = "righteous," *G* ii. 45; birthday of, *G* i. 87, ii. 33; drunkenness of, *G* ii. 69-73; as husbandman, *G* ii. 66 (see also Ark of Noah)

Nocturnal Emission, *E* ii. 15 (?)

Nose, *G* i. 77, ii. 3, iii. 5, 32, 239 (see also Smell)

Number-symbolism, angular and oblong, *G* i. 83, 91, ii. 5, 45, iii. 49, 56, *E* ii. 93, 111; digits, *G* i. 83; equal and unequal, *G* i. 91, ii. 5, 14, iii. 49; odd and even (or male and female), *G* i. 83, 91, ii. 14, iii. 38, 49, 56, 61, *E* ii. 33, 46; ratio, *G* iv. 27; salutary, *G* iv. 27

INDEX

297

INDEX

Order, in age, nature, number, rank, time, *G* i. 64, ii. 45, 47, 74, iii. 49, iv. 12, 84, 122, 157, 199, 215, 218, 230, *E* i. 1, ii. 27, 46, 58

Orphans, *E* ii. 3, 4

Oryx, permitted for food, *E* ii. 101

Ox, as sacrifice, *E* ii. 101 ; sym. earth, *G* iii. 3, 7

Pain, see Pleasure

Painting, *G* iv. 243

Palm (measure), *E* ii. 111 n.

Papyrus, *E* ii. 41

Paradise, *G* i. 6-15, 34, 56 ; sym. immortal virtues, *G* iv. 51

Pascha, name = " pass over," *E* i. 4

Paschal Lamb or Sheep, *E* i. 3, 7-18 ; sym. spiritual change, *E* i. 4

Pascher, J., *G* iv. 110 n.

Passion, see Fear, Grief, Sensual Pleasure

Passover, *E* i. 1-23 ; of the soul, *E* i. 4

Patriarchs (phylarchs), sym. by stones of Logeion, *E* ii. 14 ; sym. constellations, *E* ii. 14

Patterns, see Archetypes, Incorporeality

Peace and War, lit. and fig., *G* iii. 8, iv. 90, 197, 206, 218, 228, 229, 235, *E* ii. 11, 21, 44, 64, 68, 102

Pederasty, *G* iv. 37

Pentad, see Number-symbolism

Pentecostal Year, see Jubilee Year

Perfection, *G* i. 97, iii. 10, 12, 20, 32, iv. 30, 34, 47, 60, 66, 133, 164, 175, 177, 191, 205, 213, *E* i. 1, 8, ii. 60, 69, 76 ; sym. by Abraham in contrast to Lot, the progressive man, *G* iv. *passim* (see also Progress)

Peripatetics, *G* iii. 16 (see also Aristotle)

Perseverance, see Constancy

Persians, empire of, *G* iv. 43

Pharan (Bibl. Bered), name = " hail " or " dots," *G* iii. 36

Philistines, name = " foreigners " (*cf.* LXX *allophyloi*), *G* iv. 177, 191

Philosophy (Gr. *philosophia*), *G* i. 57, ii. 41, iii. 5, 33, 43, iv. 1, 21, 22, 42, 76, 87, 89, 93, 97, 104, 167, 191, 192, 241, *E* ii. 13, 20, 103, 117, 118, 124 n. (see also Wisdom)

Phylarchs (patriarchs), *E* ii. 14

Piety and Impiety, *G* i. 10, 55, 66, 76, 100, ii. 13, 18, 23, 43, 48, 61, 70, 82, iii. 1, 28, 43, iv. 1, 2, 10, 12, 19, 29, 42, 44, 49, 51, 53, 60, 67, 84, 133, 200, *E* i. 1, 7, 10, 12, 21, ii. 15, 26, 27, 31, 45, 47, 83, 99, 101, 105, 115 ; piety as queen of virtues, *E* ii. 38

Pillar, sym. opinion, *E* ii. 17 ;

INDEX

by paschal lamb or sheep, *E* i. 3, 7-18

Progression (in music), see Music

Promise of God, *G* iii. 55-58

Prophecy, Prophets, *G* iv. 90, 125, 138, 196, 212, *E* ii. 27, 29, 43, 49, 67 ; prophetic souls, *E* i. 4 (see also Inspiration, Logos)

Prostration before God, *G* iv. 3, 78, 113, 130, *E* ii. 83

Providence, see God

Prudence, see Virtue

Ptolemy, Claudius, *E* ii. 81 n.

Punishment for Sin, *G* i. 35, 77, ii. 14, 43, 54, 77, iii. 52, 56, iv. 4, 8, 25, 26, 50-52, 70, *E* i. 4

Puppet-show, *G* iii. 48

Purity, see Holiness, Mixture

Purple, sym. water, *E* ii. 85

Pythagoras, Pythagoreans, *G* i. 17, 99, iii. 16, 49, iv. 8, 27 n., *E* i. 23 n., ii. 33 n. (see also Number-symbolism)

Quality and Quantity, *G* iv. 181

Quintessence, see Elements

Rainbow, *G* ii. 64

Ram, as sacrifice, *E* ii. 101 ; sym. air or reason, *G* iii. 3, 7

Ram (constellation), head of zodiac, *E* i. 1

Raven, sym. wickedness, *G* ii. 36-39

Raw Meat, sym. savagery, *E* i. 16

Reason, see Mind

Rebekah, name = " constancy," *G* iv. 97, 188, 199 ; sym. constancy or perseverance, *G* iv. 92-188 *passim*

Red, sym. shameful passion, *G* iv. 170

Reformation of Character, *G* iv. 12, 233, 245, *E* i. 8, 13, 15, 16, ii. 107

Refuge, Cities of, *G* iii. 52

Reitzenstein, R., *E* ii. 38 n., 39 n.

Relaxation, see Tension

Repentance, *G* i. 82, 91, ii. 42, 43, 54, iv. 180, 233, *E* i. 13, 15, 16

Rest and Movement (incl. Change), *G* i. 87, iii. 39, 62, iv. 1, 93, *E* ii. 55, 70, 83, 91, 106

Reuben (tribe), *G* iv. 123

Revelation and Truth (Urim and Thummim), see High Priest

Revenge, *E* ii. 11.

Reverence, see Piety, Prostration

Righteousness, see Justice

Rivers of Paradise, *G* i. 12

Road to Virtue, *G* iii. 27, iv. 108, 125, 131, 226, 242, *E* i. 19, ii. 13, 26

Roasting, see Food

Robbins, F. E., *G* ii. 5 n., *E* ii. 81 n.

Royal Highway, see Road to Virtue

Ruddiness, sym. savagery (in Esau), *G* iv. 160

300

INDEX

Sabbath, *E* i. 9

Sabbatical Year, *G* iii. 39

Sacrifice, lit. and fig., *G* i. 62, ii. 52, iii. 3, 48, 102, *E* i. 3, 7, 10, 12, 17, 18, ii. 14, 31, 32, 35, 50, 99, 101; sym. communion, *E* ii. 69; sym. soul, *G* iv. 28, *E* i. 11, 98, 100; equality of, *E* ii. 99 (see also Altar, Paschal Lamb)

Sagittarius, *E* ii. 76

Salt, sym. communion, *E* ii. 69; sym. unfruitfulness, *G* iv. 52

Salutary Offerings (Bibl. "peace-offerings"), see Sacrifice

Salvation, *G* i. 71, ii. 11, 22, 25, 27, iii. 52, 57, iv. 7, 26, 27, 44, 45, 49-51, 54, 130, 198, 233, *E* ii. 43, 64

Sanctuary, see Holy of Holies

Sapphire, as colour of heaven, *E* ii. 37

Sarah, name = " ruler," *G* iii. 52, iv. 122; sym. virtue and wisdom, *G* ii. 26, iii-iv *passim*

Saturn (planet), *E* ii. 75

Scarlet, sym. fire, *E* ii. 85

Schmidt, Helmut, *E* ii. 124 n.

School-studies, see Education

Science, see Knowledge

Scorpio, *E* ii. 76

Scriptures, gen., *G*, *E* *passim*; beauty of, *G* iv. 196, 223; truth of, *G* iv. 168

Scylla, *G* i. 76

Seals, lit. and fig., *E* ii. 114, 122, 124 (see also Impressions)

Seasons, see Time

Sediment in Temple-oil, sym. impurity, *E* ii. 103

Seeing, see Sight

Seminal Principle or Substance, *G* ii. 16, 42, *E* ii. 68 (see also God, Logos)

Sense-perception, *G* i. 25, 35, 37, 38, 47-49, 52, 77, 94, ii. 3, 21, 29, 34, iii. 3, 5, 22, 32, 41, 51, iv. 1, 3, 11, 52, 88, 110, 117-121, 189, 203, 215, 239, 240, 243, *E* i. 4, 8, 22, ii. 3, 13, 16, 52-59, 69, 82, 93-100, 106, 112, 121; good senses *v.* bad senses, *G* iv. 147; sense as servant of mind, *G* iv. 215-216; (see also Hearing, Sight, Smell, Taste, Touch)

Sensual Pleasure (Gr. *hēdonē, vel sim.*), *G* i. 31, 41, 44, 46, 51, 99, ii. 7, 8, 12, 18, 22, 29, 37, 46, 49, 56, 57, 59, 61, 68, 69, iii. 10, 21, 27, 48, 51, 52, 61, iv. 15, 16, 33-42, 53, 66, 77, 79, 80, 86, 90, 99, 112, 135, 152, 154, 159, 168, 170, 173, 182, 183, 185, 191, 198, 201, 206, 210, 224, 230, 234, 238, 240, 241, 245, *E* i. 8, 15, 19, ii. 2, 3, 12, 14, 18, 31, 51, 100, 118

Serpent, sym. sensual pleasure, *G* i. 31-36, 47, 48, ii. 56, 57

301

INDEX

Servants and Masters, see Freedom

Seth, name = " one who drinks water," *G* i. 78 ; sym. virtuous soul, *G* i. 78, 81

Sheep, as sacrifice, *E* i. 7, ii. 32, 101 ; Paschal sheep sym. progress, *E* i. 3, 7-18

Shem, sym. good, *G* i. 88, ii. 79

Shoes, sym. road to virtue, *E* i. 19

Shoulder, sym. labour, *G* iv. 98, *E* ii. 108

Shoulder-pieces, see High Priest

Shur, name = " wall," *G* iii. 27, iv. 59

Sight, *G* i. 77, ii. 3, 21, 34, iii. 5, 32, 51, iv. 1, 3, 11, *E* ii. 3, 39, 51, 52, 82, 112 (see also Eye)

Silence, *G* iv. 108, *E* ii. 118

Silenus, *G* iv. 99

Silver, sym. sense-perception, *E* ii. 102

Similarity and Dissimilarity, *E* ii. 33

Sin, *G* i. 65, 68, 73, ii. 14, iii. 40, 41, iv. 60, 65, 66, 70, 73, 92, 152, 190, 245, *E* i. 8, 15, 32, ii. 41

Sinai, name = " inaccessible," *E* ii. 45 ; as scene of revelation, *E* ii. 27-49

Sin-offering, see Sacrifice

Sirens, *G* iii. 3

Skeptics, *G* iii. 33

Slavery, see Freedom

Sleep and Sleeplessness, lit. and fig., *G* i. 24, iii. 9, 55, iv. 2, 62, 94, *E* ii. 15, 82

Smell, *G* ii. 3, 21, iii. 5, 51, iv. 1, 11, 52, 214 (see also Nose)

Smoothness, of Jacob's skin, sym. frugality, virtue, *G* iv. 201, 204, 206

Sobriety, see Drunkenness

Socrates, quoted, *G* ii. 3, iii. 3 (*Phaedr.* 246 E) (see also Plato)

Sodom, name = " blindness," *G* ii. 43, iv. 23, 31 ; name = " sterility," *G* iv. 23, 31 ; sym. sense-perception, *G* iv. 52

Sodomites, sym. bad traits, *G* iv. 36, 38, 51, 52

Sojourn, usu. of mind or soul in body, *G* iii. 10, 45, iv. 42, 45, 59, 74, 178, 185, 187, 195, *E* ii. 2

Solstice, see Equinox

Sons of God, see Angels

Sophists and Sophistry, *G* iii. 19, 23-25, 27, 33, 35, iv. 87, 88, 92, 95, 104, 107, 221

Soul, gen., *G* i. 10, 11, 78, ii. 29, iii. 42, 48, 54, iv. 1, 214, 230, 243, *E* i. 17, ii. 35, 39, 71, 80 ; body and soul, see Body ; eightfold soul (reason, five senses, organ of reproduction, speech—as in Stoic theory), *G* i. 75, ii. 12, iii. 4, iv. 110 ; fivefold soul (rational, irascible, appetitive, nutri-

INDEX

tive, sense-perceptive—as in Aristotelian theory), *G* iv. 186; harmony of soul, *E* ii. 20, 38; incorporeal soul, see Incorporeality; migration of soul, *E* ii. 40; moved by itself only, *E* ii. 120; origin of soul in wisdom, *E* ii. 36; threefold soul (rational, appetitive, spirited—as in Platonic theory), *G* ii. 59, iv. 216, *E* i. 12; twofold soul (rational and irrational), *G* iv. 112, 117, 159, 218, 220, *E* i. 23, 33, 53 (see also Mind, Sense-perception)

South, *E* ii. 101; south celestial sphere, *E* ii. 79

Span (measure), *E* ii. 111 n.

Speech (incl. *logos prophorikos*), *G* i. 32, 77, ii. 42, 60, iii. 43, iv. 8, 13, 85, 88-90, 96, 102, 107, 108, 120, 132, 140, ii. 210, 214, 221, *E* i. 17, ii. 5, 16, 34, 44, 110, 111, 116, 118; speech as composed of letters, syllables, words, discourses, *E* ii. 111

Spirit, divine spirit, *G* i. 90, ii. 28, 59, iv. 5, *E* ii. 33 n.; holy spirit, *E* ii. 33 (?); vital spirit, *G* ii. 8, iii. 3

Spring (of water), see Fountain

Spring (season), see Equinox, Time

Square, see Number-symbolism

Staehle, K., *G* ii. 5 n., iii. 12 n., 38 n., 49 n., iv. 92 n., 110 n., *E* ii. 84 n., 97 n., 100 n., Appendix A *passim*

Staff, sym. rule, *E* i. 19

Stars, see Heaven

Statecraft, *G* iv. 165, 218, 236, *E* ii. 42, 44

Statius, *E* ii. 76 n. (*Theb.* iv. 225)

Stein, Edmund, *E* ii. 62 n.

Sterility, see Barrenness. Sodom

Stoics, *G* iii. 3 n., iv. 26 n., 46 n., 85 n., 145 n., 196 n., *E* ii. 110 n., 120, 124 n.

Stole, see High Priest

Stone Tablets, *E* ii. 41

Stones, of altar at Sinai, *E* ii. 30; of shoulder-pieces of high priest, see High Priest

Strabo, *G* iv. 1 n.

Strangers, see Foreigners

Sublunary World, see Elements

Sulphur, *G* iv. 51, 52

Summer, see Equinox and Solstice, Time

Sun, sym. wisdom, *G* i. 10, 57, 84, ii. 40, iii. 14, iv. 1, 51, 94, 140, 158, *E* ii. 32, 51; movements of, *G* iii. 3, *E* i. 1, ii. 75, 76, 112

Supplanter, see Jacob

Surface (in geometry), *E* ii. 61, 121

Sword, *G* i. 57

Symbolism, gen., *G, E pas-*

INDEX

INDEX

Training of Body, *G* ii. 63, iii. 12, iv. 29, 210, 238, *E* i. 6, ii. 103 (see also Athletic Contests)

Trance, see Sleep

Tree of Knowledge, *G* i. 11

Tree of Life, *G* i. 10, 55

Triad, see Number-symbolism

Tribes of Israel, *E* ii. 30 (see also Patriarchs)

Trojan War, *E* ii. 102

Truth, *G* iv. 69, 115, 125, 172, 194, 204, 206, 224, *E* i. 20, ii. 5, 9, 101, 107, 111, 116; truth of Scripture, *G* iv. 168 (see also Opinion)

Tunic, of Adam and Eve, *G* i. 53

Turner's Art, see Arts

Unbounded, *E* i. 23

Undergarment of high priest, see High Priest

Understanding, see Mind

Unity and Separateness, *E* ii. 33, 88, 118

Unleavened Bread, sym. humility, *E* i. 15; festival of *E* i. 1 n.

Uplifters, see Lampstand

Urim and Thummim, see High Priest

Valley, sym. state of soul, *G* iv. 195

Veils of Tabernacle, veil between Holy Place and Holy of Holies, sym. four elements, *E* ii. 91-95, 106; veil at entrance to Tabernacle (called "covering"), *E* ii. 96, 97

Venison, sym. character, *G* iv. 167, 222

Venus (planet), *E* ii. 75

Virginity, lit. and fig., *G* iv. 95, 99, 111, 119, 132, 143, 242, *E* ii. 3; virginity of number seven, see Number-symbolism

Virgo, *E* ii. 76

Virtue and Virtuous Man, gen., *G* i. 51, 75, 97, 100, ii. 12, 38-40, 59, 71, 76, 79, iii. 1, 8, 19-22, 27, 30, 40, 48, 51, 54, 60, 61, iv. 2, 6-16, 20, 22, 45, 61, 63, 69, 73, 80, 84, 92, 116, 129, 133, 134, 144-148, 152, 157, 166, 167, 172, 204, 206, 215, 217, 222, 225, 228, 231, 241, 243, *E* i. 6, 7, ii. 13, 23, 27, 38, 53, 54, 71, 103, 116; cardinal virtues (incl. two or more), *G* i. 12, 13, 99, ii. 23, iii. 53, iv. 11, 157, 159, 214, *E* i. 4, 8, ii. 12, 17, 112; beauty of virtue, *G* iv. 99; is motherless, *G* iv. 68; is older than vice, *G* iv. 51; is sister or brother of wisdom, *G* iv. 60, 66, 162

Vision of God, see Sight

Voice, see Speech; voice of God, see God

Voluntary and Involuntary Acts, *G* i. 21, 66, 68, ii. 45, 50, 69, 79, iii. 51, 56, iv. 1, 34, 37, 64, 65, 70,

INDEX

8 ; female as imperfect male, *E* i. 7

Wood, of ark, sym. incorruption, *E* ii. 53, 57

Word of God, see God, Logos

World, see Creation. Elements, Nature

Wreathed Wave, see Ark, Table

Writing, *E* ii. 41

Year, name = " contains everything within itself," *E* i. 8, ii. 67 (see also Time)

Youth, see Life

Zillah, *G* i. 77

Zodiac, *G* iv. 164, *E* ii. 75-78, 109, 112-114 (see also under names of Constellations)

Zoor (Bibl. Zoar), name = " mountain," *G* iv. 50 ; sym. salvation or destruction, *G* iv. 50

THE LOEB CLASSICAL LIBRARY

Latin Authors

AMMIANUS MARCELLINUS. J. C. Rolfe. 3 Vols.

APULEIUS: THE GOLDEN ASS (METAMORPHOSES). W. Adlington (1566). Revised by S. Gaselee.

ST. AUGUSTINE: CITY OF GOD. 7 Vols. Vol. I. G. E. McCracken. Vols. II and VII. W. M. Green. Vol. III. D. Wiesen. Vol. IV. P. Levine. Vol. V. E. M. Sanford and W. M. Green. Vol. VI. W. C. Greene.

ST. AUGUSTINE, CONFESSIONS. W. Watts (1631). 2 Vols.

ST. AUGUSTINE, SELECT LETTERS. J. H. Baxter.

AUSONIUS. H. G. Evelyn White. 2 Vols.

BEDE. J. E. King. 2 Vols.

BOETHIUS: TRACTS and DE CONSOLATIONE PHILOSOPHIAE. Rev. H. F. Stewart and E. K. Rand. Revised by S. J. Tester.

CEASAR: ALEXANDRIAN, AFRICAN and SPANISH WARS. A. G. Way.

CEASAR: CIVIL WARS. A. G. Peskett.

CEASAR: GALLIC WAR. H. J. Edwards.

CATO: DE RE RUSTICA. VARRO: DE RE RUSTICA. H. B. Ash and W. D. Hooper.

CATULLUS. F. W. Cornish. TIBULLUS. J. B. Postgate. PERVIGILIUM VENERIS. J. W. Mackail. Revised by G. P. Goold.

CELSUS: DE MEDICINA. W. G. Spencer. 3 Vols.

CICERO: BRUTUS and ORATOR. G. L. Hendrickson and H. M. Hubbell.

[CICERO]: AD HERENNIUM. H. Caplan.

CICERO: DE ORATORE, etc. 2 Vols. Vol. I. DE ORATORE, Books I and II. E. W. Sutton and H. Rackham. Vol. II. DE ORATORE, Book III. DE FATO; PARADOXA STOICORUM; DE PARTITIONE ORATORIA. H. Rackham.

CICERO: DE FINIBUS. H. Rackham.

CICERO: DE INVENTIONE, etc. H. M. Hubbell.

CICERO: DE NATURA DEORUM and ACADEMICA. H. Rackham.

CICERO: DE OFFICIIS. Walter Miller.

CICERO: DE REPUBLICA and DE LEGIBUS. Clinton W. Keyes.

2

NEPOS CORNELIUS. J. C. Rolfe.

OVID: THE ART OF LOVE and OTHER POEMS. J. H. Mozley. Revised by G. P. Goold.

OVID: FASTI. Sir James G. Frazer. Revised by G. P. Goold.

OVID: HEROIDES and AMORES. Grant Showerman. Revised by G. P. Goold.

OVID: METAMORPHOSES. F. J. Miller. 2 Vols. Revised by G. P. Goold.

OVID: TRISTIA and EX PONTO. A. L. Wheeler. Revised by G. P. Goold.

PERSIUS. Cf. JUVENAL.

PERVIGILIUM VENERIS. Cf. CATULLUS.

PETRONIUS. M. Heseltine. SENECA: APOCOLOCYNTOSIS. W. H. D. Rouse. Revised by E. H. Warmington.

PHAEDRUS and BABRIUS (Greek). B. E. Perry.

PLAUTUS. Paul Nixon. 5 Vols.

PLINY: LETTERS, PANEGYRICUS. Betty Radice. 2 Vols.

PLINY: NATURAL HISTORY. 10 Vols. Vols. I.–V. and IX. H. Rackham. VI.–VIII. W. H. S. Jones. X. D. E. Eichholz.

PROPERTIUS. H. E. Butler.

PRUDENTIUS. H. J. Thomson. 2 Vols.

QUINTILIAN. H. E. Butler. 4 Vols.

REMAINS OF OLD LATIN. E. H. Warmington. 4 Vols. Vol. I. (ENNIUS AND CAECILIUS) Vol. II. (LIVIUS, NAEVIUS PACUVIUS, ACCIUS) Vol. III. (LUCILIUS and LAWS OF XII TABLES) Vol. IV. (ARCHAIC INSCRIPTIONS).

RES GESTAE DIVI AUGUSTI. Cf. VELLEIUS PATERCULUS.

SALLUST. J. C. Rolfe.

SCRIPTORES HISTORIAE AUGUSTAE. D. Magie. 3 Vols.

SENECA, THE ELDER: CONTROVERSIAE, SUASORIAE. M. Winterbottom. 2 Vols.

SENECA: APOCOLOCYNTOSIS. Cf. PETRONIUS.

SENECA: EPISTULAE MORALES. R. M. Gummere. 3 Vols.

SENECA: MORAL ESSAYS. J. W. Basore. 3 Vols.

SENECA: TRAGEDIES. F. J. Miller. 2 Vols.

SENECA: NATURALES QUAESTIONES. T. H. CORCORAN. 2 VOLS.

SIDONIUS: POEMS and LETTERS. W. B. Anderson. 2 Vols.

SILIUS ITALICUS. J. D. Duff. 2 Vols.

STATIUS. J. H. Mozley. 2 Vols.

SUETONIUS. J. C. Rolfe. 2 Vols.

TACITUS: DIALOGUS. Sir Wm. Peterson. AGRICOLA and GERMANIA. Maurice Hutton. Revised by M. Winterbottom, R. M. Ogilvie, E. H. Warmington.

TACITUS: HISTORIES and ANNALS. C. H. Moore and J. Jackson. 4 Vols.

TERENCE. John Sargeaunt. 2 Vols.

TERTULLIAN: APOLOGIA and DE SPECTACULIS. T. R. Glover. MINUCIUS FELIX. G. H. Rendall.

TIBULLUS. Cf. CATULLUS.
VALERIUS FLACCUS. J. H. Mozley.
VARRO: DE LINGUA LATINA. R. G. Kent. 2 Vols.
VELLEIUS PATERCULUS and RES GESTAE DIVI AUGUSTI. F. W. SHIPLEY.
VIRGIL. H. R. Fairclough. 2 Vols.
VITRUVIUS: DE ARCHITECTURA. F. Granger. 2 Vols.

Greek Authors

ACHILLES TATIUS. S. Gaselee.
AELIAN: ON THE NATURE OF ANIMALS. A. F. Scholfield. 3 Vols.
AENEAS TACTICUS. ASCLEPIODOTUS and ONASANDER. The Illinois Greek
    Club.
AESCHINES. C. D. Adams.
AESCHYLUS. H. Weir Smyth. 2 Vols.
ALCIPHRON, AELIAN, PHILOSTRATUS: LETTERS. A. R. Benner and F. H.
    Fobes.
ANDOCIDES, ANTIPHON. Cf. MINOR ATTIC ORATORS Vol. I.
Apollodorus. Sir James G. Frazer. 2 Vols.
APOLLONIUS RHODIUS. R. C. Seaton.
APOSTOLIC FATHERS. Kirsopp Lake. 2 Vols.
APPIAN: ROMAN HISTORY. Horace White. 4 Vols.
ARATUS. Cf. CALLIMACHUS.
ARISTIDES: ORATIONS. C. A. Behr. Vol. 1.
ARISTOPHANES. Benjamin Bickley Rogers. 3 Vols. Verse trans.
ARISTOTLE: ART OF RHETORIC. J. H. Freese.
ARISTOTLE: ATHENIAN CONSTITUTION, EUDEMIAN ETHICS, VICES AND
    VIRTUES. H. Rackham.
ARISTOTLE: GENERATION OF ANIMALS. A. L. Peck.
ARISTOTLE: HISTORIA ANIMALIUM. A. L. Peck. Vols. I.-II.
ARISTOTLE: METAPHYSICS. H. Tredennick. 2 Vols.
ARISTOTLE: METEOROLOGICA. H. D. P. Lee.
ARISTOTLE: MINOR WORKS. W. S. Hett. On Colours, On Things
    Heard, On Physiognomies, On Plants, On Marvellous Things
    Heard, Mechanical Problems, On Indivisible Lines, On Situations
    and Names of Winds, On Melissus, Xenophanes, and Gorgias.
ARISTOTLE: NICOMACHEAN ETHICS. H. Rackham.
ARISTOTLE: OECONOMICA and MAGNA MORALIA. G. C. Armstrong (with
    METAPHYSICS, Vol. II).
ARISTOTLE: ON THE HEAVENS. W. K. C. Guthrie.
ARISTOTLE: ON THE SOUL, PARVA NATURALIA, ON BREATH. W. S. Hett.
ARISTOTLE: CATEGORIES, ON INTERPRETATION, PRIOR ANALYTICS. H. P.
    Cooke and H. Tredennick.

4

ARISTOTLE: POSTERIOR ANALYTICS, TOPICS. H. Tredennick and E. S. Forster.
ARISTOTLE: ON SOPHISTICAL REFUTATIONS.
  On Coming-to-be and Passing-Away, On the Cosmos. E. S. Forster and D. J. Furley.
ARISTOTLE: PARTS OF ANIMALS. A. L. Peck; MOTION AND PROGRESSION OF ANIMALS. E. S. Forster.
ARISTOTLE: PHYSICS. Rev. P. Wicksteed and F. M. Cornford. 2 Vols.
ARISTOTLE: POETICS and LONGINUS. W. Hamilton Fyfe; DEMETRIUS ON STYLE. W. Rhys Roberts.
ARISTOTLE: POLITICS. H. Rackham.
ARISTOTLE: PROBLEMS. W. S. Hett. 2 Vols.
ARISTOTLE: RHETORICA AD ALEXANDRUM (with PROBLEMS. Vol. II). H. Rackham.
ARRIAN: HISTORY OF ALEXANDER and INDICA. Rev. E. Iliffe Robson. 2 Vols. New version P. Brunt.
ATHENAEUS: DEIPNOSOPHISTAE. C. B. Gulick. 7 Vols.
BABRIUS AND PHAEDRUS (Latin). B. E. Perry.
ST. BASIL: LETTERS. R. J. Deferrari. 4 Vols.
CALLIMACHUS: FRAGMENTS. C. A. Trypanis. MUSAEUS: HERO AND LEANDER. T. Gelzer and C. Whitman.
CALLIMACHUS, Hymns and Epigrams and LYCOPHRON. A. W. Mair; ARATUS. G. R. Mair.
CLEMENT OF ALEXANDRIA. Rev. G. W. Butterworth.
COLLUTHUS. Cf. OPPIAN.
DAPHNIS AND CHLOE. Thornley's translation revised by J. M. Edmonds: and PARTHENIUS. S. Gaselee.
DEMOSTHENES I.: OLYNTHIACS, PHILIPPICS and MINOR ORATIONS I.–XVII. AND XX. J. H. Vince.
DEMOSTHENES II.: DE CORONA and DE FALSA LEGATIONE. C. A. Vince and J. H. Vince.
DEMOSTHENES III.: MEIDIAS, ANDROTION, ARISTOCRATES, TIMOCRATES and ARISTOGEITON I. and II. J. H. Vince.
DEMOSTHENES IV.–VI.: PRIVATE ORATIONS and IN NEAERAM. A. T. Murray.
DEMOSTHENES VII.: FUNERAL SPEECH, EROTIC ESSAY, EXORDIA and LETTERS. N. W. and N. J. DeWitt.
DIO CASSIUS: ROMAN HISTORY. E. Cary. 9 Vols.
DIO CHRYSOSTOM. J. W. Cohoon and H. Lamar Crosby. 5 Vols.
DIODORUS SICULUS. 12 Vols. Vols. I.–VI. C. H. Oldfather. Vol. VII. C. L. Sherman. Vol. VIII. C. B. Welles. Vols. IX. and X. R. M. Geer. Vol. XI. F. Walton. Vol. XII. F. Walton. General Index. R. M. Geer.
DIOGENES LAERTIUS. R. D. Hicks. 2 Vols. New Introduction by H. S. Long.
DIONYSIUS OF HALICARNASSUS: ROMAN ANTIQUITIES. Spelman's translation revised by E. Cary. 7 Vols.

DIONYSIUS OF HALICARNASSUS: CRITICAL ESSAYS. S. Usher. 2 Vols.

EPICTETUS. W. A. Oldfather. 2 Vols.

EURIPIDES. A. S. Way. 4 Vols. Verse trans.

EUSEBIUS: ECCLESIASTICAL HISTORY. Kirsopp Lake and J. E. L. Oulton. 2 Vols.

GALEN: ON THE NATURAL FACULTIES. A. J. Brock.

GREEK ANTHOLOGY. W. R. Paton. 5 Vols.

GREEK BUCOLIC POETS (THEOCRITUS, BION, MOSCHUS). J. M. Edmonds.

GREEK ELEGY AND IAMBUS with the ANACREONTEA. J. M. Edmonds. 2 Vols.

GREEK LYRIC. D. A. Campbell. 4 Vols. Vols. I. and II.

GREEK MATHEMATICAL WORKS. Ivor Thomas. 2 Vols.

HERODES. Cf. THEOPHRASTUS: CHARACTERS.

HERODIAN. C. R. Whittaker. 2 Vols.

HERODOTUS. A. D. Godley. 4 Vols.

HESIOD AND THE HOMERIC HYMNS. H. G. Evelyn White.

HIPPOCRATES and the FRAGMENTS OF HERACLEITUS. W. H. S. Jones and E. T. Withington. 5 Vols. Vols. I.–IV.

HOMER: ILIAD. A. T. Murray. 2 Vols.

HOMER: ODYSSEY. A. T. Murray. 2 Vols.

ISAEUS. E. W. Forster.

ISOCRATES. George Norlin and LaRue Van Hook. 3 Vols.

[ST. JOHN DAMASCENE]: BARLAAM AND IOASAPH. Rev. G. R. Woodward, Harold Mattingly and D. M. Lang.

JOSEPHUS. 10 Vols. Vols. I.–IV. H. Thackeray. Vol. V. H. Thackeray and R. Marcus. Vols. VI.–VII. R. Marcus. Vol. VIII. R. Marcus and Allen Wikgren. Vols. IX.–X. L. H. Feldman.

JULIAN. Wilmer Cave Wright. 3 Vols.

LIBANIUS. A. F. Norman. 2 Vols..

LUCIAN. 8 Vols. Vols. I.–V. A. M. Harmon. Vol. VI. K. Kilburn. Vols. VII.–VIII. M. D. Macleod.

LYCOPHRON. Cf. CALLIMACHUS.

LYRA GRAECA, III. J. M. Edmonds. (Vols. I.and II. have been replaced by GREEK LYRIC I. and II.)

LYSIAS. W. R. M. Lamb.

MANETHO. W. G. Waddell.

MARCUS AURELIUS. C. R. Haines.

MENANDER. W. G. Arnott. 3 Vols. Vol. I.

MINOR ATTIC ORATORS (ANTIPHON, ANDOCIDES, LYCURGUS, DEMADES, DINARCHUS, HYPERIDES). K. J. Maidment and J. O. Burtt. 2 Vols.

MUSAEUS: HERO AND LEANDER. Cf. CALLIMACHUS.

NONNOS: DIONYSIACA. W. H. D. Rouse. 3 Vols.

OPPIAN, COLLUTHUS, TRYPHIODORUS. A. W. Mair.

PAPYRI. NON-LITERARY SELECTIONS. A. S. Hunt and C. C. Edgar. 2 Vols. LITERARY SELECTIONS (Poetry). D. L. Page.

PARTHENIUS. Cf. DAPHNIS and CHLOE.

PAUSANIAS: DESCRIPTION OF GREECE. W. H. S. Jones. 4 Vols. and Companion Vol. arranged by R. E. Wycherley.

PHILO. 10 Vols. Vols. I.–V. F. H. Colson and Rev. G. H. Whitaker. Vols. VI.–IX. F. H. Colson. Vol. X. F. H. Colson and the Rev. J. W. Earp.

PHILO: two supplementary Vols. (*Translation only.*) Ralph Marcus.

PHILOSTRATUS: THE LIFE OF APOLLONIUS OF TYANA. F. C. Conybeare. 2 Vols.

PHILOSTRATUS: IMAGINES; CALLISTRATUS: DESCRIPTIONS. A. Fairbanks.

PHILOSTRATUS and EUNAPIUS: LIVES OF THE SOPHISTS. Wilmer Cave Wright.

PINDAR. Sir J. E. Sandys.

PLATO: CHARMIDES, ALCIBIADES, HIPPARCHUS, THE LOVERS, THEAGES, MINOS and EPINOMIS. W. R. M. Lamb.

PLATO: CRATYLUS, PARMENIDES, GREATER HIPPIAS, LESSER HIPPIAS. H. N. Fowler.

PLATO: EUTHYPHRO, APOLOGY, CRITO, PHAEDO, PHAEDRUS. H. N. Fowler.

PLATO: LACHES, PROTAGORAS, MENO, EUTHYDEMUS. W. R. M. Lamb.

PLATO: LAWS. Rev. R. G. Bury. 2 Vols.

PLATO: LYSIS, SYMPOSIUM, GORGIAS. W. R. M. Lamb.

PLATO: Republic. Paul Shorey. 2 Vols.

PLATO: STATESMAN, PHILEBUS. H. N. Fowler; ION. W. R. M. Lamb.

PLATO: THEAETETUS and SOPHIST. H. N. Fowler.

PLATO: TIMAEUS, CRITIAS, CLITOPHO, MENEXENUS, EPISTULAE. Rev. R. G. Bury.

PLOTINUS: A. H. Armstrong. 7 Vols.

PLUTARCH: MORALIA. 16 Vols. Vols. I.–V. F. C. Babbitt. Vol. VI. W. C. Helmbold. Vols. VII. and XIV. P. H. De Lacy and B. Einarson. Vol. VIII. P. A. Clement and H. B. Hoffleit. Vol. IX. E. L. Minar, Jr., F. H. Sandbach, W. C. Helmbold. Vol. X. H. N. Fowler. Vol. XI. L. Pearson and F. H. Sandbach. Vol. XII. H. Cherniss and W. C. Helmbold. Vol. XIII. 1–2. H. Cherniss. Vol. XV. F. H. Sandbach.

PLUTARCH: THE PARALLEL LIVES. B. Perrin. 11 Vols.

POLYBIUS. W. R. Paton. 6 Vols.

PROCOPIUS. H. B. Dewing. 7 Vols.

PTOLEMY: TETRABIBLOS. F. E. Robbins.

QUINTUS SMYRNAEUS. A. S. Way. Verse trans.

SEXTUS EMPIRICUS. Rev. R. G. Bury. 4 Vols.

SOPHOCLES. F. Storr. 2 Vols. Verse trans.

STRABO: GEOGRAPHY. Horace L. Jones. 8 Vols.

THEOCRITUS. Cf. GREEK BUCOLIC POETS.

THEOPHRASTUS: CHARACTERS. J. M. Edmonds. HERODES, etc. A. D. Knox.

THEOPHRASTUS: ENQUIRY INTO PLANTS. Sir Arthur Hort, Bart. 2 Vols.

THEOPHRASTUS: DE CAUSIS PLANTARUM. G. K. K. Link and B. Einarson. 3 Vols. Vol. I.

THUCYDIDES. C. F. Smith. 4 Vols.

TRYPHIODORUS. Cf. OPPIAN.

XENOPHON: CYROPAEDIA. Walter Miller. 2 Vols.

XENOPHON: HELLENICA. C. L. Brownson. 2 Vols.

XENOPHON: ANABASIS. C. L. Brownson.

XENOPHON: MEMORABILIA AND OECONOMICUS. E. C. Marchant. SYMPOSIUM AND APOLOGY. O. J. Todd.

XENOPHON: SCRIPTA MINORA. E. C. Marchant. CONSTITUTION OF THE ATHENIANS. G. W. Bowersock.